ISLAM AND MODERNITY IN TURKEY

ISLAM AND MODERNITY IN TURKEY

Brian Silverstein

palgrave
macmillan

Portions of this book first appeared in different form in:

"Sufism and Governmentality in the Late Ottoman Empire," in *Comparative Studies of South Asia, Africa and the Middle East*, 29(2), 2009: 171–185. Copyright 2009, Duke University Press. All rights reserved. Reprinted by permission of the publisher.

"Disciplines of Presence in Modern Turkey: Discourse, Companionship and the Mass Mediation of Islamic Practice," *Cultural Anthropology*, 23(1), 2008: 118–153.

"Islam and Modernity in Turkey: Power, Tradition and Historicity in the European Provinces of the Muslim World." *Anthropological Quarterly*, 76(3), 2003: 497–517.

First published in 2011 by PALGRAVE MACMILLAN® in the United States—a division of St. Martin's Press LLC, 175 Fifth Avenue, New York, NY 10010.

Where this book is distributed in the UK, Europe and the rest of the world, this is by Palgrave Macmillan, a division of Macmillan Publishers Limited, registered in England, company number 785998, of Houndmills, Basingstoke, Hampshire RG21 6XS.

Palgrave Macmillan is the global academic imprint of the above companies and has companies and representatives throughout the world.

Palgrave® and Macmillan® are registered trademarks in the United States, the United Kingdom, Europe and other countries.

ISBN: 978-0-230-10982-7

Library of Congress Cataloging-in-Publication Data

Silverstein, Brian.
    Islam and modernity in Turkey / Brian Silverstein.
        p. cm.
    ISBN 978-0-230-10982-7
    1. Islam—Turkey—History. 2. Secularism—Turkey. 3. Liberalism—Turkey.
I. Title.

    BP63.T8S65 2011
    297.09561—dc22   2010028251

A catalogue record of the book is available from the British Library.

Design by Scribe Inc.

First edition: February 2011

10 9 8 7 6 5 4 3 2 1

Printed in the United States of America.

CONTENTS

ACKNOWLEDGMENTS

I am grateful to the members of the Iskender Pasha community in several cities for their openness in allowing me to be among them for extended periods of time, and to my teachers Stefania Pandolfo, Hamid Algar, Michael Meeker, Aihwa Ong, Paul Rabinow, and Ayla Algar. Thanks also to İsmail Kara, who has been most generous with his erudition over the years, and Vince Pecora, who let me try out parts of my arguments in various knowledgeable venues. Numerous people and institutions were instrumental in the research and writing, and it is with pleasure that I thank them here: the İslam Araştırmaları Merkezi in Istanbul, particularly Recep Şentürk, Semih Ceyhan, Sema Doğan, and librarian Selahattin Öztürk; and the Bilim ve Sanat Vakfı and Nurullah Ardiç. Nazif Gürdoğan and Erol Kılıç helped get me started early on. Martin van Bruinessen, Julia Day Howell, Bruce Grant, Esra Özyürek, Yaseen Noorani, Ana Alonso, Jane Hill, Paul Eiss, Şerif Mardin, and Yael Navaro-Yashin all gave helpful comments on parts or early versions of the manuscript. For helpful assistance along the way I also thank Dick Eaton, Steve Lansing, Tad Park, Anne Betteridge, Ahmet Guida, Christine Szuter, Tom Sheridan, Ellen Basso, Dani Triadan, Dave Thompsen (University of Arizona College of Social and Behavioral Sciences Tech and image scanner extraordinaire), and Hikmet Kocamaner for his assistance and Aslı I sız for her comments as the project drew to a close.

Funding for the project at various stages came from a Fulbright Institute for International Education student fellowship, the Center for Middle Eastern Studies at University of California at Berkeley, the Institute for Turkish Studies in Washington DC, and a Fulbright-Hays Faculty Research Abroad fellowship. I am grateful for the friendly assistance of the directors and staff of the Fulbright offices in Istanbul and Ankara. Thanks also to Ali Çarkoğlu and Dean Ahmet Alkan at Sabancı University in Istanbul for their generosity and hospitality during writing.

It is a pleasure for me to make a special note of gratitude to my colleagues and friends at the University of Arizona, and especially the School of Anthropology, for the exemplary collegiality and generosity they have shown me. I feel fortunate to be able to work in such an extraordinary environment. I am also glad for the stimulating engagement of colleagues in the Department of Near Eastern Studies and at the Center for Middle Eastern Studies at the University of Arizona.

Finally, I am fortunate to have the wonderful support and companionship of my wife, Özlem; my parents, Raymond and Karen; my brother, Roger, and my in-laws, Ergun and Aslı Özgür, in Istanbul; and Chris Gutkind in London. This study could not have been done without them.

ISLAM AND MODERNITY IN TURKEY

ON ONE OF MY EARLIER TRIPS TO Turkey in 1996, as I passed through the lobby of the hotel where I was staying in Istanbul, I saw that a small group was watching a variety show on a television in a sitting area off in the corner. The show was typical of its kind and comprised a number of prerecorded skits tied together by monologues by the show's host and his conversations with guests, usually entertainment personalities. One of the pieces had evidently been recorded in a large city in Germany, with a man-on-the-street interviewer, microphone in hand, working with a roving cameraman. The interviewer would politely stop passersby, asking them in German if they would please read out loud what was written on a little card. As one of the hapless Germans started to read, it became obvious that what he or she had been asked to read was not German but a Turkish proverb, which the reader naturally pronounced with great difficulty and error. This misreading, however, produced explosions of laughter in the studio audience in Istanbul, as well as among the group of men watching in the hotel lobby, who were reacting to both the reader's pronunciation as well as the incongruousness of hearing such colloquial Turkish expressions coming out of the mouth of an urbane German.

One of the things that is striking about this instance is that the situation that produced the laughter at the failings of a well-heeled German was facilitated by Turkey's switch to the Latin alphabet (from the Arabic alphabet) in 1928.[1] Some critics—few in Turkey, more in other countries with large Muslim populations—are of the opinion that the change of alphabet is an example of how Turks have alienated themselves from their authentic identity by trying to take on all the trappings of "the West." Yet this comic skit points to ways in which this relationship between Turkey and Western Europe is more complicated. It is because Turkey took up the Latin alphabet prevalent in Western Europe that a reversal of hierarchy between Western Europeans and Turkish speakers became easy in this instance.[2] The urbane Western European is transformed into an object of ridicule in his or her unwitting encounter with "the Turkish"; the surprise for the Western European is that this piece of Turkishness at first had seemed so familiar and easily legible.

This encounter points to the ways that questions of history, identity, and power in Turkey, Europe, and the Muslim world can be broached by attending to the status of cultural forms, their relation to the past, and how and why they have changed in recent centuries. The question to ask is not what kinds of alienation have been involved in these processes (as many studying other parts of the Muslim world tend to ask regarding Turkey), but rather what understanding of contemporary Turkish cultural forms emerges when they are placed in historical context. Ought we consider the profound institutional reforms undertaken by Ottoman and then Republican Turkish authorities as an abandonment of Islamic identity and traditions (as is often claimed) or rather as unfolding within them? The answer to this question—which in Turkey is currently engaging a vast number of scholars and the public (Mardin 2006; Meeker 1994; Silverstein 2005)—is complex and necessitates a clarification of what constitutes Islamic traditions in the Ottoman and Turkish context and how and why these traditions have been changing. The stakes in such an enquiry are high. The answers Turks arrive at greatly influence the stance they have regarding the status of their own country and their identity as Muslims.

Students of other Muslim countries should also be paying close attention to these issues in Turkey. While Turkey's experience of the last two centuries differs in crucial respects from other Muslim majority countries, without closely attending to the Ottoman and Turkish experience, a general understanding of how Islamic traditions have been articulated with modernity remains seriously incomplete. What is taking place in Turkey contrasts dramatically with developments in recent decades in other important parts of the Muslim world, like Egypt, where an authoritarian single-party state and an absence of a functioning democracy have greatly contributed to the emergence of what several scholars refer to as an Islamic "counterpublic" (Abdo 2000; Hirschkind 2006). It is tempting to take the case of Islamic traditions as instances of such a counterpublic and generalize this into an analytic of Islamic traditions and modernity tout court. Much as I admire and have learned from many of the studies coming out of such an approach as specific studies of specific formations, such an analytical move would be hasty and misguided, in my view, for it would elide and obfuscate several key issues.

Take two points that are addressed as core arguments of this book: Islam has been transformed into a religion on the liberal model in Turkey, that is, as a phenomenon having primarily to do with personal choice and private belief. What are the processes through which this has taken place? Secondly, the vast majority of observant, conservative Muslims in Turkey—as described by themselves and others—do not see or experience this arrangement (Islam as a religion) as illegitimate. Why not? This book is structured around answering both of these questions. In doing so we examine the relationship between contemporary Islamic practice in Turkey, the legacies of institutional change in the late Ottoman Empire and early Republic, and more recent transformations at the juncture of culture, power, and the economy.

However, before undertaking an analysis of Islamic discourses and practices, some setup is required to establish the nature of the objects with which we will work, and this is reflected in the structure of this book. There are numerous works on Islam in Turkey, which drew attention in the 1990s as Islamist parties swept many municipal elections and performed well in national ones, leading to much discussion about an Islamic "resurgence";[3] likewise we have several social histories of Ottoman reform.[4] But what we do not have are studies of Islam in contemporary Turkey informed by a careful consideration of Ottoman backgrounds and precedents that enables us to understand the relevant contexts and histories in which Islamic discourses and practices have been unfolding, especially in relation to other regimes of knowledge and power.[5] How are we to understand the significance of the change in alphabet? What should we make of the lack of jurisdiction of Islamic law in Turkey and that there are no *shari'a* courts in the country, both having been replaced by civil law? What of the fact that most religiously observant Turks do not seek an alternative to the nation-state? What do observant Muslims in Turkey think about the country's bid to join the European Union? Are these merely the rather lamentable results of a small clique of elites who, through various repressive measures, have alienated the Turkish population from itself in the name of Westernization, civilization, or even Enlightenment liberation?

This book argues for another way of studying Islam in Turkey by proceeding from a diagnosis of the status of the Turkish present. The book situates descriptions of practices in the present against the background of histories of the institutions in and through which such practices unfold. It is thus an ethnography of these practices and an essay in that critical history of the present that Michel Foucault, following Nietzsche, called genealogy: "a form of history which can account for the constitution of knowledges, discourses, domains of objects, etc. without having to make reference to a subject which is either transcendental in relation to the field of events or runs its empty sameness throughout the course of history" (Foucault 2003f, 306). The critical history of the status of the present—genealogy—presented in Part I of this book establishes the context in which to interpret the contemporary

discourses and practices described in Parts II and III.[6] The book explores
several levels of phenomena, at several different sites: Ottoman institutional
reforms and the debates surrounding them; late Ottoman Sufis and their
bureaucratization; contemporary Sufi devotional practices and discursive
traditions in Turkey; an Islam-oriented radio station; research foundations
and think tanks; legislation regarding public and private spheres; and debates
about the EU (European Union), religion, and secularism.

THE MODERNITY THING

The term "modernity" has taken on a fetish status, is often deployed as a sign
of trendiness, and is in danger of referring to just about anything and therefore, of course, nothing. And yet for several reasons—not least that debates
about modernity and what it means to be modern are a major feature of the
landscape in Turkey—it is a concept that will be employed a great deal in this
book. There have been several approaches to the question of defining modernity or what it means to be modern, a pursuit that itself came quickly to be
on the agenda of those seeing themselves as moderns. I consider that market
capitalism—and all it implies, including colonialism and technological innovation connected to science (Marx 1990; Tilly 1985)—rationalized administrative bureaucracy (Weber 1978), and the normalization of the objects of
governance (Foucault 2003b) are clearly central to modernity (Chakrabarty
2000; Chatterjee 2004).[7] Modernity also involves certain experiences of oneself, most importantly a relation to time (implying a relation to death): time
(and indeed life itself), for moderns, is largely an empty context, with no
inherent significance (time does not, for instance, unfold daily as one more
instantiation of a sameness, which is the unfolding of God's plan, nor do
the passing days mark the approach to the Apocalypse, etc.). This essentially
secular experience of time is central to a characteristically modern temporality—the temporality of capitalism—as a mode of being in and relating to
time (Koselleck 2004, Blumenberg 1983; Chakrabarty 2000). Built into this
is a critical attitude (i.e., not merely one of rejection) toward, in this case,
religion but also toward received wisdom in general, which comes to be called
("the weight of") tradition (Weber 1978). There is an unmistakable sense
that the days we live in are qualitatively different from the past (Kant 2007),
and that, therefore, the past will not serve as much of a guide for us in the
present and future. Thus a critical stance toward tradition has tended to be
central to moderns' conceptions of themselves (Gay 1973; MacIntyre 1984).
In this context and against this background (to invoke one of the instruments
of historicism) humans, and especially the self, are taken to have a particular
status (Foucault 2007). Modern selfhood is often thought in terms of an
internal depth, the locus of true subjectivity, and who one is invited—by

various disciplines (e.g., psychology), various cultural movements (e.g., literary romanticism, new age lifestyle movements), and various politico-economic regimes (e.g., neoliberalism)—to discover and cultivate (Taylor 1989, Rose 1998). Thus modernity involves certain conceptions of human nature in terms of the definition of what humans are, what nature is, and what their relation is to one another (Outram 2005). Central to these notions of human nature is a conception of rationality, embodied in principles considered universally valid and underpinning that quintessentially modern object, "the" economy (Polanyi 2001; Mitchell 2002). Finally modernity involves the study of humans (among other objects) by disciplines with the status of science, with the aim to apply this knowledge to the management of problems (Foucault 1979; Weber 2004).[8] Another way of putting this is to say that the way social scientists have studied modern subjectivities and societies has been and is central to the ways in which those subjectivities and societies are changing. In this book we take modernity as the set of discourses, practices, institutions, and attitudes involving a particular self-consciousness and attempt to know and transform ourselves and that curious object known as society.[9]

COMMENSURABILITY AND HISTORICAL DIFFERENCE

A major question for historians and anthropologists—and others working across temporal difference, cultural difference, or both—has been how to think about modernity in geographical contexts that are not generally considered as part of its historical heartland (Chakrabarty 2000; Comaroff and Comaroff 1992). This turns out to be a more problematic set of issues than at first glance, but several commonplaces can be put confidently aside in favor of other approaches. What are, after all, the relevant contexts and units of analysis? Is "Europe" a useful starting point or such a unit? Or the "West"? If we accept (as many world historians do) that a major condition of possibility for industrial capitalism in Western Europe was the pillaging of silver from the Americas, what would it mean to claim that capitalism (and, for some, modernity itself) begins in the West and is then exported? Other scholars have produced well-informed scholarship on these issues, and we do not need to review that literature here.[10] Suffice it to say that the handy conflation of modernity with the West is problematic, for the "inside" and "outside" of the so-called West is hard to pin down, especially once one considers the conditions of possibility for the emergence of much of what we just enumerated as central to modernity. However, people in many places came under the rule of these Europeans and, as did many that did not come under direct rule, began to transform themselves and their societies along lines laid down by these Europeans. It is with these transformations, and how to conceptualize them and analyze them in the late Ottoman Empire and contemporary Republican Turkey, that we are concerned in this book.

In what ways were the Ottomans both like and unlike their imperial peers, the Habsburg Austro-Hungarian Empire and the Romanov Russian Empire? Recent critiques of hasty narrative reduction of other cultures in terms of the analytical categories of Western social science have opened the way toward greater sensitivity to the life-worlds historians and anthropologists try to portray and the ethical and political implications of such work for projects like pluralist democracy (Connolly 2005; Mahmood 2005). This book builds on this recent work but makes certain qualifications. The main question here is one of difference, that is, the extent to which the Ottomans should be considered as "other" to the so-called West. This is a question whose answer obviously depends on several variables, such as what one means by the West, how one interprets and defines the Ottomans, and what one's criteria for difference will be.

Dipesh Chakrabarty has recently written of the epistemological, political, and ethical issues inherent in the writing of histories of so-called non-Western peoples, with particular attention to the inevitability of having to conceptualize their relationship to political modernity (2000). It is, Chakrabarty argues, ill conceived to see the question of the articulation of various peoples and places with modernity in terms of their coming into a modernity that was already in progress before them but more a question of meaning and the significance people give to their lives. Yet it cannot be left to that because it is also true that the way peoples engage with capitalism is a part of the way an increasingly large percentage of people in the world have experienced their lives. How should one adequately conceptualize and understand people's lives while doing justice to the complexity of meaning and tradition, on the one hand, and articulation with capitalism on the other? "The problem of capitalist modernity cannot any longer be seen simply as a sociological problem of historical transition (as in the famous 'transition debates' in European history) but as a problem of translation, as well" (2000, 17). So in what terms and with what frameworks shall someone writing from and for the so-called Western academy describe non-Western life-worlds? Chakrabarty suggests that models of what takes place when one translates come in handy: "What translation produces out of seeming 'incommensurabilities' is neither an absence of relationship between dominant and [dominated] forms of knowledge nor equivalents that successfully mediate between differences, but precisely the partly opaque relationship we call 'difference'" (2000, 17). Chakrabarty writes that his own work in *Provincializing Europe* was an attempt "to write narratives and analyses that produce this translucence—and not transparency—in the relation between non-Western histories and

European thought and its analytical categories" (2000, 17–18). He points out how the institutionally recognized narratives of the discipline of history require that radically heterogeneous and diverse conceptions of the world—and therefore of personhood, meaningful action, and agency—must, in the final analysis, be translated into something other than what they often first appear to be or other than what they are considered to be and experienced as by participants in the events in question (e.g., peasant rebellions who leaders insist were instigated by the will of spirits or gods, or religious practitioners who derive a sense of dignity from their submission to something outside of themselves).[11] They are translated into (local chapters) of the history of capital, essentially secular histories, in which only humans—and certain ones more than others—can have agency. The implicit assumption of much of the historical work written, for instance, in a Marxist vein is that such a move of translation is considered epistemologically valid because the categories of Marxian analysis are taken to be not merely historically or culturally specific but as universal; and (precisely because they are universal) it is really only in terms of such history (which he refers to as "History" with a capital H) that politically responsible, progressive work can be done. This mode of work, in other words, "tends to evacuate the local by assimilating it to some abstract universal" (2000, 18). Chakrabarty refers to this as the analytical mode of endeavor.

We may, Chakrabarty argues, question in this kind of work an implicit model of translation that relies on problematic notions of a neutral third language, often taken to be the language of science (preferably resembling mathematics). For believing, for instance, that H_2O is a neutral way of describing the substance to which English gives the name "water," or Turkish "su," is naïvely ethnocentric. In the end, Chakrabarty argues, historians and anthropologists working cross-culturally simply have to confront the real work of constant translation between at least two systems (the cultures one studies and the concepts of social science), without recourse to some utopian situation in which we discover the language in which nature or the world itself was written. Languages and meanings being in constant flux, this means that the work of translation is both a work of interpretation and ceaseless, never coming to an end. This (as Chakrabarty calls it) "hermeneutic" mode of endeavor "finds thought intimately tied to places and to particular forms of life" (2000, 18); one hastens to add that the very work of translation, undertaken, say, by anthropologists and historians, is itself tied to particular times, places, and forms of life. I, too, find much of the best of historical and anthropological writing to be undertaken at the uneasy intersection of these two modes of endeavor—the analytic and the hermeneutic—and that is where the present study is situated.

I also think, however, that Ottoman experiences and materials invite us to build on Chakrabarty's approach to the "struggle to be at home in modernity" and perhaps to push it up a register (2000, 180). I will argue that late Ottoman Islamists were, in their own way, similarly riding along this fault line, taking the ground they were standing on and the history they were involved in as both the history of Islam *and* another history that was reorganizing their own frames of meaning and understanding of the world and themselves. They were, in other words, aware of and explicitly grappling with precisely these issues of the commensurability of ("modern" and "Muslim") life-worlds while at the same time having to deal with extremely urgent, pressing concerns regarding the form that their state and institutions should take, the kinds of knowledges that would allow them to survive in the world around them, and the nature of just and "good" governance. Moreover, these issues were perceived as all being interrelated. Crucial here, as we will see in following chapters, is that this was a slow, incremental process that unfolded over centuries, such that by the turn of the twentieth century, one could argue that Ottoman Islamists (and most other Ottomans, for that matter) experienced both universalist, modernist history and Islamic history as "their own."[12] We thus, in a sense, push all the way round the idea of historical difference here, for we will come to see how in the late Ottoman case, European thought and its analytical categories were incorporated and made Ottoman on grounds that were internal to Ottoman reasoning.

This book addresses these questions by bringing together two currents in recent theoretical work in historical and social research. One sees the Ottomans as an entity commensurable with polities to the Ottomans' north and west and emphasizes that the Ottomans were part of Europe. In this vein I take my lead from recent revisionist Ottoman and world historians.[13] The other body of work is on discursive traditions, their categories and styles of reasoning, and the particular forms of life enabled and animated by them. Here I draw upon the work of Talal Asad, Michel Foucault, and Alasdair MacIntyre. I argue that it is in bringing these two approaches together that we are able to bring into focus a historically (and historiographically) informed understanding of the relationship between Islam and modernity in the Turkish context.[14]

In attending to the relationship between Islamic traditions and modern techniques and practices in the context of Turkey, we need to keep in mind that the Turkish present is not postcolonial in any direct sense (Turkey not having been colonized).[15] This is not merely to celebrate successful resistance. Rather, the point is to recall that, in the Ottoman and Turkish case, a radical rupture does not characterize the specific contexts and imperatives of power in which Islamic traditions continually evolved while characteristically modern forms and techniques were incorporated (in spite of the rhetoric of the revolution beginning in 1923 with the proclamation of the republic by nationalists led by Mustafa Kemal "Atatürk").[16] The Ottomans were like several other powers in the political geography of Europe (especially Russia and Austro-Hungary) that were, on a global scale, close to the margin of the emergence of industrial capitalism and sought to incorporate techniques of modern governance as a way of waging more effective warfare by rationalizing and bureaucratizing the identification and exploitation of resources (Murphey 1999; Silverstein 2003; Aksan 2007). This history of the incremental reform of institutions, according to the Ottoman authorities' own criteria, has bequeathed a situation in which modernity has been experienced not as a conspiracy of outsiders but as a legacy of decisions made by earlier generations.

Much of the Muslim world and southern Europe have experienced major regime changes, not to mention revolutions, over the course of the twentieth century (e.g., consider Spain, Italy, or Greece; colonialism, mandates, independence, or deposed monarchs in the Arab Middle East, Africa, and Asia; revolution in Iran). It is important to point out that the inaugurating ideology of the Republic of Turkey founded in 1923 remains largely unchanged today: the sovereignty of the nation, embodied in a state oriented toward nationalism, developmentalism, populism, secularism, and etatism. There have been, to be sure, variations in emphases among the guiding principles of the country ("revolutionism" is no longer a daily ethic outside of certain small cliques of devoted Kemalists), but it is important not to underestimate the implications of the underlying continuity in the regime since the republic was founded in 1923. The terms "sovereignty" and "nation" have been the topic of much scholarly debate as of late, but for our purposes I merely want to point out the immense prestige that these ideas have had and continue to have for the vast majority of the population in Turkey, especially given the two "utopian" experiments that have been tried literally right next door and that did not quite go as many had hoped: Soviet communism and the Iranian revolution.

MAKING ISLAM A RELIGION: LIBERALISM AND SECULARISM IN TURKEY

Religion has been a central topic of anthropological concern since the inception of the discipline in the late nineteenth century. This has largely to do with the "nonmodern" societies with which early anthropologists considered themselves to be concerned. These societies are defined as such precisely because they were taken to be ones in which religion was "still" a major organizing factor in social, political and economic life, a quality that seemed to distinguish the peoples anthropologists studied from their own societies and themselves. Thus, religion is not merely one topic among many for people who see themselves as modern; it is a—indeed arguably *the*—key site at which definitions of modernity have been formulated (Asad 1993; 2003).[17] Not surprisingly, in many countries religion is central to discussions and debates about what it means to be modern, and Islam in Turkey is certainly a case in point.

In recent years, and increasingly since the events of September 11, 2001, one hears around the world in the media, in policy circles, and even some academic environments almost exasperated discussions surrounding versions of the question "Why doesn't Islam behave like a religion should?"[18] The "problem" seems to be that Islam continually oversteps the boundaries of the properly religious and "interferes" in the political, the economic, the public (or, conversely, the private), and so on.[19] Recent anthropological work on Islam has shown how such questions and concerns are only possible from the ground of an assumption that there is something called "religion" that is not only analytically separable from (most importantly) the political but also normatively separated.[20] This secular-liberal expectation is itself a historical and cultural product, having emerged from the North Atlantic experience of Christianity, against the background of power struggles between princes, the church, and a newly emergent bourgeoisie. This process of what came to be known as secularization thus did not merely differentiate a preexisting, essential sphere called the religious from other spheres of life; it also produced the notion of a bounded sphere of religion in the first place. "Religion" as a particular sphere of existence, centering on private belief or personal choice, is one side of a coin, the other side of which is secularism. Thus defined, religion and secularism are two aspects of the same phenomenon. That the category of religion has been deployed simultaneously in analytical and (usually implicitly) in normative modes in much social science is worth highlighting at the outset of a discussion of Islamic practice, lest we find ourselves, despite our intentions, stumbling backward into versions of the question invoked previously. How then to conceptualize the discourses and practices of religious traditions whose historicities are not identical with but are mutually imbricated with the histories of secularism just outlined?

The structure of this book reflects the advice Talal Asad has given on how to do a critical anthropology of religion. Continuing and radicalizing a line of inquiry pursued by Wilfred Cantwell Smith beginning in the early 1960s, Asad deconstructed the category of religion and the expectations it bears regarding what the place, scope, and role of a properly functioning religion is, and thus implicitly what a pathological one is (i.e. the kind of arrangement in which political modernity is considered to be impossible; Asad 1993). One of the implications of this line of work, in my reading, is that one does not need a "philosophy" of religion—because religion has no essence transcending time or place—but rather one needs histories of the term's meanings and uses in various times and places. How have prestigious formulations of what religion is and what it is not influenced the ways in which diverse phenomena have become organized and institutionalized? As we examine in detail in this book, the institutionalization of a distinction between the public and the private spheres is central to the functioning of liberal political culture, as is the centering of religion on something called personal (private) belief.[21] It is then the very transformation of Islam into a religion on the liberal model that is in question and at stake in many parts of the world, including Turkey, and has been for the last century or so. This transformation is not a forgone conclusion; it merits our attention as an object of inquiry, for this way of distributing things and assigning spheres is not natural or universal. Rather, specific historical processes produce this arrangement. This transformation is, however, essentially a fait accompli in Turkey.

The genealogy of this state of affairs is outlined in Part I of this book.[22] We will see how late Ottoman Islamic and state reform movements involving the incremental differentiation of Islam into a religious sphere were undertaken for Islamic reasons (on the basis of Islamic legal reasoning). Thus, there is an Islamic genealogy to the secularization or differentiation of Islam as a religion in Turkey (Abu-Manneh 1994; Hanioğlu 2008).[23] Thus, while it is neither the case that the privatization of Islam along liberal lines is universal or natural nor the case that any Muslim society that is structured this way is necessarily merely dealing with postcolonial legacies or with some degree of alienation from Islamic traditions, I will also argue that while it is useful to historicize the category of religion and set it aside for a moment in favor of the analytical purchase of other concepts—in particular the category of tradition—we will eventually come back to seeing Islam as a religion because it has been deliberately *made* into one as a result of processes set in motion by reasoning on grounds internal to Islamic traditions. This background is important as we then go on in Part II of the book to evaluate the status of the transformations in Islamic traditions of discourse and practice in Turkey.

Recent work on Islam has also pointed to the uncritical use of normative concepts from liberal traditions—like autonomy, resistance, and critique itself—to study allegedly nonliberal movements like many Muslim ones.[24] What is at stake in such debates is not only the nature of Islamic practice; the thrust of an argument about the "alternative" status of Islamic modes of subjectivity is also to propose an alternative model of political action and community that counters the norms of liberal political culture (Asad 1993; Mahmood 2005; Hirschkind 2006). I argue that recent portrayals of Islam's allegedly alternative relationship to political modernity need to be nuanced by pointing out that the latter in Turkey has its genealogy in Ottoman reform movements (Silverstein 2003; Meeker 2002; Mardin 2006). It is not due to wishful thinking that I seek to make such a point. Rather, I argue that the notion that Islamic traditions—their culturally defined goals and modes of reasoning and being—stand in an alternative, "counter" relation to liberal politics, in the Turkish context at least, is not an adequate conceptualization.[25] The emergence of some form of arrangement known as secularism is always historically specific, the result of a specific conjuncture power relations. Crucial to defining the status of secularism in a given context is the question of how and why it came to be found there; as a result of what kinds of calculations, reasons, and actions; and on the part of whom and in the name of what. For instance, if, as I argue, Ottoman Muslim reformers beginning in the eighteenth century had *Islamic reasons* for introducing the changes that eventually led to the country's secularism, then the status of even the *absence* of practices or institutions commonly seen in other parts of the Muslim world could itself be understood as falling within Islamic traditions. Thus while the anthropological and historical exercises of interpreting dramatic cultural and historical differences are usually exceptionally difficult, pushing up as they do against the thinkable, I suggest that it may at times be even more difficult to conceptualize historical and cultural differences when the ground of those differences overlaps with one's own, as the example of the Germans reading Turkish proverbs suggests.[26] What perspectives emerge when Ottoman and Turkish histories are considered to be in crucial respects commensurable with other European histories? What understanding of Turkey, Islam, and the "West" emerges?

This book thus illustrates what is at stake in the secularization of a religious disciplinary practice in Turkey.[27] As we will see, there may be internally coherent, Islamic reasons for these processes (e.g., "service" to the community of Muslims). This is an example of what happens when Islam articulates with liberal politics and commercial broadcast media and shows that there is a multiplicity of reasons why various groups come to participate in a liberal public.[28] One might have *religious* reasons for having a secular attitude toward religion and politics. This renders plural and heterogeneous the temporality of the public (Connolly 2005), which is a source of anxiety for statist, arch-secular people in Turkey (who have governed during most of the history of the republic but have lost power in recent elections).[29]

CONTINUITY AND DIFFERENCE IN
TURKISH ISLAMIC TRADITIONS

A new generation of Islamic scholars and historians in Turkey are reconceptualizing the Turkish present's relationship to the Ottoman and early republican past; the politics of historical scholarship and the elaboration of Islamic traditions in Turkey are overlapping. Some contemporary Islamists in Turkey engaged in this research are openly acknowledging in their scholarship and in discussions in the media and press—after decades of Islamists dismissing the reforms as anti-Islamic, elite Westernization—that had they lived through the transition to the republic, they may well have supported many or even most of the reforms, as they now realize many observant and very sophisticated Muslims did at the time.[30] The range of identities and possible subject positions during the collapse of the empire was exceptionally broad and variegated, and it was due to what individuals had experienced in the Ottoman collapse that they took up a stance regarding reforms. The structural and emotional ability of contemporary Turkish Muslims to reconnect with these earlier subjectivities may be difficult for those unfamiliar with late Ottoman and early republican Turkish cases to appreciate. This is the phenomenon to which Wilfred Cantwell Smith was referring when he wrote, "To a considerable extent . . . the characteristic quality of the Turks in the modern Muslim world seems to rest on the uniqueness of their immediate past. (The prime matter here is continuity: the unbroken sequence from their medieval grandeur, including a persisting independence—and therefore active responsibility)" (Smith 1957, 162). Reasoned decisions and calculations on grounds internal to Islamic discursive traditions, and not an abandonment of those traditions, are central to the genealogy of modernity in Turkey (Asad 1986; MacIntyre 1984).

The notion of tradition is not one for which many anthropologists have had much use since Eric Hobsbawm and Terence Ranger's (1983) influential volume *The Invention of Tradition*.[31] However, in a now seminal article, Asad (1986) argued that social scientists (and anthropologists in particular) should define Islam—like he argues Muslims themselves do—as a discursive tradition (and not, rigorously speaking, as a religion). Asad operates with the formulation of tradition elaborated by Alasdair MacIntyre in his work in moral philosophy and specifically in his controversial work *After Virtue*. A tradition, in Asad's adaptation of MacIntyre's Aristotelian notion of moral tradition, is an ongoing set of discussions (a "discourse") and practices that are closely interlinked and have been so continuously and over time. One of the most important practices is discussion and debate about correct practice. To belong to a tradition involves sincere commitment to the value and normatively binding character of authoritative judgments. Normative judgment is thus an important part of any tradition; there are better ways to do things, and therefore there are ways that are worse. Here we need to keep in mind that these discussions about correct practice are always evolving and the judgments reached are constantly changing. Stasis is not a characteristic of tradition. Indeed, Asad notes that one must wait for the appearance of the modern bureaucratic nation-state in order to arrive at an unprecedented homogenization of discourse and practice in society. However, to say that traditions are always changing does not amount to saying they are "constructions," "inventions," or that they do not exist. Living traditions change through engagement with the received, ongoing sets of discussions; doing otherwise is by definition abandonment of the tradition.

The study of traditions is thus not merely about representations but rather about matrices of discourse and practice, and crucially discourse *about* correct practice.[32] Hence, as Foucault put it, "the target of analysis [isn't] 'institutions,' 'theories,' or 'ideology' but *practices*—with the aim of grasping the conditions that make these [practices] acceptable at a given moment . . . It is a question of analyzing a 'regime of practices'—practices being understood here as places where what is said and what is done, rules imposed and reasons given, the planned and the taken for granted meet and interconnect" (2003d, 247–48). In our approach to Islam as a tradition of discourse and practice in this book, it will be with relationships between things said and things done, and with norms and reasoning, that we will be mostly concerned. To the extent that we will examine the practices in and through which Muslims work on themselves, honing certain dispositions and capacities and trying to expiate others all in the light of programs that they do not themselves make up but that are rather governed by norms, we are dealing with the field Foucault, following Aristotle's usage, termed "ethics" (Foucault 2003a; Hadot 1995; Faubion 2001).[33]

This book thus builds on this conception of Islam as a discursive tradition. I also, however, propose a corrective to recent work in this vein with respect to what I argue is an unduly narrow, localized (postcolonial Arab Middle East–centered) definition of which specific discourses and practices Islamic traditions consist of today.[34] Work among Muslim communities often undertheorizes the nature of continuity in practice and discourse, which is crucial to the functioning and definition of traditions. Muslims consider that it is important to legitimize their practice through reference to authoritatively established positions—in other words, to orthodoxy. A relation of continuity with the past is thus established, while a form of censure and reproach is to judge a view or practice to be without basis in the traditions. In the legitimacy of a given practice or discourse aspiring to "Islamic" status, the politics of continuity is central.

The notion of continuity becomes problematic in many parts of the Muslim world because of the perceived ruptures of European imperialism and colonialism. How does one, as a Muslim, consider the character of discourses and practices in recent centuries and the judgments arrived at in those contexts, vis-à-vis those discourses, practices, and judgments of previous periods? Even though certain areas of the Muslim world were not formally colonized (e.g., Turkey and Iran), the entire world was, and continues to be, shaken by the ascendance of European, "Western," non-Muslim power. Hence I argue that the issue is one of defining Islamic traditions and their relationship to modes of power. I examine the specific articulation of a branch of the Naqshbandi Sufi order with governmentality and with the institutions, habits, and temporalities associated with capitalist enterprise (Connolly 1989, Chakrabarty 2000) since Ottoman times. Foucault defined governmentality as "the ensemble formed by the institutions, procedures, analyses and reflections, the calculations and tactics that allow the exercise of this very specific albeit complex form of power, which has as its target population, as its principal form of knowledge political economy, and as its essential technical means apparatuses of security" (2003b, 244). In other words, I examine the orders' articulation with political modernity and argue for the shared historicity of Islamic traditions and characteristically modern modalities of power and subject formation; in the process I illustrate how many Sufis and other Muslims in Turkey have religious reasons for having a secular attitude toward religion and politics.

During the last few centuries, Muslims have been adapting the resources of Islamic traditions in order to understand and adequately cope with emerging situations. Keeping the notion of discursive tradition in mind, it is important to reconstruct the landscape of calculation, reason, and agency from the perspective of those in positions of responsibility to rule over a multiethnic, multiconfessional empire. In the capital of an empire—ruled by a figure widely recognized to be the caliph, stretching from Bosnia to Yemen, and scrambling to preserve its sovereignty in the face of constant military attack, especially by a Russia that was in a parallel position of importing modern techniques from points west—Ottoman ruling authorities were never in doubt that theirs was an Islamic polity and that they were governing from within Islamic traditions. Continuing to live an Islamic way of life in light of the normative proscriptions of Islamic traditions is explicitly the rationale of both rule and reform through the very last years of the empire. Indeed, as we will see, the decisions to bring the empire to an end, proclaim a republic (abolishing the sultanate), and eventually abolish the caliphate were also debated on grounds of Islamic reasoning, among others. The threads one might be tempted to imagine constituting this knot of historicity—the Islamic or Ottoman versus the secular, liberal republican—are already themselves plural, heterogeneous, and in crucial respects, overlapping.

To clarify, I am not arguing that contemporary Islamic practices are "modern" and, therefore, not traditional. As Charles Hirschkind has recently noted in his work with Muslim activists in Egypt, "Forms of modern power and authority define the conditions and provide the means by which [contemporary Islamist movements have] elaborated and pursued the task of cultivating Islamic virtues today . . . What merits our attention . . . is the way in which instrumentalities of modern power are made to operate within practices that, in their temporal and ideological dimensions, presuppose ongoing traditions of Islam" (2001, 13). In this book I draw out how these new conditions of possibility articulate with the cultivation of particular kinds of Muslim selves, oriented toward an ethical commitment to the elaboration of Islamic ways of life, by examining the discourses and practices of a Sufi order the eponym of which dates to fourteenth-century Bukhara in Central Asia.[35] Describing modern forms of Islamic practices, then, is important but not sufficient; what is significant here is the relationship between these new forms and what is considered to be a historically grounded tradition of cultivation of Islamic virtues. This is the thread tying the parts of this book together.

SUFISM IN TURKEY

Sufism (Arabic *tasawwuf*, Turkish *tasavvuf*), focused on intensified devotional techniques for living as a Muslim, has been a part of the landscape of the Muslim world since the early centuries of Islam and eventually came to be institutionalized as orders centered on sheikhs (having known chains of initiation) and their disciples (Knysh 2000).[36] In the Ottoman Empire until 1923 and briefly in the Republic of Turkey, Sufi orders were extremely important in social, political, and economic life, with a great many Muslims of various social classes and even many *ulema* (Islamic scholars) actively cultivating their devotion in one (or more) of the many idioms of Sufism available in the empire.[37] As we will see, in 1925 the republic proscribed the orders and closed their lodges (known as *tekkes*, *dergâhs*, or *zaviyes*), and it remains today technically a punishable offense to be involved in a Sufi order, as sheikh or as devotee.[38] The abolition of the orders is generally interpreted as an index of their pervasiveness among the population of the late empire; their ability to mobilize masses of people; and, hence, their ability to disrupt and challenge the institutions and authority of the new republican regime, itself attempting to mobilize the population in a populist, nationalist mode. Also important was the collapse of the orders' prestige and their association with "superstition" and irrationality, which was already a topic of debate in the later empire. Today only a small minority of people in Turkey are involved with a Sufi order, though there are no reliable statistics on the matter. However, a number of orders have continued to function in a somewhat "public secret" fashion. Indeed, the Naqshbandi order (a branch of which we examine in this book) in particular is seen by many as having played a subtle but pervasive role in the ongoing elaboration of Islamic movements with various emphases (economic, political, educational, cultural, and intellectual) over the course of the republic, especially in recent decades.[39] Regarding the place of the Naqshbandi order in Turkish republican history, Yavuz writes, "The Naqshbandi Sufi order served as the matrix for the emergence in the 1970s of the four leading contemporary Turkish Islamic political and social movements: the neo-Nakşibendi [sic] Sufi order of Süleymancı and other orders [including the Iskender Pasha group discussed in this book]; the new Islamist intellectuals; the Nurcu movement of Bediüzzaman Said Nursi, with its offshoot led by the charismatic Fethullah Gülen; and the [Millî Gençlik Hareketi] of Necmettin Erbakan" (2003, 11). The elections of November 2002 gave an offshoot of Turkey's Islamist movement, the Justice and Development (Adalet ve Kalkınma, or AK) Party—with close connections to Islamist networks and intellectuals—an overwhelming majority in the parliament and allowed them to form the first noncoalition government in 15 years. As we examine in Chapter 6, many of their policies favor a liberalization of regulation, which is in line with both their moderately conservative supporters and EU entry protocols. This and similar convergences between EU liberalization and the discourse of the AK Party modality of the "religious right" (as it is known in Turkey) make the Kemalist (statist, archsecular) establishment—not to mention the military—nervous, leading to the ironic situation whereby many Islamists in Turkey have been pro-EU entry, while the military (historically a force for integration into the West) has become a (albeit subtle) proponent of more cautiously paced reform. The current prime minister, Recep Tayyip Erdoğan, participated in the Sufi order studied in this book in the 1970s (as did many others in his party and the Refah and Fazilet Parties out of which it grew) and is generally considered both to have been a formally initiated devotee at one point and to cautiously continue to sympathize with many aspects of Sufi practice and culture. Hence the mode of religiosity of this order, described in this book, has been influential, particularly regarding their position that the faithful are not merely permitted to engage with modern technologies, but rather obligated as Muslims to do so. This has translated into a characteristic stance on the part of the order regarding issues like social justice, the environment, overconsumption, technical expertise, development, competition, boys' and girls' education, and democratization.

However, while it is important to emphasize that no reliable, relevant statistics exist, it is not the case that participation in Sufi orders is a mass phenomenon in Turkey, unlike, for example, in Pakistan, Morocco, or parts of West Africa. Rather, the study of Sufis in contemporary Turkey illustrates how Islamic traditions of discourse and practice are affected by articulation with modern technologies like mass media, political modernity, and economic liberalization. This is, then, not an exhaustive study of Sufism in contemporary Turkey, or even of a particular order. The experiences of Sufis in Turkey do, however, illustrate well the kinds of transformations Islamic discourses and practices have undergone over the last century. In portraying the devotional practices of a Sufi order, I aim to convey a sense of what it means to try to live one's life within Islamic traditions in Turkey, which itself means living simultaneously within various structures the status and historicity of which are multiple and complex.[40] The processes described here are an important case for understanding the nature and status of traditions of discourse and practice in politically and economically liberalizing environments.

REPUBLICAN DEVELOPMENTALISM, LIBERALIZATION, AND THE "MUSLIM BOURGEOISIE"

The modality of governance of the republic, often known as modernization from above (Keyder 1997), is one the republic inherited from the Ottoman Empire. That elite, highly trained technocratic experts applying positive sciences should engineer and implement reforms, and that these might involve public institutions as well as the details of personal life were features of Ottoman governance. Government through the rationalization of administration and normalization of the objects of governance—people known and intervened upon as units of populations—was well elaborated in the empire long before there was any talk of a republic. The extent to which the organs of Ottoman and later republican governmentality penetrated to local levels and reorganized religious institutions and activities is an important aspect of the relationship of Islamic traditions to modern modalities of power. Thus, as we will see in Chapters 1 and 2, it is important to remember that Islamic traditions had already been profoundly reorganized by such state projects of governance for decades in the Ottoman Empire, and thus we must place republican developments against that background.

It is generally accepted that Turkey is one of the few countries in the world where national developmentalism was largely successful in delivering development, economic integration, urbanization, and welfare, at least through the 1970s (Keyder 1987). These gains reached the population through mechanisms of social entitlements, employment, and certain carefully state-controlled forms of organization and patronage. People were identified as members of certain professional groups or economic sectors, which created expectations and client relationships along certain axes. The bargaining over the distribution of material rewards generated by developmentalism constituted "politics"; strategies were oriented toward a greater participation in the distribution of benefits. In other words, the overall success of developmentalism during much of the republic did not lead to the emergence of liberal citizenship in which individuals and groups with private interests exercise public reason in defining the rules by which they will be governed and transmit these to the state. Rather, authoritarian nationalism, emphasizing unity and collective purpose, guided by a highly trained cadre of technocrats knowing and representing the population, was the founding ideology of the new republic. This ideology and ethos continue to inspire many Kemalists, and many have commented on the extent of such people's nostalgia surrounding these earlier periods (Özyürek 2006; Bora 2006). Again, this is in contrast with the other countries in southern Europe, which all have seen one or usually several regime changes and revolutions explicitly rejecting the state ideologies common before World War II. Turkey has lived in much more continuity with that period.

The pervasiveness of modernizing developmentalism in the early decades of the republic is difficult to overstate, with this governmentality having a remarkable impact on identities and lifestyles. Islamic discourses, practices, and identities are no exception. Microlevels of bodily comportment and practice were rarely publicly discussed as such before they were rendered visible and calculable by these modern state-sponsored development programs in which domestic family life especially was "variously defined, manipulated, and generally subjected to the regulation of health, educational and welfare programs" (Ong 1995, 161). Hence, instances of renewed and intensified interest in such virtues as modesty and bashfulness in women, or the visceral qualities of experience in religiously disciplined bodies, are all linked inextricably and intimately to the governmental techniques of microlevel visibility, calculability, and objectification. Observant Muslim selves in Turkey are traversed and organized by these modern regimes of knowledge and power.

The coup of 1980 was a major watershed in the history of the country, particularly regarding religion, society, and intellectual life. While it is true that both the political Right and Left were shaken by the coup, its real weight fell on the Left, leaving it in tatters to this day.[41] Both the economic performance of the country leading up to the coup and the rhetoric of the military regime from 1980 to 1982 militated against any romantic invocations of a restoration of the previous order of things: "Thus it was not restoration but radical innovation that was called for. Consequently the tenure of the Republican elite was brief while technocratic management and radical legal-institutional innovation became the order of the day. A frantic legislative activity succeeded in clearing the administrative system of a bureaucratic and populist heritage of sixty years . . . Both the bourgeoisie and the bureaucracy recognized that the period of an expanding national economy without world market sanctioning was over and a new type of regulation was necessary" (Keyder 1987, 224–25). The formula applied was a familiar one: instant liberalization following the prescriptions of the International Monetary Fund. This amounted, as in other countries, to the dismantling of state controls and distribution policies along neoliberal lines (Harvey 2005). The processes examined in Parts II and III of this study should be seen against this background. Especially important are certain new situations and tensions that have manifested since 1980. The increasing privatization of Turkish economic and social institutions has led, naturally, to the invigoration of a capitalist class, which is, significantly, often ambivalent in its commitment to state ideologies incubated in the heavily developmentalist and statist periods. These ideologies are generally given the shorthand "Kemalism," referring to Mustafa Kemal (Atatürk), leader of the nationalist forces establishing the republic in 1923 out of the ruins of the Ottoman Empire. While rarely elaborated explicitly, Kemalism refers to the dominant ideology of the state regime for nearly the entirety of its existence, characterized by etatism, technocratic expert rule, archsecularism, nationalism, populism, and developmentalism. The new, small capitalist class, while largely owing its position to state patronage, increasingly demanded a predictable and transparent legal and political environment in which to operate according to the logic of international corporate capitalism; developing the nation fell from many capitalists' lists of priorities.

What is especially new in the history of the republic is that among these new cadres of major capital holders and players in the liberalized economy are outwardly pious, observant, and often even activist Muslims.[42] Within this "new Muslim bourgeoisie" are some who have considerable amounts of capital at their disposal and whose holdings are among the largest in the country.[43] As is the case for most of the new bourgeois class, however, the observant among them tend to be much more modest in their means. Nonetheless, they are in a position to establish companies and distribution networks for products in the environment of liberalization that has taken hold. What this has also meant is that the Kemalist elite has lost its monopoly on public discourse—and crucially its monopoly on political discourse, which is considered to be compatible with the democratic world—as new private outlets in publishing and media especially have appeared, coupled with think tanks and research foundations publishing their intellectual productions. The extent to which this is creating anxiety, and even panic, and a proliferation of conspiracy theories among the traditional Kemalist elite is difficult to exaggerate.[44] This panic has created an ironic situation: Kemalists accustomed to seeing themselves as the progressive vanguard of humanist liberation are now often seen as fighting a reactionary, rear-guard action to obstruct the actual democratization of cultural, political, and economic institutions, while a large majority of the country's observant Muslims, including most of those described in this book, appears to actively seek it. Thus the conditions of possibility for the changes described here (e.g., the radio station owned and operated by the Sufi order of this study) are in an important sense constituted by the changes in the political economy of the country since 1980, the shorthand for which is political and economic liberalization.

It is also in this context that the question of Turkey's relationship to Europe has taken on an even more urgent tone than previously throughout the existence of the republic. Çağlar Keyder summarizes the period as the context in which Turkey threw its weight behind the EU project:

> With the collapse of developmentalism during the 1970s, Turkey had entered a long period of directionless meandering. Economic transformation stalled; political reform remained a distant goal; corruption deepened. Politicians proved inept; a series of naïve attempts at forming alliances—with the Middle East, with [Turkey's] Black Sea neighbors, with the Turkic world—ended in disappointment. There was no leadership to propose a direction: petty politicking was the rule, with the same names in tired clientelistic parties forming coalition governments in various combinations. In this environment the prospect of European Union membership emerged as the only credible project with majority support. This is why the relationship with Europe once again became a sensitive issue. (2006, 73)

We turn to a discussion of Turkey-EU relations and the EU-inspired reforms in the epilogue.

ETHICS AND POLITICS OF RESEARCH

The ground that this study examines partially overlaps with the ground from which it is written. As Stefania Pandolfo reminds us, pointing to the ethical stakes involved in social research, "Commensurability [is] not just an epistemological question" (2000, 129). There is a long history of visitors to Istanbul from points to the north and west embracing Islam, as I myself did, and fashioning their lives thereafter, in myriad ways that defy summarization, as the lives of Muslims. Ottoman society included many such individuals, coming from Central and Eastern Europe, the Balkans, the Caucasus, the Volga basin, and beyond; they settled, married, and are the ancestors of many in Turkey. Moreover, a disproportionately large percentage of the Ottoman ruling classes was made up of such people. Much work has been produced on the subject of religious conversion, on the structuring of motives by the pre-conversion culture that predisposes the conversion candidate to seek something in the "new" religion, and on the various mechanisms that keep the convert in that new religion (Robbins 2004). These models of conversion no doubt have much to recommend them, yet I must admit that I do not recognize myself in them. At points in the past, many people have embraced a new religion from outside; how else can we imagine that any religions ever grew? My suspicion is that the proliferation of work on religious conversion is a sign of the times we live in, when it now seems to be religion that poses the greatest challenge to political pluralism. This is not a view I share, but it is undoubtedly widespread. The idea seems to be that we must have something important to learn by studying people who, in the late twentieth and twenty-first centuries no less, actually *choose* to adhere to a religious tradition. I do not personally feel I have much of interest to say when I am asked about my becoming a Muslim, which occurred before my research on this project began and before I met my (Turkish) wife. This is a question I am only asked, I might add, by non-Muslims or by nonpracticing Muslims. I am neither the first Muslim in my family—my mother's cousin embraced Islam when he married an Indonesian woman in the early 1990s—nor, for that matter, the first in my family to spend time in Turkey, as my aunt lived in Ankara in the 1950s teaching English to Turkish military cadets until she was overheard at a cocktail party sympathizing with "revolutionaries" somewhere and asked to leave, blacklisted, she would tell us, from further U.S. government work.

I am certain, however, that my Muslim identity had important implications for my research. I spent two years and several summers in Turkey conducting the research for this study, mainly in Istanbul but also in Bursa, Ankara, Sivas, Kayseri, Malatya, Gaziantep, Urfa, and several other smaller towns. I was received by those with whom I worked as an American Muslim. (This is how I was usually introduced by the Turkish friends and acquaintances with whom I interacted in conducting this study.) As my wife is an Istanbulite and we reside with her family when there, I am often somewhat playfully taken to be a kind of *enişte* (sister's or aunt's husband). At the same time, as is well known, the topics of Islam, religion, and secularism in Turkey are focal points for major debates inside the country. I eventually learned that some of those with whom I interacted were unsure about my intentions or who I was "working for" but felt an obligation to assist me because I am a Muslim, and there were no doubt many who politely put a distance between themselves and me, though I naturally have only limited awareness of this. However, I was warmly received by the overwhelming majority of the people with whom I had contact during my research, an experience readers of ethnographies will know is not necessarily shared by everyone doing such research. This is not to say that researching the topic of Islam in Turkey is easy. Suspicion, hesitation, and even fear saturate the field and did especially in the wake of the events of February 28, 1997 (discussed later), when I conducted the main part of the fieldwork for this study. The stakes can be very high.

The student of Islam in contemporary Turkey tends to encounter difficulties on several fronts. First are those Kemalists—mainly in Turkey, numerically few but in influential places—who perceive talk of living Islamic traditions and practices in the country as frightening reminders that the symbolisms and power structures of a previous, failed theocratic order can be mobilized to mislead a population still poorly informed about the liberating effects of secular humanism. As a foreigner working on the topic of Islam, one is then ascribed one (or indeed, ironically, both) of two positions: either one is oblivious to the danger "these groups" represent and is in the grip of Orientalist fascination with the exotic, in which case one can hardly be considered a competent and ethical social scientist (for one is denying coevalness and shared human ground between researcher and those she works with); or one is very well aware of the danger and is contributing to the political projects of these people by taking them seriously (a surfeit of coevalness, as it were).[45] It is not without some regret that I learned that these attitudes are held in certain circles in Turkey, especially among some self-described secular, modern academics. I can, however, understand and sympathize with the great deal of bitterness and cynicism on the part of those who identify with the Left in Turkey regarding the issue of religion for reasons mentioned previously having to do with the aftermath of the 1980 coup in which Leftist activists—and even Left-leaning nonactivists, including many academics—were fired from their jobs, imprisoned, and often tortured, and the Left was rendered a shambles, while many right-wing activists (some of whom later took up positions in Islamic movements) came to enjoy state patronage. It is important to realize that in the eyes of many academics and intellectuals on the Left in Turkey, the "resurgence of Islam" seen in the 1990s is a direct result of the state's patronage of the Right and its persecution of the Left after 1980. Many also see developments regarding religion in Turkey (and the phenomenon of foreigners, especially Americans, studying it) in recent decades in the context of the cold war and U.S. interventions in places like Afghanistan in the 1980s, whereby the United States would be behind the resurgence of Islam in the Muslim world generally, including Turkey, the aim having been to support whoever would fight against communism. It is thus the United States who is ultimately responsible for the Islamic resurgence in Turkey.[46] These scenarios are neither entirely baseless, nor do they begin to account for and explain the significance of Islam in Turkey, as some commentators in and outside of Turkey suggest they do.

Then there are the scholars of Islam in the contemporary world, often working on the Arab world, Iran, and South or Southeast Asia, who fail to consider the Turkish case in its historical context (about which they are evidently poorly informed) and effectively write the country off as unlikely to be fertile ground for a serious analysis of Islam and modernity due to its alleged total abandonment of living Islamic traditions. It is as if the 70 million Muslims in Turkey are somehow not fully living Islam and not truly a part of the Muslim world; those societies to the north and west of Turkey, of course, chastise them for just the opposite reasons.

An important point connected to the practicalities of fieldwork that will be immediately obvious to the reader is that this book—and especially the later chapters—takes up almost exclusively the experiences of men. While in many spheres of Turkish society interaction between men and women unrelated by kinship is a common, normal part of everyday life, those I worked with tended to observe a strict segregation of the sexes. This was not so total that I never saw women at public events or even in private homes or never spoke with them. However, I would most often be introduced to women (usually my interlocutor's wife or sister) who would then politely excuse themselves to other rooms of the house. Before starting my research I was determined to not let mine be characterized by the usual gaps regarding women's experiences and tried to come up with various ways to interact with them (usually asking a man I had come to know whose wife or sister was a participant in the Sufi order if he thought she would mind joining us for an interview, so that I might inquire as to her experiences). After a few arranged (and highly contrived) interviews, it became clear that my pursuit of such work was going to be extremely uncomfortable for everyone involved and bore the risk of impeding, or even bringing an end to, my research in general. As I conducted this research alone, without my wife or another woman as a research partner, the world of women in the Muslim community I describe in this book was largely closed to me. While in my brief interviews with women participants, as well as those with men, I was assured that devotionally there were no differences in women's and men's practices and techniques, I here record my regret and dissatisfaction regarding what I am able to say about women's experiences in the order. I can only hope that others better positioned to do such work proceed to do it.[47]

Let me emphasize here—in the event they do not become clear in the pages that follow—a few points that I am *not* arguing. I am not claiming that the Sufi Muslim formations we will examine are the only examples of authentically functioning Islamic traditions in Turkey, and I do not wish to suggest this indirectly. I also do not claim that the specific arrangements Turkey has regarding religion, politics, and public life are models for other Muslims in other times or places. This is, importantly, also a suggestion most people in Turkey politely refuse. I also do not contend that there is something natural or inevitable about the liberalization of Islamic traditions in Turkey or anywhere else. I do hope, however, that as more and more social researchers and Muslims themselves address and reflect on the various and diverse articulations of Islam and modernity, the Turkish experience will no longer be overlooked or addressed so simplistically. It is also worth emphasizing that I do not try to read recent shifts in Turkish culture and politics in terms of modern political theory because I think such theories are the only ones that are universally valid; rather I do so mainly because it is in terms of the norms of such political theory that people in Turkey have come to know and transform themselves and their surroundings.

THE CHAPTERS

The structure of this book reflects its concern with both the genealogy—critical histories of the status of the present—and the ethnography of contemporary discourses and practices.[48] The first part of the book is a genealogy of contemporary forms of Islamic practice and modes of selfhood in Turkey, establishing the status of modernity in Turkey as initiated by Ottoman reform movements. Part II examines Islamic practices as techniques of ethical self-formation, drawing on examples from a Sufi order, and showing how Islamic virtues involve the retraining of desire and continually subjecting one's dispositions to normative judgment. Part III analyzes how Islamic practices are structurally transformed by the mass-broadcast mediation and liberalization of the social, economic, and political environment, transforming the religious sphere and the place of moral discourse in public life.

Chapter 1 is a genealogy of contemporary forms of Islamic practice and modes of selfhood in Turkey. Partly due to their geographic location and the heterogeneous nature of the empire's population (e.g., regarding provenance and religious faith, including those in government service), the Ottomans had a wide range of regimes of knowledge and power, epistemologies, and technologies to draw from to continually adjust their governance to changing circumstances. I show how the incorporation of modern techniques in the empire was a decision argued and legitimated on grounds internal to Islamic reasoning in order to reverse military defeats in Balkan Europe, of which the empire was a part. Republican Turkish policies regarding Islam are largely continuations of late Ottoman restructuring and reform of Islamic and other institutions. The genealogy of Turkish secularism is grounded in Ottoman Islamic reasoning.

I illustrate this by analyzing in Chapter 2 the transformations in the status of Sufi sheikhs in the later empire and argue that their increasing bureaucratization was the extension of increased rationalization of Ottoman administration and the normalization of the objects of governance into the Islamic sphere. The proscription of the orders in 1925 was part of a series of events begun decades earlier (which is not to say that this proscription was somehow inevitable), and the experiences of Sufis in the Republic of Turkey established in 1923 have been deeply conditioned by the legacies left to the republic by the late Ottoman Empire. Thus the characteristically modern modes of power—redoubled rationalizing of administration and normalizing of the objects of governance—and the particular kinds of knowledge and subjectivities associated with them had profoundly rearticulated the nature of discourse and practice among Sufis by the last third of the nineteenth century. This was well before there was any question of a republic.

Building on recent work in the anthropology of ethics as programs of self-formation and reformulations of the concept of tradition, Chapter 3 shows how Naqshbandi Sufis in Istanbul and several regional Turkish cities work to reform their dispositions by inscribing their practices within Islamic orthodoxy. I examine these Sufis' Islamic practices as a means through which moral selves are constituted in Muslims in the form of structured dispositions. I show how people come into contact with the Sufi order (even though the orders have been illegal since 1925), and how norms of sincerity and moral integrity are significant in both the attraction of the order to those who encounter it and in members' continuing participation. I then draw out the status of the ethical selves formed in and through disciplinary practices against the background of the institutions and histories discussed in prior chapters.

In Chapter 4, I examine the Sufis' practice of *sohbet* (Arabic *suhba*, which I translate as "companionship-in-conversation") as a technique of ritualized discourse and as an example of Islamic discipline aimed at constituting a virtuous disposition toward ethical practice and avoidance of sin. In *sohbet* lessons, alongside the importance of the content of the sheikh's discourse, the relationships ("companionships") formed in the act of oral transmission and liable to constitute ethically structured dispositions in devotees are the object of careful cultivation. Central to the functioning of this "discipline of presence," as I call *sohbet*, is the role of presence and repetition in the training of affect. Such a face-to-face mode of transmission has been characteristic of many kinds of Islamic religiosity in republican Turkey (and other countries), functioning parallel to and in the interstices of official, state-sanctioned Islamic institutions like the Presidency for Religious Affairs, mosques, and religious schools.

I then show in Chapter 5 how this discipline of presence is restructured by mass-broadcast media like radio. I discuss the impact of the Sufi order's radio station on the devotional practices and institutions previously described and how the use of radio as an attempt to maintain a sense of community in the mass-mediated environment of post-1980s Turkey introduces structural changes to the group's practice. What was formerly a carefully cultivated devotional practice can now be easily conflated with informational discourse in the public sphere. While the content of a given Islamic discourse may remain, its connection to the inculcation of ethical dispositions is often now equivocal. These documented microlevel changes at the level of Islamic practice have important implications for the status of the subject as Muslim and citizen in Turkey and for the place of moral discourse in public life.

Chapter 6 situates and examines the structural significance of these changes to devotional practices and Muslim religiosity within the profoundly transforming, liberalizing environment in the country in recent years. Based on fieldwork with participants in and administrators of Islamically oriented foundations (*vakıf*), I show how the importance of civil institutions like private foundations and associations is increasing. With the liberalization of Turkish political, economic, and social life in dialogue with EU protocols, traditional associational forms like the Sufi order lose their role as a "parallel sphere" of Islamic religiosity and knowledge transmission and have to compete in a broadened, more-inclusive public sphere that now includes a much wider range and subtlety of Islamic discourses than was previously the case under the regimes of Kemalist republican elites. Foundations appear to be playing an ever-greater role in setting the terms of Islamic discourse in Turkey, through both personnel (increasing numbers of the country's most respected and sophisticated Islamic scholars participate in foundation activities like seminars) and though their writings (many such scholars write columns in the Islamically oriented daily press). Moreover, Islamic discourse appears to be adjusting the style of its reasoning to "hold its own" in a public context in which shared conservative Islamic norms cannot be assumed.

The epilogue briefly elucidates the stakes involved in reconceptualizing Islam and modernity in Turkey. Turkish Muslims do not see themselves as "models" for any other Muslim society, but rather simply see themselves as living in continuity with the histories and genealogies this book elucidates, living simultaneously within Islamic traditions and political modernity. Many self-styled Europeans and Islamists around the world posit a radical otherness between Islam and Europe. Yet many in Turkey think that what is at stake in Turkey's entry negotiations with the EU—beyond the matter of reforming Turkey in certain areas—is really nothing less than the Enlightenment project, which invoked the possibility of shared juridical norms across differences of religion and whose humanism has been the basis for several centuries of Europeans' sense of legitimacy. To claim that Turkey—despite its secularism—is outside of Europe because of its Muslim identity, that is, because of religion, would be to signal Europe's abandonment of that Enlightenment project. It thus becomes clear how important it is to adequately conceptualize the issues—as well as false problems and nonstarters—involved in Turkey's relationship to the EU and to Europe.

PART I

GENEALOGIES OF THE TURKISH PRESENT

CHAPTER 1

OTTOMAN REFORM, ISLAMIC TRADITION, AND HISTORICAL DIFFERENCE

Whose history is being made?

—Talal Asad, *Genealogies of Religion*

WHAT BECAME THE REPUBLIC OF TURKEY IN 1923 was heir to the institutional structures and administrative experience and apparatus of the Ottoman Empire, the longest-lived and arguably the strongest empire that the Islamic world has seen. Today, with a population of over 70 million, Turkey is one of the world's most populous Muslim-majority countries and also a North Atlantic Treaty Organization member currently engaging in formal talks on entry into the European Union.[1] Those administrative elites who were instrumental in the establishment of this republic had been born and launched their careers in the late Ottoman environment, that is, the reign of Sultan Abdülhamid II (r. 1876–1909) and the subsequent "Young Turk" regimes of the Committee of Union and Progress, or CUP (1908–1918). What took place in the transition from empire to republic, and what does this genealogy make of the Turkish present? The processes through which Ottomans began to consciously transform their institutions and build new ones in the late eighteenth century are usually glossed as "Westernization." This is, as I argue shortly, an inadequate conceptualization and falsifies in advance several key issues that ought to be subject to scrutiny.

In examining the historicity of cultural institutions and practices in Turkey as the heir to a genealogy of Muslim reform, the important issues concern what this reform consisted of, in the name of what was undertaken and in the context of what kinds of imperatives. The incorporation into Ottoman administration of the characteristically modern techniques of governance, like formal rationalization and generalized discipline, did not take place as a result of colonialism (Anatolia and the Balkans not having been colonized), but rather as sovereign state reform on the part of a Muslim polity. As we will see, the creation of new institutions to train experts and technicians for the military and government led to incremental shifts in the prestige of various institutions, kinds of knowledge, and types of practitioners. For instance, the new military sciences were prestigious, the schools teaching them were relatively well funded, and their graduates had very good prospects of prestigious employment. Why were they prestigious? These were taken to be the knowledges that would allow the empire to defend itself. One did not need to study Arabic or Persian (the classic Islamic languages in the Ottoman lands and considered extremely prestigious over the centuries) to acquire these knowledges; French, German, or English was more useful. Over decades, such shifts amounted to several processes that only became clear with hindsight: the sphere of the "religious" came to be increasingly constituted and differentiated as such as an effect of the institutionalization and relative prestige of other regimes of knowledge and power. This was the onset of a process that only much later came to be called secularism, after it was largely in place and not before.[2]

Thus modern techniques of governance and modalities of power were not incorporated into Ottoman governmental technologies with the goal to "Westernize" or abandon Islamic norms in favor of non-Western ones.[3] Rather the aim was the strengthening of the Muslim polity, *as* a Muslim polity, vis-à-vis military, economic, and cultural onslaught from powerful, non-Muslim polities to the north and west.[4] Ottoman governmentality incorporated many Islamic institutions, such as mosques, *medreses* (advanced Islamic seminaries), and Sufi lodges, the funding and personnel of which were administered by the state by the later half of the nineteenth century. These are crucial elements in a genealogy of Islam and modernity in Turkey. The republic emerged from and acquired the cumulative experience of these efforts, which is clear from the reasoning the new republican leaders employed among themselves and in establishing their state in the international arena.

By the early eighteenth century, Ottoman rulers began to continually take conscious stock of their institutions and their functioning and undertook to transform them.[5] Why did they do this? What were the conditions in which they did, and what were their goals? For an understanding of the ways in which Ottoman society and institutions changed in the following centuries and then of the nature of the republic that would emerge in 1923, these turn out to be crucially important questions, for the way was prepared for these later processes and events by the preceding Ottoman reform movements. One way to conceptualize Ottoman reform is to see in it incremental shifts in the prestige and influence of various regimes of knowledge and power over the last 150 years of the empire. In other words, a study of Ottoman reform can be part of a genealogy of the onset of both modernity and what would eventually be called secularism in the latter-day Republic of Turkey.[6] Given the degree to which reform of social institutions and the social environment crucial to the formation of Muslim moral selves has been undertaken in Turkey, this chapter shows how the conditions for Islamic practice in contemporary Turkey are grounded in Ottoman reforms of the last century. We will then be able to address the extent to which the transformations in Islamic devotional practices examined in subsequent chapters are to be considered as developments within Islam and evaluate what becomes of an Islamic tradition of practice in a self-consciously and profoundly reforming society like Turkey.

This chapter examines how and why a new regime of power and knowledge was incorporated in the Ottoman empire, what kinds of shifts to which this led, and especially what it made of the grounds from which Muslims—as rulers and subjects—lived Muslim lives at the time and in the ensuing conditions. It is important to sketch out this background to more contemporary, present-day developments because it allows us to evaluate the very status of modernization and reform in relation to Islamic traditions in both the later empire and republic. The combination of the Muslim identity of the Ottoman Empire's ruling classes, the empire's geographic location, and the heterogeneous nature of the its population (e.g., regarding geographic provenance and religious denomination, including those in government service) put at the Ottomans' disposal a wide range of knowledges, epistemologies, and technologies to draw from in continually adjusting their governance to changing circumstances. We will see how the incorporation of modern governmental techniques to the empire was a decision argued and legitimated on grounds internal to Islamic reasoning in order to reverse military defeats in the Balkan Europe of which the empire was a part. As the empire collapsed by the turn of the twentieth century, the political culture of the elites who would eventually establish the republic in 1923 was formed in the context of the Balkans, where most of them were also born or spent formative years (including Mustafa Kemal—later Atatürk—himself, born in Salonica in present-day Greek Macedonia).[7] I argue that the institutional reform movement beginning in the eighteenth century was not dramatically different from what other European powers like Russia, Austro-Hungary, or Spain were undertaking. Turkey is thus the heir to an Ottoman genealogy of sovereign Muslim reform without an intervening colonialism.[8] Republican Turkish policies regarding Islam are largely continuations of this late Ottoman restructuring and reform of Islamic and other institutions, and hence, as I argue later, the genealogy of Turkish secularism is grounded in Ottoman Islamic traditions. Moreover, I will argue that one see continuities not only in existing Islamic institutions, discourses, and practices but also in ones that are *absent* as well—there is an Islamic genealogy to certain institutional absences in republican Turkey.

In this chapter we will first examine the context and nature of Ottoman reform movements. Then we will explore the attitudes of the ulema, or Muslim scholars—who had held positions of influence and respect in the Muslim community for centuries—toward these reforms. We will pay particular attention to the ulema's support for the reforms and their reasons for it. We will also look at the attitudes of a new type of figure who emerged in the late Ottoman period: the Islamist intellectual. The way reform was debated by Ottoman ulema and Islamist intellectuals is a key issue in situating Ottoman reform within Islamic traditions. It is also in this broader context of reform and Islamic institutions in general that Sufis' attitudes toward reform need to be seen, which we take up in the next chapter. We examine in some detail the question of the Islamic bases for the transition to the republic by such moves as the abolition of the sultanate and then of the caliphate. And finally, I note the significance of the fact that these late Ottoman Muslim identities and stances are a topic of much interest and research by Muslim scholars in contemporary Turkey, who are seeking to go beyond the simplistic "Islamist versus secularist" or "Ottomanist versus Kemalist" approach to religious identities that has been so prevalent in much historiography in the country, including among conservative Muslims.

THE IDEA OF REFORM

Much of the established historiography of this period of Ottoman reform characterizes it as one in which Ottomans came to see that "religion" was a problem for the vitality of the empire and needed to be contained by a wide-ranging project of reform amounting to secularization (Berkes 1998). Some have interpreted Ottoman invocation of Islamic reasoning and a redoubled emphasis on Islamic unity (*ittihad-ı İslâm*) in instrumental terms as an attempt to carry out a secular agenda by making manipulative use of Islamic discourses (Lewis 1968). This view has been adjusted in recent years by scholars focusing their attention on the processes of reform and especially their rationale at the time. Rather than uncritically and retroactively projecting a later ethos of secularism back to the late Ottoman context, historians have begun to take a closer look at the specific goals and styles of reasoning characteristic of those undertaking Ottoman reforms and have concluded that while certain individuals were no doubt instrumental in their recourse to Islamic discourse, there was no overarching project to attenuate the influence and effects of Islam in society on the part of the vast majority of influential Ottoman administrators in the nineteenth century. On the contrary, the evidence suggests that the aim of the reforms was precisely to maintain, or even amplify, both the influence of Islam on society and individuals and the state's ability to accomplish this (Fortna 2002; Abu-Manneh 1994). I suggest that the appropriate term to describe the kinds of techniques used to reorganize institutions is "modern." With their reforms, the Ottomans were incorporating into their administrative apparatus characteristically modern forms of power Michel Foucault identified as governmentality, a mode of exercising power that is concerned with

> not territory but, rather, a sort of complex composed of men and things. The things, in this sense, with which government is to be concerned are in fact men, but men in their relations, their links, their imbrication with those things that are wealth, resources, means of subsistence, the territory with its specific qualities, climate, irrigation, fertility, and so on; men in their relation to those other things that are customs, habits, ways of acting and thinking, and so on; and finally men in their relation to those still other things that might be accidents and misfortunes such as famine, epidemics, death, and so on. (2003b, 235)

The concrete configurations of knowledge and power—which Foucault referred to as technologies (1979)—that constituted this regime of governmentality were rationalization of administration (Weber 1978) and normalization of the objects of governance (Foucault 1979). Rationalization consists of explicit deliberation and calculation about the functioning of institutions and distribution of resources, while normalization refers to the proliferation of grids of intelligibility, means for making measurements according to normative benchmarks, whereby an increasingly finer scale of new objects (e.g., populations and individuals) become thought of in terms of these new normative knowledges (e.g., the emergent human sciences) and are seized hold of and manipulated according to their logic. It would however be a mistake to see the reform of Islamic institutions in terms of the modern versus traditional, as if these constituted two ontologically different qualities of existence, with modern social forms inevitably triumphing over the traditional. Such an understanding misrecognizes the nature of a tradition, which I will discuss shortly. What is important regarding a tradition are the modes of reasoning through which adjustments are made and the kinds of practices and selves they enable.

OTTOMAN COMMENSURABILITY AND
HISTORICAL DIFFERENCE

In theorizing Ottoman reform, one of the major issues with which we have to deal is the question of historical difference, that is, the extent to which we should consider the Ottomans to have been different from the so-called West. One way to approach these issues of historical difference is through the concept of incommensurability, meaning "lack of common measure." The term has been used with some variations by scholars working in mathematics, the philosophy of language, moral philosophy, and historiography. For some, the term refers to a situation in which a translation of one text into another cannot be produced without serious distortion (Davidson 2001) or to "items that cannot be precisely measured by some common scale of units of value" (Chang 1997, 2). Similar to this latter definition, others have used the term to denote situations in which standards of evaluation and assessment are not shared, either because people involved may start reasoning from different premises or because they may have different conceptions of or standards for when an account or argument is considered reasonable or the claims being discussed are, at least partially, untranslatable (MacIntyre 1989).

The question of commensurability has been addressed—usually implicitly—in the work of Alasdair MacIntyre and has been influential in anthropological work recently. This is so for several reasons. First, MacIntyre forcefully and rigorously lays out an account of what some might call the historical and cultural specificity of the modern West (and in particular what he controversially sees as the post-Enlightenment West's characteristic aporias), which is a project on which many anthropologists have been working as well, especially through their examination of the historical baggage borne by social-scientific concepts. Secondly, MacIntyre gives an account of tradition that links up discourses, practices, and conceptions of the good into particular ways of life (MacIntyre 1984). In the process, he significantly complicates important concepts anthropologists and others have used, like tradition itself, culture, religion, practice, habitus (Aristotle's *hexis*), and ethics. To be sure, MacIntyre's account of how these concepts relate to one another, and what their status is in the West in the aftermath of the Enlightenment, is controversial, and I do not intend to defend his ultimate claims about this. But I find his linking up of practice, tradition, and ways of life as inspired by differing ideas of human flourishing ("excellence" in his term) useful and will take it up in the pages that follow. By analyzing Islam with the concept of tradition, we will also be in a better position to see how Islam sits with the category of religion, and specifically the historical process through which Islam was made into a religion in the Ottoman Empire. In doing so, we will also lay out an argument about the commensurability of Islamic traditions and modern social forms.

In anthropological writing on Islam inspired by work on ethics and moral philosophy, work on tradition often refers to "virtues, ethical capacities and forms of reasoning" and "how to organize [one's] daily conduct in accord with principles of Islamic piety and virtuous behavior" (Mahmood 2005, 4). One of the more subtle and sophisticated recent scholars working in this vein, Mahmood examines the women's mosque movement within the Islamic revival in Egypt by first questioning the normative liberatory subject of liberal politics, even in the analysis of those who consider themselves to be pushing up against and critiquing those norms, for example from within feminism. "This scholarship," Mahmood argues, "elides dimensions of human action whose ethical and political status does not map onto the logic of repression and resistance [central to liberal notions of the political subject of liberty]" (2005, 14). In her work, Mahmood seeks to "grasp these modes of action *indebted to other reasons and histories*" (Mahmood 2005, 14; emphasis added). She explores Egyptian Muslim women's life-worlds as instances of what she calls "operations of power that construct different kinds of bodies, knowledges and subjectivities whose trajectories do not follow the entelechy of liberatory politics" (14). It is precisely this notion of Islamic traditions as "other histories" or of "other life-worlds" that I wish to question, for the historical evidence suggests that it will be of partial but limited use in conceptualizing Ottoman Islamic traditions to lean too heavily on these notions without seeing them as deeply imbricated with modern ones.

The Ottomans saw themselves and their empire as commensurable with the other polities of Europe, especially from the point of view of warfare, but also economically, politically, and culturally, given that the Balkans were central territories of the empire, along with western Anatolia (Ágoston 2005; Murphey 1999). Indeed, the Ottoman "war machine" not only was comparable to others in Europe from the late fifteenth to early seventeenth centuries but also was in crucial respects that were important to players at that time—such as professionalization and provisioning—more advanced: "The organizational revolution which transformed European military practice and allowed for the sustaining of armies of mass mobilization for the first time came to realization only in the closing decades of the seventeenth century. This revolution in practice was initially driven by necessity rather than invention, and results were at first mostly limited to France. At the close of the seventeenth century the Ottomans were still leagues ahead of their European contemporaries in the development of centralized modes for resource extraction and allocation for use in war" (Murphey 1999, 98).

By the late seventeenth century, a new situation was presenting itself to the Ottomans: they asked themselves, "Given that it is a fact that we are in possession of the true faith, why are we losing wars to infidels?" As reflected in the minutes of divan councils between the sultan and his highest-ranking civil and religious functionaries and military commanders, as well as in advice reports known as *nasihatnâme* presented to the sultan, the Ottomans began to discuss among themselves their problems with polities bordering them on the north and west in terms of diplomacy, military power, and technique (Aksan 2007). The Ottomans did not have the luxury of abstractly hypothesizing about what ideally Islamic governance would be in a vacuum, with no global relations of power involving threatening non-Muslim polities, their military onslaught, and their interference in the internal affairs of the Ottoman polity: "For contemporary Ottomans, the basic fact in their conception of the need for reform was the continued military defeats they endured" (Findley 1980, 114). What form institutions should take and how they should function were the subject of intensifying debate by Ottoman authorities. In the Ottoman context, questions of good governance, formulated as proper Islamic governance, were always imbricated with the pragmatic issues surrounding how to govern a multiconfessional, multiethnic empire, including large populations of Christians and Jews. In other words, the Ottomans did not approach questions of how to strengthen Muslim's institutions and reform their knowledge as abstract, philosophical matters or questions of identity, at least not initially: "A kind of dynamic reaction to the trauma of helplessness in the face of defeat, so widely apparent in the Middle East a half a century later, was thus already in evidence at the topmost echelons of the Ottoman 'center.' More than that, it had begun to radiate downward and outward, provoking or preparing the way for changes in many phases of the administration and in many phases of its interactions with subject classes. The concern for military reform and for generating increased levels of resources are parts of this process" (Findley 1980, 116).

One of the most important of the reformers in the Ottoman service prior to the reign of Sultan Selim III (r. 1789–1807; considered to have been the first to try to institutionalize reforms) was Ibrahim Müteferrika (d. 1745), a Hungarian (apparently Unitarian) convert to Islam.[9] In 1731 Müteferrika published a printed booklet titled "Reasoned Procedures for the Organization of Nations" (Usul ül-Hikem fi Nizam ül-Ümem).[10] The fact that this treatise was printed is itself greatly significant, as printing in the Arabic script of texts in Turkish had only recently been permitted in the empire, as a result of Müteferrika himself petitioning the sultan to open a press in 1727 as itself an important part of reform. Müteferrika argued that it was absolutely vital to reform the empire's military, and that this could be accomplished by the Ottomans examining and learning from the experiences of other states, first and fore-most the Habsburgs (Austro-Hungary) and Romanovs (Russia): "Specifically he pointed to the [Ottoman] disorder in strategy and logistics, to the huge size of the forces, to the total lack of discipline which overrode individual courage and wisdom, and the need for accurate intelligence of the enemy" (Aksan 2007, 187). Müteferrika argued that while the Ottomans were Mus-lims and the legitimacy of the empire laid on its following the shari'a, it was not only possible but necessary to adopt successful aspects of "Christian armies" into the Ottoman repertoire.

Müteferrika's was not an isolated proposal but rather one of an entire genre of treatises that would be penned by Ottoman administrators, gov-ernors, military commanders, and ulema. The empire's problems were thus increasingly taken to be essentially technical in nature, involving organiza-tion, expertise, and equipment; in other words, the problem was not seen as a problem with Islam or the Ottoman conception of justice. Indeed, not only would the Ottomans not be compromising their Muslim identity by undertaking beneficial reforms, but it was positively incumbent upon them, as Muslims, to do so.

The eventual strategy was the well-known reorganization of the military beginning with Sultan Selim III's Nizam-i Cedid ("New Order" reforms) in the late eighteenth century and continuing under the Tanzimat after Sultan Mahmud II's destruction of the Janissary corps in 1826.[11] The Ottoman reformers also immediately realized that all of this was going to be extremely expensive. Hence they began a review of the state's income, an identification of "productive" resources, the management of finances and their expendi-tures, and an attempt to render each of these more efficient, soon leading to a full-blown administrative reform. In hindsight, these reforms amount to the onset of a new Ottoman governmentality. These techniques were eminently transposable and quickly found application in the military, schools, factories, and prisons.[12] The Ottomans began to send delegations to other European capitals to consult on the new techniques, seeking to incorporate them into their military, and requested the services of advisers from Paris, London, and Berlin. Hence the incorporation into Ottoman administration of charac-teristically modern techniques, like formal rationalization and generalized discipline, did not take place as a result of colonialism (Anatolia and the Balkans not having been colonized) but rather as sovereign state reform on the part of a Muslim polity.[13] Equally important, we should not understand this incorporation as constituting simply "Westernization," if by this term we would elide the fragmented and provincial character of many regions that would eventually refer to themselves as the "West." Indeed, such places as Spain, Sweden, Austro-Hungary, and Russia were also sending officers and administrators for training in such centers as Paris, London, and Berlin, like the Ottomans, to observe and acquire those emerging techniques constitutive of the distinctively modern forms of power.[14] The Ottomans were simply one of these sovereign polities seeking more efficient ways to maximize resources and engage in more efficient warfare. The prospects of failing to do so were already becoming clear to the Ottomans by at least the second half of the eighteenth century.

EUROPEAN PROVINCES OF THE MUSLIM WORLD

The "Noble Edict of the Rose Garden" (Hatt-ı Şerif-i Gülhane) was promulgated in 1839 and is often taken by historians to mark the intensification of the Ottoman reforms known collectively as the Tanzimat (or Tanzimat-i Hayriye, the "beneficial and auspicious reforms").[15] The aim of the reforms was to create a stronger apparatus through which to govern the empire, principally through centralization and modernization. The Tanizmat also marks a shift in the center of Ottoman power from the sultan to the bureaucracy, which had been prepared by Sultan Mahmud II (r. 1808–1839), who had died earlier the same year as the edict of Gülhane. With the edict, the sultan recommitted himself to certain principles that were implied to be already in effect but that he now intended to strengthen.[16] The edict also marks the official commitment of the Ottoman authorities, and specifically the sultan, to uphold one of the arrangements central to liberal political thought and often seen as a condition for secularism: the principle of the equality of religious adherents before the law. Both the forum in which it the edict was promulgated and its contents are significant. It was read in a garden outside the walls of the palace to a group of Ottoman dignitaries and foreign diplomats, amounting to the Ottomans presenting to foreigners in a semipublic space their intentions regarding what were, in principle, their internal affairs. The text was also published in the state's official gazette, and copies were sent to the provinces to be read publicly. The main points of the edict were that the Ottomans would guarantee the life, honor, and property of all the sultan's subjects; inaugurate a more efficient and just system of taxation and the abolition of tax farming; begin regular recruitment into the armed forces (implying that this would be regardless of recruits' religion); and uphold equality before the law regardless of subjects' religion (although this was somewhat differently worded in the Turkish and French texts of the edict).[17] The Ottomans were dealing with problems on several fronts at the time the edict was promulgated, which had led historians to debate its sincerity.

Two points are worth emphasizing about the edict. First is the circumstances and concrete form in which the Ottomans undertook liberal reform. The very existence of the empire was threatened by the insurgent governor of

Egypt, Mehmet Ali, but also by increasingly destabilizing and serious interventions by foreign powers under the pretext of protecting Christians from Ottoman despotism and predation. This had reached the point where territories of the empire were being lost (e.g., in the Balkans and the Morea, the eventual Greece), with the scenario usually being rebellion due to Ottoman misrule, which was either spontaneously local or strongly instigated through agents and material support from outside powers; Ottoman attempts to put down these rebellions were inevitably portrayed as yet another atrocity by the "savage Turks" against an oppressed Christian community, which was followed by open diplomatic and material support for the rebels by outside powers and demands for autonomy from the Ottomans. The incorporation of liberal reforms was thus something the Ottomans felt was in their interest, which leads to the second point. The reasoning behind the edict and other such reforms was internal to Ottoman Islamic discursive traditions, putting the legitimacy and desirability of the new reforms in terms of Islamic traditions as they had been interpreted by Ottoman authorities. The edict's opening lines are the following:

> It is known, far and wide, that from [the time of] the emergence of the Ottoman dynasty, the glorious precepts of the Quran and the exalted laws of the shari'a were thoroughly honored. Hence the sublime Ottoman state increased in might and glory, and all its subjects, without exception, rose to the highest degree of comfort and prosperity. In the last one hundred and fifty years, a series of mishaps and myriad causes brought about a disregard for the sacred shari'a laws and the beneficent regulations [of the sultans], and hence the former power and prosperity turned into weakness and poverty. It is an unassailable fact that states not ruled by the laws of the shari'a have no chance to prevail. Such deliberations are ever present in our [i.e., the sultan's] mind. Ever since the day of our advent to the throne, our mind has been ceaselessly engaged in thoughts on the welfare and the satisfaction of the [subject] peoples, and on the improvement of the conditions of the provinces. Considering the geographical position of the Ottoman provinces, the fertility of the soil, and the aptitude and intelligence of the inhabitants of the empire, the conviction should remain that by striving to find efficacious means, the result can be attained, with the help of God, within a few years. Full of confidence, therefore, in the help and beneficence of the Almighty and in the support of our Prophet, we deem it appropriate to establish novel regulations in order to provide our sublime state and our protected domains with the benefits of good administration. (Mustafa Reşid Paşa 2006, 336–37)

The discourse was essentially one of renewal from within established traditions of Islam and the related Ottoman traditions of statecraft. Abu-Manneh

(1994) has argued that the edict should thus be seen not as a move against those traditions but one that emerged from and developed within them. He points out that the figure generally accepted as the author of the Gülhane text, Mustafa Reşid Pasha, had been strongly influenced by his "mentor and protector" in the Ottoman administration for many years, Pertev Pasha, "who was known to hold an extremely Sunni-orthodox outlook. Indeed, . . . the ideals that were to find expression in the [Gülhane] rescript seem to have been shared by many members of the Ottoman political and religious elite, and were the subject of much discussion before the drafting of the Gülhane" (Abu-Manneh 1994, 175). In other words, the Gülhane edict was not the product of marginal modernizers with an implicit agenda to Westernize the empire, let alone secularize it, but was rather the product of reasoning and debate among mainstream (orthodox Sunni Muslim) statesmen aiming to strengthen the empire as a Muslim polity.

In the course of their reforms, the Ottomans decided that experts proficient in new disciplines were needed, as were the institutions that would produce such experts. As we have seen, the first beneficiary of the new reforms was to be the military, which was understandable, since one of the most pressing issues was precisely to shore up the empire's declining military and strategic situation. In retrospect, the foundation of the new institutions producing new kinds of knowledge and new types of practitioners of those knowledges amount to the origin of the arrangements that later in Turkey came to be called secularism. In this context secularism does not so much represent the separation of something called religion from something called public life (which it has nonetheless come to mean, in principle, for many) but refers, in practice, primarily to institutional issues of how much power is to be accorded to those whose authority derives from their knowledge of the Islamic tradition. The main issues for the Ottomans were arguably neither philosophical ones nor matters of identity. In important Muslim centers like the Balkans and Caucasus, it had become clear by the late nineteenth century that there would simply be no more Muslims there if they failed to reorganize the regime of power and knowledge, and those involved certainly did not consider it to be a matter of measures that would lead to their abandonment of the Islamic tradition, versus other measures that would not. Similar processes have taken place in other parts of the Muslim world, including the Middle East, but perhaps not so dramatically.

Most of the countries considered to unproblematically constitute a part of the present cultural and political geography of Europe were actively engaged in a similar process of incorporating (from without) as many of these modern techniques as possible by sending military and administrative commissions to Paris, London, and Berlin as observers.[18] These processes have been retrospectively normalized, aided by nationalist historiographies of those aspiring to European status, as developments within a homogeneous Europe; in the case of the transfer of these techniques to Ottoman lands, it somehow becomes a matter of civilizations. In other words, I am arguing that there is nothing unnatural about Ottoman appropriations of modern disciplinary technologies of power any more than there is anything natural about Vienna, Rome, or Petersburg doing the same. Evidence of this can be found in instances like the Prussian chief of staff Helmuth von Moltke writing in his memoirs of his experiences as an inspector, reorganizer, and trainer of Ottoman forces in the 1830s, where he compares Mahmud II—quite unfavorably—with Peter the Great of Russia, who had similarly requested assistance from Berlin, Paris, and London in the reorganization of the Russian military: "In Russia the foreigners may have been hated; in Turkey [sic] they are despised."[19] Ottoman modernizers may have been simply imitating postures originating in points further west; the important point is that Greek, Serbian, or Bulgarian modernizers were no different on this and similar scores, nor for that matter were Spanish, Russian, or Danish modernizers.

The developments described here all took place within one of the most important parts of the Muslim world, the central Ottoman lands. What in this context—which after all encapsulates particularly potently the global context of power relations Muslims have found themselves in—is the Islamic tradition, and what are the criteria of continuity according to which we might arrive at a definition? These questions, which go to the heart of the matter of Islam in the contemporary world, cannot be adequately addressed by any framework that would have us elide the history of the past few centuries outlined here. Invocations of continuity (on the part of Muslims, commentators, or both) do not constitute continuity in practice. Ever since the events outlined previously, the study of practices in and through which Muslim selves are constituted, that is, the modes of Islamic ethical subject formation, must necessarily take account of these microlevel articulations of modes with differential historicities. The important point is that these multiple historicities need to be recognized as now a feature of Islamic traditions themselves.

OTTOMAN EUROPE: THE BALKANS BEYOND DIFFERENCE AND INCOMMENSURABILITY

In the closing years of the nineteenth century, Sultan Abdülhamid's regime began an on-again-off-again emphasis on pan-Islamic unity ("ittihad-ı İslâm"; generally overrated by the Western powers and the object of hysteria, especially on the part of the British) and attempted to strengthen the ties between the empire's center and the Arab provinces (Deringil 1998). However the significance of the Balkans to the identity of the empire is clarified when one considers what the loss of the territories in the Balkan Wars of 1912 and 1913 meant for Ottomans at the time. As Zürcher writes,

> [The] importance of the Ottoman losses in the Balkan war cannot be overstated. It was a disaster in human, economic and cultural terms. The empire lost nearly all its European territories, over 60,000 square miles in all, with nearly four million inhabitants. Again, as in 1878, Istanbul was deluged with Muslim refugees who had lost everything. There were severe outbreaks of typhus and cholera and a very high mortality rate among the refugees. Their resettlement caused enormous problems and many spent the next few years in squatter towns. But the significance went even deeper: the areas lost (Macedonia, Albania, Thrace) had been core areas of the empire for over 500 years. They were the richest and most developed provinces and a disproportionate part of the Ottoman ruling elite hailed from them. Salonica, after all, had been the cradle of the [Committee of Union and Progress]. A side effect of the losses [of the multiethnic, predominately Christian Balkans] was that now, for the first time in Ottoman history, ethnic Turks became a majority of the population [in the remaining Ottoman territory]. (Zürcher 2004, 108–9)

The genealogy of social, political, and religious formations in Turkey needs to placed squarely in this Balkan context, which raises some conceptual points in the context of a discussion about Islamic traditions. Most obviously is the idea that one of the most powerful, and culturally influential, polities the Islamic world ever produced, the Ottoman Empire, was, in crucial respects, a Balkan polity. The aim here is not to replace categories like East, West, or Middle East with 'the Balkans.'[20] I refer to the Balkans here for mainly heuristic purposes, that is, if we insist on identifying the political development of the Ottoman Empire and Turkish republic with a particular geographical region, this region ought to be the Balkans, for it will prove more fruitful in clarifying the nature of things like the political culture that has been characteristic of republican social life. We need to overcome our sense of anxiety at the location of major centers of Islamic civilization outside the region now known as the Middle East, for the geography now known as Europe is an integral part of that Islamic civilization. The converse is also the case, namely, that important areas of Islamic civilization have been in what is now considered to be Europe (Andalusia and the Ottoman Balkans being two obvious cases in point). This resituating of the Turkish present in a Balkan Islamic context aids in understanding the genealogy of late Ottoman and early republican political elites and their rationalities; the structure and status of discourse and practice in Turkey; intellectual and social movements like religious revivalism and nationalism; and popular tastes, architecture, spatial sensibilities, and lifestyles.

The importance of the Balkan context thus should be kept prominently in mind when considering the transition from the empire to the republic, as a large number of figures and personnel (especially officers of the CUP) prominent in the second constitutional period (1908–1918) and who would play an active role in the nationalist resistance, independence war (1921–1922), and establishment of the republic in 1923 were born or spent formative years in the empire's Macedonian and Thracian territories in the Balkans.[21] The empire's Balkan provinces were the context in which those active in the war of independence and in the establishment and organization of the republic gained their formative experience. This was an extremely tumultuous time, in which finer principles were subject to the brutal test of efficiency and success in the face of military onslaught by more powerful enemies; the price of failure was loss of life, land, and property through what is now called ethnic cleansing. These experiences figure prominently in the rationale of the early republican elites, who were clearly acting and organizing in and for a world characterized by this type of environment, and who had no illusions about the fate of those polities felt by their neighbors to be weak. This is what the front line of the Muslim world vis-à-vis Europe had come to look like by the twentieth century and goes a long way toward explaining why a majority of ulema enthusiastically supported the 1908 CUP coup against Abdülhamid and the restoration of the constitution.

NATIONALISM AND MUSLIMIFICATION

One of the features of the Balkans most destructive to Ottoman efforts at self-preservation (and, of course, so liberating in the eyes of the respective populations) was nationalism. To the extent that rural populations could be infected (as the Ottomans saw it) with the new ideology, it was much easier to get them to see the Ottomans as foreign and thereby incite them to rebellion. Clearly, by the time of the Balkan Wars, nationalism was the only game in town; it was being used most effectively by former subject populations in the series of rebellions and disasters by which the Ottomans effectively lost their former heartlands in the Balkans. The officers prominent in the subsequent Turkish nationalist resistance movement came out of this environment, and it has clearly marked the character of Turkish political culture ever since.

By 1915, one out of four Muslims living in the remaining Ottoman territory was a refugee from the Balkans or Caucasus or the child of one (Zürcher 2000, 160). If we consider that very few of these refugees would have been Kurds or assimilated into Kurdish environments, it follows that a very high proportion, probably more than half, of the non-Kurdish Muslim population of what would become republican Turkey were of Balkan or Caucasian extraction.[22] This provenance, along with the extreme brutality of the violence many of them suffered and witnessed prior to and during their migration as well as the fact that many of the Ottoman officers that were commanding Ottoman armies dealing with these events in the Balkan Wars and Caucasus were themselves from the Balkans and Caucasus, goes a long way toward explaining the tone and emphasis of what Zürcher has called the period's "reactive nationalism," an increasingly beleaguered and pragmatic effort by Ottoman leaders to prevent these events from happening again (e.g., at the hands of remaining minorities like the Armenians, leading to the latter's deportation and massacre; Zürcher 2000, 160, 172).[23] Muslims in the Ottoman Empire were among the last to take up nationalism, only doing so after it was taking hold among some Balkan Christians: "Ottoman Muslim nationalism became very strong . . . after 1912. The fact that at least a quarter of the Muslim population of Anatolia now consisted of *muhacirs*, refugees—or children of refugees—from areas in the Balkans, the Black Sea region or the Caucasus that Christian states had conquered, added bitterness to the ethnic tensions. These people remembered how they or their parents had been forced to leave their ancestral homes, often more than once, and were determined not to let this happen again" (Zürcher 2004, 117).

A further example of the impact of Balkan social and political tendencies can be seen in the effects of nationalism as the model of the republic's political sovereignty that emerged from the Balkan Wars, World War I, and the war of independence. The loss of the Balkans and the region's multiethnic, predominantly Christian population was followed by forced migrations, expulsions, and exchanges, as well as informal pressure on remaining minorities, such that the population of what became the Republic of Turkey had been dramatically homogenized from a multiconfessional and multiethnic one into a 98-percent-Muslim one on the model of the formation of nation-states in the Balkans (which saw the violent expulsion of hundreds of thousands of Muslims and their flight toward remaining Ottoman and, later, republican territory). This process, in turn, led to an interesting situation for the republican elites after 1923, for the nascent bourgeoisie of the late Ottoman period had been predominantly composed of (mostly Greek and Armenian) minorities, who were also considered in a sense to stand between the Muslim majority of the empire and Europe. This bourgeois class was now gone. Çağlar Keyder describes the ensuing situation for the new republican (Muslim Turkish) elite identity vis-à-vis Europe thus:

> The social removal of ethnies considered alien . . . had the effect of purging the ambivalence that the nationalist elites would otherwise have had to wrestle with. This removal of the material anchoring of Western practices and lifestyles made it possible to imagine a fictional West with no immediate material reference. It could, therefore, be presented in rhetoric in an

idealized version with no damaging or dislocating effects. Once the negative dimension was eliminated, modernization could be presented as an entirely positive project against which no defensive posturing was necessary. The elites did not feel any colonial resentment; *they did not see themselves as belonging to a world different from the one they sought to emulate.* (Keyder 1997, 50; emphasis added)

Turkey thus, in a sense, emerged on the front line of the assault by polities that were in the process of incorporating techniques of discipline and governmentality (imperial Russia and Austro-Hungary) outlined above. The history of the late Ottoman Empire and republican Turkey today may be considered an extended and ongoing experiment in the chain of events entailed by the engagement of a sovereign Muslim polity located on the near margin of the heartland of industrial capitalism with specifically modern forms of power and their attendant modes of subjection.[24] The structure of the positions from which problems were identified and analyzed and the measures proposed to solve them—in short, the relations of power and force and the conditions for strategic calculation and agency—bears in the Turkish case the clear and explicit traces of a sovereign polity attempting to incorporate modern forms of power in order to prevent its own domination by nonbelievers, as would eventually be the case of so much of the Muslim world. What this entailed, of course, was the production and application of new kinds of knowledge that existing institutions were not producing but that had to be gleaned elsewhere. The incorporation of modern disciplinary techniques was, to be sure, a bringing in from without, but from the perspective of the history of Islam there is nothing new about this per se.[25] What was new, however, was the relative authority and prestige accorded to those knowledges, the proliferation of which was considered to enable Muslims to defend themselves (e.g., military engineering and medicine; sanitation and hygiene; etc.). The process of incorporation of new technologies of governance discussed in this chapter does not appear to have been experienced by the Ottomans as a capitulation to the hostile enemy's cultural imperialism even in later periods, for, as Keyder has pointed out, "Unlike other nationalists of the Third World, the Ottomans did not feel particularly resentful toward the West. Having withstood overt colonization and preserved the integrity of the state, they perceived their predicament in the paradigm of the European interstate system and in the perspective of intricate alliances and enmities that fueled the world of the Great Powers" (1993, 22).

ISLAMIC GENEALOGIES OF OTTOMAN REFORM

It is crucial to situate a discussion of late Ottoman Islamic traditions in the context of the imperatives of power outlined previously, for these loomed very large and concrete in the minds of Ottoman Muslims, especially those in and near the capital, to an extent that may be underappreciated by scholars more familiar with developments among Muslims in other regions. The reforms just discussed had a major impact on Islamic institutions, discourses, and practices, which we will also see included Sufis. These changes in Islamic institutions are well illustrated by looking at two important processes: transformations in the Islamic scholarly establishment, the ulema, and the emergence and rise in importance of noncleric "Islamist intellectuals."[26] (They are also well illustrated by the photograph in Figure 1.1.) For decades, the historiography of Ottoman modernization and reform considered the ulema as a

Figure 1.1   "Medreset'ül-Mütehassısîn derûnendeki Sultan Abdülhamid Han-ı Evvel Kütüphanesi. Salonlarından biri." [A room of the Sultan Abdülhamid Library in the Mütehassısîn Medrese.] This *medrese* was established in the series of *medrese* reforms of 1914 as a kind of postgraduate institute of advanced Islamic studies, at the pinnacle of the Ottoman *medrese* system. What is remarkable about this photograph of the library of one of the highest institutes of Islamic learning in the Ottoman Empire is how indistinguishable it is from other contemporary libraries throughout the world attached to institutions that were not particularly "Islamic."

Source: Photo from the İlmiye Sâlnâmesi of 1334 [1915/1916].

reactionary force opposed to reform.[27] More recent, careful work on materials produced by the ulema themselves paints a much different picture. Analysis by historians of writings by and debates among ulema, their published articles in journals appearing in the late nineteenth and twentieth centuries, and their unpublished memoirs has led to the conclusion that practically all of them supported the notion that institutions in the empire and among Muslims in other geographies needed profound and urgent reform generally.[28] In the Ottoman context of the late nineteenth and early twentieth centuries, this translated into the ulema's increasing support for the opposition to Sultan Abdülhamid, which by the end of the nineteenth century meant support for the CUP, a clandestine circle of reform-minded constitutionalists composed of émigrés and a significant number of military cadets.[29] İsmail Kara summarizes the ulema's transformations and evolving attitudes: "This process can be seen as a substitution by the ulema of the turban [in favor of] the fez, their increasing use of an 'intellectual' language, their critical attitude towards classical institutions like the caliphate and their increased acceptance of the teaching-thinking-perception clichés of the time. In short, this change meant an 'intellectualization,' in the modern sense of the word, of the ulema" (2005, 164).

This evaluation of the ulema's stance in the sociopolitical landscape of the late Ottoman Empire is very significant on several levels. First, in the contemporary politics of history and historiography in Turkey, this approach renders problematic several assumptions and approaches to the history of the late empire and early republic. Summarizing a great many nuanced positions, one can say that the more Kemalist, secularist, modernist historiography has emphasized the ulema's (and indeed all Islamic players' and institutions') backwardness and their obstruction of progress (a theme that, in fact, dates to the later empire itself, as it was propounded by many European Orientalists and echoed by some in the empire). Meanwhile, many writers in the republican period identifying themselves as Islamist or conservative and generally, with a degree of hostility toward the Kemalist reforms, have tended to portray the ulema as a bastion of authentic Islamic identity and tradition essentially unchanged since the early years of the empire and standing alongside the allegedly pious sultan in his heroic efforts to maintain the empire (which they emphasize was the caliphate). This new generation of scholarship rejects both of these approaches, and it initially pointed out that the merest perusal of the actual writings of the Ottoman ulema and the Islamists in question renders these approaches utterly misguided.[30]

Second, this recent scholarship establishes that a conception of Ottoman reform and modernization that sees enlightened secularist reformers on the one hand and religiously inspired opponents of change on the other is laughably inadequate and untenable. Again, several issues are at stake. The reason why such a perception has reigned for so many years has obviously to do with the interrelated writings of westerners on the topic of Islam and modernity (i.e., Islam as an obstacle to modernization, much the same as they saw religion in general) and the relative lack of interest on the part of early republican elites in exploring internal debates about modernization among the empire's Islamic scholars.

Third is the matter İ. Kara referred to as intellectualization. On this point, two phenomena were in play during this time: the emergence of the intellectual as a type of person, which was closely linked to the spread of print journalism and writing for and the reading of periodicals; the increasing familiarity of the ulema with this emergent sphere; and the eventual transformation of many of the prominent ulema of the day into this newly identifiable intellectual.[31] This is very significant because it illustrates quite dramatically that the idea that Islamic modalities of knowledge, on the one hand, and modern ones, on the other, existing in ontologically different spheres is too simplistic, and rather we see what the imbrication of Islamic and modern regimes of knowledge and power looked like in the writings and persons of many ulema, and even Sufi sheikhs (as we see in the next chapter).

Finally, if Ottoman ulema and Islamist intellectuals were arguing for not only the legitimacy but also the dire necessity of reform on grounds internal to recognized, established, and authorized Islamic reasoning (i.e., based on established sources and in an authorized style of argumentation), then it follows, if we take Islam as a tradition of discourse and practice, that there is an Islamic genealogy to reform and modernization in the late empire and hence in republican Turkey. As we shall see, the ulema's and Islamist intellectuals' alignment with the opposition to the sultan led to exceptionally wide-ranging and profound interrogations of things like the meaning of "Islamic governance"; the role of Islam in state and society; the status and roles of Islamic knowledge in relation to other kinds of knowledge; the rights, duties, and political representation of Muslims and non-Muslims in a multiethnic and multiconfessional polity; and how to address all such issues in a context of powerful, colonizing, non-Muslim European imperial power. Most of these topics are ones that many parts of the Muslim world have been grappling with over the course of the later twentieth century. Ottoman ulema had these issues squarely on their agenda by the late nineteenth century (the ulema doing so much later than the bureaucracy, which was debating them at least 50 years earlier). The point here is not merely to emphasize that the Ottomans engaged with these issues first among Muslim polities. Rather this is significant for its effects, intended and otherwise. First among these is that in the context of these debates about what Islamic institutions are, and what good governance in Islam is, the ulema were at the forefront of the debates that eventually led to debates about the caliphate, its legitimacy, and its necessity. Second, this means that the Ottoman ulema and Islamist intellectuals (and, as we shall see in the next chapter, Sufi sheikhs) were among those who prepared the ground for the radical transformation of the state, first restoring a constitutional monarchy with the monarch as caliph, then splitting off of the caliphate from the monarchy, then abolishing the latter, and finally abolishing the former and proclaiming a republic.

İ. Kara has done the most to excavate the nearly forgotten richness and subtlety of the late Ottoman and early republican periods' Islamist figures, their worldviews and reasoning, and the historical context in which these were formed.[32] As his studies are based on meticulous, exhaustive work with published and unpublished texts (including many from private, family archives) written by late Ottoman Islamists, it is worth quoting him at some length. He summarizes the frameworks in terms of which late Ottoman administrators, intellectuals (including a great many Islamist intellectuals), and even many ulema had come to see themselves:

- The Ottoman state, the Muslim world and Muslims themselves are in a general state of stagnation, regression, and collapse [the terms commonly used at the time included: *tedenni, tevakkuf, inhitat, inkıraz*].
- In the Ottoman empire and Muslim world immobility and torpidity [*atalet, cümûd*] are predominant.
- Islam is like "a fur worn inside out." These adversities do not come from the most perfected of religions, Islam, but rather from rulers/administrations [*idareler*] who have distanced themselves from Islam's essential sources, from its principles, and its directives, and come from the *ulema* and Muslims who permit this to happen.
- The fundamental reasons for this stagnation and regression are the negligence [*ihmal*] and mistakes of the *ulema* and administrators [*idareci*], alongside the ignorance of the people [*halk*]. (İ. Kara 2001, 20)

For those who read the writings of prominent Ottoman ulema, particularly those in the central provinces of Anatolia and the Balkans, the sense of profound crisis leaps off the page, as does the evidence of a search for radical solutions as the last, final hope for the community of Muslims (*umma*) to stay on its feet. The solutions needed to be effective, hence feasible, and wide ranging, as there was a recognition that one field's problems (e.g., massive ethnic cleansing of Muslims and loss of core territories with majority Muslim populations linked to military failure) were connected to others (e.g., insufficient military academies and schools), with both connected to insufficient state revenues, and so on. Solutions late Ottoman ulema and Islamists tended to come up with were centered on the following:

- Restoring progress and advancement [*terakki, teâli*].

- Developing models of an 'active' type of person and a dynamic kind of society by foregrounding concepts like jihad, effort and exertion [*sa'y*], and reinterpreting and changing the contents of concepts like *tevekkül* ['resignation and trusting in God'], *fakr* ['poverty' or humility before God], *dünya* ['worldly affairs'], *zühd* ['pious asceticism'].

- Leaving behind Islamic history's and culture's traditional frameworks, mentalities and institutions which have been destroying and altering Islam, and returning to the 'era of prosperity' [*asr-ı saadet*, the ideal political and social organization of the time of the prophet and first four Caliphs], to the sources [Quran and sunna, precedent of the prophet], and to pure Islam. Rediscovering Islam as at ease with knowledge and reason by opening the doors of *ijtihad* [interpretation of sources] and to make this Islam predominant in life again.

- Alleviating ignorance and enlightening minds with a new understanding of education and teaching. Related to this, generating an eagerness for progress, and the founding of associations and organizations that can take a leading role in political, religious, and cultural movements.

- Struggling against despotic, absolutist regimes. (İ. Kara 2001, 21)

Both the relatively early appearance of these attitudes among Ottoman Muslims (in the second half of the nineteenth century) as well as their extremely wide currency need to be emphasized, especially for those more familiar with Muslim reform movements elsewhere. Note also that Ottoman Muslims in a sense did not have the luxury of reflecting on these issues in an abstract way, as a matter of identity, and then leaving it at that. The situation was dire and called for concrete measures; Ottoman ulema were prominent in debating these.

OPPOSITION, CRITIQUE, AND ISLAMIC TRADITION

In what sense can it be said that the grounds from which the ulema and Islamists articulated their opposition to the Abdülhamid were *Islamic*? In a seminal article, Talal Asad, building on the work in moral philosophy by Alasdair MacIntyre (1984), encouraged those seeking to define Islam as an object of anthropological knowledge to see it as a discursive tradition (Asad 1986). On this account, Islam is best considered a matrix of discourse and practice, and crucially discourse about correct practice. Such discourses evolve over time, as practitioners engage with the received sets of vocabularies, sources, and styles of reasoning that come to characterize the tradition. The most important debates are either directly or indirectly about correct practice: what is best to do or feel in a given situation. It is important to note, as Asad does, that stasis is not a feature of a discursive tradition. (Hence the classic portrayal of tradition as static, with something called "modernity" being dynamic, is an effort by some calling themselves modern to congratulate themselves according to their own criteria.) Thus traditions are "living" when they are evolving through being elaborated by practitioners making a sincere effort to ascertain right practice in terms of the discussions and debates received from the past (as they are considered to be of use in making one's way in the present). Finding such discussions, vocabularies, and frameworks to be of little value and abandoning them is by definition to abandon the tradition.

It is worth noting in passing that Asad is not suggesting that only Islam ought to be approached this way; other so-called religions, and even other formations, could also be approached as traditions, discursive or otherwise. Indeed, his later work deconstructs the category of religion by showing the historical and cultural specificity of its emergence and the problematic assumptions and expectations it carries. In his work, I take Asad as suggesting that the concept of tradition is arguably more useful for those studying what have hitherto been called "religions"—especially those traditions other than Christianity—than the category of religion itself. In this book, I largely take up Asad's approach and suggestion. One of the effects of approaching Islam this way is that the way is opened to examining the very historical processes through which—in our case in the Ottoman Empire and republican Turkey—Islam has been turned into a religion.

Ottoman ulema support for the opposition to Abdülhamid built momentum in the final years of the nineteenth century, which is the period during which many ulema started to form alliances with the CUP.[33] What is important for our discussion is to ascertain the extent to which this opposition to the sultan and cooperation with the CUP ought to be seen as internal to evolving Ottoman Islamic traditions. What were the rationales for this ulema and Islamist support? In this connection, one may refer to Asad's discussion of *nasiha*, or moral advice, in Islam, a role bolstered by the well-known hadith "al-dinu al-nasihatu" ("religion is moral advice beneficial to the recipient"): "*Nasiha* signifies advice that is given for someone's good, honestly and faithfully. It also has the meaning of sincerity, integrity, and doing justice to a situation. *Nasiha*, then, is much more than an expression of good intention on the part of the advice giver (*nasih*): since in this context it carries the sense of offering moral advice to an erring fellow Muslim (*mansuh*), it is at once an obligation to be fulfilled and a virtue to be cultivated by all Muslims" (Asad 1993, 214). Important here is the notion of the duty of the Muslim to criticize political authority, which can be contrasted with Enlightenment conceptions (such as Kant's [1991]) of critique as a right: "The virtuous Muslim is thus seen not as an autonomous individual who assents to a set of universalizable maxims but as an individual inhabiting the moral space shared by all who are together bound to God (the *umma*)" (Asad 1993, 219). Thus the intention and mode of critique in *nasiha* is central to its position in the practice and reformation of Muslim moral personhood. With this in mind, let us turn to actual texts written by ulema addressing themselves to the sultan.

Among the writings that are exemplary in this regard is a petition by a group of scholars affiliated with the Cairo-based journal *Kanun-i Esasî* (Constitution), and penned by a prominent scholar, Köprülülü Sheikh Aliefendizâde hoja Muhyiddin, in 1896 demanding that the sultan reconvene the Ottoman Chamber of Deputies (parliament) and reinstate the constitution, both of which had been more or less moribund since Abdülhamid's ascent to the throne in 1876. The petition was forwarded to Abdülhamid himself and included the following lines:

> If . . . your exalted person [the Sultan] will deign to reject the desire for the opening of the Chamber of Deputies, the ruin of the government of Islam by the evil hand of [your] regime seems certain, [and] that is why all efforts to prevent this outcome are legal [according to shari'a] [*wajib*] . . . Deign to consign this petition to a judicial system guaranteed by a constitution, and we shall all once more be your subjects! We shall once more consider you as the giver of life to religion [*din*] and nation [*millet*] . . . It has been promised [in the Quran] that this religion would be improved by a reformer every hundred years. Hasten to acquire this title of reformer! The reformer of this century will be he who inaugurates a Chamber of Deputies and who gives freedom to the Islamic community [*millet-i İslâmiye*]. [Without divulging] this matter to friend [or] foe, we send this petition to your exalted office [the Sultan]. We pray as a favor from God that you will, before fifteen days have passed, realize an auspicious and noble act in proportion to the moral and worldly nobility of your office. If not, until our last breath, we shall make all efforts necessary for the glorification of religion and the liberation of the country [*vatan*], O our Sultan. (qtd. in İ. Kara 2005b, 167; translation modified; see İ. Kara 1998 for the Ottoman Turkish texts)[34]

We may note the initial tone of admonishment and moral correction addressed from one Muslim to another, for the good of religion and the country. For the author of this text, criticizing the sultan is his duty as a Muslim and scholar keen to help what he sees as a ruler straying from the path of just, good governance and endangering the entire community with his absolutism and despotism (*istibdad* and *zülm*, the terms increasingly used by the opposition to describe Abdülhamid). Nothing less than the sultan's legitimacy as ruler of the empire was at stake.

Another important (though this time anonymous) text published initially in the pages of *Kanun-i Esasî* and then as a pamphlet was titled "A Patriotic Call in Response to the Religious Efforts of Their Excellencies, the Ulema." In it we read the following: "The criminal attempts of cruel people, beginning with our sultan himself, are ruining and damaging the strong edifice of the distinguished religion of Mohammed; they are trampling on religious laws; and the Islamic community [*millet-i İslâmiye*] is oppressed and sighing and groaning. Even so the ulema are incapable of uttering even a couple of words! O ulema of the Islamic religion, where are you? God has entrusted the ulema with the duty of moral guidance [*nasiha*] to tyrants, so won't your silence before these dangers be interpreted as—God forbid!—your approval of the oppression of despots?" (İ. Kara 2005b, 171–72; translation modified; Turkish text given in İ. Kara 1998, 14–15).

One of the important rationales for critiques of the ulema by these kinds of writers is that the ulema had become too submissive to the authority of the ruler of the day, whereas according to hadith, obedience is only due to one who follows canonical law (*ma'ruf*). The legitimate grounds for demanding a constitutional government lay in the notions of consultation (*meşveret*, from the Arabic *mashwara*) and its semantic relative, council (*şûra*).[35] The legitimate ruler is he who consults, and the argument put forth here (as it had been for decades by Ottoman Tanzimat reformers) is that the mechanism for consultation is a Chamber of Deputies.[36] It was, then, precisely as *nasiha*, moral counsel from one Muslim to another, that ulema were demanding from the sultan the restoration of the constitution and functioning of the Chamber of Deputies. Calls by and for the ulema to join the opposition to the sultan were also made on grounds internal to Islamic discursive traditions, and were articulated as *nasiha*, *khutba* (sermons; the title of a series of propagandistic pamphlets written at the turn of the century inciting Ottoman intellectuals, notables, and the ulema to revolt against Abdülhamid), *irşad* (guidance), or *davet* (invitation).

Moreover, and this is a crucial point, the ulema presented these Islamic modes of argumentation and reasoning in the relatively new venue of the mass-circulation periodical and printed pamphlet. As such, these texts were read by—and often alongside the writings of—figures who were not trained as, or writing from within the, ulema, but who were also articulating positions on the problems facing their society, like issues of economic, military, and diplomatic weakness; the relative merits and roles of religion and science; and the forms of good governance. Increasingly, ulema found that their writings elicited responses—both supportive and critical—from nonulema, which in turn demanded responses from the initial *alim* (sing. of ulema) author. This led incrementally to what Kara refers to as the intellectualization of the ulema, whereby the ulema's discourse, and even to an extent their role in public criticism and debate, came to resemble the role of that new type of Ottoman figure, the intellectual. While the vocabularies still showed marked contrasts and differing emphases, what was considered to be a convincing argument and a competent, credible proposal on the part of ulema and nonulema intellectuals had come to resemble one another. This is a point that is not well known to those unfamiliar with the history just alluded to yet one that is crucially important for an understanding of the relationship between Islamic and modern regimes of knowledge and power in the Ottoman Empire and later in the republic.

Another important thread of these new intellectuals' critiques of what they saw as the despotism of the sultan is their indirect or even open casting of doubt upon his status as caliph. There were several lines of attack here, and we cannot examine them in detail, but some scholars argue that in doing so many Ottoman ulema were playing into the hands of powers like the British. The British were concerned about the influence of the caliph on the Muslim population in their colonies, and especially India (where support for the caliph was high, indeed often higher than in Ottoman territories), and devoted a great deal of effort to producing tracts denouncing the illegitimacy of the Ottoman sultan's claim to the caliphate, often on grounds that the caliph must be a member of the Prophet Muhammad's tribe of Quraysh. It could well be the case that Ottoman ulema who doubted the legitimacy of the Ottoman caliph ultimately played into these efforts; however, what I want to emphasize here is simply the fact that the legitimacy of the Ottoman sultan as caliph had come to be an issue debated among some Ottoman ulema, foreshadowing debates about the caliphate in the transition to the republic.

After the promulgation of the first Ottoman constitution in 1876 and its suspension in 1878, one of the main points of debate among the ulema was the proper place and form of consultation, or *meşveret*. Discussions of constitutionalism and representative assemblies were closely linked to the concept of *meşveret*. By the close of the nineteenth century, there were extremely few Ottoman ulema who disputed that, first, consultation with either the ruled or their representatives and taking their views into serious consideration was a religious obligation, and second, that a parliament or chamber of deputies with legislative power limiting the power of the sultan was the legitimate form of such consultation. *Meşrutiyet*, the term that was used for constitutional governance, was based on the abstract of the term *meşrut*, meaning "bound by conditions" (from the Arabic root generating şart, "condition"). The sultan, and the administration itself, would be bound by the constitution. Eventually, and in the context of rapidly spreading nationalism among minorities and increasingly among Turkish-speaking Muslims, the idea of direct or indirect consultation with the population ended up at the principle of the sovereignty of the nation (which was the principle in terms of which groups were demanding their independence from the empire). Many Islamists came out strongly opposed to the institutionalization of this principle. Said Halim Pasha, for example, wrote that among the masses (*kalabalık*) is usually the last place "truth and wisdom" are found, and hence a mere numerical majority ought not be the foundation of sovereignty (İ. Kara 1997, 167). Constitutional governance institutionalizing consultation was thus taken to be the legitimate form of Islamic governance. Again, the concrete historical context of imperatives was crucial here, for many Islamists considered that constitutional governance was not so much the exercise of a certain right but that it represented "the government strengthening itself, the soundness of law, and securing oneself in the face of foreign interventions" (İ. Kara 1997, 54–55). By the end of World War I, the combination of these debates among Islamists and the behavior of the sultan in acquiescing to the demands of the allies had put the prestige and legitimacy of the sultan's status as caliph seriously in question. Legitimate governance, it was argued, is through consultation, just as the early caliphs had done. As a prominent Muslim scholar wrote in 1909, "The concept of Sultanate (on the other hand) implies subjugation and usurpation of power, and builds on the idea of despotism [istibdad]. This is why, in this time of liberties [devr-i hürriyet], the concept of Sultanate has to be circumscribed, since some of its meanings are inconsistent with the constitution."[37]

THE REPUBLIC AS AN ISLAMIC GOVERNMENT?

The relationship between the caliphate and the nation was increasingly debated in a context in which the basic units of Ottoman and Muslim politics were being rethought by Ottomans. The Chamber of Deputies naturally brought to the fore the question of how to conceptualize and institutionalize the polity. National sovereignty came to be increasingly prestigious, especially when it was invoked by hitherto subject populations to legitimate their rebellion (liberation as they saw it) from the empire. We must appreciate that the world had not yet seen the common twentieth century debates about the relationship between Islam, nationalism, and democracy at this point; these late Ottoman Islamists were thus not jaded by the trials and failures of many later attempts.[38] While not shared by all, it is important not to underestimate how widely prestigious were the attempts to legitimate representative political institutions as performing the function previously performed by the caliph, especially on the part of figures who were, by all accounts, very sincere and conservative in their Muslim devotions and identity. Arguing for the abolition of the caliphate and its replacement by a national assembly, in other words, was not seen to be a position only to be taken by those who had, for all intents and purposes, abandoned Islamic traditions and were imitating the West.

At the end of World War I, the sultan-caliph Mehmet VI (Vahidettin) acquiesced to victorious entente (primarily France, Britain, Russia, and Italy) demands, and his government signed the Treaty of Sèvres in 1920, which among other things envisaged the total demobilization of the Ottoman armed forces, the occupation of large swathes of Anatolia by entente forces, and the creation of a Kurdistan and Armenia in the east of Anatolia. Greek forces had landed at Izmir (Smyrna) in May 1919, and it became clear that the Turks were going to have to fight for whatever territories they wished to retain on nearly every front, meaning that the military was the only hope. It was in this context that the nationalists, led after May 1919 by Mustafa Kemal, rallied.

They repudiated the Treaty of Sèvres, declaring it null and void, whereupon the sultan had the sheikh ul-Islam promulgate a fatwa, declaring the nationalists rebels and that it was *fardh* (religiously incumbent) for Muslims to kill them. The nationalists countered by having the mufti of Ankara (where the nationalists had made their headquarters), Rıfat (Börekçi)—subsequently the first minister of religious affairs in the republic—issue a fatwa declaring the sultan to be under an occupation that was distancing him from his duties, and that it was *fardh* for the faithful to rescue the caliphate.[39] Importantly for our discussion, the rallying cry to join the "nationalists" (as they have come to be known in historiography) was in fact largely presented as a call to jihad against the infidel invaders. The nationalists themselves were very careful to declare their aims to be the rescuing of the caliphate, as it had been captured and was being held hostage. While many in the country, including among the nationalists, retained an emotional attachment to the position of the sultan-caliph, Vahidettin was henceforth considered by the nationalist leaders to be doing the bidding of the country's enemies. When the sultan and several in his retinue fled the capital on a British ship after the Grand National Assembly voted to abolish the sultanate on November 1, 1922, he was widely considered to have disgraced himself. For a little over a year, Vahidettin's cousin, Abdülmecid efendi (d. 1941) was nominated by the Grand National Assembly to serve as caliph without the title of sultan.

Interestingly, the bill to abolish the caliphate was penned by one Safvet efendi (Safvet Yetkin after the surname law, d. 1950), a Sufi sheikh who was a deputy in the first Grand National Assembly (*meclis*).[40] Introduced in the assembly in March 1924 as backed by 53 deputies, the bill was titled "Proposed legislation abolishing the caliphate and expelling the Ottoman dynasty from Turkey." The introductory paragraph justifying the proposal, as well as the discussion of the first article of the bill, shed much light on the reasoning shared by a great many who had been participating in the late Ottoman Islamist movements. I quote them at length here:[41]

> The existence of the caliphate in the Republic of Turkey has not allowed Turkey to free itself in its domestic or foreign politics from a double-headedness. Turkey, which in its independence and national life accepts

no partnerships [to its sovereignty], has no patience for an explicit or even implicit dual nature. It has been an absolute constant that this [Ottoman] dynasty—which for centuries has brought calamity on the Turkish nation and now, through deeds and promises, has caused the demise of a Turkish empire—under the cloak of the caliphate will be an even more effective threat to the existence of Turkey. This dynasty is a pure danger for everything having to do with the situation and strength of existence [*kuvvet-i mevcudiyet*] of the Turkish nation. Fundamentally, the caliphate or imamate in early Islam was created as having the meaning and function of government [*hükümet*]. Because of this, alongside the current Islamic government [i.e., the republican government] which is charged with performing all worldly and spiritual duties, there is simply no reason for the existence of a separate caliphate. This is the reality. In order for the Turkish nation to preserve its security/soundness [*selamet*] it cannot choose any course of action other than conforming to the truth [*hakikat*]. (qtd. in M. Kara 2002, 108)

After a vote in the Grand National Assembly moving to debate on the bill, Sheikh Safvet begins with the bill's first article: "The Caliphate is dissolved. Since the caliphate is [already] inherent in the meaning and concept of government and republic the [separate] office of caliphate is abolished" (M. Kara 2002, 109). Crucial in the reasoning behind the abolition of the caliphate is not that religion is not important or that the new republican state wishes to distance itself from Islam. On the contrary, the republican state is justifying its abolition of the caliphate on grounds that the functions of the caliphate are now carried out by the new government itself:

The first and foremost of the fundamental duties of the republican administration [*idare-i cumhuriyet*] is to maintain the glorious judgments and commands of Islam [*ahkâm-i celile-i İslâmiye*] . . . As the noble Davud (peace be upon him) and others among the apostles responsible for the administration of public affairs [*idare-i umur-u âmme*] with the justice and benevolence that the lord [God, *hak Taalâ*] commanded had an effect on many affairs, the noble Quran referred to these noble individuals with the honored title of caliph. Justice is among the divine attributes [of God]. Attaining this glorious attribute is what it means to be the vice-regent [caliph] of God on Earth. God said, addressing Davud (peace be upon him): [Safvet gives in Arabic] "We did indeed make you a vice-regent [*halifeten*] on Earth." And then he continues, [in Arabic] "So judge [*fahkum*] between men in truth [*bilhakki*]" [Quran, Sad 38:26]. Thus it is understood that the true meaning of caliphate, vice-regency, is executing government [*hükümet*] between men in truth [*hak*] and justice. As the noble messengers were protected against all great and small sins and were just in all their actions, they were each a vice-regent of Allah on Earth.

The seal of the prophets, our dear Prophet [Muhammad] was the greatest and most esteemed caliph. After our dear Prophet, the four select companions were also given this glorious title. Because each one of these honored individuals, who were superior people, entirely contented themselves with their glorious prophetic works, and in their management of public affairs, as this was the age of felicity [time of the "rightly guided" first four caliphs]; [they] truly ensured justice and benevolence. A prophetic miracle [hadith] says, "The caliphate, that is, a government based on justice and truth will last for thirty years after [my death]." Thirty years later, with the period of the caliphate of Imam Ali, the Umayyad government appeared with oppression and hatred, and the foundations of justice began to be shaken. From this noble hadith it is demonstrated [sabit] that from the point of view of the religion of Islam, the caliphate is executing rule through truth and justice . . . No one imagined that such absurdities [as calling Yazid and Walid II "caliphs"] could be a slander against Islam. This plainly shows that any Islamic government that manages public affairs through justice and truth, that government is a successor [caliph] to Allah on Earth. Those governments that deviate from justice and truth are quite distant from that honored title. With the passing of centuries and cosmic events, there is one truth that humanity has found through experience, and that is that since the [time of the] noble prophets a government founded on justice and truth can only be found in a republican administration [idare-i cumhuriye]. In fact, at the time of the rightly guided [first four] caliphs, the public opinion [efkâr-ı umumiye] of the mass of companions [cumhur-ı ashab] prevailed [hâkim idi]. Consequently, since the execution of governance through truth and justice today only exists thanks to a republic [cumhuriyet] and since the government of our country [hazıra] is, thanks be to God, a republican administration, the essential nature of the caliphate is reasonably and logically completely manifest in the spiritual dimensions [şahs-ı mânevesi] of the Grand National Assembly. Thus, as the essence [hakikat] of the caliphate as the religion of Islam means it is manifested in the spiritual dimensions of this great assembly, the [notion] of the honored station of caliphate as being external to the Grand National Assembly is contrary to the realities of Islam and is meaningless . . . At this point whatever needs to be done to prevent such an oddity is up to [this] illustrious body [the assembly itself], which is in possession of the essential meaning of the caliphate. (Safvet, qtd. in M. Kara 2002, 109–10)

The Sufi sheikh Safvet efendi, who was author of this text of major historical moment, the law abolishing the caliphate, was prominent in the public life of the orders during the second constitutional period (when, as we will see, he was the publisher of the journal *Tasavvuf*). The justification for the abolition of the caliphate was patently not that the state had no business regarding religion, or that religion was no longer important to the legitimacy of the new republican state. Rather, the reasoning was that if the meaning of "caliph"—such as we know it from canonical sources like the Quran and hadith—is "he who ensures the management of the affairs of the community according to justice and truth," and if the consensus among Muslims is now that this is best done through a republic, then it logically follows that that republic is carrying out the function of the caliphate and there is no reason for a separate caliphate to exist. In other words, since on grounds internal to Islamic traditions legitimate governance has now passed to the republican administration, the republic *is* an Islamic government.

Another classic argument (often cited as the more sophisticated among those argued) in favor of the abolition of the caliphate from the point of view of Islamic jurisprudence (*usul ul-fiqh*; drawing on discussions of the Quran more than hadith) is that put forth by the Minister of Justice Seyyid Bey.[42] Seyyid Bey had had a *medrese* education, then graduated from the university's faculty of law, where he then taught *usul ul-fiqh* (methods of jurisprudence) in particular. He had been a member of the Ottoman Chamber of Deputies after 1908, and was after his tenure as minister a deputy in the second Grand National Assembly. Seyyid Bey took the floor in the assembly during the debate over the legislation to abolish the caliphate, and made a long presentation on "the essence of the caliphate from the point of view of shari'a" (which was subsequently the title of a published booklet of his text). In his opening lines he said, "We are making a major revolution in the history of Islam" (Seyyid Bey 1997, 259) and for this reason everyone needed to give his candid views on the matter, as the decision needed to be done with full awareness and knowledge of the issues involved. Seyyid Bey thus situated the work of the assembly on the question of the caliphate in the context of the history of Islam. He quickly came to his point of departure, which was that "caliphate means government [*hükümet*], it is directly a matter of the people [*millet işidir*], and depends on the era in question" (261). He then goes on to note that in the Quran, there is no verse regarding the form of the caliphate, but that the Quran does give two normative formulas: regarding consultation (*meşveret*; "Their affairs are [determined] by shura among them," *al-Shura*, 42:38) and rulers (*ulu'l emre*; "Submit to Allah, the Prophet and the ruler [*emir*; Seyyid Bey translates this as *idare*] among you" *Nisa* 4:59).[43] Reiterating the same Quranic verse cited by Safvet efendi about Davud, he argues, "From this it is evident that the aim of the Caliphate is to dispense and distribute justice [the term in Islamic jurisprudence being *tevzi'-i adalet*]. Having respect for the truth, giving the right [one] what he justly deserves, abolishing falsehoods, defending people's rights: the role and duty [*vazife*] of the caliph is to strive for these aims. Which is in fact the same role and duty of government" (Seyyid Bey 1997, 262–63).

Seyyid Bey's discussion is a long one, corresponding to some 60 pages of print, and we cannot go into all its details, but we can emphasize certain parts of it pertinent to our purposes. He goes on to discuss the meanings of the term "imam" in the Quran, which often is used to mean "leader," as it is in the verse Bakara: "[Allah] said [to Abraham]: 'I will make thee an imam to the people.' [Abraham] pleaded: 'And also [imams] from my offspring!' [Allah] answered: 'But my promise is not within the reach of evil-doers'" (Quran 2:124; translation modified). He discusses this term because he says the position of imam, leader, has similarities with caliph. Summarizing, he says that while all caliphs can be considered imams, not all imams can be called caliphs. Regarding the verb derived from the root for caliph, "*istihlaf*," it is used in the Quran in the sense of appointing a successor in the affairs of justice: "There is no verse in the Quran [regarding appointing a caliph] besides these" (Seyyid Bey 1997, 264). Addressing himself to the several scholars of Islam who were deputies in the assembly, he asks, "Are there any other verses besides these, sirs?" to which he receives two replies, "No" and "There are hadiths," both confirming his exposition (as hadith are not verses of the Quran). In short, he argues, there is nothing explicit in either the Quran or the hadith about such matters as to how the caliph should be appointed, what a caliph's qualifications are, or whether it is proper (*vecib*) for the people to appoint the caliph under any circumstances and in any era. Now, he asks, while there are many hadiths regarding how to cut one's finger-nails and groom one's beard, what could be the wisdom behind there being no hadiths on these issues regarding the caliphate? "This is because, contrary to what is commonly thought, the question of the caliphate is simply not one of the fundamental religious [*dinî*] issues, it is a political one: it changes according to time and custom [*örf, âdet*], and depends on what [a given] time makes necessary. This is why our lord the prophet Muhammad preferred to remain silent on the issue of the caliphate . . . In short, the Prophet Muhammad completely left the matter of the caliphate up to the *umma* [the community of Muslims]" (Seyyid Bey 1997, 265).

In effect, the Grand National Assembly, when establishing the parameters of its own sovereignty, called upon the Islamic scholars in its midst to evaluate the transfer of sovereignty from the caliph to the assembly itself. These scholars then in effect identified the question of the caliphate as not essentially a religious matter per se but rather one of worldly leadership, provided that governance is done according to principles of justice and truth. Having been given the question of the caliphate and sovereignty to adjudicate upon, they kicked it back to the assembly, *but did so on grounds internal to Islamic reasoning*. This is the crucial point: the abolition of the caliphate and the situating of sovereignty solely in the hands of the Grand National Assembly was done internally to Islamic reasoning. Once this is accomplished, as there is no need to go back over the justification for this earlier debate, subsequent discussion takes place on the acquired territory of the arrangements ensuing from this decision.

Now, some may be quick to suspect this formulation as having been little more than a rather manipulative and selective reading of Islamic legal reasoning with the aim to deflect criticism that may be leveled at the assembly from more religiously conservative circles. I think it would be misguided to solely see the bill in these terms, for there is no evidence that either its author or the many who spoke or wrote in support of it were anything other than utterly sincere in their views on the matter. Seyyid Bey, Safvet efendi, and many of the other Sufi sheikhs and *medrese*-trained ulema who were deputies in the first elected Chamber of Deputies were leading figures among the late Ottoman Islamist movement, and we thus should not underestimate the extent to which their views were sincere, the product of profound soul-searching, both widespread and exceptionally compelling in the climate of their day, given all that the country had experienced in recent years. In this connection, and recalling our discussion previously, it is significant that prominently displayed at the front of the room during the first Chamber of Deputies was a large framed inscription reading: "Ve emruhum şûra beynehum" ("Their affairs are [determined] by shura among them").[44]

THE RELIGIOUS STATUS OF A CONTEMPORARY ABSENCE

One of the main arguments of this chapter is perhaps a counterintuitive one, namely that the absence of certain "Islamic" features of Turkey's contemporary institutions was itself established on Islamic grounds. Most important in this regard are the status of rule in the country and the transition from the Ottoman Empire to the Republic of Turkey. While this process has commonly been seen as simply a distancing of the new republic from Islam, new scholarship in recent years has revised this view and has tried to situate the events of the transition in the context of their occurrence. A more realistic appreciation of the options that were facing people as the Ottoman Empire was collapsing can now be elaborated, and this is what I have tried to contribute to in this chapter. It is important not to lose sight of the fact that the rationales and parameters for debate about republican reforms—including those pertaining to religion and the state—were based, naturally enough, on experience during late Ottoman times. Only then can we adequately appreciate the relationship between republican and late Ottoman Islamic discourse and practice. This is a feature of Turkey's past and present that is not well known by students of other parts of the Muslim world and can lead to rather simplistic conceptions of the status and nature of certain Islamic traditions and institutions in the country and of their absence. In the next chapter, we build on this conceptualization of transformations in Islamic traditions, institutions, discourses, and practices and explore parallel developments among Sufi orders in the late empire and republic, establishing important contexts in which to interpret the book's subsequent chapters.

CHAPTER 2

SUFISM AND MODERNITY FROM THE EMPIRE TO THE REPUBLIC

SUFI ORDERS WERE PROMINENT AND WIDESPREAD IN the Ottoman Empire but were officially banned by the new republican state in 1925, and it has since been a punishable crime in Turkey to be involved with a Sufi order as a sheikh or as a disciple. Why were the orders banned? What then becomes of Sufi practice in such an environment? The short answer many of the Sufi men I worked with in Turkey gave me is "Sufis in all periods of Islam, and in all parts of the Muslim world, have been harassed. But no one can destroy Sufism, because it is a matter of the heart [*kalb işi*]."[1] Nonetheless, it is the case that many are dissatisfied that they are not able to practice their religion as they please (many adding, for my benefit no doubt, "like one can in America").[2] From the point of view of the history of Islam and Muslim communities, how should we conceptualize Sufism in the country in the wake of this? How should we conceptualize it from the point of view of the history of the state, religion, and politics? To do this adequately, I would argue that we need to examine in some detail how and why Sufi orders in the late Ottoman Empire had been restructured according to the new regimes of knowledge and power we described in the previous chapter, for this will provide an important context in which to interpret the proscription of the Sufi orders in the new republic in 1925 and the nature and place of Sufi discourse and practice in the republic subsequently. This chapter parallels somewhat the discussion in the previous chapter but examines particularly the experiences of the Sufi orders with the Ottoman reform movements we saw. We examine the situation regarding the orders in the late empire and their eventual proscription, for their illegality is one of the more striking features of the landscape of Islamic practice in Turkey, especially given how important the orders were in earlier centuries in the same geography. We then examine in detail the events surrounding the abolition of the Sufi orders and closing of their lodges. We will thus have established the historical status of the Sufi orders in contemporary Turkey, an important step in understanding the nature of the Sufis and Sufism in the country today.

Sufi orders were a major feature of the social, political, and economic landscape of the central Ottoman lands of the Balkans and Anatolia in the later empire. Studies of Sufism have long emphasized the point that throughout the Muslim world, there is a plurality and diversity of forms and practice among Sufi orders. Much of this diversity has to do with the form and function of the articulation of Islamic institutions with other social, political, and economic institutions in a given context. Indeed, there is such a diversity that Michael Gilsenan has argued that we ought not try to find some transhistorical, *sociological* significance to the term "Sufi order" (*tariqa* in Arabic): "The term [*tariqa*] is not in any useful sense a sociological classification . . . It does not denote a set of common defining characteristics which go to make up a distinct type of social entity and mark it out as a special form of association with a characteristic pattern of social relations. On the contrary, in itself it conveys very little about important problems such as distribution of and accession to authority, or mode of entry, or content of membership of any group which designates itself a *tariqa*" (Gilsenan 1973, 4–5). These latter matters are indeed a matter of specific times and places. This book takes a fairly standard approach to the question of defining Sufism per se. Throughout the centuries, many Muslims have cultivated an interest in Sufism, in its history, its practices, its ways of life, its literature, its poetry, and its architecture. However, in my experience few who have not sincerely placed themselves in the hands of a sheikh, for personal, devotional, and practical advice would consider (or describe) themselves as Sufis. What differentiates Sufi groups from other associations of an Islamic character to be found all over the Muslim world (and those in Turkey, such as the Nur cemaati or Millî Gençlik Hareketi) is that Sufi orders are structured around the relationship between a *mürşid* (sheikh), with a known and recognized chain of initiation, and *mürids* (disciples). As in many other parts of the Muslim world, a great many Ottoman Muslims (including ulema) cultivated their piety through affiliation with one or more of the orders.[3] The orders were largely fiscally and administratively autonomous as institutions in the central Ottoman lands until the late eighteenth century.

The Sufi lodge (*tekke*, *dergâh*, or, less commonly, *zaviye* in the Turkish-speaking context) has been the center of the associative life of Sufis throughout the history of most of the orders. Here, traveling Sufis would be accommodated, students housed, a sheikh often lived with his family, and a kitchen functioned.[4] During the last century of the Ottoman Empire from

1820 to 1920, it is estimated that there were between two thousand and three thousand *tekke*s in the core provinces of Anatolia and Rumelia (the Balkans; Kreiser 1992, 49). Estimates put the number of *tekke*s in the capital of Istanbul alone at around three hundred by the late nineteenth century.[5] The upkeep of most lodges was provided by a foundation (*vakıf*), from which modest stipends to some residents and provisions, such as food for the kitchen, were ensured. State policies concerning such foundations were therefore of extreme importance to the life of the *tekke*s and orders. When the state sought to inaugurate a new policy toward the Sufi orders—as the republican administration did in 1925 when it proscribed the orders and closed their lodges—this involved new procedures in the administration of foundations.

OTTOMAN GOVERNMENTALITY AND NAQSHBANDI SUFIS

As we saw in the last chapter, the late eighteenth century marks the onset of major Ottoman reform movements. Over the course of the nineteenth century, Sufi orders were incrementally reconstituted in the field of Ottoman governmental power too. The level of penetration of new techniques of organization, of new kinds of knowledge, and of new normativities and forms of reason was subtle but pervasive. Among the major effects of the dissemination of the optic and practice of governmentality was the increasing individuation of people into productive subjects, and it increasingly became the individual that the state was interested in for its interventions.[6] The aim was the flourishing of productive capacities through a concern for the welfare of the population (especially their attendant productivity), amounting to the incipient exercise of what Foucault termed biopower, which "brought life and its mechanisms into the realm of explicit calculations and made knowledge-power an agent of transformation of human life" (1978, 143).

The main mechanisms were formal bureaucratization of the Sufi orders—marked most dramatically, as we will see, by the establishment of the Assembly of Sheikhs—and the increasing rationalization of the conditions for Sufi practice, meaning that more and more aspects of the life of the orders would be subject to explicit calculation, according to emergent criteria of reason and performance, as targets of policy. These new means of exercising power simultaneously redefined and transformed the objects upon which they were exercised; the kinds of knowledge that individuals were increasingly proficient in (especially about themselves and in terms by which they came increasingly to define themselves); and the kinds of activities they increasingly spent their days doing—in other words, these means transformed the kinds of subjects they were.

Concurrent with this bureaucratization one witnesses the steps by which the Sufi orders were transformed from corporate bodies, addressed as such by the state, to an instance of "populations," thought of as composed of individuals who can be compared and exchanged as the objects of rationalized procedure (Foucault 2003b, 240–44). The various qualities of the Sufis needed to be rendered visible in order for them to enter into the calculus of governance; hence one witnesses a proliferation of examinations, a systematization and stricter control of diplomas and certification, and surveys in the sphere of the Sufi orders, thereby situating hitherto localized processes on grids of calculation and analysis. Able bodies were to be accounted for by this new optic and technique of governance, and the juridical apparatus was to take hold of them as much as necessary in order to render them productive (as opposed to *zayi*—unproductive, a term increasingly used, by Sufis and others, to describe Sufis and their institutions).

We are especially concerned with a branch of the Naqshbandi order in this book, one of the oldest orders in the Muslim world and first documented in the Ottoman capital Istanbul in the late fifteenth century (Algar 1990 ; LeGall 2005). The Naqshbandi order became one of the preeminent orders in the central Ottoman lands of Anatolia and the Balkans as well as the capital Istanbul after the first quarter of the nineteenth century, with members including many Ottoman Islamic scholars as well as statesmen and bureaucrats.[7] The eponym of the Naqshbandi order, Baha al-Din Naqshband (1318–1389), was born near and spent much of his life in Bukhara, in Central Asia.[8] The first Naqshbandi center in the Ottoman Empire was established by Molla 'Abd Allah Ilahi from Simav, who became a disciple in Samarqand and then returned in the second half of the fifteenth century to establish a Naqshbandi circle centered on the Zeyrek mosque (which would be an important Naqshbandi center again in the twentieth century, under Abdülaziz Bekkine efendi, a sheikh in the branch of the order studied here). However, the prominence of the Naqshbandiyya in the central Ottoman lands, and not least the capital, is tied to Mevlana Khalid "al-Baghdadî" (d. 1827) and his successors. Indeed, sometime after the mid-1860s, a Naqshbandi lodge was established directly across from the seat of the Ottoman government, the Sublime Porte (Bâb-ı Âli).[9] It seems plausible that this is a result of Mevlana Khalid's view that the piety of Muslims is ensured through the piety of their rulers:

> If the *umma* [Muslim community] had gone astray, it was because of its rulers. Thus following Sirhindi, Shaikh Khalid seems to have regarded as a foremost duty of Naqshbandi-Mujaddidi shaikhs to seek influence upon rulers and to bring them to follow *shari'a* rules. He seems to have regarded the central part of his mission to be to insure the supremacy of the *shari'a* in society and state. Only then would it be possible to restore virtue and righteousness to the life of Muslim society and to the acts of the ruler and his men. This is undoubtedly an exposition of the basic principles of

the Naqshbandi-Mujaddidi order. It was a sober call for a community to live according to its own Orthodox beliefs. Basically it was a moral and religious call. (Abu-Manneh 1982, 14–15)

This is a view that also seems to have been passed down to subsequent generations of Naqshbandis up to the present (as we will see in later chapters), as they notably did not seek to cultivate their devotions through reclusion but sought to influence those in positions of authority and power, who would in turn influence those around them and society in general.

For many of the Sufis I worked with, the difficulties Sufis have experienced during the republic are not that different in quality or quantity than difficulties many Sufis have experienced over the centuries in many Muslim polities and are to be taken as a test (*imtihan*) of oneself and of one's resolve to avoid sin, moral corruption, and temptation. A strong, not to say violent, distaste for Sufism has hardly been limited to Turkey's republican regime. In the Muslim world, it has not been uncommon for religious personalities, including Sufi sheikhs, to be exiled from their countries of origin or long-time residences by ruling authorities. Countries like Syria, Egypt, Iraq, Iran, and Tunisia come to mind, but in fact, most states with a Muslim majority have found it expedient or necessary at one point or another to expel Sufi sheikhs from their territory. Sheikhs of the order discussed in this book, Khalidi Naqshbandis, were subject to such treatment by Ottoman authorities on several occasions (discussed in detail later).[10]

As we saw in the previous chapter, as the empire collapsed during its final decades, the prestige of those regimes of knowledge and power considered to be effective in the concrete defense of the homeland and its Muslim population (now figured as something called the Turkish nation) in the face of invasion is difficult to exaggerate.[11] Searching questioning of the scope and functioning of Islam in such a society was under way, and most everyone agreed, for instance, that all schools needed to be teaching modern disciplines.[12] Resources were extremely limited. Among those with a Sufi background, and indeed among many sheikhs themselves, there was little desire to devote many resources to Sufi institutions like *tekke*s in such conditions. While the new nationalist administration in Ankara initially took no measures against the orders and basically confirmed the status of sheikhs as bureaucrats (alongside imams, *hatibs* [preachers] and muezzins [reciters of call to prayer]), in 1925 the Grand National Assembly abolished them for reasons we will now examine.

HÜSEYIN EFENDI'S DOSSIER

In 1918, a Sufi sheikh in the Ottoman capital found himself filling in blank spaces on a printed questionnaire sent to him, as it was to all other sheikhs in the city. This is what he wrote in response to the questions:

My name is Hüseyin Şerafeddin. I am one of the grandsons of Mehmet Ali Pasha. I follow the Mezheb of Imam-ı Azam Ebu Hanife. In 1904 I took an oath [*müstahlef oldum*] to the Halvetiye-i Uşakiye Tarikat. In the presence of my sheikh, I was trained in the path [of Sufism; *terbiye-i seyr-i suluk eyledim*]. My dear sheikh is among the notables [*rical*] of the Uşakî tarikat at Kal'a-yi Sultaniye [Çanakkale]. He passed away in 1916.

I was born in Istanbul in 1872. My father is Mehmet Recai Pasha, retired from the Çanakkale artillery commanders.

After completing the Rüştiye Mektebi and upon my graduation from the Mekteb-i Mülkiye-i Şahane, I studied Arabic to a practicable [*tatbikat*] level and the text of the Gülistan [Persian] with Kırımlı [Crimean] Hacı İbrahim efendi at Bayezit Cami. I read and write French and speak Greek. For formal correspondence, I use [*kitabet*] Ottoman, which comprises three languages [*üç lisandan mürekkeb*]. I have no published works.

I previously worked in the Ministry of Justice [*adliye*], and for more for than 20 years, I have been working in several secretariats of the Directorate of the Central Registries [*defter-i hakanî emaneti*] . . .

[Our] *dergâh* was rebuilt and reanimated in the name of Deniz Abdal by your humble servant [Şerafeddin himself] in my garden (which was empty land) located near the Prefecture on Tramway Street in the Deniz Abdal neighborhood. The work was done by my dervishes.

As is customary in the Halvetiye-i Uşakîye [order], our devotions [*ayîn*] are practiced on Monday and Friday nights. At present nothing has been determined regarding succession or appointments, and our *vakıf* documents are in order.

Besides the Rüştiye teacher, Ahmet Fazıl efendi, I have no assistants. Though outwardly [*zahiren*] it appears that I have more than two thousand dervishes, in reality [*hakikatte*] there is not more than one. (qtd. in Albayrak 1996, 79)

Here we have Halveti Sufi sheikh, son of a military officer and grandson of one as well, a graduate of the prestigious modern style schools that had come to produce the empire's bureaucrats (as opposed to a *medrese*, an advanced Islamic seminary),[13] with good knowledge of French, and passable Greek. Alongside his education at the Mülkiye, he studied Islamic sciences in lesson circles at major mosques in the capital, including one of the largest and most prestigious, Bayezit, where he studied with a certain Ibrahim efendi, of Crimean Tatar origin. He presumably learned French at the Mülkiye; his knowledge of Greek, his sheikh's affiliation, and his father's place of appointment suggest that he hailed from the Çanakkale area of the Aegean region. While Hüseyin efendi cannot be said to be entirely typical of Sufi sheikhs of the late Ottoman period, anyone familiar with this period, its institutions, and the kinds of subjects associated with them will not find him particularly exceptional or unusual.

Why was Hüseyin efendi filling in the blanks on a questionnaire? Why was this questionnaire sent to him and other sheikhs by the Meşihat, the offices of the sheikh ul-Islam (chief mufti of the empire)? And what does what he wrote on this questionnaire, and especially the very fact of his filling it out, tell us about the status of the Sufi orders in the late empire and the kinds of people who composed them? The transformations that the social and institutional life of the Sufi orders underwent in the nineteenth and twentieth centuries are illustrative of several important transformations in Ottoman cultural and religious practice, most importantly the profound and subtle shifts taking place in the status and functioning of different types of knowledge and their practitioners and the corollary shifts in the relationship between modes of selfhood and subjectivity, on the one hand, and regimes of knowledge and power, on the other. These shifts in the later empire are a still poorly mapped-out dimension of the broader changes that we examined in the last chapter.

It appears that incorporation into Ottoman governmentality, as described in the previous chapter, was initially experienced by Sufis as an encroachment upon their autonomy, and the measures to be discussed in following pages were at times resisted by Sufis (indeed, one should exercise caution in not overstating the degree to which the directives regarding the orders were actually carried out or the degree to which newly created institutions were actually functional). This incorporation was done incrementally over the course of the nineteenth century. By the twentieth century, the evidence suggests, however, that many Sufis themselves actively promoted the incorporation of the orders into what was considered to be a regime of reform, as a last hope to give back to the orders some semblance of an important role in the life of their communities (M. Kara 2005, 533–36). At a time when anti-Sufi invective was proliferating, we will see that many senior Sufis were themselves of the opinion that without a program of modernization or reform (*islah*), the orders, and Sufism in general, were not likely to make a contribution to Muslim life in the future.

Reform of Sufi institutions mirrors in many respects broader programs of Ottoman reform already fairly well documented, which are themselves analogous to (and, I have argued, should indeed be seen as commensurate with) other reform movements in eastern and southern Europe. The concerns of Sufis, the problems they identified as the most pressing, were similar to those many felt the Muslim community faced as a whole: weakness and paralysis deriving from knowledge and practice of traditions being at a low level relative to what they were in the past. However, a simple return to earlier practices was generally not proposed by Ottoman Sufis in the nineteenth and twentieth centuries. Reform proposals referred to an energized reconstitution of institutions and practices by making use of modern techniques, like bureaucratization and centralization of curricula and courses for training sheikhs drawn up by scholarly committees, and the examination of Sufi lodges and the practices of their members, especially in rural areas, by teams of inspectors (M. Kara 2005, 536, 538). It would therefore be misguided to see these processes simply as the orders "submitting" to the imposed force of "the state." Rather, as we will see, these modern technologies of power were thought by many Sufis to be productive of outcomes they themselves sought. These new regimes of power and knowledge were absorbed into society through capillary mechanisms, like schools and institutions reorganized according to the latest knowledge produced by the human sciences, which increasingly inspired the reforms and suggested their targets. As we will see, these mechanisms both allowed them to penetrate down to the minutiae of everyday life and rendered the orders and individual Sufis more productive and effective according to their own standards.

THE SUFI ORDERS AND STATE DISCIPLINE

As the Ottoman *'ilmiye* (Islamic scholarly) hierarchy was increasingly linked to the Ottoman state through *medrese* and court reorganizations throughout the nineteenth century, the Sufi orders saw a parallel tendency toward reform and bureaucratization, with their personnel increasingly reporting to and dealing with—indeed in the end becoming—state bureaucrats.[14] While a particular interest on the part of the state in the affairs of the Sufi orders was no doubt heightened by the abolition of the Janissary corps and the closely associated Bektashi order in 1826,[15] the incremental incorporation of the orders and their institutions actually predates this.[16] Until the early decades of the nineteenth century, the orders were basically autonomous in the administration of their foundations (*evkaf*) and in the appointment of their sheikhs, two key indexes of their economic and social functioning.[17] From this point on, the orders become increasingly subject to the broader centralizing projects of the Ottoman state, which were set into full motion under Mahmud II (r. 1808–1839). In 1811 and 1812, he issued a decree (*ferman*) bringing the foundations of the various orders under the auspices of the newly founded Directorate of Imperial Foundations (Evkaf-ı Hümayun Nezareti).[18] The main points of this decree were the following:

1. The central *tekke* of a given order should be the one where the eponym of the order is buried, and the administration of the order's affairs should be organized from here. [This was particularly relevant in rural areas.]
2. Those sheikh positions vacated upon the death or departure of the previous sheikh should be filled by appointment of the central *tekke*, and the views of the sheikh ul-Islam [i.e., the ulema corps] should be consulted.
3. In the appointment of sheikhs attention must be paid to the authority and capacities of the individual candidate, while the appointment of unqualified sheikhs through bribery, gifts, etc. must be prevented.
4. The foundations of the orders must be under the administration of the Directorate of Imperial Foundations. (M. Kara 1985, 982)

The orders thus found that their hitherto administrative and financial autonomy was being eroded, as they were in effect being incorporated into the sphere of state governance, itself undergoing transformations.[19] Their finances were now incorporated into the broader finances of the empire, while their internal affairs (e.g., the appointment of sheikhs) were, albeit in a limited fashion, subject to the scrutiny of the offices of the Meşihat, that is the *'ilmiye* hierarchy of the ulema. One of the issues repeatedly raised in discussions about the orders was the problem of "cradle sheikhs," that is, the appointment, upon the death of a sheikh, of one of his sons to the position, often despite his youth and lack of authoritative knowledge and credentials. While members of the orders themselves would return to this theme from this period through the 1920s and some would argue that the practice had led to a serious degeneration of the orders and of Sufism in general, the practice of appointment of the sheikh's son as successor (*evladiyet*) was itself never prohibited altogether, even in the profound administrative reforms later in the century. A major source of this problem appears to be the fact that sheikhs in the Ottoman lands commonly lived with their families in a residential area of the *tekke*s themselves. With the appointment of a new sheikh from outside this family, the widow of the deceased not only had lost her husband but also would be essentially left homeless, possibly with children.

Following the dramatic suppression of the Bektashi order in concert with the destruction of the Janissary corps in 1826, Mahmud II issued another decree in 1836 pertaining to the orders, which stipulated the following:

1. Each member of an order should wear garb particular to that order.
2. Each dervish should carry identity papers with the seal and signature of his sheikh.
3. Certificates of authoritative knowledge of the order's traditions [*icazetnâme*] must not be conferred to unqualified dervishes, and when they are to be conferred the opinions of not one but several sheikhs must be sought.
4. In the appointment of sheikhs attention must be paid as to whether the candidate is indeed a member of the order associated with the vakıf deeds.
5. More than one sheikh position must not be given to the same person.

6. Items belonging to the tekke such as banners, flags, and musical instruments must not be removed from the premises, not even on the pretext of 'sending off Hajj pilgrims' or 'receiving returning ones.'

7. Those who do not participate in canonical worship, or in recitations of Awrad or Tawhid dhikrs, but merely wish to attend the 'song and dance dhikrs' must be excluded. (M. Kara 1985, 983)

The Ottoman state's policy toward the orders amounted by the midnineteenth century to so many efforts to bring them more fully under inspection and control as part of its broader project to render more visible and calculable an ever increasing number of microlevel, daily social practices and institutions, mainly through the requirement that they be registered (and thus recognized) by the legal order. As such, the reform of the Sufi orders is essentially an extension and application of measures first introduced in the military and educational institutions. Similar processes had been under way in Egypt since 1802, culminating in Ottoman viceroy Muhammad Ali's decree investing all authority over Egyptian Sufi orders, as well as *tekkes, zaviyes,* and shrines there, in the sheikh al-sajjada.[20] These reforms of the administrative and fiscal policies regarding the orders represent one of the more direct examples of the incorporation of that characteristically modern form of power Foucault referred to as governmentality—rationalization of administration coupled with a normalization of the objects of governance, first and foremost individuals constituted as members of populations—into the social life of Sufi orders.[21] In the process, the nature of Sufi practice and the ethical selves formed in and through these practices would also be transformed subtly, as would the nature of power in Ottoman society. Identities were becoming more minutely documented; the minutiae of dress and bodily comportment were increasingly matters of political concern, and knowledge of Sufi traditions was increasingly subject to the normativities of examination by experts.

THE MECLIS-I MEŞAYİH: SHEIKH AS BUREAUCRAT

One of the most important of these transformations was the establishment in Istanbul in 1866 of the Assembly of Sheikhs (Meclis-i Meşayih) as a body reporting to the offices of the empire's chief mufti, the Sheikh-ul Islam (Meşihat-i Islâm).[22] With slight changes, the assembly would exist until 1917.[23] This move effectively handed a significant amount of control over the Ottoman Sufi orders to the ulema. While it must be said that, compared with other times and places in the Islamic world, the Ottoman ulema were comparatively accommodating to the existence of the Sufi orders (and, indeed, many of the ulema were themselves members of one or more orders), it is nonetheless true that the foundation of the assembly coincides with tenure of a sheikh ul-Islam who is known to have been close and sympathetic to the orders and to Sufism.

In the context of the reforms that had gained momentum with Mahmud II and continued under the Tanzimat, in 1863 preparations were begun to establish the Assembly of Sheikhs, which was in fact established three years later under the tenure as sheikh ul-Islam of Refik efendi in 1866 (M. Kara 1985, 985, 990). Refik efendi (d. 1872) was Bosnian and had seen official duty in Damascus, where he was apparently initiated into the Naqshbandiya by a deputy of Mevlana Khalid, Sheikh Abdülfettah Akrî, and also studied the works of Ibn Arabî.[24] The assembly was tied to the office of the sheikh ul-Islam and took on responsibility for the administration and inspection of all Sufi orders and lodges found in and around the Ottoman capital of Istanbul.[25] The founding of this institution represents in some respects an important departure from tradition for the Ottomans; in other regards, it is typical of the measures the Ottomans felt to be necessary in the context of their general recalculation of resources and the reorganization of the disciplines of knowledge through which they identified and analyzed those resources. What the creation of these institutions certainly did do was put the Sufi orders and their assets under the eyes and pens of the sheikh ul-Islam and the ulema, thereby tipping the scales in favor of the ulema in the struggles over resources, influence, and prestige between the Sufi orders and the *medreses*.

Alongside the insights it furnishes regarding the social life of the Sufi orders in the later empire, the founding of the Assembly of Sheikhs and its subsequent reorganizations are important indicators of the nature of the administration of Islamic institutions the Ottoman state had come to pursue by the middle of the nineteenth century. These processes of identification and reconstitution of the Sufi orders within a realignment of the state vis-à-vis Islamic institutions also furnishes insight on the transformations in the nature of Ottoman governance more broadly, as the state attempted to deal adequately with life-and-death confrontations with powers to its north and west. While the decree of 1812 had already begun the reorganization of the various *tekke*s through arranging them hierarchically under central (*merkez*) *tekke*s, the founding of the Assembly of Sheikhs further reorganized the *tekke*s, attaching them to central *tekke*s not according to their affiliation but rather according to their geographic location. Initially there were 35 such central *tekke*s, but this was reduced to 15 in the Central *Tekke* Regulations (Merkez Tekâyâ Talimatnamesi) of the Assembly of Sheikhs Charter (Nizamnâmesi) of 1915 and 1916, while five Mevlevihânes and eight Naqshbandi *tekke*s functioned as autonomous (*müstakil*) centers (Aydın 1998, 96). The changes are also indicative of the changing relationship between Islamic institutions and the field of administration, which increasingly came to influence the activities higher-level authorities in Islamic institutions were expected to carry out.[26]

Between 1868 and 1869, the Assembly of Sheikhs convened under the chairmanship of the Yenikapı Mevlevihânesi sheikh Osman Salahaddin Dede, and was composed of five sheikhs from different orders: Sadiye, Kadiriye, Sünbüliye, Halvetiye, and Naqshbandiye.[27] In 1878, the number increased to six, with a member from Rufaiye.

It does not appear to be known at present how these members or the orders to be represented were chosen, but that the chairman was a Mevlevî is no doubt related to Sultan Abdülaziz's (r. 1861–1876, himself a member of the Mevlevî order and a *ney* [reed flute of particular significance to Mevlevîs] player) continuation of the policy of officially sponsoring the Mevlevîs to entirely remove any trace of Bektashis. (It is known that during his visits to the Balkan territories, Sultan Mahmud II insisted on having Mevlevî ceremonies practiced in various places, in an effort to supplant the Bektashis.) This state sponsorship of the Mevlevîs came to an end under Abdülhamid (r. 1876–1909), when an entirely different policy regarding the orders was put into place, to be discussed shortly. In 1875, a nonsheikh official observer (*nazır*) was added to the assembly, along with a secretary (*kâtip*) with the qualifications of a teacher (*müderris*); in 1891, a registrar (*mukayyid*) went to work. Between 1892 and 1897, the chairmanship was actually vacant. In 1902, the observer was removed, and in 1911, under the tenure as sheikh ul-Islam of Musa Kâzım efendi, the number of members was reduced to two.

The founding of the assembly also saw the routinization of bureaucratic procedure in the appointment of sheikhs. Whereas previously upon the death of a sheikh, the post normally passed to one of his sons (*evladiyet*) or to another authorized figure (*hilafet*), this appointment process was now detoured through an approval by the Assembly of Sheikhs. Now the candidate would be subject to an examination (*imtihan*) of his knowledge of Islam and of the traditions and practices of the particular order (*ulûm-ı dîniyye ve vezâif-i tarîkat*). In the case of a *halife* being nominated (and not an *evlad*), the candidate's *icazetname*(s) were to be checked and registered by the assembly.[28] As was previously the case, sheikhs under the new regulations were permitted to execute other functions and professions simultaneously, usually imam, muezzin, or caretaker of a mosque. The orders had thus lost their administrative autonomy and fiscal immunities and exemptions.

DESPOTISM, CONSTITUTIONALISM, AND THE SUFI ORDERS

As noted in the previous chapter, in recent years the historiography of the late empire and early republic has seen much reformulation and reinterpretation. Despite longstanding consensus among historians to the contrary, recent work has shown that there was no single attitude on the part of the Sufi orders with respect to the restoration of the constitution in 1908. In particular, the Naqshbandi order is usually considered to have been singularly emphatic in its denunciation of the restoration.[29] The available evidence, in fact, suggests that the overwhelming majority of those orders that were indigenous to and widespread in Anatolia, Istanbul, and the Balkans enthusiastically received the news, as did the scholarly, ulema class.[30] İsmail Kara attributes this attitude on the part of a majority of sheikhs mainly to two factors: First, although Abdülhamid had surrounded himself with sheikhs from a number of Sufi orders, particularly the Shadhiliyya and Rufaîyya, these orders were popular almost uniquely in North Africa and Syria; that is to say, he did not cultivate particularly close relations with any of the orders traditionally widespread in Anatolia, Istanbul, or the Balkans. Second, Abdülhamid increasingly curbed the influence and power of the orders traditionally strong in the empire's heartland and sent some sheikhs from just about every of the locally prominent orders into exile. If there is now a widespread belief that Abdülhamid was somehow the partisan of the Sufi orders, İ. Kara sees this as meaning that present-day scholars believe what only illiterates in the provinces and rural, low-ranking religious functionaries believed at the time (i.e., Abdülhamid is the ally of the Sufis).[31] In other words, while Abdülhamid is commonly (and largely correctly) associated with a policy of *ittihad-i İslam* (pan-Islamism)—hence the interest in strengthening ties between Istanbul and the Arab provinces—this did not translate into a generally positive situation for the Sufi orders popular in the central Ottoman lands, which on the contrary, found their activities under surveillance by Abdülhamid's spies and their sheikhs exiled.[32] One can conclude from this that Abdülhamid was not especially sympathetic to Sufism per se but rather looked on the orders instrumentally, as tools of broader policy—much as the Committee of Union and Progress (CUP) would in subsequent years.

The available evidence suggests that the Naqshbandiyya, usually considered to have been among the most conservative[33] of the orders (meaning in the post–1908 context, supportive of the sultan against the CUP), is no exception to these observations. Like the other orders, the Naqshbandis saw many of their numbers sent into exile by Abdülhamid. Among Naqshbandi sheikhs alone, we know that the prominent sheikh of the Kelâmî Dergâh, Esad (Erbilî) efendi, was exiled to Iraq in 1900 for eight years; Feyzullah Efendizâde Mehmet Ali efendi was exiled to the Yemen; sheikh of the Erzincan Naqshbandi dergâh and later representative in the first republican Grand National Assembly Fevzi efendi was exiled to Damascus; Ahmed Hüsameddin efendi from Bursa was exiled to Trablusgarb (Libya); and that Hüsrev Pasha Dergâh Sheikh Seyfullah efendi was also exiled. Records show that the prominent and senior Naqshbandis, like the majority of other Sufis, embraced the constitutional movement and, at least initially, enthusiastically supported the CUP against the sultan (İ. Kara 2001, 70–78). Upon his return to Istanbul after 1908, Esad efendi severely criticized Abdülhamid's "despotism" (*istibdat*) in his opening speech at the founding of the Cemiyet-i Sûfiye (Committee of Sufis; discussed below).[34] He is quoted as having said that "during the dark age of the cursed period of despotism both *shari'a* and *tarikat* were shrouded and concealed" but that now by the grace of Allah "the age of beloved freedom [*hürriyet*] and time of good fortune which is the sign of constitutional governance [*meşrutiyet*]" had come. He then continued: "Our first duty [*vazife*] is to pay our debt of gratitude to those honorable gentlemen [the CUP], who turned the Muslim world from decline [*tedenni*] to progress [*terakki*], from mean baseness to sublimity, who succeeded in accomplishing a service pleasing to God that is deserving of honor and sanctification, and who have truly been prepared to sacrifice their own lives for the safety and security of the homeland and the nation."[35] Esad efendi's sentiments, illustrative of the opinion of many sheikhs and ulema toward the CUP in the early days after 1908, appeared in print in the weekly journal *Tasavvuf*, one of several that proliferated in the liberalized atmosphere for the formation of associations and public articulation of opinion between 1908 and the onset of the Balkan Wars in 1912.

NEW SOCIAL FORMS AND A NEW PUBLIC SPHERE

An important set of sources for the study of the worldviews, practices, and institutions of Sufis after the revolution of 1908 is newspapers published by Sufi circles. In the wake of 1908 there was a proliferation of associations and committees, through which an increasing number of groups (e.g., based on concerns regarding nations and minorities, religion, class, gender, etc.) experimented with discussing both what they considered to be their own affairs and those of a public nature, frequently making demands for measures upon the CUP government and criticizing views opposed to their own (Tunaya 1998). The media through which such discussion took place were newspapers and gazettes of various formats (daily, weekly, bimonthly, etc).[36] Several were published by and for Sufis, the most prominent of which were *Ceride-i Sûfiye, Tasavvuf,* and *Muhibban*.[37] The point can only be alluded to here, but the importance of the expansion of newspapers and gazettes lies in their function as a sphere in which issues and policies would come to be debated in a fashion in which the specific person of the author did not stand in the same authorizing relationship to the texts' truth, as was the case in a more traditional scholarly idiom.[38] Criticism of excesses of power and of the malfunctioning of institutions; searching interrogations of the options available to observant Muslims as they try to deal with the political, economic, and cultural challenges of a powerful West; and new literary genres and even linguistic idioms—such issues were not treated (initially) in books but rather in newspapers and gazettes.[39] Hence, new types of individuals, the reader and writer of newspaper articles (culminating in that new type known as the intellectual), are emblematic of the constitution of a new sphere, in which an unprecedented type of discourse is emerging, one that stands in a new relationship to the exercise of power and a new configuration of the political itself: "As the subjects of publicity—its hearers, speakers, viewers, and doers—we have a different relation to ourselves, a different affect, from that which we have in other contexts" (Warner 1992, 377). Islamic discourse now enters this new field of politics as a public issue in a new way, that is, one that concerns people *as* a public, a gathering of private individuals participating in the formulation of what would come to be known as "policy"—a new semantic application of the term "*siyaset*."[40] As an indication of the spirit of the times, an article in the first issue of *Tasavvuf* was "Tasavvuf ve Meşrutiyet" (Sufism and constitutionalism).[41] This is, in other words, a part of the history of the emergence of the bourgeois public sphere in the late Ottoman Empire, in which a space is cleared by the press for not merely the announcement of information (as the early newspapers had been) but also for the open deliberation of issues now considered to be susceptible to such treatment, one of which was the place and function of Islam in the life of the community and of individuals. The publication of journals and gazettes by Sufi circles represents the articulation of Ottoman Islamic traditions with that new field of power.

Upon the restoration of the constitution, a constant stream of Sufi sheikhs who had been exiled by Abdülhamid to places like Yemen, Iraq, and Libya also began to return to the capital, where many of them began to participate in this new landscape for organizing and expressing themselves. In particular, many sheikhs expressed in print and speech their opposition to Abdülhamid and their complete support for the CUP. Among those returning from Libya was a certain sheikh Naili Bedevi efendi, who set about organizing the Cemiyet-i Sufiye-i İttihadiye (the United Sufis Association), which is known solely from the preparatory documents drawn up by him and subsequently published in the Sufi journal with known Bektashi sympathies, *Muhibban*; upon his death in 1908, the project was not realized.[42]

The main organizing principle for the new association was to be *ıslahat* (reform, improvement, or correction): "In order to distinguish the true from the false [*sahihi sahteden ayırmak*], or, more appropriately, to rectify mere imitation [*taklid*], there can be no doubt that the Sufi orders are in need of reform [*ıslah*]."[43] This was, of course, also one of the main principles of the CUP, and the term "*ittihadiye*" in the name of the planned organization is certainly a reference to this spirit. Improvement and correction of the Sufi orders according to principles recognized as their own was to be the project. The aim of the association was to be the following: "By turning the *tekke*s into spiritual [*ruhani*] and political [*siyasi*] schools, to enlighten [*tenvir etmek*] their disciples and dear sympathizers [*muhibban*] through moral and social discipline and education [*terbiye-i ahlakiye ve siyasiye*], thereby permitting the institution of the *tekke*s [*tesis-i tekayan*] to pursue their true goals [*mekasid-i asliye*] and carry out the necessary and inevitable reform [*islahat-ı mukteziyye*]."[44]

Another issue the association aimed to address was a question of incorporation, both in form and function: "The *tekke*s' documents relating to the assets of their foundations should be examined, and those found to have gone to waste should be indemnified [*zayi olanlar tazmin edilmelidir*]. Dervishes and travelers must not be the only ones allowed to enter the *tekke*s; the *tekke*s are open for the public [*umum insanlar*]. No one should be asked, Why did you come? or When will you leave?"[45] This represents a thoroughgoing interrogation of the basic status and function of the *tekke*s—and on the part of a sheikh, no less—dating from 1908. The next article calls for inspectors (*müfettiş*) in order for the *tekke*s to regain a certain internal orderliness and regularity (*intizam-ı dahili*), explicitly stipulating that such inspectors should be qualified and authorized (*yetkili ve yetenekli*) persons "of the Way" (*ehl-i tarikat*; i.e., Sufis themselves). Furthermore, the inspectors' work to redress irregularities (*aksaklıkların giderilmesi*) should not be limited to Istanbul but should include the *tekke*s and *zaviye*s in the state's other regions.

SUFIS AND REFORM

While the United Sufis Committee was never in fact convened, a parallel organization that did see the light of day was the similarly named Committee of Sufis (Cemiyet-i Sûfiye).[46] This was a semiofficial organization, whose honorary president was no less than sheikh ul-Islam Musa Kâzım efendi himself.[47] Its acting chairman was the sheikh of the Kelami dergâh, Muhammed Esad (Erbili) efendi, while Sheikh Safvet and İzmirli İsmail Hakkı were on the directing committee. Sheikh Safvet (d. 1950) was a very active sheikh in the last decades of the empire, as publisher and editor of the journal *Tasavvuf* (which functioned as the unofficial organ of the Cemiyet-i Sûfiye) and president of the Assembly of Sheikhs. Safvet is also an interesting example of the kinds of subject positions and identities common at the time but that became almost literally unthinkable over the course of the republic. Safvet efendi was a member of the Ottoman Chamber of Deputies (from Urfa) after 1908 and was a vocal supporter of the constitution and the CUP (at least initially) and scathing in his denunciation of Abdülhamid and his "despotism."[48] Safvet efendi (later Safvet Yetkin after the republican law on surnames) was also a member of the first republican assembly. As we saw in the last chapter, he was the MP who wrote—and argued on the grounds of *fiqh* (Islamic legal reasoning) for—the legislation to abolish the caliphate and to expel the remaining members of the Ottoman dynasty from the country in 1924. İsmail Hakkı is well known for his modernist approaches to philosophy, *kelam*, and *fiqh*, emphasizing such standards as classification, indexes, and bibliographies.[49] The committee made a point of holding meetings in the form of seminars or conferences at its central offices, located directly across from the Molla Gürani mosque in the Topkapı tramway street, at which members would present the results of research (*tedkik*) they had conducted.[50] The second article of the committee's charter declared that it would not be involved in politics, although at the inaugural meeting of the group, Muhammed Esad efendi referred to the "inauspicious age of despotism" (*devr-i menhus-i istibdat*) of the recent past, hardly a politically neutral way of referring to the reign of Abdülhamid.[51] Scholarly efforts of the committee included the eventual preparation of a large encyclopedic work encompassing the whole of the history of Sufism. Steps were taken in this direction, with letters having been sent out to a number of scholars known for their interest and competence in the field, such as Mehmed Ali Aynî.[52] In addition, there seems to have been an effort to gather together books and manuscripts relating to Sufism into a library of Sufism (M. Kara 1980, 287–88).

The Ottoman Chamber of Deputies (Meclis-i Mebusan) would eventually discuss and debate the changes to the charter of regulations of the Assembly of Sheikhs, and one of the most insistently raised issues appears to have been the question of the degeneration of the orders and *tekke*s in general. In fact, by 1913, members of the Chamber of Deputies were not only pronouncing the orders degenerate but also openly advocating the closing of the *tekke*s. Yunus Nadi declared, "All of these *tekke*s and *zaviye*s, which have sunken to dens of stupefaction [*tembellik yuvası*] [should] be abolished, their revenues and allowances cut off and added to the education [*maarif*] budget."[53] In the same year, in the pages of the journal *İctihad* (known to be unsympathetic, even hostile, to Sufism), Kılıçzâde Hakkı wrote of the Sufis, sheikhs, and dervishes,

> It has become a divine obligation [*farz*] to announce cihad [*ilan-i cihad*] against the softas and dervishes. And we shall say to the people [*halk*], 'You have listened to the softas, sheikhs and dervishes for six hundred years. And you have reaped nothing but disappointment and frustration [*hüsran*] from it. It is a fact that you have experienced this, and repeatedly. Now it's time to listen a bit to those the softas and sheikhs call 'atheists' [*dinsiz*], those observant [*dindar*] of the Truth of the Quran [*hakikat-i Kur'aniye*],

partisans [taraftar] of scholarship and science [ulum ve funun] and of the opinions of the masters [efkar-ı ahraran].'⁵⁴

The debates that took place in the Chamber of Deputies on the topic of the Assembly of Sheikhs are indicative of the sentiments of a great many in the late Ottoman period with respect to Islamic institutions, their efficiency, and their performance, even—and this is a crucial point—on the part of those who were pious and conservative regarding Islamic practice. Many were of the opinion that the tekkes had performed important services in the past and made important contributions to the Islamic tradition but that they had now fallen far from that point and were in need of reform at the very least. In this connection, Şemseddin Bey (Ertoğrul) suggested that a reconciliation, even assimilation, of the tekkes with the medreses would be beneficial, and that in order to do this, modern sociology should be employed (M. Kara 1980, 313–16). The director of personnel (Memurin Müdürü) at the office of the sheikh ul-Islam, Bahri efendi, argued in the chamber that the Assembly of Sheikhs had itself been neglected for years and that in its new form its duty was nothing less than to save the tekkes from their own idleness (316–18).

There is evidence that many Sufis were themselves reaching similar conclusions, though their proposals did not go so far as to amount to the abolition of the orders. Alongside the diagnosis that Sufism had "degenerated" were attempts to ascertain the reasons for this.⁵⁵ As we have seen earlier, attention was focused on the problem of "cradle sheikhs," the transfer of sheikhhood upon the death of a sheikh to his son, who was often far from the most qualified and authoritative in his knowledge and practice. The difficulty in suppressing the practice derived from the fact that sheikhs generally lived in the tekke premises with their families; if the sheikh position did not stay in the family, the now headless family would be forced to move and look for housing. According to Tahirü'l Mevlevî (one of the last generation of Mevlevi sheikhs, d. 1951), there were only two options: either abolish the practice of evladiyet (passing the sheikh position to a son), or make sure the sons of sheikhs are properly trained ahead of time by opening a special school for them, a medresetül-meşayih (M. Kara 2002, 59–61). The students of this school would not merely study Sufism as one more class in their curriculum. The medresetül-meşayih was meant to be a kind of vocational training, by and for practicing sheikhs, and in 1913 a meeting was adjourned to discuss its establishment. It is interesting to note the figures involved in this project and their backgrounds: former sheikh ul-Islam Musa Kâzım efendi; chairman of the Assembly of Sheikhs, Elif efendi; member of the Assembly of Sheikhs, Sukûtîzâde Muhammed Şerif; Yenikapı dergâh, Mevlevi sheikh Abdülbaki efendi; director of the Primary Education Department of the Ministry of Education, Ziya Bey; director of Scholarly Foundations [Müessesât-ı İlmiye-i

Vakfiye] and member of the Chamber of Deputies from Bursa, Tahir Bey (M. Kara 1980, 112). Despite the interest on the part of Sufi circles, support for the idea was apparently not widespread enough for resources to be allocated to it, and the *medresetül-meşayih* remained only an idea.

With the Central *Tekke* Regulations (*Merkez Tekâyâ Talimatnamesi*) of 1915 and 1916, the central *tekke*s would be responsible for the correspondence between the *tekke*s in their zone (e.g., ensuring that state decrees and decisions pertaining to the *tekke*s were announced to all the *tekke*s under their responsibility and that the requests and correspondence from these *tekke*s were forwarded to the Assembly of Sheikhs) and had rights of administration (*denetim*) over them. This was carried out in each *tekke* district by a team of two individuals selected by secret ballot from among the member sheikhs. Also according to the provisions of the *talimatname*, *tekke*s would be subject to continuous inspection, and the records of these inspections (*yoklama ilmühaberi*) would be kept in the central *tekke*s. Once a year, a certified general inspection register would be forwarded to the Assembly of Sheikhs by each central sheikh (Aydin 1998, 97).

The level of detail and scale of the intervention of this apparatus of administration can be gleaned from the fact that the regulations stipulated that, for at least one hour a week, a member of the order would give a lesson (*vaaz*) on its aims and purposes as well as on Islam and ethics, while the sheikhs of the central *tekke*s were obliged in principle to work toward the unity (*ittihad*; probably meaning "coordination") of the *tekke*s, sheikhs, and dervishes in their zone. The Assembly of Sheikhs charter (*nizamname*) published in the newspaper *Takvim-i Vekayi* on July, 18, 1918, was expanded by eight articles (*talimatname*), "organizing everything down to how cooking vessels, spoons and cups were to be cleaned."[56] Quite obviously, all of these regulations loaded an enormous amount of administrative rights and responsibilities on the shoulders of Sufi sheikhs, in general, and the sheikhs of the central *tekke*s, in particular. They were thoroughly bureaucratized; the sheikhs were now state bureaucrats, with an important amount of their day's time and their own energies spent in the various practices through which their institutions were to be governed. The sheikhs were not permitted to leave their posts without appointing a deputy (*vekil*) responsible in their absence, and the sheikhs were required to send monthly reports on the *tekke*s in their zone to the Assembly of Sheikhs.

Now that the offices of the sheikh ul-Islam were responsible for approving the appointment of new sheikhs, how might they even know who a given sheikh's deputies or sons are? A central technique of bureaucratic administration is the survey, through which objects are constituted in relation to normative grids of visibility and calculability.[57] In 1918, this institution organized a survey of Sufi sheikhs (as part of a broader and ongoing collection of biographical data on the ulema), by sending out printed forms, on which responses were to be written in the spaces provided. Both the fact of the survey's occurrence, and the information contained therein, are extremely revealing of the nature of Islamic institutions and personnel, as well as their governance in the empire at that time.

The questions printed on the forms next to spaces for the respondent's answers were the following:

1. Respondent's name, pseudonyms, name by which generally known, nickname; if he is from a prominent family the nature of the relation; religious creed [mezheb-i i'tikadı] and practice; of which tarikat is he a member; the period of his service from the time he joined [intisab] to the time he took the oath [to become sheikh]; the name and pseudonyms of his sheikh.
2. Date and place of birth; name and pseudonyms of father.
3. In which public and/or private schools [resmî ve hususî mekteb ve medrese] or from which private teachers [muallim-i mahsus] did you study which disciplines, sciences [ilm ve fen] and languages, and to what level; whether you received any certificates, diplomas or awards, if so their dates; what languages you write or only speak; if you have any published or printed works or compilations their topics, when and where they were published.
4. Are you at present or have you in the past been in official service [i.e. worked for the state]?
5. The name or names of the dergâh-ı şerif of which you are sheikh, its location, and the date of your appointment.
6. Founders and date of construction of the tekke?
7. The name of the tarikat that the dergâh belongs to and whose principles are being practiced [erkânı icra edilmekte olan]; times and evenings of ceremonies. Beside the current sheikh, are there any other appointees in the dergâh, if so who are they responsible to; the dergâh's rules and practices and if it has an officially registered deed of trust as a vakıf; if not, what are its established customs and practices [teamül-ü kadîmi].
8. If the respondent has assistants [hulefa], what are their names and pseudonyms, place and date of birth; how many serious ('full degree') [inabe eden] dervishes do you have?[58]

It was to this questionnaire that our Hüseyin efendi responded.

THE ABOLITION OF THE ORDERS AND
THE CLOSING OF THE LODGES

It is striking that between 1920 and 1925, the nationalist movement's leader, Mustafa Kemal, and those around him in the movement did not take hostile actions against the orders, and it is well documented that the nationalists worked closely with Sufi sheikhs in mobilizing the population in support of their efforts.[59] Indeed, the constitution of 1924 included in its article 75,

"No one may be persecuted on account of the religion, *madhhab* [school of *shari'a* jurisprudence] *tarikat* or school of philosophy to which he or she belongs. Provided they are not contrary to public order and decorum [*asayiş ve umumî muaşeret*], all types of religious ceremonies (*ayin*) are permitted" (qtd. in M. Kara 2002, 101).

Law number 429 was promulgated on March 3 of the same year, abolishing the Ministry of the Shari'a and Evkaf, and establishing the Ministry of Religious Affairs. The former ministry had existed only since 1920 when it was created as an alternative to the Meşihat, the office of the sheikh al-Islam in Istanbul that had collaborated with the Western powers against the nationalists. Article 5 of this law stipulates that "all appointments and dismissals of imams, *khatibs*, *va'iz* [preachers], shaykhs, muezzins, caretakers and various personnel to and from all mosques and *tekke*s shall be undertaken by the Ministry of Religious Affairs." Sheikhs, *tekke*s, and *zaviye*s were thus officially recognized and placed under the control of the new ministry, itself a part of the streamlined and more tightly structured administration in Ankara. In other words, imams of mosques and sheikhs of the Sufi orders were made state bureaucrats, as they were in the later empire. This incorporated form of social and legal life of the orders in the new republic was, however, short-lived.

The turning point was the Sheikh Said rebellion in the (predominantly Kurdish) southeast of the new republic, beginning around February 13, 1925. It is clear that Mustafa Kemal and his close associates were badly shaken by these events and used them as an occasion to deal swiftly and decisively with numerous individuals and movements suspected of being less than enthusiastic in their support for the ongoing reforms. The legal grounds for doing so were prepared by amending the High Treason Law of 1920 (previously amended in 1923) to include on February 26, 1925, the "use of religion for political purposes" and on March 4, 1925, the establishment of independence tribunals. The amendment enabled sentencing of Sheikh Said and dozens of others to death, and the tribunals continued through 1926 (Zürcher 2004; M. Kara 2002).

In July 1925, a commission of inquiry sent from Ankara to Istanbul to ascertain the situation of the *tekke*s there reported that the majority were close to ruin (*harap durumunda*; Jäschke 1972, 36).[60] In September, the Cabinet of Ministers prepared a bill to close the *tekke*s, and this bill was subsequently debated in the assembly.[61] On November 30, passage of law number 677 formally abolished the orders and closed the *tekke*s (M. Kara 1980, 322–29). The *tekke*s with mosques attached or that were also used as mosques would continue to be used solely as mosques; those not used as mosques would be used as schools, and those unable to be so used would be sold, with the proceeds going to the education budget. Titles such as *hoca*, *sheikh*, *baba*, and *dede*, given to leaders of religious communities, were banned, as was wearing turban and robes for all but official (i.e., state) functionaries (e.g., imams and muftis) while conducting their duties.[62]

THE PRESTIGE OF REFORM AMONG MUSLIMS AND SUFIS

Much has been made of the severity of the new republican regime's policies toward the Sufi orders, and not without reason, but one ought not lose sight of a few qualifying points. First, the notion that the state should proscribe or enforce certain items of dress is hardly unique to the new regime; sartorial policies had been an integral part of the Ottoman political repertoire. The fez, for instance, was banned by the republican regime, but it should be recalled that it had been compulsorily introduced by Mahmud II in the first place, replacing turbans for most Ottoman gentlemen. When the Janissary corps was destroyed by Mahmud in 1826, the closely linked Bektashi order of dervishes, whose eponym was regarded by the corps as their patron saint, was also suppressed; the order was officially dissolved, properties and foundations confiscated, and many buildings given over to other orders (particularly the Naqshbandiyya), and the wearing of distinctively Bektashi garb and headgear was forbidden (Birge 1994, 74–78). Also, the confiscation of orders' properties and the exiling of sheikhs was common in Ottoman times.

What did the Sufi sheikhs themselves think of the proscription of the orders and the closing of the lodges? Obviously the atmosphere was not conducive to vocal public protest (on this or most any other issue for that matter). Yet one can get a sense of the feelings different categories of people had by reading between the lines in the proceedings of debates and meetings from the time and, most insightfully, by reading the memoirs of sheikhs and those who turned in those circles (many of which were not published until recently and remained in manuscript form in private).[63] A prominent sheikh from Bursa, Mehmet Şemseddin efendi (d. 1936), wrote in his memoirs on May 10, 1926 (not long after the proscription in November 1925), a postscript to an earlier entry called simply "Sufi lodges" (*tekâyâ*) written in 1924,

> Ten months after I wrote the above entry entitled Sufi lodges the Grand National Assembly took notice of the maliciousness emanating from the lodges, and because it had become clear that a large number of the orders—contrary to the fundamental principles of Sufism—had become profitable operations, all of the lodges were abolished in the session of September 1341. Since the true vocation of the Sufi is a matter impartially and disinterestedly between God and his servant, in the eyes of Sufis entering the vocation such things as the lodge's monthly stipends, revenue, or residence have no value whatsoever. Perhaps because they abused (alet

etmek) the exalted Sufi vocation they are responsible. I humbly said years ago to my brethren [other Sufis] that this would happen, that a solution needed to be thought of and that the vocation needed to be protected from maliciousness and hypocrisy. And as a matter of fact what I thought has more or less come to pass. (qtd. in M. Kara 2001, 16)

Reflected here, more than the oft-repeated accusations that Sufis were mostly obscure charlatans opposed to science, reason, and progress (accusations that both less-religious figures and more-devout Islamists often leveled), is that they were also reaping material advantage and profit from their positions. Our diarist suggests that he saw some of that and suspects that this is what brought the hammer of the new regime down on the Sufis. Not only is this unbecoming of a devout Sufi, it is also, Şemseddin efendi says, contrary to the "true" nature of Sufism, which ought to be between God and the individual. This is also an index of the extent to which many observant Muslims—Sufis included—had come to see Islam and Sufism largely as a private matter, a crucially important point for our study. However, many other conservative Muslims saw the proscription of the lodges as merely one of a whole slate of anti-Islamic measures the new regime in Ankara was determined to carry out, signs of their inherently irreligious, not to say atheist, nature. What does Şemseddin efendi say to this?

> Now, the opposition [to the new regime] says, "Religion has been lost." But I ask, "What of it has been lost? What was there before such that now it's gone?" And let me say this, I have never been a member of a party, I am merely a lover of truth and justice. Wherever I see propriety, goodness and truth, that's which side I'm on. I wonder if these gentlemen tried to go to pray and someone told them, "You won't be going to the mosque anymore"? No, whoever wishes can go to the mosque, church, synagogue, tavern or brothel. As long as one doesn't harm another no one will prevent him. Well the same with fasting, and the other [duties incumbent on Muslims]. "Well, women don't wear Islamic dress [tesettür] anymore" [they say]. Fine, but I still see plenty of ladies with veils and coverings on. Does anyone tell them, "You're going to take this off, and you're going to go around naked"? No. So let whoever wants to wear a sack do so, and whoever wants to go around without coverings do so. Up to a certain point this can't be seen as going against common decency.[64]

Again, prominent here is Şemseddin efendi's approach to Islam as a religion, that is, having primarily to do with personal choice (going to a house of worship or going to a tavern). Also argued here is that, since no one prevents a Muslim from performing the duties incumbent upon him, like fasting or worship, it is improper to even think that something essential has been lost in Islam in Turkey. While the discontent among some of the religiously conservative in the early republic was considerable, it is nonetheless important to recall the fact that many observant Muslims had long since come to see Islam in terms of religion on the liberal model, that is, primarily a matter of personal choice and a private issue. That this is reflected in the memoirs of a Sufi sheikh is an excellent indication of the sensibilities of a great many observant Muslims and their attitudes toward the reforms going on in the young republic.

It is striking to see in the minutes of the assembly debates over proscription of the orders that almost no one came to the defense of the orders and *tekke*s (M. Kara 1980; 2002). This was true among the numerous MPs with a *medrese* education and even among those with Sufi backgrounds, such as Sheikh Esad Erbilî (former chairman of the Assembly of Sheikhs), Sheikh Safvet (editor of the important Ottoman second-constitutional-period journal *Tasavvuf* and author of the bill to abolish the caliphate), and Chelebi efendi (former sheikh [*postnişin*] of the important Konya Mevlevi order's lodge [Mevlevihane]; M. Kara 2002). The incremental steps leading to the proscription had seemed to the vast majority of prominent people involved to be reasonable, if unfortunate.[65] To many, then and today, proscription of the orders was merely, as one of those I worked with put it, "locking the doors of the *tekke*s which were in any case already closed."[66] The subtleties of this point may be difficult to appreciate for those unfamiliar with the transitional period from the late Ottoman to republican environments, which is why I take the time to examine this period here. Only very recently have scholars interested in something other than Kemalist or Islamist apologetics paid serious attention to this period.[67]

The main point to understand here is the near collapse of the residual prestige of the Sufi orders, and Sufism in general, in the wake of the collapse of the empire. This prestige was already in tatters by the Ottoman second constitutional period, beginning in 1908. Indeed, the vast majority of those who considered themselves to be working and living in contribution to Islamic traditions from within generally accepted that Sufism was an important part of the rich Islamic heritage, but it had, for all practical purposes, ceased to function and was unlikely ever to again. The issue was brought to a head by the dramatic dimensions of the political, military, and economic problems facing Ottoman Muslims, which we saw in the last chapter, and the broader issue of the scope and function of Islam in Ottoman society in general. At a time when Muslims themselves were interrogating the very nature of Islam and Islamic institutions and practices in an attempt to reinvigorate these practices, many came to consider Sufism a luxury that Ottoman Muslims in the heartland of the empire could not afford (İ. Kara 1997).

The empire needed schools to provide training in modern disciplines and Islamic sciences; the Sufi lodges, almost without exception, needed major repairs. Resources were extremely limited. Which does one choose? All of the available evidence suggests that, even among Sufis themselves, the answer was obvious.[68] Here is how Şemseddin efendi, a former Sufi sheikh, wrote about the situation *medreses* and Sufi lodges were in vis-à-vis modern institutions of training in his memoirs:

"But the medreses have been closed, lodges chained [shut], places of worship abolished" [they say]. Well, the medreses are not teaching disciplines appropriate to the times. Our current affairs cannot be managed [*idare olunmak*] with the old grammar and syntax, logic and reason. Instead of that we have excellent schools. Military lycées and academies, medical schools, schools of administration [*mülkiye liseleri*], coeducational teachers colleges . . . And they all give excellent meals to their students. Not like the old half a bread-cake and a bowl of wheat soup in the medreses.

And the lodges? 95 percent of them had been transformed [on paper] in order to be embezzled, had practically become profitable operations, and while a few of them were able to keep up appearances most of them couldn't even do that. Is there any reason to object that an institution has been abolished that did no service to religion, nor to the nation [*millet*], nor to the country [*vatan*]?[69]

Another aspect of changes in Sufi culture over the last 80 years is arguably equally important, even if underappreciated. It is that much of the criticism of Sufism and Sufi orders, from the later Ottoman period to the present, has centered on "superstitions" and "charlatans," and especially on those who were felt to manipulate the ignorant for personal gain. In the late Ottoman context of collapse of an entire political, economic, and social order, radical interrogation of the underpinnings of that order were to be expected and, indeed, proliferated.[70] In this context, the severest condemnation of superstition and obscurantism was a major feature of the discourse of reform. This reform discourse was considered to be the only hope for the *umma*—the moral and political community of Muslims—(particularly since in the later Ottoman environment this term came to be identified with the nation) to defend itself against (infidel) aggression, such as had just brought on the collapse of the empire.[71] On this point we again appreciate the immense prestige of the nationalist forces and administration established in Ankara from Şemseddin efendi's memoirs:

And then they say the Caliphate is gone. Well I ask, what Caliphate? The Ottoman Caliphate? That disappeared on its own. For as the vanquished in the great war the victorious states offered and forced us to accept such a peace that we would be left with neither rifle, canon, nor pistol nor any kind of means to defend ourselves. [The Caliphate] was going to become one of their colonies. Now is there even a Caliphate at this point?! From the beyond, Allah gave life to a man from Anatolia [Mustafa Kemal]. With nothing, absolutely nothing—no canon, no guns, no army, no money, nothing—with incredible exertion and effort a government of Turkey was established. And it expelled a hundred thousand well-equipped and strong [*mükemmel*] enemies. After that, of course they [Mustafa Kemal and the nationalists] wouldn't accept a Caliph who tried to give his country away as a gift to foreigners. At least if he had stayed out of it, or forget materially at least had lent his emotional support he might have retained his office. But no, right alongside the enemies they [the Caliph and the Sultan's administration] tried to interfere with the efforts of these self-sacrificing, loyal ones [the nationalists] by bringing out fatwas declaring them to be wicked rebels. This shocked the government of Turkey, and they said, Enough of the Caliphate! Fine, but couldn't they have just kept the Caliphate but put someone else in the post? They couldn't. The Turkish Caliphate was over. And from the point of view of Islam, for those Muslims in the Sunni mad-hab government means republic [*cumhuriyet*] anyway.[72]

Indeed, such was the prestige of the military that this Sufi sheikh sees it as the most competent institution in the country, even more than the civil service (mülkiye): "The government should be a military government [*hükümet-i askeriye*], because there is orderliness [*intizam*] in the military. If they carry out good governance and justice, it will be an excellent government. There isn't this kind of orderliness in the civil service. What the civil service messes up they later make the military do." (Text in M. Kara 2001, 17). It is important to not underestimate the immense prestige that the nationalist forces, led eventually by Mustafa Kemal, garnered in the eyes of a very large majority of the population. This can also be appreciated when we recall that, compared to other revolutions, for instance the Russian one unfolding next door to Turkey during World War I, the new regime found it necessary to kill only a very small number of people. The fact is that very few people had strong feelings of disapproval toward the nationalists around Mustafa Kemal, at least in the early years. This is not to deny that there was resistance to the new regime but only to emphasize that it was not a mass phenomenon (with the possible exception of areas of the predominately Kurdish southeast of the new republic, a case that we cannot examine at length here). The Sufi sheikhs lost their titles, positions, and salaries, but they were not executed as a class like many sheikhs and ulema were in the Soviet Union (though, again, a limited number of specific individuals implicated in alleged crimes against the new regime were indeed executed).

The notion that alongside knowledge of the canonical sources and practice of canonical worship there are yet "other sources" of Islamic authority continues to be controversial among observant Muslims, in Turkey and elsewhere. The effects of decades of discrediting and casting doubt on Sufism have been considerable in Turkey, and many Sufis with whom I worked in the Gümüşhanevi branch of the Naqshbandi order were very concerned that there should be no straying from the path of *sunna*, the exemplary precedents of Muhammad. These Sufis remained in that particular branch because they had not detected any such straying.

Abdülaziz Bekkine efendi (1895–1952), trained in late Ottoman *medreses* and lodges and sheikh of the Naqshbandi order studied in this book from 1949 to 1952, said in response to a question about the lodges (*tekkes*) closure, "My son, those *tekkes* deserved to be closed. Among them the ones that were maintaining [*muhafaza etmek*] Islam had dramatically diminished. And so Allah closed them" (İ. Kara 1991, 20). This remains today a very common sentiment among Sufis and those sympathetic of Sufism in Turkey, that by the end of the empire the orders had become too contaminated by superstition and ignorance, both incompatible with Islam. Today one continues to find an ambivalence on the part of participants in this order on the issue of the lodges, and it is clear that their ability to reestablish them is not a high priority for them.

Mustafa Kara has summarized the stances of sheikhs regarding the proscription of the orders and closing of the *tekkes* thus:

1. For those familiar with the press during the Second Constitutional Period and those who knew the so-called 'Tanzimat intellectuals' calling for a revolution in religion, education and society the decision did not come as much of a surprise.
2. Those resigned dervishes with an attitude of "conforming to events" or "all is the will of God" also said that there was not much to be upset about. Some among these, taking into consideration the circumstances of the period, continued to pass on Sufi culture by other means, and ensured that the torch was passed on.
3. Those who were upset at the closure were concerned that with the collapse of religious-Sufi life society itself would also collapse.
4. Some of those who complained about Law 677 [closing the orders] had found that their source of income had vanished and had to struggle to make a living.
5. Some Sufis of the opinion "we'll take the good with the bad" did not care much about the lodges and tombs [of saints and luminaries], continued on their journey in the depths of the heart, and looked on events through rosy glasses without seeing much that could upset their tranquility.
6. Those who looked at events from the point of view of the merits of policy preferred to keep quiet.
7. In an environment characterized by new public order regulations and the Independence tribunals, some Sufis were silenced out of fear. (M. Kara 2001, 18)

SUFISM AND GOVERNMENTALITY AT
THE CLOSE OF THE EMPIRE

Ottoman governmentality incorporated many Islamic institutions such as mosques, *medrese*s, and Sufi lodges. These are crucial elements in a genealogy of Islam and modernity in Turkey, which is why we have taken them up in the first part of this book. As the reforms considered central to the empire's ability to maintain itself centered on military sciences and other disciplines not traditionally associated with Islamic knowledges, these latter came to be— in practice if not yet in principle—differentiated as a distinctly "religious" sphere. One did not need to learn Arabic, for instance, in order to learn and apply the new military sciences; in fact, knowledge of French, English, or German was much more useful for reading textbooks and understanding the lectures of visiting teachers. Over the decades, schools teaching the new languages and disciplines became the most prestigious and the best funded from the state. The effect of this was an incremental shift in the relative prestige of newly differentiated knowledges. This is the genealogy of what only much later came to be called secularism in Turkey. It was already well under way by the second half of the nineteenth century.

Sufi orders were a major feature of the social, political, and economic landscape of the central Ottoman lands of the Balkans and Anatolia in the later empire. As in many other parts of the Muslim world, a great many Ottoman Muslims (including ulema) cultivated their piety through affiliation with one or more of the orders. The orders were largely fiscally and administratively autonomous as institutions in the central Ottoman lands until the late eighteenth century. It had already become clear to the Ottoman authorities by the late eighteenth century that the creation of new types of (initially military) institutions demanded by the increasingly dire military and strategic situation on their north and west frontiers was going to be extremely expensive. This realization led immediately, naturally enough, to a review of the ways in which fiscal resources—taxes—were being collected and administered in the empire. This review led, in turn, to the formulation of new procedures and new ways of defining objects as useful resources—including, crucially, people. Over the course of the nineteenth century, the Ottoman Sufi orders were incrementally reconstituted in the field of Ottoman governmental power. The level of penetration of new techniques of organization, of new kinds of knowledge, and of new normativities and forms of reason was subtle but pervasive. Among the major effects of the dissemination of this optic and practice of governmentality was the increasing individuation of people into productive subjects, and it increasingly became the individual that the state was interested in, in terms of interventions. Welfare would now be defined by attending to the needs of the population at the level of the processes of life itself (birth rates, health, labor, rest, disease, death, etc.), which was accomplished by the amplification of bureaucratized procedure with expertise about "humans" generated by practitioners of new sciences (administration, psychology, pedagogy, nutrition, sanitation, hygiene, etc.; the *sciences humaines*). These new means of exercising power simultaneously redefined and transformed the objects upon which they were exercised, the kinds of knowledge that individuals were increasingly proficient in, and the kinds of activities they increasingly spent their days doing—in other words, transformed the kinds of subjects they were.

The aim of these Ottoman reforms, as we have seen, was not to rationalize society and certainly not to do so as part of a process of Westernization; the aim, quite simply, was to strengthen the empire and the functioning of its institutions and thereby the community of Muslims. Rationalization of procedure was a consequence of the deliberate transformation, creation, and destruction of institutions; the decision to change a practice or institution into a particular desired outcome inevitably entails explicit calculation of the nature of the units in question and of the directions in which changes may take place.[73] By 1908, Islamic institutions such as *medrese*s and *tekke*s had been incorporated by the Ottomans into the generalized discipline of a regime of governmentality, and the authority of sheikhs (and therefore the functioning of the orders' Islamic traditions) was exercised simultaneously in characteristically modern and Islamic modalities. During these periods, the Sufi orders were not outside the field of modern power; that field was part of the conditions of possibility for the very continuation of Islamic traditions themselves.

PART II

DISCIPLINES OF PRESENCE

CHAPTER 3

EVERYDAY ETHICS AND DISCIPLINARY PRACTICE

In the road just below the back gate to the courtyard of the İskender Pasha complex in Fatih, we run into Ahmet. I had been thinking about him recently, especially during my visits to the complex, but was told that he came around rarely these days; running into him like this is quite a coincidence. He smiles, we embrace, and he reaches into his pocket and pulls out a date, saying, "Here you go, a date." I laugh, and gesture, patting my heart with an open palm, implying, "No, no . . . thanks." He smiles, holding up the date insistently. The other guys we are with are talking among themselves, not paying too much attention to us. I take it, and we continue to talk. I notice that he doesn't give one to anyone else, only to me. It is a little uncomfortable, but everyone is chatting. I'm holding this sticky thing in my fingers, not knowing if I should eat it now or later. In the midst of the banter, I pop it into my mouth, work the pit out and drop it on the ground, and I ask about Yusuf *amca* ("uncle" Yusuf), how his health is, and how the garden of the tombs at Süleymaniye is shaping up.[1] Ahmet nods, says he's not bad, that he comes to Süleymaniye nearly every day in the morning, makes *ziyaret* (a visit) to Mehmed Zahid efendi, and tends the garden and his gravesite. "Actually," Ahmet says, "he was asking about you today. The date was from him."

* * *

I START WITH THIS VIGNETTE BECAUSE, AMONG both Muslims and non-Muslims, in the past and present, mention of Sufism often has brought to mind wonders or charismatic acts (*keramet*) worked by sheikhs or saintly, pious figures.[2] This was definitely not a major concern for the Naqshbandis I worked with, and indeed, though I myself never brought the topic up, they seemed to be keen to discourage me and other disciples within earshot from attaching any interest to such things.[3] Yet there would be moments when they were playfully suggested, like in the instance with the date, and these little "inside jokes" contributed to the ethos of companionship and lightheartedness I noted among many of these Sufis, which is characteristic of a certain kind of attitude and style of life I shall attempt to describe in this chapter. Uncle Yusuf was an extremely gentle man, with a youthful face and a trim beard, who just exuded positive energy. He was recovering from a serious illness, which slowed him down. Now retired, he had been involved in the order for decades and was apparently one of the more devoted to the previous sheikh of the order, Mehmed Zahid Kotku, and was his driver for a time. Mehmed efendi had even arranged Uncle Yusuf's marriage. He had apparently taken his sheikh's death pretty hard, and he still spoke of Mehmed efendi as if he had seen him a few hours earlier. Uncle Yusuf embodied many things for this community: most importantly, a link with the past, including the last Ottoman-era sheikh (Kotku). Despite this, he had a positive demeanor toward the (at the time of my research) current sheikh, who was likely younger than Uncle Yusuf himself, and a certain wise yet humble playfulness, which I will suggest in this chapter we consider as a certain kind of ethical disposition. Indeed, a sense of *keramet* that is especially widespread among Sufis (and most famously popularized by Ibn 'Arabi in his *al-Futuhat al-Makkiyya*) is that one of the most important signs of a given sheikh's special qualities is his "miraculous" ability to get people to abandon bad habits and forbidden things in favor of ones that are licit and encouraged in Islam.[4]

Many social scientists studying Islam and Sufism in Turkey take up the topics because they see them as constituted primarily of personal networks and assume that these networks are important in social, economic, and political life in the country. Especially among so-called Islamist political movements, Sufi orders are considered to be influential. This may well be the case, and there are connections between some of the ruling Adalet ve Kalkınma Party (AKP) cadres and this Sufi order (and perhaps others), including in their general approach to Islam, the nature of good governance, and modernization, which I discuss shortly. But another (and in my opinion, more important) reason why the study of Sufism is a useful window into Turkey is that certain Sufi groups (and others that are offshoots of Sufism, like the Nurcus) have had a significant impact on the formation of Muslim sensibilities in the country, especially regarding engagement with characteristically modern social forms, practices, and regimes of knowledge and power.[5] Naqshbandis in particular, as we saw in the last chapter, had been close to the apparatuses of power in the later Ottoman Empire, especially during the reign of Abdülhamid, and Mevlana Khalid's views on influencing those in power appears to have been continued by subsequent sheikhs after the abolition of the orders in the republic, as we shall see in the pages that follow.

Let me clarify at this juncture an argument I am not making in this study. Some of my social-scientist colleagues with whom I discuss the topic approach the study of Sufis in Turkey from the point of view of a presumed, implicit, cost-benefit analysis members of a Sufi order would seem to be running in their minds (some taking this approach also pursue the "networks" analysis mentioned previously). Accordingly, for the researcher (and by extension, for the member herself), the relevant question would be the following: "What do people get out of participating in these Sufi orders?" I have had enough conversations that gravitated in this direction to sense that some readers will be scanning these pages for an answer to this question. For reasons that should become obvious, my response is that I do not find this to be a particularly useful approach to the issue and that a better approach is a more obvious one: participating in these Sufi orders is a way for people to become the kinds of Muslim selves they want (or believe they are supposed) to become and gives them techniques for understanding, defining, and reproducing a certain kind of ethical self. In this sense, we may approach Sufism as similar to certain schools of ancient philosophy such as Pierre Hadot has described them, that is, in consisting essentially of "the practice of spiritual exercises . . . not as a theoretical construct, but as a method for training people to live and to look at the world in a new way" (Hadot 1995, 107).[6]

Having established in previous chapters the historical status of Islamic traditions of discourse and practice after the transition to the republic, we now turn to an account of such traditions in the present. What are the connections between these traditions and particular kinds of ethical subjects? Continuing to examine Islam as a discursive tradition (and not, for instance, merely a set of beliefs), we explore categories, styles of reasoning, and practices in and through which Muslim selves are formed. The relationship between power and subject formation comes especially into focus as we discuss the formation of dispositions to feeling and action. This turns out to be more important for an understanding of the relationship between religion and the political than, say, the influence of religion on party politics or vice versa (though we will address this as well). We are approaching here a particular understanding of the relationship between repeated actions, dispositions, qualities of character, and human nature.

These Sufi Islamic traditions of practice involve, as William Connolly puts it, "embodiment in repetitive practices that help to consolidate the dispositions, sensibilities, and ethos through which meaning is lived, intellectual beliefs are settled, and relations between constituencies are negotiated" (2005, 56). We are building here on several critiques of approaches to religion that see it as primarily consisting of a set of beliefs or meanings that can (and ideally should be) separable from "the materialities of culture" (Smith

1991; Asad 1993). The expectation that religion has a proper essence that can be separated from practice has a complex genealogy and is an integral part of secularization, but Asad usefully summarizes this with reference to Christianity, as when "faith had once been a virtue, [but] now acquired an epistemological sense. Faith became a way of knowing supernatural objects" (Asad 2003, 38–39).[7] Considering faith to be a "mode of knowledge" parallel to reason means essentially that "rituals and exercises are understood to *symbolize* a belief or faith already there, not to participate in the very constitution of faith itself" (Connolly 2005, 57). The liberal distinction between private faith and public reason thus tends to ignore the issue of how one is supposed to have a disposition to come to faith in the first place. A focus on "religious symbols," such as in the discourses of some of those involved in the head scarf debates in Turkey and in France, entirely elides the fact that a particular thing (practice, way of dressing, eating, or talking, etc.) may not be a symbol of something else (or a "political statement") but may rather be a "medium through which embodied habits, dispositions, sensibilities, and capacities of performance are *composed and consolidated*" (Connolly 2005, 57). Most religious traditions have a large accumulated body of knowledge about and techniques for the education of the senses, and Islam is no exception. Alongside this, it is important to acknowledge that nonreligious forms of social life also have similar "body-brain-culture resonance machines," to use Connolly's term (2005, 57), through which certain ways of doing and speaking both imply and reinforce certain kinds of selves that are supposed to interact in accordance with certain norms. This is a crucial analytical framework and level for us to be operating on, for it brings to light both the relationship between discourses, practices, and modes of selfhood, as well as how these modes relate to the nature of the public. Once we see this visceral, sensorial level, we can appreciate that this is the level on which the heterogeneity of the public is an issue, and we turn to this in later chapters.

For these Muslims, Islam—and Sufism in particular—does not consist of sets of beliefs set down in treatises meant to abstractly systematize reality. This community, like many communities of Muslims, does have texts at its core, namely the Quran and collections of hadith, as well as monographs on historical figures in Islam and Sufism and topical essays on various beliefs and practices in Islam and Sufism. Many of the texts this community produces and reads are on ethics (*ahlak*) and are best thought of as guides in the art of living (Kosman 1980).[8] In other words, Sufism for these Muslims is not merely a system of thought; rather, it consists of practical means for the cultivation of the proper life of a Muslim. Important here is the idea that it is necessary to work on oneself, with the assistance of a guide, and that through such work one must transform oneself, for there is a better condition of humans (their telos) than the one they are generally in without such work. Moreover, the practitioner's embodiment of this work in his or her transformed dispositions transmits and recapitulates the history of the knowledge about attempts to do such work. These accumulated attempts, and the discourses defining and evaluating them, are what we mean by a tradition (MacIntyre 1984). As this history, the history we have outlined in earlier chapters, is turned into bodily practice, it contributes to the dispositions to action, sentiment, and reason of its practitioners. This also becomes important when we go on to explore the temporal and historical heterogeneity of the public in contemporary Turkey.

THE SPACE OF SUFISM IN CONTEMPORARY TURKEY

In the decades after the abolition of the Sufi orders in 1925, which we saw in the last chapter had been severely discredited and maligned beginning in the late Ottoman period, it appears that the numbers of their adherents declined sharply, while several of the orders did continue to function in a secret fashion, quietly among circles of people in the know. The Sufis I worked with did not usually refer to the order as a *"tarikat"* (the usual Arabic term for Sufi order), but rather as a *cemaat* (Arabic *jama'a,* or "community"), which not only is at least partly due to the ban on Sufi activities but also may be a legacy of the late Ottoman period, when the term *"tarikat"* may have begun to take on the tone of shadiness that it carries for many people in Turkey today (connoting charlatanism, etc.). Today there are no Sufi lodges as such in Turkey, although their traditional functions do not go entirely unfulfilled. The Gümüşhanevi branch under discussion here is well known for its activities among personnel and students at universities. A number of branch members informed me that this orientation continues the scholarly identity of Ahmed Ziyaüddin Gümüşhanevi (d. 1893), the internationally renowned scholar of Islam who expanded this branch in the Khalidiyya lineage of the Naqshbandi order.[9] It seems likely that the growth of interest in this branch of the order among university professors and students dates to the period of Abdülaziz Bekkine efendi. According to *mürid*s (initiated members loyal to the sheikh) who participated, in warm weather, Aziz efendi used to hold *sohbet*s (lessons, more on which in the next chapter) after *juma'* (Friday) prayers, on a raised platform, shaded under trees behind the Ümmü Gülsüm mosque in the Zeyrek neighborhood of Istanbul, where he was the imam. In colder months the *sohbet*s would take place in his wooden two-storied house behind the mosque (Ersöz 1992).[10] There were usually many students and academics in attendance (including the Islamist-nationalist writer Nurettin Topçu), especially from Istanbul University, which is an easy walk from Zeyrek. Several accounts by participants in these *sohbet*s attest to their power and subtlety, including that of the Egyptian Turkologist and Cairo University professor

Ahmad Sa'id Sulayman (d. 1991), who spent some 20 months in Istanbul in the early 1950s: "I was deeply impressed by the sheikh [Abdülaziz] efendi's *sohbet*s. Frankly, in Egypt I had been a member of the Bayyumi *tarikat* long enough to be permitted to initiate others as a *khalifa* [deputy to the sheikh], but I must admit that among those groups in the old wooden house I just melted away [*eridim*]" (qtd. in İ. Kara 2004, 18).[11]

While Sufi orders became illegal in 1925, enforcement of the relevant laws has varied over the decades, with a minor relaxation noted just before the 1950 general elections (the first truly competitive ones), in which the Democrat Party (DP) emerged victorious over the Republican People's Party (Cumhuriyet Halk Partisi or CHP). To an outsider, the DP resembled the establishment CHP considerably, with the notable exception that a major part of their platform was to bring the average person—and especially those in rural areas—closer to the state. Since at the time, as in many countries around the world, religious adherence was generally higher in rural areas than in cities (this was just as the massive rural-urban migration was beginning in Turkey), this meant, almost by definition, that the DP tended to take a softer line on matters of Islamic observance than the CHP had. The DP was very popular initially and stayed in power for the next ten years but by then had managed to alienate enough of the country that when their rule was brought to an end with a military coup in 1960, it did not provoke widespread opposition.

In 1952, Mehmed Zahid Kotku (d. 1980) took up leadership of the *cemaat*, continuing and increasing its popularity among student circles. Starting in the 1960s, Kotku encouraged his initiated followers to be active in worldly affairs, specifically in capacities that would enable Turkey and the Muslim world to stand up to cultural, political, and economic domination by the West. Echoing ideas expressed since the late Ottoman period, Kotku considered Western domination to be based on the West's clever development and use of technology, albeit in a way that is out of balance with ethical considerations concerning family life, the environment, and so forth. Kotku made it clear not only that was there no problem with Muslims industrializing their societies based on the latest technology, but also that it was positively incumbent upon them to do this (Gürdoğan 1996). This was the context in which the continually growing numbers of attendees at Mehmed Zahid efendi's *sohbet*s during the 1960s began to take their places in increasingly influential institutions such as the State Planning Organization (SPO; Devlet Planlama Teşkilatı), created in the wake of the 1960 coup to coordinate industrialization through investment and allocation of subsidized inputs and foreign exchange. The SPO quickly became an extremely powerful mechanism for political bargaining over scarce resources (Keyder 1987, 148).

The idea of freeing Turkey from the logic of the Western-dominated capitalist market also led to Kotku's suggestion to establish the Gümüş Motor Company (the name invoking the memory of the nineteenth-century Naqshbandi scholar Ziyaüddin Gümüşhanevi), with Necmettin Erbakan (who was later to become prime minister) as its director. However, the company did not last long. Having lost the investment in the motor company, many in the *cemaat* concluded that there was a direct connection between being able to create an alternative market and moral economy, and the political-economic environment in which transactions take place. In other words, they would need to participate in institutionalized politics.

Political parties with a primarily Islamic orientation date to the early 1970s in Turkey, though constitutionally, a party cannot have religion as its basis, and hence so-called Islamic parties tend to euphemize themselves. The short-lived National Order Party (Millî Nizam Partisi, MNP), led by Necmettin Erbakan, was founded in 1970 by deputies in the assembly who until that time had been in the Justice Party (itself largely a reformation of the DP that had been banned after the 1960 coup). It was closed in 1971. The year 1972 saw the founding of the National Salvation Party (Millî Selamet Partisi, MSP), which was a part of coalition governments in the country through most of the 1970s, until it was banned (with all other existing parties) in the wake of the coup of 1980. It appears that Mehmed Zahid efendi played a role in the founding of the MSP (Çakır 1990), and it is probably the case that many of those attending Mehmed efendi's lessons were inclined toward the MSP. Thus it does appear to be true that there was a link between this Naqshbandi Sufi order and Islamist political parties, especially during the 1970s, which is when certain members of the current AKP cadres are reputed to have attended Mehmed efendi's lessons. It is significant that many of the major figures in the MSP and then later Refah Partisi (RP) came out of the İskender Pasha community, which was once famous as a center for the Naqshbandi order. Preeminent among these political figures are Necmettin Erbakan (prime minister from 1996 to 1997) and current Prime Minister Recep Tayyip Erdoğan (from 2003), who both participated in Mehmed hoja's *sohbet*s in the 1970s.

During the mid- to late 1970s, the political landscape in Turkey was utterly radicalized into Right and Left, with youth groups and gangs sympathetic to, or directly organized by, each side, viciously and murderously attacking and counterattacking each other publicly. A number of those on the Right who considered themselves to be politically conservative (*muhafazakâr*) emphasized the language of Islam and that Islam is the bastion of true

Turkish culture and values. A coup in 1980 brought an immediate end to the street-level violence, and the military administration and the then-elected government under general-*cum*-president Kenan Evren began to emphasize what came to be called the "Turkish-Islamic synthesis" (*Türk-İslam sentezi*) as a formulation for national identity. This was an attempt to preserve nationalist sentiments while drawing on the heritage of Islam as culture and general ethic, a move that appeared to be the height of irony to many secular, liberal Turks, given that it was championed by a military man. The aim really was to remove any remaining wind from the sails of the Left and to appropriate the discourse of Islam for the mainstream while reexerting state control over Islamic institutions. These efforts, by all accounts, largely achieved their goals.

Upon Kotku's death (also in 1980), leadership of the community passed to his son-in-law Esad Coşan.[12] Coşan's appointment was not without controversy, since Kotku had himself been trained by the last generation of Ottoman sheikhs, and several longtime Kotku disciples found it difficult to place themselves in the hands of someone of Coşan's generation. Coşan was nonetheless well respected for his knowledge of Islam and Sufism as a professor at Ankara University's theology faculty, and he began to attract younger generations of disciples. Coşan continued and intensified the *cemaat*'s engagement with daily life and with the modern technologies that Kotku had encouraged through his *sohbet*s and publications. In his publications, Kotku exhorted Muslims to seek the best possible education for themselves and their children (boys and girls), including knowledge of Islam as well as of "secular" disciplines such as economics, laboratory sciences, management, and medicine. Reflecting these concerns, a member of the order in Istanbul told me about the kinds of people who tended to gravitate toward the order:

> There are generally a lot of engineers [in the order], people from technical schools. A good example is [former president Turgut] Özal and [Necmettin] Erbakan. I, too, came out of a technical university, but now I'm a professor of communication. So engineers showed more interest [in the order]. [Esad hoja] brought together more engineers. They all have a university education. They think more practically, they're more productive people, more competent, they accomplish more . . . It's always better to be the hand that gives than the hand that takes. So one needs to be able to always give, and to be able to do this, one needs to produce. Be it knowledge, a service, a product, you must produce it and produce it well, produce it beautifully. Quality is very important; so is beauty. And constantly trying to do better, more beautifully, trying to be a better person, a more beautiful person. So there is a kind of competition here. One competes with oneself. Constant competition. Didn't Marx say this? "Without struggle there is no progress." So competition is important. Competing

in goodness. There is a hadith: "Compete at goodness; try to make one another good." Do you know Arabic?[13]

In referring to a hadith, the speaker situates what he says in the context of a concern for orthodoxy. These emphases on education, training, and competence can also be seen in the *cemaat*'s publishing and media projects, most prominently the monthly magazines *İslam* from 1983 and *Kadın ve Aile* (Woman and the family) from 1985, in addition to publications by the Seha publishing house.[14] From 1994, the emphases could also be heard on the *cemaat*'s radio station and, for a brief interim, in its daily newspaper *Sağduyu* (Common sense), and on a television station that was short-lived in the late 1990s. While there is mention here of Marx, the orientation toward productivity and service may also be an index of the atmosphere that had developed since 1980, in which the economy had been opened to foreign capital and ownership and norms of international capitalism and a general ethos of enterprise increasingly came to set the tone in the country.[15]

Refah Party candidates won many of the country's major municipal elections in 1994 (including Istanbul and Ankara). In the national elections of 1995, Refah emerged as the leading party, with the most seats in the national assembly and a major role in the ruling coalition, including the prime ministry. It is difficult to exaggerate the suddenness with which Islam seemed to become the main issue in politics and culture, and the key issue for social science research in Turkey, only to be dropped unceremoniously a few years later.[16] (A resurgence in interest, though on a smaller scale, later occurred in 2002 in the wake of the AKP wins.) Questions about the continued existence of Sufi orders and Sufi practices were revived, and attempts were made to make sense of the rise of Refah in terms of its connections to these orders. Even within the orders themselves, members engaged in discussions among themselves about whether or not the orders should clarify their views on party politics.

Within the İskender Pasha community, discussions began in the early 1990s about whether leader Esad hoja should become involved in party politics, either in an established party or as founder of a new one (Çakır 1990). In the end, he did not enter party politics, and the *cemaat*'s relationship to Refah during the years of Refah's rise and time in power was often strained. It appears that several points of disagreement centered on what could be called a struggle for authority and prestige. As a key player in the MSP–RP formation, Necmettin Erbakan was reported to have made critical remarks suggesting that he himself had and should have more authority among Muslims than Esad hoja. Some observant Muslims, including many in the order, were apparently uneasy with the extent to which Erbakan seemed to be trying to fashion himself as something of a religious authority, which, given his engineering background, was a hard sell for some. Disagreement between the party and this Sufi order spilled out into the open by 1990, when Esad hoja, under his well-known pseudonym Halil Necatioğlu, published an article in the order's journal İslam titled "The Indisputable Value and Superiority of the Islamic Scholar [*Alim*]" (Necatioğlu 1990). The article was directed specifically at Erbakan and the Refah cadres, as the implicit ending of the title was "over the politician." However it needs to be noted here that members of the order were not monolithic in their politics in that the order did not speak with one voice regarding party politics. A significant number of members of the order supported the Motherland Party (Anavatan Partisi, ANAP), which was the party of former president Turgut Özal (president from 1989 to 1993). Özal had only thinly veiled his sympathy for Naqshbandi Sufism, and his mother is buried in the Süleymaniye cemetery (near Mehmed Zahid Kotku and Ahmed Ziyaüddin Gümüşhanevî; Çakır 1990, 17–76). I note here for future reference the significance of the order's support already in the 1990s for a party (ANAP) identified in Turkey as more "liberal" in the classic sense than "religious" per se, an issue to which we return in subsequent chapters.

Erdoğan was elected mayor of Istanbul in 1994, proving to be extremely popular in the eyes of many of the city's enormous population who had felt marginalized by previous municipal administrations because of their status as recent migrants to the city, their relative poverty, their residence outside the city's prestigious neighborhoods (including many squatter settlements), as well as their conservatism, especially regarding religion (White 2002). Yet even many who did not share this profile grudgingly admitted that his administration was quite efficient and competent, especially regarding infrastructure. He was clearly a rising star in the Refah Party.

In February 1997, the military officers on the National Security Council essentially presented an ultimatum of measures that the Refah–True Path coalition government would have to undertake to reverse what the council saw as explicit "Islamicizing tendencies" in the bureaucracy and even in the armed forces. The government resigned in June. The event is remembered as "28 Şubat" (February 28), which came to be used as a euphemism for the beginning of a crackdown led by the military against "political Islam." Commentators generally agree that the ultimatum represented a statement by the generals of the measures necessary to prevent them from carrying out a coup d'état.[17] Following 28 Şubat, the military continuously made it known in meetings with politicians and in published statements that it considered one of the gravest threats to the country's security to be those who wish to exploit religion for political purposes. The armed forces directed considerable energy toward combating such people. Elected officials, such as the then-popular mayor of Istanbul (at the time of writing prime minister) Tayyip Erdoğan, were tried and spent time in jail. Journalists and writers were harassed and arrested. Most importantly for this discussion, associational life for the outwardly pious was more restrictive. An incipient trend to stage conferences and symposia on Islamic or Ottoman topics (often with the support or participation of municipalities) waned.

In 2001, after months of thinly veiled tensions within the new Fazilet Party (after the Refah's closure by the constitutional court) over several issues, including the party's conception of state-religion relations and the inability of members critical of Erbakan to rise in seniority, several Fazilet members, including Erdoğan and the charismatic Abdullah Gül, founded the Justice and Development Party (AKP, mentioned previously), made up of several Fazilet and other party transfers as well as intellectuals and technocrats. Again, many of the founding members of the AKP had experience with the İskender Pasha community, and the exceptionally high training and competence of the cadres, their own adherence to Islamic norms in their personal lives, and their attempt to fashion a politically liberal Muslim society can be seen, at least in part, as a legacy of their İskender Pasha experience.

It is against the background of these developments over recent decades that both participation and scholarly interest in Sufism have risen, even though the statutes banning orders have not been changed since the early years of the republic (Kafadar 1992). Books are published on the orders in general and on this or that particular order; magazines publish dossiers; scholarly journals publish articles. Many publications are quite hostile to the orders, to be sure, but many are not. The continuing existence of the orders is, in short, an open secret; just how open depends almost literally on the month, if not the week.

ENCOUNTERING SUFISM

The question of why and how a member becomes involved in an order seems to be one of the most pressing on the mind of the outsider. It is a doubly difficult issue. First, and most importantly, members themselves sometimes have ambivalent feelings about the period of their entry into the order, for it refers implicitly to the time when they were not involved in what they have hitherto taken to be central to the cultivation of an ethical self. Queries about this time in their lives usually led those younger men I worked with to become a bit embarrassed and speak of themselves as a bit naïve (or "young") in the past, leading to a friendly, conspiratorial tone of complicity with their present self and with me.

The second point here is that this period of entry into the *cemaat* is not consistently experienced as a crucial, existential moment whose qualities are central to successful participation in the order, in the culture of Sufism, and in the cultivation of an ethical Muslim self. While one does hear of dramatic life changes and "unveilings" among members, this is tied to the kind of life the person was previously leading and not to the nature of entry into the order. There was only one time during my research that existential emptiness was proffered as a main factor in members having decided to join, and that was by the (then) executive director of the foundation associated with the order: "Often one feels a kind of spiritual emptiness inside [ruhi boşluk], so one starts trying to numb one's feelings. Some drink, some gamble, for instance. When one first comes to Sufism, the number of people who don't have some kind of supernatural experience is about zero. The first four months or so are extraordinary. One really feels transformation [in oneself]." While this member refers to a supernatural experience, he quickly links this to the transformation one feels in oneself, suggesting that this is itself the kind of supernatural thing he is talking about. Thus, narratives of introduction to the order are not focused on something resembling mystical experience such as is given in classic Western accounts of Sufism.

At the time I conducted my research in the late 1990s, it was clear that the *cemaat* had continued to draw members primarily from among academic circles under Coşan. This was reflected in the claim by most of the people with whom I spoke in Istanbul and Anatolian cities that they had encountered the group during their studies at various universities. This has much to do not only with the experience of university study in Turkey, mainly the practicalities involved in finding housing, but also with the kind of exploration and experimentation typical of university students in many countries. Finding suitable accommodation is one of the major concerns of incoming university students in Turkey (as elsewhere), and with changes to Turkey's laws regarding foundations (*vakıf*), there was expansion of private, foundation-operated dormitories run as a nonprofit activity. University-operated dormitories were at the time of my research often very rough around the edges in Turkey, with such details as bedding, laundry, and showers, not to mention security of property, often leaving much to be desired. By contrast, private (usually foundation-operated) dorms are usually cleaner and more intimate, as there is a sense of shared purpose among those staying there. In response to a question about how he learned of the foundation's dorms, a young member said, "Through my brother. He stayed at one of the *vakıf* yurts in Ankara, and I visited him. I liked the atmosphere." Also important in this regard is that until they go away to the university, Turkish youths tend to be so tightly enveloped in their family that many I worked with recalled their departure from home as being accompanied by a degree of trauma. Many members of the *cemaat* told me they were terrified at the prospect of leaving home for an extended period for the first time in their lives to go to a totally unknown city and live in close quarters with complete strangers. It is thus understandable that any contacts before arrival were welcome. A member in Sivas, originally from Siirt, in the Kurdish southeast near the border with Iraq, related, "In Siirt I had a *hoja* from Sivas at the Imam-hatip lycee, and he said to me, 'I hear you're going to Sivas [to study].' 'Yes, *hojam*, I am,' I said. 'Well, then, here's an address. Go there when you arrive, they'll take care of you.' And I said, 'Oh, my, I really appreciate it because I'm totally helpless [*çaresiz*]!' So I came, and found the [branch office of the foundation affiliated with the order], and was really warmly received." In giving the contact information for the foundation in the city to which the student was heading, it was understood that the foundation, its community, and its dormitories had an Islamic identity. It was not, however, always clear in advance that the community was in fact structured around a Sufi order.

ISLAMIC TRADITION, ORTHODOXY, AND SUFISM

The realization that the foundation was related to a Sufi order was not always smooth, not only among those who were skeptical toward them due to the "danger" they had been taught such groups posed to the secular order of things, but also among those coming from more religiously conservative backgrounds who were skeptical that such *tarikat*s were less than orthodox. The member from Siirt again:

> Before coming to the [theology, *ilahiyat*] faculty here at Sivas [in 1994] I didn't really know much about *cemaat*s, *tarikat*s. I'd heard of something called the Nurcus, Millî Gençlik vakfı, I knew of these, but I'd never had any contact with them. When I came I didn't know what these *cemaat*s were doing, what their particular traits were. And I asked myself, "I wonder why there are so many different *cemaat*s? Why not one, but many? Shouldn't there be just one?" So, it was with a bit of a prejudice that I approached *cemaat*s . . . [and] that's the way I approached this one, too. As much as possible I wanted to follow from the outside, to observe from outside to see if these people were doing something wrong or not. Now, since the theology faculty is teaching us about Islam, this is what we are trained specialists in [*ihtisas*]. So, after one or two years my knowledge had started increasing. I got to know Islam better, really got acquainted with it; what is hadith, what is *sunna* [exemplary sayings and deeds of the prophet], what is contained in the Quran, what is proper conduct, what is improper . . . So, it was with those eyes that I looked at the *cemaat*. Since I *know* what Islam is, what it isn't, that's how I looked on the *cemaat*. According to the Quran is there anything wrong here? According to hadith? I thought about this for a long time, and in particular I listened to the *sohbet*s of [Esad] hoja efendi. What I'm talking about now was in about 1996, and during the

whole time I'd been observing: their activities, their ideas, what they talk about, and so on. And I was participating at the same time. At the [foundation's] student housing, and at the foundation [itself], there used to be a lot of *sohbet*s. So, I found the *cemaat* to be in accordance with the Quran and sunna. I made a decision, "Well, there is no straying [*sapma*] here, no acts outside the Quran and sunna. I can work within this *cemaat*, it suits me." And at the moment, it's going well.

Several things are worth pointing out about this member. First is his status as a university student, and in particular as a student in advanced Islamic studies, getting the highest level of training in Islamic disciplines available in regional cities in the country. From his high school he already had training sufficient enough to be an imam, or prayer leader in a mosque (i.e., he knew Arabic well, had memorized the Quran, knew the *farz* and *sunna* prayers required for worship services, and was trained in cantillation). This knowledge was now being deepened and broadened with advanced training in methods of generating normative judgments about correct practice (*usul ul-fiqh*), methods for understanding various types of hadith, as well as methods for interpreting the Quran (*tefsir*). This is, in short, a Muslim who is, comparatively speaking, extremely knowledgeable about Islamic traditions. The second point to emphasize is that it was in light of these broader Islamic traditions that he evaluated this Sufi order. This is an index of an important attitude on the part of the *cemaat* regarding its own Islamic identity and how it relates to others who are observant (but not initiated members of the order) and indicates well the Naqshbandi mode of Sufism. A member of the order in Sivas said of his encounter with the order, "At first, there isn't really a 'Sufi' atmosphere. After all, you can't really explain Sufism directly anyway. And since [entry into the order] is something based on request [by the prospective disciple], they didn't really direct us to Sufism at first. It was more just about Islam. The first steps are not about Sufism." The focus is on Islam per se, and proper Sufism was often described as simply Islam. Those with whom I worked in conducting my research emphasized continually that their practices were nothing more and nothing less than Islam itself: "This is true Islam. Being able to live as our Prophet lived, this is Sufism. Now, obviously it isn't possible to really live like him. But we can try—try to do like him, try to do like the Companions [*sahaba*]. It's about not retreating into one's own shell, but being together with people, talking with them. You know, Ibrahim Abi, 'enjoin the lawful and prevent the forbidden.'" The invocation of the companions of the Prophet Muhammad is significant, and we return to the figure of the companion and the function of companionship in this order and in Islam in the next chapter. So we have here an attempt to not only believe certain things but also do certain things in emulation of an established pattern laid out by those whose example is taken as normative. We also see here an emphasis that contrasts with some apparently classic approaches to Sufism that tend to be emphasized in Western literature, such as reclusion for intensive spiritual exercises (Schimmel 1975). Rather, as has been noted by others regarding Naqshbandis, the emphasis is on cultivating piety in daily interactions with people (captured in one of the order's formulations of its doctrines: "solitude among the multitudes" [*halvet dar enjuman* in Persian]; see Algar 1976).

Naqshbandis in Turkey today often refer to themselves and like-minded (not necessarily Sufi) Muslims simply as "*ehl-i sünnet*," or "people of the tradition."[18] A member in Istanbul related, "What is important for us, that is, compared to other groups, is if [a group] is on the path of the people of the sunna [*ehl-i sünnet*], if it's a real Sufi order, if it has a *silsile* [chain of initiation], if it doesn't do things contrary to the Quran and the example [*sünnet*] of our Prophet, then this is a proper Sufi order, that is to say it is a Sufi order on the path of the people of the sunna, and [its members] will always be brothers to us. They merely take one path, while we take another." Naqshbandis' identity as Sufis is imbricated into their identity as Sunni Muslims to such an extent that a Turkish Naqshbandi sheikh of recent decades has written, "True Sufism is submission to God's Book and imitation of the *sunna* of His Messenger; it is reliving, by inner state and outer deed, the auspicious age of the Messenger and his Companions; it is the very essence of Islam."[19] We recall that the title of one of the order's monthly periodicals during the late 1980s and early 1990s was, simply, *Islam*. Today, visitors to a number of the websites associated with the order are presented with a number of menus, among which "Islam" is listed more prominently than "Sufism" or "the Naqshbandiyya." Particularly in its self-presentation to outsiders, and more especially non-Muslims, the emphasis is clearly on Islam and Muslim identity over Sufism. This is significant in a number of respects, particularly in that many members, and certainly Esad Coşan himself, were aware that a veritable "Sufi industry" has developed in the West, cultivated for the most part by (often well-intentioned) romantics with little knowledge of or sincere interest in Islam. Coşan and this community preferred to emphasize Islam over Sufism in the order's publishing and broadcasting projects.

Thus the first encounter with the *cemaat* is usually through a friend or close acquaintance, who may recommend one go talk with this or that person (who ends up being a member), or who may take the novice to hear a sheikh or deputy. Upon making contact with the *cemaat* in the form of the *vakıf*, students were usually placed in either a dormitory run by the *vakıf* or in shared apartments also operated by the *vakıf*, the rents of which were generally below market rates. Then (again largely for the outsider) there is the question of why one stays once introduced, especially since there are many other groups on the Turkish landscape oriented toward a Muslim identity, such as the Nurcus. The most often repeated explanation of what they specifically liked about Sufism, in contrast to these other social groups and associations aiming to reinforce Islamic identity and practice in Turkey, was that "it has a clear [known] source [*belli bir kaynağı var*]." The source referred to here is the understanding that the teachings and practices of the order are traceable back to the Prophet himself, and the *silsile* of transmitters of the disciplines is known to all.[20] That this chain of transmission is known to the people in the order is taken to be a sign of authenticity of both the group itself and the kinds of experiences one may have in relating oneself to it. This sensibility is an embodiment of the kind of authenticity of oral transmission by chains of known transmitters characteristic of hadith scholarship.[21] By way of analogy with *isnad* (the known chain of morally upright transmitters of hadith), Sufi orders' transmission of their traditions of spiritual discipline over time in the form of *silsile*s is taken to be an assurance of authenticity. Indeed, this principle of the authoritativeness of the source was often cited as the most important reason why a member of the order continued to associate with it rather than with one of the other groups in Turkey oriented toward the observant and pious (e.g., Nurcus).[22]

Another theme that recurred in members' discussions of how and why they initially got involved with the order was the atmosphere, mentioned previously: they were warmly received, and they liked the feelings they got from people. More specifically, many identified a certain sincerity on the part of the people they met in the *cemaat*, and that touched them. One interviewee said, "Sincerity [*samimiyet*] is part of one's psychology, whether one likes it or not. Whoever shows you more closeness, when you realize it's not a game, then a certain affection [*meyil*] comes out. So, naturally, that warm reception that I got at the first moment frankly touched me [*beni etkilemiştir*]. Now he's graduated, but that first friend who received me I will never forget. I was greeted with an extremely beautiful reception. These things are very important."

A disciple in Istanbul related,

> The people in this community [*cemaat*] are truly sensitive [*hassas duyguları olan*] people. For instance, once when I was [back in my village in Anatolia] a kind of inspector came, from Ankara. Now just from this man's way of looking at things, his gestures, I don't know, but without even talking with him I just felt that he probably had a connection to the community [i.e., Sufi order]. Why? This party [i.e., political movement] has a certain way of doing things, and its people [too]. [Outsiders], well, for example they talk a lot, and they constantly interrupt you. They put on airs, too. But people who have been brought up in this community have a certain

kind of gentleness. They're more dignified. I mean, no matter how important they are, there is a certain unpretentious modesty. They have a certain sympathy for the people around them. They are interested in things like books and scholarship, in beautiful things. So I have seen this, that in people who have been [in the community] for five, six, seven years this care, this sensitivity gets formed. And in politics [too]. Among the people I've been talking about the number of "showman" types is small, almost none. And today, even if someone comes from an Islamic background it's possible that they can do bad things, like they might be a cheat in their business life. But I have myself seen that among the people coming from a background in this [Sufi] community, rich or humble, there is very little of this kind of deviation.

This sense of value in the moral integrity of people is also a major factor in disciples' decisions to stay in the *cemaat* once they encounter it. It also reveals the direct link established between the validity of statements and moral stature:

> What was most important for me [in my joining the Sufi order] was that I got acquainted with [it] through a *hoja* in Siirt . . . who was trained [*yetişmiş*] in the community [i.e. order], in Ankara. He was a student of [Esad] Hoca efendi, at the theology faculty [of Ankara University]. Then, when I saw something beautiful inside, I stayed, for in light of the information they gave me, I found it to be appropriate [*uygun*]. You know, when you believe someone to be on the right path, you will feel more positively toward that person. Your relations will become more sincere [*samimi*], and you will grow to like them even more. Your love gradually increases [*sevginiz gittikçe artar*], your affection [*meyil*] increases. So, my entry into the *cemaat* was through someone else, but what kept me in it, made me like it, has to do with the knowledge I acquired from it and from my own evaluations of it.

This member brings out a connection between moral stature and sentiment, which is a crucial dimension of this community. Having positive feelings toward someone leads one to start acting in certain ways; there is a connection between feelings and actions. This was an issue brought up repeatedly by members, and it turned out that this visceral level of feeling was one this community was often operating on, as we will see later.

Interestingly, there was often a noticeable difference in the way older generations spoke of their introduction to the order when compared with younger generations. Here is how a more senior member who joined the order in the late 1960s related his experiences then:

So, I became a disciple of Mehmed Zahid efendi, began to follow the lessons of this perfected man [*mübarek zat*] in 1967 or 1968. I met him for the first time at a sermon [*hutbe*]. A friend of mine took me. We went for Friday worship, and he was climbing up to do the *hutbe*, I couldn't even see his face, but up, up he climbed. He had broad shoulders, and without seeing his face, I was already entranced [*hayran*] by him. And when he turned around and I saw him for the first time I said to myself, "In all my life I've never seen such beauty!" Not in my own family, not from another teacher, not in another mosque. In fact, in Beykoz, Hajji Osman efendi was also a very beautiful person, had a lovely face. And I thought, as I wept, "I'll surely never see such beauty again." Once Mehmed Zahid efendi was talking about great people [*büyük zatlar*], not about himself, and said that at a *sohbet* of the great saints [*büyuk evliya*] you should sit facing them, because just by seeing their faces, one is enlightened [*feyz verir*]. So even if he came down without giving a *hutbe*, if I'd only seen his face I'd have been reborn. Just as if I'd received the lesson [i.e., been formally initiated into the Sufi order] I was enlightened by his face.

This kind of moment-by-moment account, as if relating a dream with minute descriptions of sentiments and feelings, was clearly part of a specific recitational genre. It is difficult to tell if these older members actually lived their first encounters this way at the time (maybe they had been primed to do so by their environments) or if they learned subsequently to code their initial encounters this way, as a gesture of devotion and as part of the cultivation of certain dispositions and qualities of character, especially in the retelling of such account for younger generations' edification. But it is interesting for our discussion that the speaker mentions the importance of being in the presence of "greats" or those with a refined moral stature, being in their line of vision, and being able to watch them.

One may interpret this as allowing for a kind of mystical effect to take place, and I will argue in the next chapter that such an effect is indeed what is intended, but it is also one that has to do with the influence that a respected person's presence has on one's conduct. Being in the presence of a sheikh can be so forceful that it has the effect of being formally initiated into a Sufi order. Several senior Naqshbandis explained to me their understanding that people are influenced most in their behavior by other people. For the proper formation of character, then, one should try to always be with "good people," defined as those who seek the approval of God, and only God, and are not led astray by such things as popular fashion, prestige, or power. The Quranic verse, "O ye who believe! Fear Allah and *be with those who are true in word and deed* [*al-sadiqin*]" (Quran 9:119, emphasis added) was frequently cited in this context.

SUFISM AS AN ETHICAL PROJECT: *NEFSİN TERBİYESİ*

The first time I met Ahmet, who we encountered at the opening of this chapter, was over a cup of tea, in the reception room of the İskender Pasha courtyard, on a Wednesday. There were not usually many people around at such a time: a few elderly men chatting, some salaried foundation employees coming and going into offices, a few young men mostly engaged in the renovation work going on in the larger meeting rooms next to the reception room, and a significant number of transients and misfits of various sorts. Ahmet was the kind of fellow who must have been much more common in the old days, before February 28 (1997). He would come to the mosque, with the aim partly to simply *be* there, that is, to be together with the people who gather there. He was still participating in the *sohbet*s but wished the environment could be more intense. His head was shaven, and his skin was darkened by long exposure to the sun during his work in the garden of İskender Pasha or at Süleymaniye. He usually had his pant legs rolled up; his clothes were ripped and dirty; he carried buckets of rubble from the reception room being renovated and sprayed water from a hose to clean tools and wheelbarrows. When they saw him go by, others around the mosque courtyard would smile at me and gesture toward him, "There's a real dervish!"

Such work, conducted by members of the order on a voluntary basis, was just the kind of effort a neophyte disciple would be expected to engage in as part of the process of disciplining his *nefs* [*nefsin terbiyesi*]. The term "*nefs*" (from the Arabic *nafs*), translated variously in English as "ego," "lower self," or "base instincts," recurs in the Quran, such as in Sura 79:40, where the Muslim is admonished to "fear the place of his Lord and hinder the *nefs* from lust." The *nefs* is thus the cause of sin, of blameworthy, evil acts. Disciplining the *nefs* is akin to an ethical project in the sense Aristotle, Foucault, and MacIntyre have outlined. Paraphrasing Foucault's reading of Aristotle, we can posit four issues regarding any ethical project, "the answers to all of which must be derived from the discourses and practices of a given sociocultural environment," in our case Sufi Islamic traditions (Faubion 2001, 90). First, what is the substance, the material to be worked on? Second, what set of norms orients the effort to make oneself into an ethical subject? Third, what training or exercises (ascesis) does the given project require? And fourth, what is the ultimate end that can be attained (telos; Faubion 2001, 90–91)?

The *nefs* is often likened to an appetite that must be tamed. This taming, or disciplining of the *nefs*, is indeed one of the most important activities Naqshbandi Sufis feel they are engaged in. Many of the books published by Kotku and Coşan are on the topic, as are many chapters of others. A member of the order in Sivas told me,

It's kind of like in the circus—the animals there. One gives them little food, breaking them in and training [*eğitmek*] them, not giving them the things they want. Maybe one animal wants to go out today; nope, we're not going to. To the extent that the reins are in our hands, we'll take the horse where we want to go. But without a horse, one can't go anywhere, one definitely must have a horse. So, Sufism does this. It disciplines the *nefs*, and this thing called *nefs* is actually us ourselves [*biziz*]. Me. You know, we say, "I don't want any" [*canım istemiyor*]. That me—self—is the *nefs*. "I" don't want to go out. "I" am bored. That term "I," this is the *nefs*. "The self inside [*içimizdeki ben*]," they say. So, the point is to discipline [*terbiye etmek*] this. Because [otherwise] one goes where it wants to go; one acts as it wants us to act. The reins, the bridle of the horse, must be in our hands. This is the goal. And we have no choice but to make use of this [*nefs*]. The goal is *not* to kill or destroy the *nefs*. To kill the *nefs* is not a big deal. But to discipline it, *that's* tough.

A thorough discussion of the metaphysics of the *nefs* in Islamic thought and Muslims' techniques for struggling with it is beyond our scope here, but one should understand that one of aims of the exercises we have been describing is clearly not to eliminate the *nefs*.[23] The aim, in other words, is not release from desire but rather to try to desire the correct things, most importantly the approval of God. Indeed, the community had taken up as a kind of motto the Arabic formulation often used in training adepts in the disciplining of their nefs: "*Ilahi anta maqsudi wa ridha ka matlubi*" (Allah, you are my goal and your approval is what I seek).[24] One should not be sidelined by seeking things other than God's approval. The *nefs*' desire for fame, power, or money are well known, but there are also less obvious, more insidious ways in which the *nefs* can derail one's work on oneself, and there is much discussion of this informally and in texts. Another member in Sivas related several ways in which one's *nefs* can sneak up on one:

As one rises through stages [of emotional and spiritual maturity], şaytan [Satan] truly starts to present different kinds of games to you, plays out different scenarios—this is very important. As one rises through stages, there are things that make one stray [*saptıranlar var*]; that's what we've heard.[25] It's very dangerous because you don't know you're being deceived. For instance, how might one be deceived? [Maybe someone says to you] "Ah, look at you, look how beautifully you perform your prayers!" I remember this example from one of *hoja* efendi's *sohbet*s. "Mashallah!" they might say. But at that moment you're finished if you really think that way! [İnsan o anda gider, yani] If you think, "Hmm, really?" Or if you say, "Well, I've seen a lot of shaytan in my time," [şeytanı gördüm diktim] [and now I don't have to worry about it] you've also had it. All of a sudden your efforts will fall to nothing.

Emphasized here is that one ought to work on oneself and one's dispositions and actions, and doing so makes one into a better person in the eyes of God. However, one must be on guard lest the effects of this work on oneself either go to one's head and make one ease up on one's efforts or subtly develop into a sense of superiority or haughtiness, especially with regard to one's obligations as laid down in Islamic orthodoxy. This is one of the forms that these Sufis' disdain for what they see as some other so-called Sufis' laxity or heterodoxy takes: their utter disregard for those who call themselves Sufis but who do not even fulfill the merest of their responsibilities in light of the *sunna*.

SPIRITUAL EXERCISES

The foundation affiliated with the order ran two nonprofit dormitories in Istanbul at the time of my fieldwork in the late 1990s: one in the heart of the old city and one just beyond the Byzantine walls. Each had around 30 student residents, the one beyond the walls all male, the other with about a 3 to 1 male-to-female ratio, men and women on separate floors. Each dorm had about ten residents who were on scholarships that covered the students' room costs. Not all student residents were members of the *cemaat*, however, since membership was not a condition of residence in any formal sense. More important to fitting in at the dorm was residents' general observance of Islam in their daily lives, for example, in their discipline in prayers and care in their social relations and lifestyle.

A typical day for those residing in one of the *cemaat's* dormitories would begin predawn when the lights were turned on in the sleeping rooms, while the resident on duty that week said in a soft tone, "Friends, let's do our morning prayers, *inshallah.*" After making their way out of the room, down the hall, and past the Atatürk memorial (with flag and bust), residents would head downstairs, then past the laundry room, past a ping-pong table, and into the washrooms. These were immaculately clean and well appointed like the rest of the facilities, with a row of doored lavatories on the right, eight sinks on the left, and facing them, a trough with eight spigots at waist height for ablutions.

Canonical worship was then performed upstairs in the room also used for socializing, where low divans rimmed the room. The senior student on duty who usually acted as imam would swing around on his haunches to face the congregation and lead a brief *khafi* (silent) *zikr* and *du`a* (supplication). He then would ask, "Who will start?" Then began the recitation of *Evrad-ı Şerif* (sing. Arabic *wird*), which a quorum of at least around ten tries to do every morning after *fajr* prayers. The recitation takes about 40 minutes and is entirely in Arabic, with the *abi*, or elder brother (relatively more knowledgeable, senior resident disciple) on duty, asking different people to take turns. Those who presented themselves more prominently, with a visible desire to recite, would do so without the text of the prayers before them. However some took recourse to a neighbor's copy to refresh their memory if they strayed or could not remember and someone else did not correct them out loud first. This daily recitation of *Evrad* was also an occasion for members to memorize these prayers, the accomplishment of which is understood to be a sign of a *mürid*'s spiritual progress. He is thus able to perform the recitations himself and for others and can teach it to others. The recitation was closed by a short silent *zikr* of 33 *Subhanallah*, 33 *Alhamdulullah*, and 33 *Allahu akbar*, to which 33 *Istaghfurullah wa alaytu l-alayh* are often added.

For many Muslims, including the Sufis I worked with, *zikr* or "remembrance of God" was done after worship but much more often takes the disparate form of a certain daily vigilance, a careful monitoring of one's conduct and sentiments to avoid not only falling directly into sin but also, more importantly, forming improper habits and dispositions. "It is easy to acquire bad habits" was a phrase I heard often. As such, we see here a particular understanding of the relationship between repeated action, dispositions, qualities of character, and human nature. While several approaches in social science have emphasized that human dispositions are to a large extent culturally constructed (just to what extent is a matter of debate), these approaches have also emphasized the point that it is in the formation of such dispositions and in their largely unconscious working in the channeling of conduct and desires that the maintenance of hierarchies and social relations of domination actually operate. The work of Pierre Bourdieu has been most influential in this vein. I do not wish to dispute that the maintenance of hierarchies like social classes largely operates through such mechanisms (i.e., rather than through outright physical violence). However this approach elides important aspects of the concept of practice such as it has been developed in the work of Aristotle and those inspired by this work, such as Alasdair MacIntyre.

Crucial for this other tradition of thinking about practice are conscious efforts to form certain dispositions in oneself through what we may call, following Pierre Hadot, "spiritual exercises" (Hadot 1995, 128). Hadot uses this term to translate the ancient Greek ascesis and means by it "inner activities of the thought and the will," which are not to be confused with the asceticism of later Christianity. That the focus is on inner transformations also should not suggest that these exercises do not have a physical, bodily dimension. In particular, what Hadot says of the Stoics' approach to philosophy is very apt as an account of the approach toward Sufism of those I worked with:

> In [the Stoics] view, philosophy did not consist in teaching an abstract theory—much less in the exegesis of texts—but rather in the art of living. It is a concrete attitude and determinate lifestyle, which engages the whole

of existence. The philosophical act is not situated merely on the cognitive level, but on that of the self and being. It is a progress which causes us to *be* more fully, and makes us better. It is a conversion which turns our entire life upside down, changing the life of the person who goes through it. It raises the person from an inauthentic condition of life, darkened by unconsciousness and harassed by worry, to an authentic state of life, in which he attains self-consciousness, an exact vision of the world, inner peace, and freedom. (Hadot 1995, 83)

Several points are worth emphasizing here, for they very much resemble our Sufis' approach to Sufism and Islam. First is the whole approach to pedagogy and ethics. For these Muslims, Sufi doctrine did not consist of abstract treatises meant to abstractly systematize reality. As such, many of the texts on Sufi ethics (*ahlak*) this community produces and reads (such as the series *Tasavvufî Ahlâk* by Mehmed Zahid Kotku) are handbooks in the art of living. In other words, Sufism for these Muslims consists of practical means for the cultivation of the proper life of a Muslim. Second, one does this by working on oneself with the assistance of a guide, and through such work one ought to transform oneself, for there is a better condition of humans. Indeed, in the case of Islam, it is this perfected state, as it is often called, that is one of the proximate goals (though it is important to note that no one would actually claim to *be* in a state of perfection, for this would be tasteless and arrogant). So we have here also the notion of telos: that human nature has a goal, and this goal is not set by humans themselves but rather is inherent in their nature. Third is the emphasis put on the transformation the practitioner goes through, and the term "conversion" is especially apt here (discussed shortly).

In order to effect this transformation of the disciple, the guide has at his disposal several techniques, many explicit and some esoteric and implicit. These include getting the practitioner to constantly be in a state of ritual purity (i.e., making sure one has taken one's ablutions and is ready for canonical worship, which in the case of women would also involve covering one's head). Hence, above and beyond the widespread view among Sunnis that modesty in women requires them to cover their heads in the presence of non-kin men, these Sufis have yet another reason: one should always be in a state of being ready for worship and "mindful" of God. This was explained to me by a senior deputy who had been in the order since the days of Zahid Kotku as having several purposes, but most generally, that one in such a physical state will also feel different and will thus be less susceptible to be influenced by "the devil." In other words, through these techniques of reformation of oneself, it becomes easier to do good deeds and avoid doing evil ones.

A widely used technique for cultivating mindfulness of God is several types of *zikr* (from the Arabic *dhikr*), or formulations of "recollections" or repetitions of the divine names and attributes as a method of continual presence and submission, as an aid in continually monitoring one's conduct.[26] Again, these are considered to be techniques handed down since the time of the prophet, as a disciple explained to me:

> There are various types of *zikr*. There are those who do it standing up, sitting down, voiced [*cehri*], silently [*hafi*], and so on. Now, what does it mean to say, "Allah, Allah"? What is the essence of saying it? What if we say something else? These suggestions [*telkin*] for *zikr* go all the way back to our Prophet, peace be upon him. It has come down to us through our Prophet's having said it. So, this isn't something like a lesson [*ders*], made up [by the speaker], and so on. These suggestions are all connected [to the Prophet].

The relationship between *zikr* and the sort of mindfulness that helps one to achieve a heightened sense of one's purpose in life was explained to me by a member in Istanbul: "These are means of being mindful of Allah. When you don't do *zikr* it will almost never cross your mind to contemplate why you're in this world, or the fact that you have certain responsibilities toward Allah. So on this point *zikr* is truly important. It reminds you [to think about] why you came to this world, that you have responsibilities, that you are being tested and you need to pass this test successfully. So in my opinion this is why *zikr* is very important; it's one of the foundations [upon which things are built]."

Related to this conception of *zikr* is *rabıta*, the link or "bond" between the sheikh and the disciple. The mechanics and details of this technique of spiritual realization have been outlined elsewhere (Abu-Manneh 1990), but we may mention here that in this Sufi order there are three kinds of *rabıta*: the *rabıta* of death, often sequentially the first; the *rabıta* of the guide, or sheikh; and the *rabıta* of presence (of Allah). In these kinds of *rabıta*, the practitioner is invited to imagine herself as having died, as in the presence of the sheikh, and as in the presence of God ("like he's as close to you as your jugular vein," as one disciple put it) respectively.[27] Imagining one's own death is often an extremely sobering and even terrifying experience, especially for novices, and it appears to be for this reason that it is one of the first techniques that disciples are invited to cultivate, in order to instill a certain attitude and set of dispositions in themselves. Specifically, the practitioner is meant to reorient his assessment of what is significant and to appreciate the ephemeral nature of such things as fame, power, and fortune, while gaining a perspective on the reality and importance of pleasing God.

It should, however, be mentioned that *rabıta* is a point of practice that occasions some controversy. Problematic for some who encountered the *cemaat* and subsequently disassociated themselves from it was the practice of concentrating one's attention and affection so enthusiastically on the sheikh that it became confounded with one's devotions, which should naturally be reserved for God alone. Those with whom I worked took care to emphasize that the techniques of *rabıta*, which they all practiced, made it less formal and less structured than worship but that it needed to be done very carefully. One *cemaat* member in Sivas told me that *rabıta* was nearly cause for his departure from the *cemaat*; it was only upon careful reflection and consultation over the course of his theology studies at the university that he found *rabıta* acceptable and continued to participate in the *cemaat*. The environment of generalized hostility toward the orders in republican Turkey, and especially a heightened contempt for charlatanism examined earlier, including among the more observant and pious, may have led to the diminished profile of *rabıta* in favor of *sohbet*. If this is the case, it is not the first time the practice has been secondary to *sohbet*. In both Ahmad Sirhindi's *Maktubat* and Fakhr al-Din Kashifi's *Rashahat `Ayn al-Hayat*, the emphasis is on *sohbet* over *rabıta* (Abu-Manneh 1990, 286).

THE GARDEN OF SPIRITUAL EXERCISE

Ahmet expressed a common feeling among the members I worked with that participating in the Sufi order brought him peace (*huzur*), for he had learned discipline that kept his mind on track. As he put it, "In what God says one really finds peace." A deputy for Esad hoja said in a sohbet, "Once someone struggles with his or her *nefs*, they become an entirely different person!" Ahmet related to me, "When I walk to Süleymaniye, for instance, I find a spiritual balance [*manevi denge*]." The garden and cemetery behind the grand Süleymaniye mosque was where Ahmet and some other members were working to clear the weeds and thickets that had overgrown the place, even encroaching to near the graves of Mehmed Kotku and the other Gümüşhanevi sheikhs buried near him next to the tombs of Sultan Suleiman ("the Magnificent" or "the Law Giver," as he is known in Turkish) and his Ukrainian-born favored wife Hürrem Sultan (Roxelana). I began to accompany him to the cemetery and then started to go there directly. Despite their polite protestations, I also began to help them in their work, starting in midmorning, and taking a break for a sandwich provided by Uncle Yusuf, who oversaw our efforts.

It was a bit jarring, minutes after stepping off the tramway at Bayezıt into the bustling square in the very middle of this city of over 12 million people, to then be working with a scythe, pulling stalky weeds and grasses, with soil, grass, and chafe caking my arms and face. The work was of course backbreaking, with the sun pounding down on us. But it was a singularly powerful experience to look up from one's work, head swirling, the sun forcing a squint, to see the cascading domes of the Süleymaniye mosque towering above. Every now and then someone would say to me, "OK, Ibrahim, that's enough, why don't you take a break," which I declined with a smile, partly because I felt it was some kind of (albeit playful) test of my resolve on their part, and partly because I was shocked at how out of shape I seemed to be. After about a week's work, the cemetery was really taking shape. Others were always already there by the time I arrived, and my own contribution was quite negligible, but nonetheless it was gratifying to see the effect. Instead of a walled-in sea of six-foot-tall weeds with the tops of a few tombstones visible, there was now a tidy cemetery with raked gravel between the long Ottoman gravestones. Besides Ahmet, all of the other workers were young; teenagers, 20 years old at most. One of my other acquaintances, Hamid, from Türkmenistan in formerly Soviet Central Asia, came from time to time. He was in the process of gathering himself and returning home for a while to do his military service and maybe get married. He was not too worried about serving in the Turkmenistan army, unlike how most Turkish men I know feel about serving in the Turkish army. "If you've been abroad, and know a foreign language, they make you a secretary or driver or something like that," he said nonchalantly. He had been in Turkey a couple of years, having completed a course in automobile mechanics in the central Anatolian city of Konya (where he became affiliated with the order)and got himself certified to work on Mercedes Benz automobiles. "Do you think I could go to Europe with that?" he asked me. We checked out websites for mechanics courses in Germany, as he knew a few words of German in addition to his fluent Russian, but he eventually decided to return to Türkmenistan and try to go to Europe from there. It is not uncommon to meet students from the Turkic-speaking parts of the former Soviet Union in Turkey. Like Hamid, many of them come to either study at Turkish universities (where they, like most Turkish students, generally try to enter departments like engineering, medicine, or management) or complete certification or training courses.

THE GUIDE

Many Sufis claim that everyone needs a sheikh, whether they know it or not, and behind this claim is recognition of the need for upright, "mature" guides to train, discipline, and work on the self. But not just anyone is fit to be a sheikh, and one must be careful in the matter of finding a sheikh because he will have an enormous influence on oneself, as a disciple explained to me:

> No one can just appoint or designate someone as sheikh off the top of his head. These kinds of things have their particular signs [alamet]. After all, is it easy to connect oneself to such a person, to live Islam, to discipline one's self [nefsi terbiye etmek]? But alongside him, kneeled before him . . . in the context of the words he says, we find a direction for ourselves. This amounts to the sheikh being in control [kontrol]; he controls people.

Personally, I myself . . . well, I know, I've experienced this. So, being disciplined by someone like him is much better [than not having a guide].

Community members felt that it is important to be with someone who is aware of his responsibilities toward his disciples in order to instill in them the proper *adab* (moral etiquette; Messick 1993). As Faubion has noted, "The ethical field is certainly a normative field. Yet . . . it is very often also a field of ideals that actors are less obliged than encouraged to realize. It is a domain of obedience" (2001, 90). We have already seen that constituting a will to obey is part of what these disciplinary practices are oriented toward.

In speaking of the importance of a sheikh, members often discussed the disciplining of the *nefs* and the fact that the sheikh is in possession of proper technique that renders him worthy of attention. Trying to discipline one's *nefs* on one's own, I was told, can be unnecessarily circuitous and lead to one chasing one's tail; much better results are obtained by doing so under guidance, hence the role of the sheikh. A member of the order put it thus:

When we connected with hoja efendi, there is a hadith which says, "Ulema are the heirs [*varis*, from the Arabic *warith*] of the Prophet." A *varis* is like a *vekil*, as in, you go in my place. So, ulema are the *varis* of the Prophet in our day. After all, there is no Prophet right now, right? So what should we do, are we just helpless out here? Of course not. Maybe it isn't obligatory [to be under the guidance of a sheikh], but from the point of view of living Islam, it's very important. There is his *varis*; there is the going and learning of discipline [*terbiye*] from him, and there is also our own disciplining of ourselves. Now, which is better? Of course the discipline undertaken under supervision [*gözetim*] is more productive [*kârlı*] because his knowledge of these sciences [*ilm*] is well honed [*sivrilmiş*]. He's come to the point of a restful disposition [*saman*].

Moreover, the affective impact of Esad hoja not only was important to the continual, repetitive disciplining of the *nefs* but also was a large part of the atmosphere many of the men I worked with spoke of that kept them in the group once they were introduced to it.

In their early decisions to stay with the *cemaat* once they had encountered it, sheikh Esad hoja's lack of pretension was reported to have been impressive to many I spoke with. Despite his respected status as a professor, and in apparent contrast to a number of other *hoja*s, Esad hoja would encourage others to correct him if he was found to be in error. As a (then) recent graduate from the Sivas Ilahiyat faculty related, "hoja efendi once said [at a *sohbet*], 'If you ever see me do something contrary to Quran or sunna, by all means alert me.' See, I like that. Other *hoja*s may not say something like that." It was, among other things, Esad hoja's general demeanor that impressed people, and that despite the fact he was a knowledgeable scholar, he was very modest. Indeed, several people told me that what first attracted them to this order, and sometimes through it to a more pronounced Muslim identity, was the qualities of character people involved in the order had. Also attractive to many who were in the order, like this member, was that being a member did not require adherence to a kind of personality cult regarding Esad hoja:

There are people who like hoja efendi, and there are some who aren't too interested. Among [the *cemaat*] there are also a few who are very, very zealous [*tutucu*].[28] Overly tied to him. Everything they say starts with, "hoja efendi this" or "hoja efendi that." For instance, I myself have read one of his books. I love hoja efendi, but I only read one [of his] books. Some of these people go and read all of his books, they always walk around with one in their hands. Or, they saw hoja efendi once in their lives, but they'll say, "Oh, yes, I know hoja efendi personally." So there is a bit of a hierarchy among my friends at school in this sense, but most of them are like me, not overly, extremely zealous. Anyway, you know zealot types, they're generally illiterate [i.e., ignorant] people.

REPENTANCE AS CONVERSION

It is often said that the Muslim's setting down the path of *seyrüsülûk*, of initiatory training in the specialized disciplines of Sufism, is a kind of rebirth, characterized by what is usually referred to among those I worked with as an inner and outer purification (Knysh 1999, Schimmel 1975). Both are part of a whole, and one cannot be conceived without the other.[29] Outer, bodily purification is characterized by a redoubled effort to be continually clean and to be in a state of perpetual ritual cleanliness after ablutions, ready for worship and prayer, which the devout Muslim is presumed to be engaged in at least five times throughout the day. The main feature of inner purification is abandoning those habits that lead one to stray from the path God has chosen for humans and to avoid sin. The technique for accomplishing this is *tövbe* (from the Arabic *Tawba*), repentance, which carries associations of "turning to" in the Arabic. The first sign of *tövbe*, of turning to God, in the believer is sincere regret and sincerity in one's determination not to repeat acts that will necessitate repentance again. Evil and being a bad person was explained to me as generally harming others and putting oneself first over God and others. Central to *tövbe*, then, is a certain set of sentiments.

Tövbe is an important theme in the Quran, where sinners are encouraged not to lose faith in the mercy and compassion of God: "Say 'O my Servants who have transgressed against their souls! Despair not of the mercy of Allah:

for Allah forgives all sins, for He is oft-forgiving, most merciful'" (39:53). Moreover, those who repent are assured that God loves them: "For Allah loves those who turn [*tövbe*] to Him constantly and He loves those who keep themselves pure and clean" (2:222). As the Turkish language is not closely related to Arabic, but has many Arabic loan words, the semantic extension and subtleties of meaning and association among words derived from the same root in Arabic are lost to most Turkish speakers. However, it is important to realize that part of the disciplinary apparatus within which newcomers to Islamic devotional practices like the Sufi ones described here are initiated is study of Arabic. For many practitioners without a previous upbringing in an observant family or study in an *imam-hatip* school whose curriculum included Arabic, the simultaneous learning of new practices and the semantic universe of Arabic had the effect of amplifying the intensity of the transformations they felt in themselves.

Ahmet illustrated these spiritual techniques well. He was somewhat older than most of the other disciples, "around 40" he would say. He had already tasted a lot of what life has to offer, he told me, only some of it worthwhile. He had been in the gold business in Adana, buying and selling. "We used to walk around with so much money, bags of it." Times were good, and cares few. But it eventually seemed "empty" [*boş*]. "I started to feel an emptiness inside me," he related. He decided to put himself in order, which quickly entailed distancing himself from his friends. "We were doing all kinds of things," he shook his head with a smile, lowering his voice so others in the room would not hear, "gambling, drinking . . ." he trailed off. Then, by chance, he heard Esad hoja on the radio, which he later learned was the local Adana broadcast of the station AKRA. "He was relating how, on the day of Judgement [*kıyamet*] God will place a Quran before us, and if you can't read it, he'll be very sorry [*üzülüyor*]. The Quran-ı kerim was sent by God, through Jibrail, transmitting the word [*kelam*] of God, and it is written in the Quran. Well, I heard that, and I immediately decided to learn Arabic. I've just recently started," he said with a smile.

He decided to come to Istanbul, where he felt he could make a fresh start, getting some distance from his previous life and finding a more pious atmosphere. He went straight upon arrival to the mufti of the Fatih quarter, telling him of his desire to learn Arabic, and was handed off to another fellow, "younger than I was!" as he put it.[30] The fact that he was put into the hands of people younger than he was an eye-opener, compounding his sense of helplessness, but he kept silent, with the feeling that he was starting at the beginning of a long project. Equally important was his sense that he needed help in rearranging his moral judgment. The fact was that he was entering into a different environment and hierarchy—one where his status was quite low.

"Being together with good people," Ahmet told me, "is to be forgiven; being together, forgiving, praying sincerely, speaking truthfully. Wherever good people are, we need to find them." The Gumuşhanevi Naqshbandi order was for Ahmed just such an environment of "good people." His words were also likely inspired by Quranic passages relating to *tövbe* and repentance, particularly Sura 9, often called "The Repentance": "Fight and slay the pagans wherever ye find them. And seize them, beleaguer them, and lie in wait for them in every stratagem. *But if they repent, and establish regular prayers and practice regular charity, then open the way for them: for Allah is oft-forgiving, most merciful.*"[31] In my conversations with him it became clear that among the most important concerns for Ahmet—and several of the older, non–student age Sufis I encountered—was forgiveness or to be forgiven (*af edilmek*). I never pressed him on just what kinds of wrongs or sins he had committed or felt he did; maybe there were even legal problems, or maybe not. But it was clear that Ahmet felt that by 40, he had not lived a "good life" and was at this point preparing to spend the rest of it trying to please God in hopes of being forgiven. In my conversations with him, in which I would begin by posing questions about the role of the sheikh in Sufism, and about devotional techniques like *rabıta* and *zikr*, he would inevitably return to this theme of forgiveness and repentance. Sufism was, for Ahmet, quite simply an effective way of returning to the moral life God commanded for humans. "After the age of discernment, around 12, 13, what you do gets recorded by the angels. It goes into the computer," he said with a smile. "Reason [*akıl*] is our greatest blessing [*nimet*]." Again returning to his main theme, he added, "When we forgive [others], God multiplies our good deeds a thousand times."

The environment provided by the Naqshbandi order was thus primarily, for Ahmet and many others, a place where one could be with good people, and Sufism was itself primarily, as he put it, simply "continually being with God. Not abandoning things [şeyleri terk etmemek]." And then he used the classic metaphor of ores and metals: "It's like being pure gold," rather than gold alloyed with other, less pure metals. The figure of testing ores and metals to ascertain the purity of their components contains the roots of the notion of *fitne*, meaning "discord" or even "anarchy." Sewn discord is taken as a kind of test of the moral fiber of Muslim societies.[32] On another occasion, at which Ahmet was not present, the deputy for Esad hoja giving the *sohbet* at İskender Pasha mosque came around to a discussion of moral character and how one is often put to the test in today's society: "Distinguishing and separating out good from evil is like separating metals to take out the gold, and this is *fitne*. Who is it that has the most difficulties in Turkey today? It is the knowledgeable, the scholars [*alim, mürşidler*], those who are thinking [*fikr edenler*]."[33] This kind of discussion was also typical of the way that criticisms tend to be directed at the powers that be by the order, that is, indirectly and without explicit reference to those targeted; the point is clear enough, however, and rarely misunderstood.

But more importantly, the general status of the present is, in a sense, taken to be one of moral chaos and discord, creating a situation in which the believer is constantly tested: will she do the right thing despite overwhelming pressure to do otherwise? Those who are perennially mindful of God will find that they are in a better position to do so.

ISLAM AND NATIONALISM

During a lunch break from our work in the cemetery one day, Uncle Yusuf began speaking of the importance of learning and scholarship in Islam and decried the situation of Muslims today: "Look around. These days Muslims are among the most ignorant people in the world. We barely deserve to be called Muslims." As if to drive the point home, to an extent many conservative Turks would likely be sensitive about, he added, "Have you ever seen greater enemies of scholarship and learning than the Mongols? They ravaged and destroyed libraries and cities, for what?" invoking the historical memory of people Turkish schoolbooks say were "Turks." There was nervous laughter and nods all around, and Hamid, identifying himself—as a Turkmen—as a descendent from these hordes, said not without irony, "I guess that's us, huh?" Everyone chuckled.

It was in moments like this that the sensibilities of members of the *cemaat* distinguished themselves from much of the discourse of the political Right with which they tend to otherwise associate themselves. While political party sympathies of the members of the order during my fieldwork in the late 1990s tended to be for the various reincarnations of the Islamist parties Refah-Fazilet, RP-FP (recalling that the AKP did not yet exist), I did meet a couple of members who declared their support for either the MHP (Milliyetçi Hareket Partisi, or Nationalist Action Party) or BBP (Büyük Birlik Partisi, or Party of Great Unity), the latter an offshoot of the former, which adds an Islamic element to their shared ultranationalist platform. The vast majority of the members I worked with had a decidedly ambivalent attitude toward nationalism. On the one hand, they knew and expressed that there is really no place for nationalism in Islam; what is important for one's identity is that one be a Muslim and live as such, while one's origins—national, ethnic, or otherwise—should not be an issue. On the other hand, nationalism, the sense that one is a Turk and distinct from Arabs, Greeks, Armenians, Iranians, and so on, is profoundly embedded into the consciousness of schoolchildren in Turkey. Turkish students of history are taught that at the end of the Ottoman Empire, the Arabs treacherously cooperated with European imperialists ("infidels" in the language of the religiously conservative) to dismantle the empire, thereby betraying their Muslim brothers. Moreover, Turkish students are taught, these Arab neighbors were so incompetent and naïve that they then allowed themselves to be duped by these infidels and taken over as colonies and mandates. The compelling notion of the *umma*, or the political and moral community of Muslims (transcending nation-states), is in Turkey set squarely against the background of this experience and carries little practical force (we recall our discussions in earlier chapters). Indeed, I found that many Turks I spoke with harbored, even if ever so subtly, ready to change it upon reflection, a sense of superiority relative to other, neighboring Muslim peoples (Arabs on the one hand, and Shi'ite Iranians on the other). Yet when Uncle Yusuf spoke of Central Asian Turks and Mongols in such unflattering terms, the group around us sitting in the shade of the tombs of Sultan Suleiman and Hürrem Sultan, nodded approval and offered up anecdotes of their own.

WHY SUFISM?

Many of the members I worked with said that before engaging seriously with this *cemaat*, they explored other groups, such as the Nurcus or other *tarikat*s. Most of the members came from religiously conservative families, and only in a very few cases did I meet people who had dabbled in Leftist groups; ultranationalist explorations were somewhat more common. The Nurcu movement is probably the most widespread of non–state sponsored Islamic movements in the country and has received a good deal of attention in Turkish media and domestic and foreign scholarship.[34] They are also undoubtedly a favorite topic of research because of their professed emphasis on technological progress, while their uneasy relationship with the state accords them a prestigious "persecuted" status in the eyes of some foreign researchers. Many of the young men I worked with had encountered the Nurcus and had explored them a bit. Almost without exception, those who had been briefly involved with Nurcus related to me that they were put off by what they felt to be the secrecy of everything about them. Those I interviewed said that, given the harshness of the environment in Turkey for outwardly pious people (especially after February 28, 1997, and before the election of the AK Party in 2002), it can perhaps be understood that one would practice a strategic dissimulation of one's intentions or the status of one's actions. But the people I spoke with expressed their dissatisfaction with an apparent Nurcu sensibility that leads to secrecy even within the observant community (*umma*). Without my prompting, this was the issue many of the young men I spoke with returned to in discussing the Nurcus, like this member of the order in Istanbul: "Another thing [I like] about this [Naqshbandi] *cemaat* is that there is no secrecy. I mean, if I'm on the right path, why should I hide anything? Why should I be wary of people? They should be wary of me. Some other *cemaat*s have this kind of secrecy, and it isn't good. If you're right, why are you hiding it? OK, it's one thing to hide yourself from enemies of Islam, but why hide yourself from Muslims? What I know to be correct I will say to any and all Muslims, without hesitation."

In response to my queries about why members got involved with this particular order rather than another one, the response was often that this *cemaat*'s way of doing things was but one among many; however, they found this one to be most appropriate. Practicalities like the fact that this was the first one they encountered were also freely mentioned as reasons. Another point was brought up by the director of the *vakıf* at the time of my research when he said, "Many *tarikat*s are not especially open to the public [*halk*], even to locals. It's usually families who introduce people they know into the group. They also don't have many public activities to speak of, such as talks or conferences [like we do]."

Among Naqshbandi groups functioning in Turkey at the time of my research was a group centered in Adıyaman, northeast of Gaziantep. Perhaps most interesting about the relationship between this group and the İskender Pasha group is not what I heard about the former group from members of the latter, but rather what I did not hear. For during the entire duration of my research and discussions about the status of Sufism in Turkey and about the Naqshbandi order in particular, only two or three times was this other branch ever mentioned. Was this due to a lingering sense of factional schism? So as to not seem like I was trying to gather information on any and every order, but staying to my stated goals of understanding the practices of one group, I did not seek information on this other branch from the members of the İskender Pasha group. In a conversation with the (then) *vakıf* director, however, this other group came up:

> There's the Adıyaman group, near Adana, they're also Naqshbandis. We don't really have relations with them. They're a little strange. For instance they have this practice, for 15 days a girl will go to the lodge, to do "service" [*hizmet*], and then go back home. Now, this is just strange. After all, women shouldn't go around by themselves anyway. Some groups get into different things: around here in Fatih there are people in skullcaps and baggy trousers; Nurcu's shave their beards. They don't prove [the authoritative Islamic source of] any of this. The prophet never said anything about black *çarşaf* [loose black sheet covering the entire body except for face and hands] for women, for instance, so my wife doesn't wear it.[35]

A few conversations I had with members contrasted the *cemaat*'s emphasis on the diligence and effort that is necessary in the disciplining of the *nefs* with the apparent pretense of some other groups to have transcended the necessity of such efforts. My information on such groups is solely secondhand, derived from conversations with people more or less denouncing them. In one such conversation, in Sivas, references to other groups came up in a conversation on the importance of diligence and mindfulness (of God) and stages of spiritual advancement (*makam*):

> [Some people say], "Hey, look, we've really covered some [spiritual] ground here [*bir yerlere geldik*], you know. I bet if we don't do our prayers [regularly] it's OK now." We hear about this. It's so wrongheaded, there are truly perverse [*sapık*] *tarikat*s out there, in Turkey. They say they've come to a particular point, and prayers and worship [*ibadet*] are waived [*kalkmış*] because they've [allegedly] "risen through the stages" [to spiritual maturity]. Now, could there be anything more ridiculous? So then why weren't they waived for our Prophet? There are these kinds of things, particularly these days. In fact, as a result of them, [people] attack Sufism.

While my experience with other *tarikat*s is limited, it seems safe to say that from my discussions one may generalize that foremost among the reasons why members preferred the Sufi order to other Islamic groups was the perceived authenticity of what is said and practiced as well as the sense of fully participating in the *umma*, the community of believers, without separating oneself off by a veil of secrecy. As far as the reason for selecting this particular order over others, one parameter was practicality (i.e., this was the first group they encountered, and they liked it). Among those who did look around but decided to align with this group, the reason was primarily the sense of continuity of practice and technique, the authenticity of which is vouchsafed by the known chain of morally upright transmitters from a known source. Also significant was the lack of a clique mentality or veneration of a family lineage, with a simultaneous emphasis on what are widely held to be simply the recognizable tenets and practices of orthodox Islam. As one member contrasted this community with others: "You hear 100 *ezan* [from the Arabic *adhan*, 'call to prayer'], 99 of them are usually fake [*sahte*]. You can find the real one; it's the one done from the heart [*kalp*]. Love is the way of affect [*muhabbet yolu*]. There are definitely good people everywhere, and I am going to assist and protect them. This has nothing to do with age, beards, or skullcaps at all."

This particular Sufi order has been numerically small, not a mass phenomenon, but also disproportionately influential in Turkey, having an impact on Muslim sensibilities generally and on political, social, economic, and religious tendencies specifically. We have seen in this chapter how this branch of the Naqshbandi order approaches the phenomenon of Sufism as an ethical discipline oriented toward the cultivation of a particular form of virtuous life: "Virtues are dispositions not only to act in particular ways, but also to feel in particular ways. To act virtuously is not, as Kant was later to think, to act against inclination; it is to act from inclination formed by the cultivation of the virtues. Moral education is an 'éducation sentimentale'" (MacIntyre 1984, 149). What is the connection between actions and sentiments, and why does this order focus on this connection? In the next chapter, we examine in more detail the mechanics of this disciplinary tradition by focusing on one of the group's main devotional practices.

CHAPTER 4

DISCOURSE, COMPANIONSHIP, AND SPIRITUAL EXERCISES

A few minutes have passed since the *ezan* (from the Arabic *adhan*) sounded from the loudspeakers on minarets in the mosques of the Fatih neighborhood of Istanbul as worshippers make their way to *'asr* (afternoon) prayers and the following *sohbet* on this, like most other, Sunday afternoons.[1] They come to the Iskender Pasha mosque's courtyard gate, down the steps, to the ablution fountain.[2] Friends and acquaintances nod and smile to one another, rolling down their sleeves as they rise from the stools by the ablutions fountains. Inside they perform the canonical worship then break ranks for recommended *sunna* prayers and brief individual *zikrs*. After prayers, about half of the male worshippers gather in the main part of the mosque under the dome to listen to the week's *sohbet*. Women tend to perform their prayers and listen either in the balcony overlooking the mosque's main room or in an activity room downstairs in the basement, to which loudspeakers have been wired, and from which there is more coming and going, and children.[3] The imam who led the prayers, we'll call him Murad hoja, often acts as a deputy (*vekil*) for Esad hoja, who was abroad—mainly in Australia—beginning in 1997. Murad hoja shakes hands with and greets friends who had previously been standing in the prominent positions around and just behind him for prayers, while a young assistant turns on the light above the pulpit raised in the front-left corner of the room. He makes his way up the pulpit's ladder and sits under a framed *kilim* (flat-woven tapestry carpet) and wooden inlaid calligraphy.

Murad hoja now begins what he and the audience refer to as a *sohbet*. The *sohbet*, like those of the recent sheikhs in this Naqshbandi *silsile* (chain of initiation) Mehmet Zahid Kotku and Esad Cosan, is structured around the reading and discussion (*izah, şerh*) of hadith (accounts of exemplary sayings and deeds of the Prophet Muhammad, which alongside the Quran are the canonical sources of Sunni Islamic traditions).[4] The hadith is first read in Arabic and then translated and interpreted, giving examples from daily occurrences and historical anecdotes. In this manner one, two, or often three hadith are read and interpreted, lasting a total of about an hour and a half. There is very little coming and going during the *sohbet*, no talking among listeners, almost no note taking, and rarely are questions asked. On very few occasions does a listener jot something down on paper. At the end of the *sohbet*, supplicatory prayers (*dua*) are said, asking God to accept the efforts of the *sohbet* and prayers of its participants; then there is an abbreviated version of the Hatm-i Hacegan, an invocation of the memory of earlier pious personalities, Naqshbandis, Sufis, and other Muslims, with special emphasis on figures in this branch's Gümüşhanevi *silsile*, and then a *zikr*.[5]

* * *

In a home in the old center of Urfa, an ancient city in southeast Anatolia near the Turkish border with Syria, an out-of-town visitor joins eight men gathered on a Friday night after the last prayers, as they tried to do every week. The gathering is hosted by a man in his fifties know to be a pious, scholarly local personality, who leads the group in a study and discussion of hadith. Again, each hadith studied is first read in Arabic, then ways to translate it are discussed, leading into its interpretation, with examples given from daily occurrences and historical anecdotes. About a dozen hadith are read and interpreted, lasting a total of two and a half hours. This *sohbet* is among a fairly learned group. Note pads are out, and notes are taken in them as well as in the margins of the books, while a young man swiftly refilled glasses of very strong tea, placing them before the group sitting on the deep-red-toned and overlapping carpets. At the end of the *sohbet*, *dua* are said. This then also leads to a *zikr* and brief ritual recitations of cycles of prayers and invocations of the memory of Sufi luminaries considered to be predecessors in the Sufi Order.

* * *

SOHBET: DISCOURSE AND COMPANIONSHIP AS ISLAMIC PRACTICE

DURING MY FIELDWORK IN THE LATE 1990S with the Gümüşhanevi branch of the Khalidi Naqshbandi order, members would gather like in these two examples to hold *sohbet*s, resembling in outward form a lesson. I had been attending *sohbet*s such as these and socializing with members of the order for several months in various cities in Turkey when I realized that practically no one had ever been discussing the classic themes of Sufism emphasized in Western literature on the topic, such as "intimate experience of God" and "self-effacement [in the Reality of God]" (Knysh 1999, Schimmel 1975). Not only were these techniques not discussed during *sohbet*s; they were also not discussed among the many followers. It became quite obvious that the members of the order simply were not particularly concerned with these themes on a daily basis. Yet I was repeatedly told that these *sohbet*s were this Naqshbandi Sufi order's main devotional activity alongside the canonical five daily prayers.

What members clearly were very concerned with, however, and what was a constant topic of lessons and informal discussion, was the good (*iyilik*) and morality (*ahlak*), and how one can become predisposed to ethical practice and avoid sin. As such, for the practitioners who I came to know, Sufism is essentially an ethical discipline (the term they used was "*terbiye*," Arabic *tarbiya*), a self-reflexive effort to constitute moral dispositions (*hal-tavır*) in oneself through repetition according to precedents considered to be binding and authoritative.[6] These practitioners' concerns with ethical practice and the formation of their dispositions suggest that in analyzing such practices our focus should not be on something called "mystical experience," but rather on disciplinary practice, which Asad defines as "programs for forming or reforming moral dispositions (organizing the physical and verbal practices that constitute the virtuous . . . self)" (1993, 130). Hence I suggest that Sufi practice is best approached not through a speculative calculus of "real Sufi" *experience* (or its absence) but rather through an analysis of the relationship between traditions of discourse and practice and the kinds of ethical selves associated with them. Indeed, the great Naqshbandi Sufi and scholar of Islam Ahmad Sirhindi wrote that on the day of resurrection one will be questioned not about one's practice of Sufism but about one's adherence to the shari'a (Friedmann 2000, 41).

The central concern of the Naqshbandi Sufis with whom I worked was thus not the so-called mystical union with God (and annihilation of the self) so often cited in Western literature on Sufism. Their concern was with the disciplining of the base self (*nefs*) in order to form a proper disposition to do the good (*iyilik*) as commanded by God. As we shall see, in the Sufi practice of *sohbet* (from the Arabic *suhba*)—which I translate as "companionship-in-conversation"—the kinds of relationships formed in the act of oral transmission of texts and interpretations are considered liable to constitute a morally structured disposition in the devotee and are the object of careful cultivation through what I propose to call disciplines of presence. These practices are effective as means for cultivating an ethical self, partly due to the fact that the status of the events in which they take place is equivocal. As Sufism and Sufi orders are illegal in Turkey, *sohbet* is a genre that thrives on ambiguity.

One of the corollaries of the differentiation of public reason and private faith (considered the proper site of religion as it is taken as a matter of personal choice or preference) is a particular understanding of the connection between discourse, practice, and subjectivity: preconstituted individuals are expected to exercise secular reason (i.e., without recourse to religious authority) in their deliberation on affairs considered public. This should all take place without force; otherwise, the will expressed by the individuals involved cannot be taken as genuine. A great deal of recent work on the relationship between language, power, and the formation of subjectivities has deconstructed the relationship between subjects and power implicit in such conceptions of the public and have drawn attention, in part, to the processes through which dispositions of the will are formed in the first place (Connolly 1999). Similarly, in this chapter, we examine Islamic traditions oriented toward the formation of certain dispositions of the will and the modes of sociability produced by and sustaining them by looking at the practices of this group of Naqshbandi Sufis.

We will pay particular attention to this practice of *sohbet* as a technique of ritualized discourse and as an example of Islamic discipline aimed at constituting a virtuous disposition toward ethical practice and avoidance of sin. In *sohbet* events, alongside the importance of the content of the sheikh's discourse, the relationships ("companionships" as these Sufis refer to them) formed in the act of oral transmission and liable to constitute ethically structured dispositions in devotees are the object of careful cultivation. Central to the functioning of this discipline of presence is the role of presence and repetition in the training of affect. This discipline of presence embodies a certain implicit ideology these and many other Muslims have about how people influence one another and about the relationship between language use and this interpersonal influence. This metaphysic of influence can be seen in their ethic of companionship, which they understand to be central to the formation of a moral self, specifically through the inculcation of dispositions toward ethical practice and avoidance of sin. The embodiment of voices in bodies has traditionally been a condition for the functioning of these disciplines.

Several points are important to note in the discussion that follows. Part of the way these disciplines work (i.e., part of what makes them effective according to practitioners' own standards of effectiveness) is that ideally one reaches the point where it is no longer necessary to go through a conscious calculus to avoid most daily temptations to error; one's desires have already been honed and conditioned so that one does not even want to fall into such situations in the first place. Another important point is that much of the operation of these disciplines is implicit, even to many of the Sufis involved, especially younger ones; knowledge about how they work is somewhat esoteric. While an awareness of how these disciplines work is not quite the stuff of secrecy, nor is it explicitly discussed, and as practitioners come to an awareness of the importance of the pragmatic dimensions of companionship and discourse, this is taken to be a part of their spiritual and ethical maturity. We will see that there are probably several reasons for the esoteric nature of this knowledge, including the fact that Sufism and Sufi orders are illegal in Turkey. But I think it would be a mistake to ascribe its esoteric nature simply to this prohibition, for many traditions of Sufi practice and doctrine exist with secrecy at their core (Schimmel 1975).

CONVERSATION, ORTHODOXY, AND COMPANIONSHIP

Those I worked with emphasized that it was in emulation of the normative precedent, or *sunna*, of Prophet Muhammad that they practiced the order's main spiritual exercises, *sohbet* (discussed shortly) and *zikr* and had anything to do with Sufism. This emphasis on the emulation of *sunna* can be seen in the writings of Mevlana Khalid (Abu-Manneh 1982). Important here is the role of precedent in the formulation of right practice.[7] There is, thus, a strong sense of belonging to a tradition, in the sense we have been developing in previous chapters, and the fact that the heart of *sohbet* among Naqshbandis is the reading of hadiths is significant. By structuring their main group activities besides canonical worship around the discussion of hadith, and in a form self-consciously referring to what they feel to have been the privileged mode of transmission of knowledge between Prophet Muhammad and his companions, Naqshbandis embody what they take to be a quintessential mode of Islamic religiosity, namely, the formation of a moral disposition through companionship and discourse.[8] Hence, those I worked with were quite confident in their orthodox Muslim identity and displayed a polite but informed disdain for anyone who doubted this. While much of the criticism directed at them came from less-observant people fearful of their danger to secularism, occasionally more observant visitors hostile to Sufism would appear at the mosque. During one *sohbet*, in the context of a discussion of the importance of studying hadith and understanding them, the deputy leading the *sohbet* related a story of a stranger who arrived for morning prayers one day: "He had a long, full beard, and he was quite sure of himself [i.e., arrogant in his demeanor]. We performed the worship, and after morning worship we do a *zikr*. Now, this fellow says, 'Why are you doing this? Don't you know this is wrong?' 'Oh, is that so?' we say. 'Yes, this is from Satan!' he says. Well, we then passed to the reception rooms [of the Iskender Pasha complex], where we were going to have a small breakfast. This fellow then sat down and tried to cut a watermelon with scissors!"

This combination of self-righteous arrogance, an overly zealous, censorious nature, and uncouth ignorance is commonly associated in Turkey with those few who have come under the sway of groups known as Salafi (also suggested by the imam's reference to the visitor's "long, full beard"). With their common abandonment of adherence to one of the four schools of Sunni jurisprudence and rejection of Sufism, many observant Muslims in Turkey consider them to be beyond the pale of orthodox Sunni Islam.[9] A member in Istanbul situated recent developments in the context of centuries of tradition.

> Imam Ghazzali is an important person in Sufism . . . He said, "The way to true knowledge is through Sufism and faith [iman]." Sufism is done through practice and knowledge. You both worship, that is, put [teachings] into practice in your daily life, and you know what you are doing. This is why in the Naqshbandi branch all the hojas are people who have had a very rigorous training. They have all had a very serious education. They are all scholars [alim], they all know Islamic law [fiqh], they all know hadith, all the branches [of Islamic learning]. This is fundamental in Naqshbandi traditions. Personal qualities pass from person to person. One's maturity, beauty, erudition pass to and are reflected in those around one. So for this reason, no matter how much technology develops, it isn't a danger to the technique of giving lessons because there is still a face-to-face relationship, there is still a lesson setting [sınıf sistemi], the hoja comes and gives the lesson. There's debate, participation, and so on.

We see here again the functioning of a tradition of discourse and practice, through which conscious efforts to form oneself are done in the light of normative judgment from reasoned grounds.

The term "sohbet" is used in modern, everyday Turkish to mean "conversation." But in Islamic sources it has a more technical meaning of companionship, including shades of fellowship and discipleship (Trimingham 1998, 311; Schimmel 1975, 366). Sohbet consists of "keeping the company of the shaikh and of one's fellow disciples in accordance with precise behavioral norms" (Algar 1992, 213), with the "disciple's firm conviction in the exclusive effectiveness of [one's] shaikh's suhba" (215). There is also a sense among Sufis both that companionship is intimately linked to conversation and, conversely, that conversation engenders companionship (Gümüşhanevi n.d., 444). The most common explanation of the significance of sohbet in Islam that members of the order gave me is the same one a famous Naqshbandi sheikh gave in the late nineteenth century:[10] "Hazreti Abu Bakr, the great loyal one, was in hijret [exile] in the cave with our Prophet, and the Qur'an relates: When they were in the cave together, [Abu Bakr] was the second to the second. The Lord almighty tells of the sohbet between Hazreti Abu Bakr and the Prophet of God: 'Don't despair! God is here with us,' [the Prophet] consoled him.

Thus, Abu Bakr is called the companion in *sohbet* of the Prophet in the cave. This is where the Sufi [*tarikat*] notion of *sohbet* comes from" (Gümüşhanevi n.d., 445). For Sunni Muslims, Abu Bakr is considered to have been the companion of the Prophet Muhammad who was most favored to succeed him in the leadership of the community of Muslims and continues to be revered as the first caliph (successor), having in fact succeeded him.[11] When Prophet Muhammad was forced into exile, it is related that he spent some very intense sessions in a one on one relationship with Abu Bakr, in which they conversed intimately (i.e., participated in *sohbet*). *Sohbet*, then, is what Prophet Muhammad did with the one who is considered by Sunnis to have been his dearest companion (*sahib*). In Arabic the term "*sohbet*" itself derives from the same root as the word *ashab* or *sahaba*, "companions," and the two terms participate in the same semantic extension. *Sohbet* is what, by definition, *sahaba* do. Thus the figure of the companion in Islam is modeled on the companions of Prophet Muhammad, those who were closest to him during his lifetime, sought out and frequently kept his company, and strove to assimilate his teachings. Their significance can hardly be overstated, as it was they who transmitted the hadith and the Quran before these were written down and compiled, ensuring a critical structural role for companionship and face-to-face speech—"presence"—in the transmission of Islamic knowledge (Messick 1993; Meeker 1994).

In Sufism, those who attend the *sohbet* of a given sheikh—who is then known as their *sheikh-i sohbet*—are said to be his *sahaba* ("companions"), and members of the *cemaat* would occasionally refer to an absent member or close sympathizer of the *cemaat* as a *sahib* in their conversations with me.[12] The account of the companionship and *sohbet* between Abu Bakr and the prophet is fairly common knowledge among Muslims; specific to some Sufi groups (including the one of our study) is the tradition that part of what the prophet gave to Abu Bakr while in the cave was certain specific techniques of spiritual discipline, namely, silent (as opposed to voiced) *zikr*. The Iskender Pasha *cemaat* continues to practice a silent *zikr*.[13]

Sohbet is thus a practice in that specific Aristotelian sense Alasdair MacIntyre uses the term, involving "standards of excellence and obedience to rules as well as the achievement of goods. To enter into a practice is to accept the authority of those standards and the inadequacy of my own performance as judged by them. It is to subject my own attitudes, choices, preferences and tastes to the standards which currently and partially define the practice" (MacIntyre 1984, 190). As such, to understand the practice of *sohbet*, it is important to recall that Islam is for its practitioners, and others, a moral tradition, involving the ongoing elaboration of normative judgment about correct practice. Indeed, as Asad's (1986) notion of discursive tradition emphasizes, an important practice among Muslims is precisely discussion and instruction about correct practice. Discussion, disagreement, and dispute are, moreover, not signs of a tradition "in crisis" but rather a sign of one that is vibrant; stasis is not a feature of traditions on these accounts.[14]

Hence my use of the notion of practice differs again somewhat from Bourdieu's prominent work on practice. Refashioning the notion of habitus from Aristotle, Bourdieu (1977; 1990) expunged the aspects of it that pertain to explicit, conscious efforts to transform oneself in favor of a conception of habitus that sees the implicit, unconscious reproduction of economic classes as what is taking place through its formation "in the final analysis" (Bourdieu 1977, 83).[15] Specifically elided in this conception of habitus is the ways in which the inculcation of dispositions may also be part of explicit disciplines specifically aimed toward the constitution of these dispositions self-consciously in practitioners (Mahmood 2005), an important feature of Aristotle's pedagogy for the formation of the ethical self (Burnyeat 1980; Foucault 2003a). As MacIntyre comments, "The educated moral agent must of course know what he is doing when he judges or acts virtuously. Thus he does what is virtuous *because* it is virtuous" (1984, 149). As such, the specific status of selves produced in and through discursive traditions, as well as their historicity, is equivocal in a practice approach that focuses solely on the implicit and unconscious workings of habitus.[16] Hence a habitus-based notion of disposition formation such as Bourdieu's, while appropriate to certain orders of phenomena, are less useful in interpreting the kinds of disciplinary programs outlined here.

The Muslim subjectivities produced through practices like *sohbet* are thus profoundly ethical in the sense that Muslims (among other things) are sincerely trying to ascertain what correct practice is. Obviously, Muslims are not the only ones doing so. What the norms are that guide such attempts and allow judgment about correct practice and the style of reasoning through which this is all done: such are the things that define this as an Islamic tradition and not another kind of tradition. For these and many other Muslims, the formation of a certain kind of moral Muslim self is connected to certain ways of using language and certain conceptions of what the human is. This overlaps with the field often known as language ideology, which looks at "the cultural system of ideas about social and linguistic relationships, together with their loading of moral or political interests."[17] We will see how the formation of a moral self in these Islamic traditions is embedded in networks of companionship and contexts of disciplinary discursive practice. They are disciplinary in the common, dual, English-language senses of the term, namely, that they have to do with techniques for reforming one's dispositions by disciplining or training aspects of the subject by reinforcing habits and focusing attention and in the sense that these techniques are explicitly codified and taught.

VOICE AND TEXT IN ISLAM: ISLAMIC LOGOCENTRISM

In the act of *sohbet* we have the quintessence of what we may call an Islamic logocentrism, or the locating of truth at a source of speech.[18] The model for this mode of transmission is revelation and the prophet being commanded to recite or read (*'iqra!*) a text preexisting in heaven, *umm al-kitab* (Messick 1993; Fischer and Abedi 1990). Just as the truth of revelation here is a hearing and reciting, the disciple is being trained to develop a disposition to ethical conduct in a context of presence with the sheikh or his authorized substitute (*vekil*), rather than merely through solitary reading of relevant texts.[19] In his book *The Calligraphic State*, which has been very influential in the development of an anthropological sensitivity to the role of written texts in the Islamic tradition in the formation of ethical subjects, Brinkley Messick ends his treatment of *darasa*, or roughly "pedagogy," with a brief discussion of what he calls "heard texts." In the context of the transmission of knowledge in Islam, hearing a recitation and taking no notes, no dictation—in short, no writing—is a mode with "a model both in the initial transmission of the Quran and in its subsequent recitational use in ritual. It is in the 'heard' texts mode that instruction most closely approximates the ideals of the legitimate transmission of knowledge." Messick continues: "The fully reproduced presence of an original text . . . is associated with an authoritative conveyance, via the voiced and heard word, across the human linkages between a teacher and the students assembled in his presence" (1993, 92).

These instantiations of heard texts are obviously much more difficult for social researchers to study because they are enunciations whose inscriptions may not be found in a written document, itself available to us in an archive. Messick has drawn out here the implicit sense among many Muslims that the oral mode of transmission of knowledge is more secure than the scriptural, written mode. "The oral remains authoritative for the written, not the other way around," as Fischer and Abedi put it (1990, 105). Indeed, the explanations of this attitude given to me by those with whom I did my research, and by scholars working within these traditions, are essentially the same ones Plato puts forth in his famous critique of the written word as inferior to the spoken in *Phaedrus*.[20]

Plato raised two main objections to the notion that writing itself is a preserver of the truth. First, Plato points out that when people write things down, they tend not to commit them to memory, which meant for Plato that they have not internalized the piece of information, and there is then no way that it can become knowledge. This seems to be an attitude shared by many of the Muslims I got to know during my research, particularly with regard to the memorization of relevant *suras* of the Quran for worship (*salat*), and it is Plato's second criticism that most concerns us here: "The fact is, Phaedrus, that writing involves a similar disadvantage to painting. The productions of painting look like living beings, but if you ask them a question they maintain a solemn silence. The same holds true of written words; you might suppose that they understand what they are saying, but if you ask them what they mean by anything they simply return the same answer over and over again" (1973, 97).

Plato is objecting that one can never get the kind of knowledge from a book that one can get from a knowledgeable person, for the simple reason that if one is reading a text, and does not understand it, it is not possible to ask the text to explain itself: "They simply return the same answer over and over." To ascertain the meaning of a text one cannot understand, one always needs to ask someone; the text alone cannot help you.

There is a further danger with the written word, Plato says: "Besides, once a thing is committed to writing it circulates equally among those who understand the subject and those who have no business with it; a writing cannot distinguish between suitable and unsuitable readers" (1995, 77). Just because a person has "read" a text, in other words, says nothing about whether that person has understood it. The written word allows teachings to circulate among people who might not have the proper education to understand them. In a Muslim context, this sensibility is concretized in the fact that it has historically never been the case that upon collecting all of the relevant books of hadith, *fiqh*, and *tafsir*, retreating somewhere alone and studying them, one could emerge as a qualified, authoritative *faqih*, or jurist of the law. It is, rather, a question of with whom has one studied the relevant texts. The classic texts of the Islamic tradition on their own are often difficult and ambiguous, just like texts in any other literate, scholarly tradition. As such, they cannot in any practical sense stand on their own; one text does not simply beget another. As Plato notes, "If it is ill-treated or unfairly abused it always needs its parent to come to its rescue; it is quite incapable of defending or helping itself" (1973, 97). We also recall that, as we saw in our discussion of tradition, not all interpretations of texts that are the basis of a tradition are equally valid. This is why it is important, for both Plato and Muslims, to study texts in a context of authorized, knowledgeable people to whom one can turn for answers in case of incomprehension.

Written texts are unquestionably central to the Islamic tradition. It is neither a notion of the facticity of the written word that undergirds their relationship to authoritative truth nor merely that texts are an important mnemonic device, instrumental to a more fundamental and important discipline of moral self-formation: memorization. This role of texts as instrumental to the formation and reproduction of embodied dispositions is important to recognize, as a number of subtle studies have done.[21] Thus they form a crucial part of a matrix of oral, face-to-face interaction in which these texts are discussed, interpreted, and debated.[22] It is therefore misleading to see texts as simply "central," a point that is at the heart of all those critiques that could be leveled at Orientalist traditions of scholarship that focus on questions of textual influence. Given the traditional Orientalist method of seeking the meaning of texts in their alleged origins or in the antecedent texts that allegedly "influenced" the one under study, it is not surprising that students of Muslim societies have been slow to acknowledge this social, pragmatic function of texts. Moreover, given the materials at the historian's disposal, it is usually more difficult to understand how texts functioned in a given context than what they refer to, even though the topics may well be obscure today.

Islamic traditions, thus, tend to be ones in which truth (revelation in the Islamic formulation) is located at a source of speech. To the extent that this oral source of truth is primary, while scriptural texts are considered to both *represent* that originally oral discourse and serve *performatively* as technologies in the disciplined reproduction of ethically structured dispositions in the pious believer that would permit him or her to attempt to access their meanings, the Islamic tradition is explicitly *logocentric*.[23] What ensures accurate transmission, then, much as Plato argued, is not scriptural accuracy but rather the moral fabric of the transmitters: in the Muslim case, their commitment to the truth, their commitment to the value of knowledge, and their fear of God (who would certainly punish them for their errors or shortcomings in transmission and for leading others astray).

AN ETHIC OF COMPANIONSHIP

Thus, given the structure in Islam of knowledge legitimated by reference to written texts (Quran and hadiths), which are themselves established as authentic due to their status as being grounded in a transmission from the unmediated, actual presence of the prophet himself (through his companions [*sahaba*]), Sufism is taken by the practitioners I worked with to be squarely within Sunni tradition. Indeed, Naqshbandis have elaborated a mystical technique of spiritual realization out of the status of companionship, namely, through *sohbet*, institutionalizing and replicating a logocentrism that suffuses Islamic traditions.[24] The reason for this emphasis on face-to-face presence of seeker and one considered ethically mature is that these relationships are considered to be the ones most liable to lead to certain sentiments—the technical term here being "love" (*sevgi; muhabbet*, from the Arabic *muhabba*), discussed shortly—and, hence, dispositions to ethical practice.[25]

Several senior Naqshbandis explained to me their understanding that people are influenced most in their behavior by other people. For the proper formation of character, then, one should try to always be with "good people," defined as those who seek the approval of God, and only God, and are not led astray by such things as popular fashion, prestige, or power.

One of the Sufi order's foremost scholars of its own traditions is İrfan Gündüz, longtime affiliate of the order, formerly professor in the department of Sufism at Marmara University's theology faculty in Istanbul, and at the time of my research, a member of parliament. He writes,

> The Naqshbandi order has but one sole method, and that is *sohbet*, the method of love (*sevgi metodu*). One calls companions (*ashab*) those who: take in (*almak*) Islam's existential aspects (*hal tarafı*) from our Prophet; its inner (*deruni*) aspects; its perception and feeling (*duygu*); those who learn/ receive through *sohbet* [*sohbet yoluyla almak*], from the sight of (*gözünden*) our Prophet, from the words/speech of our Prophet, and those who have been together with (*aynı mecliste bulunarak*) Him so that they have been influenced by his magnetism (*onun megnetik etkisinden*); and those who hear His noble conversation . . . The essential feature of *sohbet* is that it is the method that aims to put us together with good people, with sincere, faithful (*sadık*) friends. The point is that states/conditions (*haller*) are contagious (*bulaşıcı*). (Gündüz 1995, 86–87)

"Taking in," "perceiving," "being together," and "influence": Gündüz is laying bare here the ways in which *sohbet* is felt to be effective, namely, through *affect*. *Sohbet* is the harnessing of a metaphysic of influence in order to form proper, morally structured dispositions to do what God commanded as the good. The term Naqshbandis use to describe this power of influence in the formation of a virtuous habitus is love (*mahabbet*, or commonly *sevgi*). Love, as a technical term among Naqshbandis and other Sufis as it is in Islamic scholarship generally, is that capacity humans have to influence one another and to make people develop certain sentiments and desire to be like another (Trix 1993, 133–57).[26] This was explained to me by a member in Sivas, a medium-sized city in central Anatolia.

> God loves the one who loves his servant, and we should do things for the love of God. He who does so, they say, will surely taste faith [*iman*] . . . But how should one love? What does one do to the object one loves? For example, I love you for the praise of Allah. Let's say you're my brother. Now, what is the sign [*alamet*] of my loving you? I will do the things you do, won't do things you don't do, don't like, right, Ibrahim abi? Or, I will enjoy [*hoşuma gitmek*] the things you enjoy, and so on. You enjoy being

with such people, and without realizing it your conduct starts to resemble theirs because you want them to approve of you, and you respect them.

Emphasized in this and classic Sufi notions of love is less "possession" of the object of one's love than submission or obedience to it. As such, the specific kind of discipline here is akin to those monastic disciplines Asad (1993, 125) studied that involve the constitution of a will to obey and in which obedience is a virtue. The imam at Iskender Pasha (at the time of my research), put the role of love thus in a *sohbet*: "We must love [*sevmek*] our Prophet Muhammed (peace be upon him). We should always ask, 'What can we do to develop or increase this love?' To love him means to follow his example [*sünnet*]. There can be no opposition to [his example]. Let us attain spiritual development in his love, by observing the *sünnet* of the prophet."[27] The model behavior meant to be reinforced here through the cultivation of a capacity to love (i.e., submit to the beloved) is, of course, to submit to the will of God. Love entails here a metaphysic of influence, with direct bearing on the constitution of habits and dispositions (Kosman 1980). As a young disciple explained to me,

When one sees hoja efendi, there is a real spiritual influence [*manevi ektilişim*]. Humans are such amazing beings, one is morally and spiritually [*ma'nen*] influenced by the people one stands next to. If one's friend is good, one will be influenced by this goodness. If the friend is bad, one will easily acquire bad habits [*kötü alışkanlık kolay edinir*]. So, we want to spend our lives with [*düşüp kalkmak*] good people because it has its benefits. When I see hoja efendi, for instance when I go to "his side" and listen to his lessons [*ders*], the effect . . . believe me, it's so powerful. One feels a certain atmosphere [*bir hava hissediyor*]; it's really something felt, something lived, one really can't explain it. God willing, have you ever seen hoja efendi, Ibrahim abi?

Sohbet harnesses and institutionalizes this conception of love into a discipline of companionship as a technique for the formation of moral dispositions. In other words, it is clear that while *sohbet* in practice consists of discourse, it is not the informational content that lends the proceedings their status as disciplinary practice (though the heuristic value of hadith lessons is certainly not to be underestimated). Rather it is the conditioning of habits, and their channeling toward subsequent ethical practice and avoidance of sin, that is primarily meant to take place in these *sohbet*s. The contagion aspect of sentiment was expressed well to me by a *vekil* after he had finished conducting a *sohbet*: "This is real stuff [*bu gerçek bir şey*]. For instance, the hand holds a pomegranate, the mouth starts to water." The discipline of *sohbet* is simultaneously centered on the interpretation of canonical sources (hence only to be done by those with authoritative knowledge of them and control of the hermeneutic apparatus to approach them) and on the constitution of the disposition necessary as a precondition for such interpretation to be received and effective.

MATERIALITIES OF AFFECT: INSIDE AND OUTSIDE OF AGENCY

Recent work on the cultural and historical particularity of the liberal locating of true agency in the autonomous individual has critiqued "critical" scholarship for not holding itself sufficiently open to difference in this area, arguing that, for instance, an account of liberation based on the autonomous intentions of individuals, or a continual analytical focus on instabilities or indeterminacies in meanings, is based on an implicit account of the self that is not universal (Mahmood 2005).[28] Several versions of such critiques have been put forth, including a classic one from a Marxian tradition by Vološinov written in the late 1920s. As part of a broader reappraisal of the relationship between language, meaning, and sociopolitical-economic hierarchy, Vološinov rejected what he called "Romanticist, individualist subjectivism" that would posit an inner realm of pure experience as the basic unit of analysis, which is then drawn upon by speakers at the moment of expression. Instead, Vološinov argues that the act of expression actually organizes experience rather than merely externalizing it or being caused by it: "The experiential, expressible element and its outer objectification are created, as we know, out of one and the same material. After all, there is no such thing as experience outside of its embodiment in signs. Consequently, the very notion of a fundamental, qualitative difference between the inner and the outer element is invalid to begin with. Furthermore, the location of the organizing and formative center is not within (i.e., not in the material of inner signs) but outside. It is not experience that organizes expression, but the other way around—expression organizes experience" (Vološinov 1986, 85). We can expand Vološinov's work on verbal expression to issues of bodily comportment and agency more generally. A significant feature of his formulation is that it is a rejection of the identification of subjectivity with autonomous, spontaneous experience and its replacement with the notion of socially constituted experience. Simultaneously, he rejects the inner-outer division because the condition for experience is bodily engagement with the social world and the dispositions to subsequent action that ensue from such engagement. Expression and utterance are, as Vološinov points out, "determined by the actual conditions of the given utterance—above all, by its immediate social situation" (1986, 85). That one's apparently innermost experiences are neither temporally nor logically constituted prior to social engagement is also assumed by practitioners of *sohbet*, as well as many others attempting to live as Muslims. We can thus begin to make sense of the repeated injunctions of leaders in the order and among many other Muslims for Muslims to act "responsibly," to act ethically, and to pay attention to things from personal hygiene and housecleaning to conduct. Such things are felt to be central, consciously or unconsciously, to the formation of structured dispositions constitutive of virtues. Dewey made a similar point when he likened ideas, dispositions, and economic status to one another because of their profoundly socially constituted nature: "The notion that intelligence is a personal endowment or personal attainment is the great conceit of the intellectual class, as that of the commercial class is that wealth is something which they personally have wrought and posses" (Dewey 1984, 367). The question, then, is not to what degree one is constituted as a person in relation to others; even less is whether it is a matter of trying to find a way out of this intersubjectivity to the "core" of "the ethical Muslim self." For the desire for autonomy that such concerns presuppose can by no means be considered to be natural or unproblematic, though they have become the unspoken center of liberal political thought.[29] Obscured in the process are the ways in which agency and action in the world have to be judged according to criteria, which are, in the final analysis, culturally specific.

Thus, I am not arguing that *sohbet* be taken as an alternative, deliberative sphere (Benhabib 1996). These structured conversations (which have the quality of lessons) may be an occasion for listeners to question a given interpretation of a hadith, and a dialogue may ensue; rarely, however, does this occur. *Sohbet* is not an instance of persuasion (implying participants of equal status) or coercion (involving external force) among deliberative public individuals who have suspended issues of status. Rather *sohbet* is entirely structured around and saturated with relations linked to status, specifically moral status and the extent to which participants are considered to be ethical beings and mature in their knowledge of Islamic traditions. As such, central to *sohbet* is that modality of power Arendt (1968) referred to specifically as authority (as distinct from persuasion and coercion), characterized by a moral obligation to obey, due not to the compellingness of an argument but to the status of the source of the demand and in an environment of shared norms.[30] And yet *sohbet*, as many people told me and as Gümüşhanevi teaches in *Jami' ul-Usul*, should simultaneously be characterized by sincerity (*samimiyet*) and intimacy (*ihlas*). An ability to accommodate these qualities simultaneously and, as it were, naturally, without experiencing them as inherently contradictory, is part of the moral habitus, or structured disposition, *sohbet* is meant to constitute.[31] We will see that it is the shared background of shared norms (in this case the normative character of *sohbet* as a disciplinary practice) that participants bring to *sohbet* events that becomes problematic when *sohbet* is recontextualized on the radio.[32]

The discipline of *sohbet* on one level incorporates an institutionalization of the necessarily social, communal nature of Muslim self-constitution, emphasizing the context of a community of moral subjects. There is a tension between the ideals and function of *sohbet* as a mode of sociality and that regnant in modern civil society, structured around an idealized liberal, autonomous, self-sufficient subject. It is simply evident to those I worked with—and arguably to most observant Muslims in general—that the constitution of the self cannot take place in any way but relationally, in the context of a community; this is the reason for the insistence on the moral fabric of society on the part of many Muslims. Central to the functioning of "influence" is repeated interaction with specifically structured environments, through which virtuous habits and dispositions are embedded.[33] At this juncture I want to emphasize two levels on which we are operating as we continue our analysis: one is the historical status of Islamic traditions of practice given the genealogies outlined earlier in this book; the other has to do with how the traditions examined here sit with other programs, prioritizing other modes of subjectivity, and actualizing other conceptions of telos.

So far, I have been examining in some detail the discourses and practices of a group of Muslims who have a relatively heightened sense of their Muslim identity and are quite proficient in the Islamic traditions in and through which certain Muslim subjectivities are sustained. What I do not want to suggest is that this is the only authentically functioning mode of Islamic religiosity in Turkey. Recalling our discussion from earlier chapters, it may even be the case that a certain *inattention* to some issues often taken to be within the purview of Islamic traditions—for example, certain matters of law—themselves have an Islamic genealogy to them and should be seen in relation to the unfolding of the history of Islamic traditions.

DISCURSIVE TRADITION AND THE PRAGMATICS OF UTTERANCE

The reason why *sohbet*s are not occasions when listeners interject to question a particular interpretation of a hadith is that *sohbet*, as a devotional practice constitutive of a virtuous habitus, turns on the pragmatics of language and how speech is used as effective action in specifiable cultural contexts, pointing to what is *accomplished* in the act of utterance in contrast to what information is being conveyed (Austin 1975; Wittgenstein 2003). The main action to be accomplished here is the constitution a specific disposition in the hearers, through the relationships entailed in the conditions in which the speech takes place (Rosaldo 1982). Those I worked with had a conception of the self and body as intimately reworked and constructed through repeated action (Mauss 1979), and therefore representing a kind of "second nature," whereby it is the very processes and forces of the body itself that are harnessed in the formation of a particular kind of predisposed self.

In the efficacy of *sohbet*, the centrality of the pragmatics, and less the representational content, is clear from the unfolding of a relatively informal *sohbet* held on the occasion of my visit to a senior member of the order accompanied by a young friend of mine, also a member. Our host began by invoking the memory of the numerous Sufi luminaries whose tombs were located in the neighborhood of his home in the Eyüp district of Istanbul, which is well known as a center of Islamic piety, scholarship, and pilgrimage to the graves of saints (foremost among them the eponymous companion of Prophet Muhammad, Abu Ayyub, reputed to have fallen in an early Muslim siege on the Byzantine city). After speaking for roughly 40 minutes, telling anecdotes meant for our edification about his moving encounters with sheikhs in the order, dreams he had in which the sheikhs influenced his decisions and behavior, instances of the exemplary behavior of the sheikhs, and stories about the qualities of the prophet, he said, "Well, I started the *sohbet* from there. We could have started from someplace else [*başka taraftan*]." This was surprising, and broke the tenor and tone of the *sohbet*. I had not assumed that he had prepared his text in detail ahead of time, beyond perhaps a few mental notes of themes or anecdotes to touch on. Nonetheless, I later realized that in this slight sentence, inserted here in a *sohbet* that continued on for more than an hour, Erkan Abi revealed first that one must choose what to start with, as a matter of competently executing a *sohbet* and second, that its execution is not tied to the information conveyed. In other words, the technique does not hinge upon the detailed, accurate recounting of specific information, and there is not a topic that must necessarily be the beginning or end (in this case, for instance, there was no interpretation of hadith). I had never before heard such reflexive metacommentary on a *sohbet* uttered by someone giving one, for a more authoritative *vekil* would not say something like, "This is where I decided to start, but we could have started otherwise," and to be sure I never heard of Esad hoja say, or even allude to such a level metalinguistically. Everything normally proceeds as if one is attending a previously arranged talk or lesson; the skill of the speaker in gauging the audience and opening the *sohbet* appropriately ensures a seamless edifice. This was an instance of Erkan Abi's lack of polish in performing *sohbet*, but it was also a "slip" that was enormously revealing, for it draws one's attention away from the content of his discourse to the way it functions.

Erkan Abi had made it clear that he was undertaking a *sohbet* as such when he formulated his intention (*niyyet* from the Arabic *niyya*) to do so by verbally articulating such intention and praying that it (i.e., our undertaking) please God. This was then followed by other cues that we had entered into another discursive "space" such as his formal, teacherly tone of voice and the relative lack of cues (e.g., sentence intonation, not making eye contact) inviting the listeners to immediate verbal response. These were "keys," in Goffman's (1981) terms, with which to interpret the status of the discourse to transpire, as *sohbet*. But the relationship of contiguity between *sohbet* and ethical habitus formation—that is, the fact that *sohbet* is continuous with the formation of certain dispositions—is generally occulted in *sohbet* events, as those leading *sohbet*s (unlike Erkan Abi) do not let on as to the technique involved. As such, this indexical relationship that is maintained between *sohbet* and its attendant dispositions is a matter of esoteric knowledge, since the contextualization cues (Gumperz 1982) that would aid participants in understanding the *sohbet* as a practice are equivocal. The pragmatic purpose of the *sohbet* is never openly elucidated, and the realization of this pragmatic level of functioning is itself taken to be a sign of ethico-spiritual advancement and maturity. This accounts for a major share of the esoteric aspects of this order's practices and also elucidates the cryptic suggestions made to me by senior members of the order that "Sufism is both more and less than you probably think it is": more because there is much more than meets the eye that is going on in any given *sohbet*; less because it is, in a sense, merely one more of the various disciplines in Islamic traditions through which Muslims train themselves toward ethical practice. In the process, however, a number of virtues are simultaneously cultivated, most important of these solidarity and friendship among people with a heightened awareness of morality and the sentiments that are considered to attend to such relationships: love, compassionship, and submission.

Clearly, then, in *sohbet* we have a situation that is not adequately analyzable in terms of what speakers' language is *describing* (Wittgenstein 2003; Tedlock 1983). The discourse is not merely meant to convey information, describe a state of affairs, or convince participants in a reasoned debate; it is to be thought of as action, meant to accomplish something, most significantly the establishment of certain relationships in and through which a metaphysic of influence leads to the constitution of virtuous selves modeled on the exemplary precedent of Prophet Muhammad. In other words, the truth of Sufi utterance here is not so much in its representational value but rather in its being or not being, or to use Austin's (1975) term, "felicitous"; the pertinent question to pose about a given *sohbet* is not "Was it true?" but "Was it done well?" To argue that the efficacy of linguistic disciplines in Sufism hinges on the pragmatics of utterance is not, however, to say that the *sohbet* discourses I have described is entirely non- or antirepresentational.

Naturally, the content of the sheikh's hadith lessons is important, and disciples are expected to take what he says very seriously. So much so, in fact, that I was told by one disciple, in response to a question about what kinds of issues he brought to the sheikh, that "you had better only bring important issues. But equally important, only ones that you want to hear a clear decision on, because once Esad hoja gives you his opinion on what to do, you had better do it!" Clearly, during *sohbet* the sheikh or his *vekil* is not just filling in time. *Sohbet* content is meant to be taken to heart by listeners and to become a part of their daily practice and the continuous devotional exercises members of the *cemaat* tended to undertake.

AMBIGUITY AND THE STATUS OF THE EVENT

In the legally hostile environment toward Sufism that is post–1925 Turkey, *sohbet* may be seen to function by virtue of ambiguous footing, that is, the potential for ambiguity on the part of listeners as to how they are meant to take what is being said, the status of what it is that is being said, and the specific illocutionary force it is intended to carry (Goffman 1981). For instance, a noninitiate might hear the verbally articulated intention to do, hold, or have a "*sohbet*" but may not ascribe any devotional sense to this term, assuming merely that a conversation or "talk" will ensue. Being able to recognize situations for what they are intended to be by brethren and to recognize that the landscape is veritably saturated with such pious efforts is, for members, an important part of the moral and spiritual maturity they strive for. Given that the mechanics of *sohbet* turn around the pragmatics of utterance, and much less around content, the situation for Sufis in Turkey today has also become generative of what Morson (1981) refers to as "boundary works," that is, events or texts that do not have a status that is entirely clear to the uninitiated observer, and therefore, the meaning of which may be ambivalent.[34]

Since Sufi meetings are by definition forbidden in Turkey, it is simply not possible for groups with a Sufi identity to meet publicly *as* Sufis. Until February 1997, one of the order's main public activities was the symposium or conference on a theme in Islamic or Ottoman history or culture, often sponsored and organized by a foundation (*vakıf*). As the head of the foundation informally affiliated (through overlaps in personnel) with the order said to me, "Modern Sufism largely consists of *vakıf* projects, like organizing seminars, symposia, and education. You can't get up and hold seminars loudly proclaiming, 'We are Naqsbandis,' but you do seminars about more general topics, in order to give people information." Some of these conferences were specifically dedicated to the legacy or memory of the former sheikh, Mehmed Zahid Kotku, and his training, spiritual techniques, and social, ethical, and moral influence on others. In this sense, the group can actually work with the ambiguities inherent in the issues of footing outlined previously. Is any given conference organized by the *cemaat* an instance of *sohbet*, that is, a Sufi Islamic discipline? Is it just an academic exchange? The answer depends on one's intentions in and modality of attending—for example, as an instance of moral edification about exemplary figures in one's traditions, as an instance examples to be emulated, or as an instance of informational exchange.[35]

One of the main public activities of the order is to organize symposia through their affiliated foundation, the foundation through which the order carries out much of its social and education activities. These symposia are open to the public. But in the event outsiders would have attended, the symposium would probably have represented a different event for them. For active and formerly active members of the order, this was an occasion to deepen their knowledge of Islam as observant Muslims trying to please God. It was also an occasion to deepen their knowledge of the particular Sufi tradition of which they have chosen to be a part. Knowledge per se is, in fact, something Esad Coşan has cultivated almost as a virtue, and many observers have commented on the disproportional percentage of members who have completed a university education. Indeed, in the eyes of many other orders, the Iskender Pasha group is quite intellectual and scholarly.

It can then seem like one thing is going on, for instance, a scientific conference, but in fact something else is taking place. It is this fact that has both allowed for the continued existence of Sufi associational life and transformed it. Now most activities are organized through a foundation, which is a legitimate form of association and incorporation in Turkey today. There are many foundations, offering modest scholarships and organizing symposia, the personnel of which are actually involved in the structured relations of seeker and knower of a Sufi order. As a result of this imbrication in the institutions of the modern state, new kinds of knowledge have become prestigious and sought, such as techniques of financial and personnel management, website construction and computer languages, and English.[36]

SUFI PRACTICE IN THE TURKISH ENVIRONMENT

We have seen how the formation of a virtuous self in this Islamic tradition is embedded in networks of companionship and contexts of disciplined discourse. The metaphysic of influence linked to an ethic of companionship understood to be central to the functioning of the constitution of morally structured dispositions to do good has been embodied in what I have called disciplines of presence; the embodiment of voices in bodies is a condition for the functioning of these disciplines. The force of *sohbet* utterance inheres in the equivocal, dissimulated status of the event that is transpiring. Thus, *sohbet* activates a certain metaphysic (influence of hearts) without the knowledge of many of the participants, but it is understood to be having its effect on them nonetheless. In other words, the "activity" or "action" that participants in a *sohbet* are party to may be ambiguous, as the status of the utterances constituting it is equivocal. The pragmatic action here is the formation of virtuous dispositions—a desire to submit to the will of God and to avoid sin—but the specific connection between *sohbet* attendance and such formation is not often elucidated in the context of a *sohbet*. The indexical features of the discourse (its relationship to the context in which it is being uttered) are occulted; it is never made explicit that the pragmatic effects of the fact of the discourse are what are sought, alongside and even over the content conveyed. But this does not mean that it should not be considered as part of a disciplinary practice, for as Asad notes, "Discourse involved in practice is not the same as that involved in speaking about practice. It is a modern idea that a practitioner cannot know how to live religiously without being able to articulate that knowledge" (1993, 36).

This works well in the contemporary Turkish environment, where the reason for the ambiguity is arguably twofold: first, again, these meetings, and Sufi orders themselves, are illegal; second, a growing sophistication in one's knowledge about how these practices work is considered to be the stuff of ethical-spiritual advancement (along several stages or stations [*derece* and *makam*]) and maturity. While *sohbet*s explicitly extol the virtues of coming together with those who are *sadıq*, or faithful and morally upright, those leading *sohbet*s would not explicitly make the reflexive point that the very *sohbet* contexts in which these exhortations are being made were themselves instances of such situations (which not only would be both risky, considering the prohibited nature of the gathering, but also could be considered in poor taste, as the speaker would be explicitly ascribing a virtuous status to himself).

The practices just described are oriented toward the formation of a moral self in and through ties of companionship and contexts of disciplined speech. The metaphysic of influence—"love"—understood to be central to the constitution of ethically structured dispositions oriented toward the good has been embodied in what I have called disciplines of presence. Behind these disciplines is an implicit theory of influence, the heart of a pervasive but subtle ethic of companionship, which holds that being with morally upright individuals entails one's *desiring* to also be a virtuously predisposed person; desire is thus disciplined through *sohbet*. Such face-to-face interaction has been an important feature of Islamic disciplines more generally over the centuries, as we saw in our discussion of logocentrism in Islam, and has been characteristic of many kinds of Islamic religiosity in republican Turkey (and elsewhere), functioning parallel to and in the interstices of official, state-sanctioned Islamic institutions like the Presidency for Religious Affairs, mosques, and religious (*imam-hatip*) schools (all of which are run by the state in Turkey). It is specifically face-to-face presence and its function in the constitution of dispositions that is undergoing transformation as a result of two main changes in Turkey: the expansion of privately owned mass-broadcast media and political and economic liberalization. Hence, this chapter serves as a baseline from which to evaluate these processes and what happens to Islamic discursive traditions in them in the next chapters, where I explore the proposition that the period of a "parallel religiosity" alongside officially sanctioned modes of religiosity may be coming to an end.

As heated debates unfold in Turkey and other parts of the world about the role of religion in public life, the processes described in this chapter are important for an understanding of Muslim modes of sociability such as they are cultivated and practiced reflexively. Are there tensions between *sohbet*, as this has traditionally operated in the formation of virtues, and the norms of civil society, in which religion is considered a matter of private, personal preference, while the public is the domain of secular reason? Building on this description of *sohbet* as it continues to function, I consider in the next chapter the ways in which the absence of the sheikh made itself felt, and how an attempt to overcome this was made by broadcasting *sohbet*s on the radio, multiplying questions of mediation and mechanical reproduction. I discuss the ways the group is attempting to work out a space for the functioning of moral discourse in public life. The relationships cultivated through *sohbet* are subject to reformulation in the context of the expansion of mass-broadcast media, specifically the use of radio by the order itself, whereby Islamic disciplines articulate with liberal models of public citizenship.[37]

PART III

ISLAM AND LIBERAL PUBLICS

CHAPTER 5

MUSLIM SOCIALITY AND MASS MEDIATION

SINCE 1994, AROUND THE TIME WHEN THE Refah Party won many important municipal elections in Turkey (including Istanbul and Ankara), the branch of the Naqshbandi order we have been examining had owned and run a radio station, AKRA.[1] In the atmosphere following the military's ultimatum of February 28 (1997), Esad hoja relocated to Australia, from where he made trips to Europe and North America, but never to Turkey. Esad hoja's move to Australia brought to a head questions regarding the structure, functioning, and even purpose of a Sufi order in the late twentieth century and focused discussions in the community about the role of broadcast media in the life of that and other Muslim communities. Esad hoja's move to Australia, and the conjuncture of economic, political, and technological contexts in which this happened, thus accompanied profound transformations in the structure and functioning of this order and in its relationship to broader Turkish society; indeed, I will argue that these transformations mirror transformations in Turkish society itself, specifically in regards to modes of religiosity, sociality, and those particular sociopolitical forms known as the public and civil society.

The transformations described in the pages that follow thus illustrate larger processes at work in Turkey and in many Muslim communities around the world. Many Islamic traditions of practice like *sohbet* are oriented toward the formation of a moral self in and through certain kinds of ties of companionship and contexts of discursive practice. Many of these Muslims would thus largely agree with Pierre Hadot when he writes, "True education is always oral because only the spoken word makes dialogue possible, that is, it makes it possible for the disciple to discover the truth himself amid the interplay of questions and answers and also for the master to adapt his teaching to the needs of the disciple" (1995, 62). This chapter explores how it is specifically this context of oral, face-to-face presence and its function in the

constitution of dispositions that is undergoing transformation as the lives of
the Sufi order in this study—and those of Muslims more generally in Turkey
and elsewhere—are increasingly articulated with mass-broadcast media in
which discourse increasingly takes the form of information and content to
be deliberated upon (Habermas 1989). The issue then becomes one of what
kinds of discourse—what genres with what historical status—and according
to what norms do such deliberations unfold. I argue that the radio broadcast
of the *sohbets* we examined in the previous chapter and their availability in
audio format was a step in the transformation of *sohbet* from what I have
described as a disciplinary practice into a generalized Islamic discourse analogous to and commensurable with other kinds of public discourse. Many of
these other kinds of discourse also have their attendant practices, to be sure,
namely, liberal civility characteristic of a classic public sphere. We will recall
that in such a public, a particular kind of secular reason is both crucial and
differentiated from religion in particular ways. What we see, in other words,
in the transformation of *sohbet* is a concrete instance of the transformation of
an Islamic tradition of disciplinary practice into a religion in the liberal mold.

MUSLIM PUBLICS

Recent studies have shown how media such as radio, television, audio cassettes, compact discs, and the Internet transform the quantity and content of
discourse among Muslims (e.g., the numbers and gender of participants in
negotiations of meaning and the specific kinds of reason articulated; Eickelman and Anderson 1999; Armbrust 2000; Hirschkind 2006; Miller 2007).
However, recent sociopolitical and technological changes also involve subtle
transformations in important features of Islamic discursive practices, like the
ones we have been examining, that are by definition oriented toward the formation of certain kinds of moral selves. In other words, the proliferation and
increased access to such media technologies involve subtle shifts in the relationship between discourse and practice and, more specifically, in the status
of discourse *as* practice. This is important for groups like the one studied here
who have a linguistic ideology regarding the role of language in the formation
of an ethical subject.

The expansion in Turkey of private radio since the mid–1990s and the
broadcast of "religious" programming is effecting the functioning of the kinds
of Islamic disciplinary traditions of practice we explored in the last chapter
(Öncü 1995). In one sense, this reproduces older shifts, debates, and anxieties
about the relationship between voice, mechanical reproduction, and the pragmatics of ethical subject formation (Benjamin 1968; Eickelman 1978). Work
on this question regarding the reproduction of words and sound and the
relationship between this reproduction and social forms in Muslim contexts

often examines the issue by taking up the matter of controversies surrounding the introduction of printing, which we examine at the end of this chapter (e.g., Messick 1993). Many of those I worked with took a decidedly long-term perspective on matters of media technology and Islamic traditions, stating that many of these technologies have come and gone over the years. For this reason, it is worth examining these earlier debates, which we do after exploring the case of how radio broadcast of Esad hoja's *sohbets* is changing Islamic traditions and leading to discussions among the religiously observant about the relationship between discourse, practice, and the institutions in and through which ethical Muslims selves can be formed.

It is on this point that I want to address the recent, now voluminous debates about "Islam and the public" (Salvatore and Eickelman 2004; Salvatore and LeVine 2005). Discussions about the relationship between the public sphere and Islam are arguably reflections of an attempt to be more theoretically sophisticated in describing the relationship between Islam, religion in general, and political modernity. What historical processes led to the emergence of a public? How is this related to capitalism and a bourgeoisie? What cultures and styles of reasoning were supposed to be part of such a public, and who was supposed to participate? Who, in practice, actually has participated? And what happened to religion in all of this (Meyer and Moors 2006)? It turns out that accounts of the emergence and functioning of a public, and public sphere, rehearse debates about the specificity of Western modernity in a nuanced and sophisticated way, attentive to both the norms and substance of political culture.

Armando Salvatore has recently argued that "maybe paradoxically at first sight, a transnational Islamic public is probably the most visible and perhaps most powerful instantiation of an exit strategy from the Westphalian frame—into a simultaneously subnationally and transnationally based type of 'sphere' that satisfies some key presuppositions of Habermas's communicative action, without fitting into the bounded character of a national citizenry" (2007, 49). Important to Salvatore's argument that some Islamic movements are likely to articulate transnational normative and substantive cultures of publicness is that, first, he tends to be talking about Muslims in postcolonial states or in Western Europe; second, he (I believe rightly) claims that these postcolonial states have generally failed to include most of their populations into their regimes of developmentalism and have also thus generally failed to deliver on their promises of welfare; and third, largely as a result of this, these states' legitimacy is practically in tatters (2007, 50–51). It is important for an understanding of Turkey and for a more comprehensive appreciation of the relationship between Islam and conceptions of the public to realize that none of these three points is quite the case in Turkey, certainly nothing like the extent to which they are in the countries to which he refers. However, on one point, Salvatore's observations are especially relevant to Turkey, and that is the centrality he gives to *maslaha*, or the common good or public interest. We saw in previous chapters that Ottoman reforms were usually carried out precisely in the name of *maslaha*, through *islah*, "renewal" or "reform." We also saw that it was as an incremental continuation of such renewal and reform efforts, keeping in mind the concrete historical contexts in which they took place, that late Ottoman and early republican institutions, discourses, and practices were formed. Admittedly, Salvatore was brushing broad strokes, and he concludes the article in which these issues are discussed by pointing out that it may be the case that very little can be said, in general, about Islam and publicness and that one must proceed on a case-by-case basis. We continue, then, our examination of Turkey as such a case.

One caveat, however, is important here. I agree with the critique of public-sphere debates as largely taking for granted the dubious claims to being grounded in nature (e.g., the autonomy of reason), explicitly or implicitly made in much liberal political theory since the time of writers like Locke (Somers 1995). I do not think that the issue of the relationship between Islam and the public sphere is necessarily *the* issue students of Muslim social formations during the last two centuries must address; it happens to be a crucial issue in Turkey because Turkey has explicitly committed itself to remaking itself in relation to political modernity, in some sense for decades, but most concretely in its recent European Union integration reforms. I develop this line of argument in the next chapter.

MASS MEDIATION AND MUSLIM SOCIALITIES

The question of the relationship between spoken, written, and printed words and embodied virtues in Muslim communities in recent centuries has been central to several discussions of Islam and modernity (Messick 1993; Eickelman 1978; Hirschkind 2006). There have been generally two kinds of concerns in such works, which we may call epistemological and disciplinary. The contrast between them is more one of emphasis, and the frameworks of such studies often overlap. On the one hand are studies that have focused on the implications for social relations of authority deriving from and upholding textual interpretation (Graham 1987; Messick 1993; Mitchell 1991, 128–60). On the other hand are those studies that explore the pragmatics of language use, paying particular attention to the ways in which language is central to the formation of a certain kind of person (Hirschkind 2006; Asad 1993). Where such studies converge is in exploring the connection between technological developments, the transmission of knowledge, and the reproduction of the human dispositions for appreciating that truth or knowledge.

This is an old concern, going back at least to the treatment we saw Plato give to it, but it is also one that is reflected in more recent Ottoman history. The focus on texts and debates about their interpretation and transmission is thus not merely a focus on "meanings" (though it is that as well) but more a matter of orientations, demeanors, perceptions, and sensory experiences that make up a particular kind of life. This is the same visceral level we saw operative for the Sufis in the last chapter.

Very few observant Muslims in Turkey denounce television, radio, or the Internet per se on religious, moral, or even "cultural authenticity" grounds, and none of those I interviewed and interacted with, inside the order and out, did.[2] I spoke with a manager at the AKRA radio station run by people affiliated with this Sufi order about how the establishment of the station changed things for the community.[3] He quickly related it to the broader changes Turkish society has been undergoing, by way of an interesting anecdote about Tayyip Erdoğan, who was then mayor of Istanbul and at the time of this writing is the country's prime minister:

A newspaper was established [by the order in the 1990s], a television station, a radio station, health clinics, and there is the Internet. These all changed everything [for us]. And also, maybe the most important thing is that before, as far as I saw, religious communities and secular communities were distant from one another. They weren't familiar with one another's organizations [yapılar]. The same goes for their [political] parties. But especially the private television stations [established in Turkey beginning in the 1990s], they changed the face of Turkey, everything. After that, these groups became more informed about [haberdar] one another. For instance, groups who saw one another as traitors came to the realization that, be it on the Right or the Left, they are both working for the homeland [vatan]. Tayyip Erdoğan was once asked (I read it in a reportage on him), "Is there anything you regret in your life? Many people see you as rather perfect [mükemmel]; you've accomplished a lot in your life." He said, "There is one thing I regret: that I didn't interact more with people outside of my own environment, didn't have more dialogue with them. I regret that I wasn't able to do this, not enough." So you see, Turkey has come to this point. In this sense, lots of things have changed among us.

For this person, who sees himself as an observant Muslim, along with an evaluation that the proliferation of privately owned mass-broadcast media brought massive changes to Turkish society, comes an estimation that one of the most important features of this proliferation is that one hears points of view that contrast with those held by the people one tends to socialize with on a day-to-day basis. This then recontextualizes one's own views; the structural significance of holding one view and not another changes. But it is one thing to "hear" someone's views and another to understand them. People from different backgrounds, that is, different constituencies coalescing around region, class, or religious observance, are increasingly "communicating" with one another through mass media. What happens to discursive genres like *sohbet*, which is both like and unlike communication, in such a context?

Cassette tapes of Coşan's *sohbet*s had been available for several years by the late 1990s, as had a more limited number of videos, and groups sometimes listened to or watched these in small gatherings in many cities and towns across the country. At the same time, many of the regional offices of the foundation affiliated with the order, as well as travel agencies run by affiliates of the order, would organize excursions to go see Esad hoja, either in Istanbul or in another location where he was spending time and holding *sohbet*s. I was told by several people that listening to these tapes was done either to reinforce a connection to Esad hoja that one already had or in anticipation of eventually going to see him. It was not the case that everyone I met who had listened regularly to such tapes did in fact go to see Esad hoja, but rather they expected that one day they would. Esad hoja's departure to Australia, new disciples' entry into the order after this, and the expansion of the order's media projects (especially their radio station) changed the place of mass-broadcast media in the functioning of the community's practices and the voice-presence-virtue formation we have been examining. The expansion of these media activities—starting with a publishing house in the early 1980s and magazines in the early 1990s—to include a newspaper, radio, and television station (short-lived though the newspaper and television station were) coincided with certain changes in the political economy, legal frameworks, and infrastructure of the country. As we saw earlier, the coup of 1980 and the resetting of institutions toward a right-of-center, world-market orientation is the background against which the order's use of radio should be seen.

In conversing on the significance of their radio and publishing concerns, those involved in their production and members of the order in general often referred to the notion of rendering service (*hizmet* from the Arabic *khidma*). One of the radio station's managers said of the media projects, "The fundamental point is to be of service to people, to be useful [*faydalı*], [and] to transmit information [*bilgi*] to Muslims." *Hizmet*, or taking care of the needs of others, has an important place in Islam and is considered by many authorities to be a pious act.[4] I was told by some who were involved in setting up the station that the debates about the religious permissibility of such a station for the community were extensive. These debates centered on the question of the permissibility of listening to music in general then, within this, on the permissibility of listening to singing and singing by men versus women and on the nature of programming, particularly the amount of sermons, Arabic lessons and Quranic exegesis to be included, at what hours, and so on. A *fiqh* [Islamic legal reasoning] committee was part of the station's governing body,[5] formed to research such issues, and it concluded that music and singing per se were not illicit, but that care must be given to the lyrics of the songs and lifestyles of the artists, one major effect of which was that the station played only Turkish music (initially "classical" or "artistic" [*sanat*] music, eventually more popular genres, but with a meticulous elision of Arabesque), Sufi music, and occasionally music from other Muslim cultures (see Stokes 1992).

The radio would usually start to be received in a given region in Turkey when a local sympathizer (*muhib*) established a receiver to pick up the satellite signal; [6] beginning some ten years later, it would also be carried over the Internet. Many members of the order expressed to me that the overall effects of the radio on the daily practices and life of the community were beneficial, given the fact that Turkish society—including rural areas—was increasingly saturated with broadcast images and discourses already. An important part of the broadcast programming on the radio station was previously recorded and (until 2001) live *sohbet*s by Esad hoja. It was also frequently related to me by the men I worked with that their sisters, mothers, and wives who spent more time at home were practically full-time listeners.[7] Station managers at the time of my research claimed AKRA had been one of the most widely received private radio stations in the country in its early days.[8] (A recent survey of 4,500 people from across the country shows that this is definitely not the case now; it does not even appear to be the station through which the largest percentage of people claims to listen to "religious" programming [Radyo ve Televizyon Üst Kurulu 2007].)[9]

I mentioned in earlier chapters that in the context of Islamist party gains in the 1990s, debates began in Turkey regarding what was called (mostly by skeptics) "Muslim capital." While some groups of observant Muslims in Turkey no doubt do dispose of considerable capital, it was clear to me that the Sufi group that I worked with was not one of them. The near bankruptcy of many of their projects and initiatives was a constant topic of discussion, and members were exhorted to find it in themselves to support them. The urgency and gravity of the situation could be clearly felt in these appeals.[10] Thus it is also important to point out that the media initiatives (e.g., their magazines, *Sağduyu* newspaper, and radio station) associated with the *cemaat* were businesses and were subject to market pressures like any other.[11] Attempts were made to attenuate this pressure by converting choice into a moral responsibility to support "good" businesses and services, but the compellingness of this quickly subsided in the eyes of those I worked with.

Managers impressed on me that theirs was a commercial radio station, deriving its operating budget from income generated and that this income came mainly from advertising. There was an entire department devoted to selling advertising, and they were by far the most serious of the employees I met. An indication of the place of advertising at the radio is suggested by the fact that the station asked in an online survey whether listeners prefer the products and services advertised on AKRA, and that 85 percent of respondents are reported to have said yes. This would clearly be a marketing tool for the station's advertising department. Audience and market came to be important factors in advertising decisions. At the time of my research, however, advertising was barely covering the station's operating expenses; if there were some Muslim businessmen making a handsome profit in the Turkish media business, those at AKRA were not among them (see Figure 5.1).

RADIO *SOHBET*: MEDIATION AND PRESENCE

Local participants in the foundation's activities were encouraged during live radio-broadcast *sohbets* with Esad hoja or a deputy and in various meetings to listen to the station. The foundation ran two dormitories in Istanbul—along with several subsidized apartments—for university students, at the time of my research, and several in regional cities with universities, which had partially

Figure 5.1   Photo taken in the AKRA FM studios, on the Anatolian side of Istanbul, in the late 1990s. On the left appears "AKRA FM" in Arabic script calligraphy, and beneath it in Turkish (in Arabic script), "seni seviyorum" (I love you). On the right is a world map and "the world listens to AKRA" in Turkish (in the currently used Latin script).

Source: Photo taken by author.

assimilated the functions of Sufi lodges (*tekke*, *dergah*) since the proscription of the Sufi orders and the disappearance of the lodges from the landscape in 1925. Esad hoja's *sohbet* on the radio (during the time of my fieldwork) at 8:00 P.M. would be the occasion for gathering in a common room, with sofas, cushions on the floor, and copies of the community's (short-lived, but relatively high-quality) *Sağduyu* and other newspapers.[12] This room was also where the television was, which was turned on solely (I was told with a smile suggesting otherwise) to watch the evening news on Channel 7, known for Islamist sympathies. One disciple related his experience of structured listening to the radio in the dorm:

[This is] one of the special qualities of the *cemaat*: its responsibility to inform. For instance, [the foundation directors] felt, "Let's educate these guys staying in our houses [apartments and dorms]." So, they recommended AKRA to us: "Look, at 8:30 in the evening [Esad] hoja efendi gives *sohbet* every day on AKRA. Listen to him, it would be a good idea," they said. Of course, we took this suggestion well, and we started listening at home. In fact, we got so into the habit that at 8:30 everyone would leave his lessons, gather in a room, and we'd turn on the radio. He would speak for a half an hour, and we'd drink our tea. Then we'd evaluate and discuss what he spoke about. I think we eventually heard most of his talks. They play them from cassettes, and it seems they don't have enough so they repeat them. So, that's how I got acquainted with hoja efendi's views.

This is an example of someone who only became familiar with Coşan and probably Sufism itself after entering the dorm and listening to *sohbet*s on radio. If a more senior *abi*, or relatively more experienced "big brother" (often no more that a few years older than the others), was in the group listening, he would often start the discussion afterward, or questions would generally be directed toward him, deferring to his relative authority. In the absence of such a person, the subsequent discussions were more decentered, with few patterns emerging from one to the other; some might even excuse themselves and leave without participating in the discussion. Discussions generally attempted to deepen an understanding of the *sohbet* by recontextualizing it and deriving generalizable principles from it that can be applied in various daily life situations. Comments by the *abi* often took this form, expounding on a principle that was emphasized in the hadiths read by Esad hoja, illustrating other life situations in which the hadith and discussed topics might be relevant, and so on. Sometimes discussions would arise regarding the meaning of the Arabic terms or the semantic extension of their roots. Thus an attempt was made to create a time and place for listening to Esad hoja's *sohbet*s analogous to the face-to-face *sohbet*s; however, the intimacy and compellingness of the face-to-face events had dissipated. The urgency to not miss a *sohbet*, characteristic of the face-to-face ones, was increasingly lacking.[13] The fact that Esad hoja's *sohbet*s were carried over radio, rather than television, was important to many members of the *cemaat*:[14]

> Radio speaks more to a person's imaginary [*hayal dünyası*]. I remember I used to listen to the radio. I didn't have any organized relationship to [the station], but I knew about it. I especially liked the *sohbet*s, the stories, and I would try to organize my life accordingly. For instance, the *sohbet* programs, for getting information; AKRA is very good for this. And there are people who are truly connected to [the radio] in their hearts, whose love is really from the heart. In that sense, AKRA really holds a special place in their world. Especially for religious people, it's even more important. I mean, there is sincerity and affection [*muhabbet*]. I think it's more effective than television. It's definitely effective; that's not even debatable.

As of early 2007, some 88 percent of listeners to radio stations in Turkey listened through a radio, while only 6.2 listened through the Internet (RTÜK 2007, 81). However among AKRA listeners, 51 percent listened through the Internet and only 36 percent through the radio (AKRA FM). I see two main reasons for the large difference, though I have conducted no systematic research on the topic. First, the RTÜK study shows that use of the Internet to listen to radio is more prevalent among both younger and more-educated listeners, which, as we saw in earlier chapters, are both features of the profile of those who tended to be members of the *cemaat* and participate in Esad hoja's *sohbet*s. Hence, it is not surprising that this continues to be an important audience (those who happen upon the station accidentally would be listening through the radio most likely, and thus would not be in a position to participate in the online survey). Secondly, it is likely that an important percentage of AKRA listeners are outside of Turkey and are Turkish speakers living in Europe, Australia, and North America, from where they would not receive a radio signal and would rely on the Internet broadcast.[15]

It is important to emphasize here that it will not be helpful to think of our problem as one of *sohbet* as a preexisting "ritual," having little, if anything, to do with "media," newly articulating with media by being broadcast on the radio: "It may very well be interesting and important for us, as anthropologists, to theorize the kinds of shifts that occur in the self-understandings and practices of a particular social group when, for example, a 'traditional' ritual is performed especially for television cameras. But we must also remember that the ritual is itself already a medium, with its own distinctive mechanisms and possibilities of objectification and translation. The problem, then, is less the meeting of 'culture' and 'media,' and more the intersection of two or more systems of mediation" (Mazzarella 2004, 353). Face-to-face interaction is thus not to be construed as "immediated," or not already mediated. Keeping in mind Derrida's critique of logocentrism (1976), we should see such face-to-face interactions as already structured by the dispositions and expectations built into those who participate in them.[16] However, mass-broadcast media are transformative of the kinds of relations we examined in the last chapter that have been generative of virtuous Islamic dispositions and of the kinds of associations in which they are reproduced. We can say, in short, that in the process of redefining the nature of the community and participation in it, the presence-practice-disposition equation is reformulated by the mediation of broadcast discourse as information. However these processes of reconfiguration of the ethical self cannot be understood in isolation from state projects of political modernization and economic liberalization that have defined the nature of the objects of governance and the modality of intervention in them (Foucault 2003b; 2008). It is through such processes of governmentality outlined in earlier chapters that things like the status of the family, of individuals, and of groups have largely been defined and transformed. Alongside the inherent interest of documenting such transformations and how they have been historically articulated with longstanding religious traditions, what is at stake in such transformations can now be formulated as the place of moral discourse in public life. Each of the terms in this phrase—"place," "moral," "discourse," and "public"—carries important weight, and it turns out to be how they are defined and lived that has a large bearing on their theoretical and practical importance in liberal democracies. Keeping in mind the histories outlined in earlier chapters, how ought we theorize the reformulations of presence described here? It is worth taking a moment to explore these issues against the background of earlier shifts.

PRECURSORS IN MECHANICAL REPRODUCTION

The expansion of radio is not the first time Muslim communities have dealt with issues of technological innovation and religious traditions. Toward the end of the eighteenth century, a French traveler in the Ottoman capital of Istanbul noted with astonishment that a bookshop had piles of copies of a work by Ibn Sina that had been printed in Rome in 1593, of which the shopkeeper lamented that he simply could not rid himself.[17] By contrast, manuscript editions of the same work were eagerly sought items despite their considerably higher price (Kuneralp 1992, 2). Printing had existed in Ottoman lands since the fifteenth century, apparently starting with the (Sephardic) Jewish community expelled from Spain in 1492 and later followed by Armenian (1567), Greek (1627), and European diplomatic and expatriate communities, all establishing their presses with the (apparently unwritten) stipulation that they not print any books in Turkish or Arabic. Permission to print works in the Arabic script was famously granted in 1727 by Sultan Ahmet III.[18] However, what is rarely noted is that a century and a half before this permission, a decree (*firman*) issued by Sultan Murad III in October 1588 had permitted the trade and importation of Arabic-letter works in Arabic, Persian, and Turkish.[19] Thus, by the time permission was granted by Ahmet III to begin printing Turkish- and Arabic-language works, printed works had been available in Ottoman lands for over a century, mostly printed in Western Europe (notably Rome) and then imported.[20] It was a pile of precisely these printed works imported from Europe that our French visitor had noted in the Ottoman capital. What was the impact of these printed works on the social reproduction of knowledge? This European's encounter with a pile of printed works in the book bazaar of Istanbul sheds considerable light on the matter of mechanical reproduction in the transmission of Islamic disciplinary traditions and stands as a precursor to the more recent changes we are examining in detail in this study.

In 1727, the same Ibrahim Müteferrika we met in Chapter 1 petitioned Sultan Ahmet III for permission to establish a printing house in partnership with one Sait efendi, son of the Ottoman envoy to Paris, Yirmisekiz Mehmet Çelebi.[21] Ibrahim Müteferrika was, we recall, a well-known scholar, translator, editor, statesman, and reformer who worked in the domestic and foreign services of the Ottoman state.[22] Today, he is probably most famous as the founder of the first Arabic-letter printing press in Ottoman lands and is also known as the author of a widely read treatise, *Risale-i İslamiye*.[23] Müteferrika composed a long petition to the sultan titled *Vesiletü-t Tibaa* (The means of printing), which enumerated ten benefits of printing. It was in the context of the broader reforms we examined earlier that Müteferrika made his proposal to establish a printing press in the name of reinforcing the empire and assisting Muslims to face the increasing challenge of the "Franks" to the west. The petition was careful to ensure that only works of a practical, and not religious, nature would be printed. The sultan's decree explicitly stipulates that permission is granted provided that works of law (*fiqh*), Quranic exegesis (*tefsir*), hadith, and theology (*kelam*) not be printed, in favor of dictionaries and works of history, medicine, astronomy, geography, logic, and travelogues.[24] The further condition for approval, presented in the text of the *firman* itself as the reasoning behind the permitting *fetva* (nonbinding legal opinion) obtained from the contemporary Sheikh ul-Islam Mevlana Abdullah, was that "several educated persons be appointed as proofreaders."[25]

The third of the ten benefits of printing Müteferrika enumerates in his petition is that "students of the sciences" studying from printed books are "safe from mistakes and are secure from wasting time . . . It becomes unnecessary to compare many texts in order to obtain a correct understanding, and this facilitates learning in the sciences" (Atiyeh 1995, 289). Of course, the fact that a work is printed does not vouchsafe it from error. Indeed, the ninth enumerated benefit refers to the Arabic, Turkish, and Persian works printed in Christian countries that were available in Ottoman lands and denounced their poor quality, characterizing them as full of misspellings and mistakes and of poor legibility. Moreover, Müteferrika continues, Christians are plying these books in trade and gaining substantial sums; Muslims ought at least take the upper hand in this trade in books in the three languages mentioned.

Both the quality of the printed texts and the authority of the established scholars of the law are assured in the scholars' role as proofreaders. That Müteferrika should mention this explicitly twice, and that it should figure prominently in the authorizing *firman*, suggests a point at which this business of printing of books in Arabic script was bound to be contentious, namely, that the control of the reproduction of texts was slipping out of the hands of the guilds of scribes, who occupied entire sections of bazaars, and of the ulema who supervised their products.[26] It appears certain that this point was, in fact, the crucial one for both advocates and opponents of the introduction of printing among Muslims (Messick 1993).

Due to various difficulties, Müteferrika would only eventually print some 17 titles over the course of 16 years, of runs from five hundred to one thousand. It seems that the main obstacle was public indifference to the printed works (Kuneralp 1992, 3). In other words, the mere appearance of these printed works did not apparently induce much desire for them. What this suggests is that it is not possible to infer a direction to social change simply from the presence of a given technology of mediation or the products of it. Such new technology, printing in this case, always emerges in a preexisting context of social practices, institutions, and culturally defined goals, which condition its reception.

Benedict Anderson has pointed to the role of what he termed print capitalism beginning in the late fifteenth century in Western Europe in the constitution of a consciousness of shared temporality, a necessary (though, he does not argue, sufficient) precondition to nationalist thought (1991). In contrast to the culture of the scribe, Anderson emphasized, print culture represented the inception of mass production and consumption of narratives susceptible to constituting consciousness of common interests among emergent liberal bourgeois and, in some cases, nationalist classes: "If manuscript knowledge was scarce and arcane lore, print knowledge lived by reproducibility and dissemination" (Anderson 1991, 37). The circulation of very large numbers of identical texts both required printing for its condition of possibility and was central to the formation of a bourgeois public, for the idea that anyone is, in principle, able to participate provided they follow the norms of reason and argumentation central to the self-conception of such publics. One might object, however, that book printing is not literacy, and in order for the transformations to which Anderson refers to occur, it is clear that transformations must have taken place in other spheres (e.g., education), to which the idea of manuscript versus print culture would have been related.[27]

Thus, Anderson argues that a specific regime of technology and power—print capitalism—was important for the emergence of a consciousness of simultaneity across vast spaces and that this was necessary to the constitution of a sense of community in the nation and to the practice of nationalism (1991, 36–46). Yet compelling as this formulation is, the notion of print capitalism is analytically underelaborated in important respects and elides key aspects of the fact that writing and printing have certain specific functions as technologies of mediation in local cultural formations and relations of power. Manuscript and print texts do not instantaneously establish similar relations among people in various historical and cultural contexts merely by their presence. What was arguably important in the impact of printed texts in the Muslim world is the institutional and social setting in which they have been used. Messick (1993) argues that the crucial issue here has to do with how the relationship between texts and authority is changed with printing, mass access to texts that comes with printing, educational reforms, *and* mass education. In this vein, Eickelman writes, "With the spread of mass higher education in the Muslim world, access to the Qur'an as well as to other books and the ways of knowing inculcated by them, has shifted in form. Religious authority in earlier generations derived from the mastery of authoritative texts studied under recognized scholars. Mass education fosters a direct, albeit selective, access to the printed word and a break with earlier traditions of authority" (1992, 259). Mass-institutionalized education and printing transformed the nexus that encompasses scriptural text, authority, and the moral subject, and this is an important background against which to situate more-contemporary developments in media technologies and Islamic traditions.

Thus, while we acknowledge that certain media enable and reinforce certain relationships between people, voices, texts, bodies, and so on, it should be clear that this is not a technological determinist argument. The relationship between media technologies and social change has been given a classic treatment by Raymond Williams several decades ago, with specific attention paid to television (1992). Williams argued against a technological determinism that would see the key parameters in the study of this relationship as being found in the nature of the technology in question, as this would largely determine the direction of social change. Rather, technology is a good site for studying social change, Williams argued, as it inevitably leads us back to the heart of social process and power, because the effects of a given technology are not determined by the nature of the technology itself but rather by preexisting relations of power structuring discourses, practices, and desires in a given environment. While Williams was more concerned with the relationship between mass media and the maintenance of certain hierarchies, our adjacent concern is with the purposes to which mass-media technologies are put, purposes that may be difficult to translate into another context and that may be culturally specific. What is primarily determinant of the nature and logic of the effect of mass mediation, in other words, are the historically and culturally variable practices and purposes to which media technologies are put.[28]

What the example of the introduction of printed texts (before printing itself) to the Ottoman Empire shows, then, is that there is nothing natural or universal about the desirability of printed over manuscript texts. The same can be said, for that matter, about scriptural writing in general.[29] The presence and circulation of printed texts per se seems to have had a negligible effect on the functioning of Islamic institutions in the central Ottoman lands, at least until the late nineteenth century. When Müteferrika petitioned for and set up his press, however, he was, in effect, altering the economy of power within the scholarly and educational establishment. The rapid reproduction of books that are all identical may be a positive feature of the development of a certain class of people (e.g., bourgeois selves constituted around private interest) but not necessarily others (e.g., scribes). It is a question of what sorts of modes of relations among people—what kinds of sociality—one wants to establish, reinforce, or impede and a question of how the printed text will function in an environment in which other modes of transmission of knowledge already exist.[30] As Mazzarella writes, "The formal and material properties of a medium arise out of and crystallize a socially and historically determinate field of possibilities. Having emerged, the medium then recursively remediates each new social context to which it becomes relevant, often at great spatial and temporal removes from its origins. Insofar as it requires and enables particular social relations, a medium starts to appear definitive of certain socio-historical forms—colonialism, nationalism, transnationalism. This process should not be confused with technological determinism . . . We are registering the historical effect of mediation" (2004, 358).

Carey has made a similar point regarding the invention of the telegraph in the mid-nineteenth century, which with its foundational role in the expansion of mass circulation daily newspapers, "produced a new series of social interactions, a new conceptual system, new forms of language, and a new structure of social relations" (1992, 70). In examining religion, language, subject formation, and the liberalization of media in Turkey, we are witnessing "new social interactions," "new conceptual systems," "new forms of language," and "new structures of social relations." I would argue that we are in a similar situation when we turn to the reproduction of *sohbet* on the radio. Reaching more people and minimizing limitations of time and place, this would appear to be an unmitigated "benefit" for this community of Muslims. However, the broadcast of *sohbet* renders problematic its relationship to the kinds of spiritual exercises we explored in the last chapter. How so?

AMBIVALENCE OF FRACTURED PRESENCE

Among members of the community, there was a degree of ambivalence with regard to Esad hoja's absence. On one hand, the nature of Sufism and the connection between the sheikh and disciple is supposed to be one that would not be profoundly affected by one's ability or inability to actually be with the sheikh on a regular basis. On the other, there are numerous sayings in sources about the importance of being together with one's sheikh and with morally edifying company.[31] Each of these views was present in the statements of members of the order. Much of the ambiguity of sentiment about the absence of Esad hoja hinged upon the value of actually being in the presence of the sheikh. Many of my interlocutors fluctuated back and forth on this point, but their claims that his absence was not debilitating were usually linked to statements about their ability to hear his lessons on the radio. The following comment by a disciple was typical:

> Being connected [*bağlı*] [to hoja efendi] has a different significance [than merely listening to him]. Religiously [*dinen*], in Sufism there is the phenomenon of receiving the [initiatory] lesson. If one has received the lesson, one is considered differently, and among ourselves we say, "That one has received the lesson," [*dersli*] and so on, meaning his or her degree of attachment is a bit higher. Others listen to [hoja efendi], like him a lot, and take his suggestions to heart but may not take the lesson [i.e., become a formal initiate]. And this doesn't constitute a negative situation from [our] perspective. Doing it is an advantage, perhaps even a point of preference from time to time. But, there are even those who have received the lesson by telephone. The aim, not physical unity, is the most important. Spiritually [*ruhen*], thinking, and believing the same thing is a serious unity [*birlilik*]. Physical unity is nice, but it just isn't possible now. The world is small, anyway. It's even hard in Turkey.

Face-to-face *sohbet*s with Esad hoja were not held that often outside of Istanbul when he was in Turkey, but it was important that people felt that if and when they wanted to they *could* travel to see him. The radio *sohbet*s were initially, for those already in the order, a placeholder during those absences, which could ideally be overcome through excursions or trips organized by regional offices of the foundation associated with the order or by travel agencies run by affiliates of the order. The fact that relatively few of those who considered themselves to be members of the order likely participated in such outings to see Esad hoja does not diminish the emotional role the radio *sohbet*s fulfilled as bridging the times when one was not able to attend in person. Thus, statements about Esad hoja's absence not being debilitating generally assumed the preexistence of a disposition formed in the context of face-to-face *sohbet*s, so the effects of Esad hoja's absence were not felt to be so destabilizing. His radio *sohbet*s could thus both assume and reinforce the morally structured habitus discussed in the last chapter, a formation whose relationship to the *sohbet* context, we recall, is crucial but implicit. If absence and broadcast mediation enable one to activate dispositions previously formed in the context of presence, what kinds of dispositions do they allow to be formed in the first place?

Very often, those who claimed that Esad hoja's absence was not so significant eventually also mentioned that they did miss the "atmosphere" (*ortam*, or *hava*) of his *sohbet*s in person, like the following member of the order: "It was passed on through discussion, debate, at the mosque. Everyone would come, children would come, women. Everyone would come and talk with one another. And what was important was that everyone saw one another as brothers and sisters. There was an incredible amount of mutual assistance and support. What the *hoja* said on Friday about Muslims in general is even more widespread in Sufism, that people help one another, they are friends, they can depend on one another. Helping people is worship. Serving people, helping them, giving." In particular, it was in connection to those who were newly entering the *cemaat* and their experience of it without Esad hoja that the issue of context and presence inevitably arose, and we saw this in Ahmet earlier. In Esad hoja's absence, of course, *sohbet* lessons continued and were led by a deputy. The broadcast of Esad hoja's own *sohbet*s on the radio was also clearly significant, and attempts were made to listen to them regularly. There are important differences, however, in the way people spoke about the face-to-face and radio *sohbet*s. After they began to be broadcast, there was more emphasis in discussing the function of *sohbet* on "service" (*hizmet*) to the community through informing rather than on the disciplinary functions of restructuring one's dispositions. There was a subtle continuum from one to the other, especially for those who used to attend Esad hoja's *sohbet*s and then listened on the radio.

An index of the change from face-to-face to radio *sohbet* was bodily posture. During face-to-face *sohbet*s by Esad hoja or a deputy, listeners sat on the floor, upright, careful not to let their bodies go limp or display lack of attention, in various postures modeled on those taken while listening to Friday sermons at mosques. Listeners to radio *sohbets* did not display the same care. Tea was often served, and one might even scan the headlines of a newspaper while listening. Clearly, the context into which the *sohbet* is inserted and the sentiments and attention it is in proximity to are quite different in the two situations. *Sohbet* was thus subtly being transformed from a discipline of presence into something else, as it was mediated by radio and broadcast. How do these shifts relate to the differentiation and transformation of spheres of social life—into domains like the cultural, economic, religious, and political—that has been under way in the late Ottoman Empire and republican Turkey? We arrive again at the social function of broadcast media in a Muslim community and its articulation with both preexisting modes of communication and ethical practice (Eickelman 1992; Hirschkind 2006).

MEDIA IDEOLOGIES AND THE QUALITIES OF SOCIALITY

It is important to recall that the simultaneous expansion and penetration of privately owned mass media into everyday life is occurring alongside a liberalizing of conditions for discussion and debate regarding identity and the political in Turkey. In other words, the expansion of these mass media since the mid–1990s creates new conditions of possibility, but what is specifically enabled depends on these broader developments. What norms regarding politics and conduct are considered desirable and prestigious? As we have seen, these are not necessarily generated internally "by" the media in question but rather are defined in a context of power relations of which mass media are only a part. As we saw in the context of our discussion of print media and institutional change in previous centuries, the appearance of these media and their effects are intimately bound up with other practices and institutions and the relations of power that are established, altered, or inhibited. Hence, it would be misguided to approach the use of mass media by the community of Muslims discussed in this book by merely assessing the "impact" of media on discursive practices, for the latter are already mediated. As Mazzarella points out, it is not so much a matter of media meeting preexisting cultural practice but "more the intersection of two or more systems of mediation" (2004, 353).

However, it is also the case that definitions of how media work and of their efficacy in the formation of certain kinds of selves according to particular norms are culturally variable.[32] We might call these, in analogy to linguistic ideologies, "media ideologies." What distinguishes work at the interface of a given tradition (recalling our discussion of tradition in earlier chapters) and mediation is that most religious traditions have the following: first, normative concepts (i.e., grids in terms of which judgments can be made) regarding what the human is and established methods for renewing

these concepts; second, reflexively elaborated techniques that involve pragmatic dimensions of language and that have a history of generating discourses about themselves; and third, an understanding of how language
works and what its role is in the constitution of particular kinds of selves.
These are somewhat different issues than the problem of the relationship
between media, mediation, and culture in general. They overlap with the
field often known as language ideology, which looks at "the cultural system of
ideas about social and linguistic relationships, together with their loading
of moral or political interests" (Irvine 1989, 255).[33] Moreover, as we saw in
the last chapter, this linguistic ideology—or cultural system of thinking about
how language works—is itself part of specific practices and is in the case we
are examining relatively esoteric. What a given group thinks mass-broadcast
media do to linguistic practice is important, especially for groups like the
Muslims we are examining who have elaborated disciplinary practices out of
linguistic practices like *sohbet*.

Islamic practices structured around the disciplines of presence described
earlier, as techniques of formation of a moral self, are under strain, and the
use of radio as an attempt to maintain a sense of community actually introduces structural changes to the group's devotional practice. To Muslims like
these, who have elaborated an important disciplinary tradition of ethical self-
formation out of the cultivation of disciplines of presence, the anonymity and
mass broadcast of knowledge and information is problematic. The transformation of utterance and companionship into broadcast information redis-
tributes voices and bodies and thereby redefines the nature of the community
and of participation in it. The radio was transformative, both in terms of the
kinds of relations that are generative of virtuous dispositions and of the kinds
of contexts in which these relations reproduce themselves. The *sohbet*s broadcast on AKRA in the name of service to Muslims are now merely another
instance of Islamic content on one of tens of radio stations operating in the
country. In substituting radio listening for face-to-face *sohbet*, it may become
difficult to sustain the quality of relationships central to the functioning of
the disciplines described here, which are not the sole means for inculcating
dispositions subtending ethical conduct and the life of an ethical Muslim
community, to be sure, but a set of Islamic traditions oriented to this end
with a long history nonetheless.

This means that there is a qualitative difference in the kinds of selves
formed through these practices of listening, and I argue that what were previously specific Islamic disciplinary practices of listening and companionship
now overlap with the kind of deliberation central to liberal political culture
and the consumer orientation of capitalism. There are tensions between
the ideals and function of *sohbet* as a mode of sociality and that regnant in

modern civil society; they sit uneasily together, but there are ways in which each codes its accommodation of the other.

NOSTALGIA FOR IMMEDIATION?

Mazzarella recently noted that "as anthropologists of media and globalization we confront a world in which cynicism about the social functions of the media and romanticism about the authenticity and value of culture are equally widespread. These two phenomena are, moreover, related, and their interrelationship arises, in part, out of the profound ambivalence that a heightened self-consciousness about the mediated quality of our lives has produced" (2004, 356). On the status of language and media in Islamic disciplines and institutional modernization, I had an insightful conversation with a respected media analyst, researcher, and author known to have Islamist sympathies, who was at the time on the communications faculty at one of the best private universities in Istanbul: "Turkey has experienced, to a much more profound extent than any other country, a fracture [*kırılma*], and change in the value put on the word, on speech [*sözün değeri*]. Previously, the ulema's word had a social value. It had an influence on social relations. In Turkey words have been left empty. There are no rules now; who said what, where, why, how, to whom, no longer has any importance. There's a verbal anarchy [*söz anarşisi*]." My interlocutor is expressing here the kind of logocentric epistemology and sensibility we saw earlier, whereby knowledge is traceable to speakers and linked to the authoritative status of the one pronouncing them (Messick 1993; Graham 1987; Derrida 1976). There are a number of anxieties and destabilizations that are perceived to accompany the move from face-to-face interaction ("immediation" in Mazzarella's [2004] phrasing) to mass broadcast, as the tie between the truth of statements and the authority of speakers is broken (see Basso 1989). One cannot simply replace one kind of mediation with another, for embodied voice, scriptural text, and radio broadcast are all different in the structure and qualities of the relationships they establish between people.[34]

The radical fracture of words from their source is, for this specialist, the defining feature of the Turkish Muslim experience of modernity: truth recedes out of reach. There is here an intimate linkage of the effectiveness of words to convey meaning to institutional transformations. Not only are, as he put it, "words cut off from their source" but also the classes of people (ulema in this case) who historically have been in a position to authoritatively interpret meanings are not being reproduced, he claims, and the modern subject is left at the mercy of the charms of surfaces. This amounts to a succinct argument for the existence of a crisis of logocentrism in the modern mass mediated environment and its inevitable relation to the problematic authoritativeness of institutions and statuses for Muslims in the modern world.

These concerns were reflected among many of the members of the order, among whom there was similarly a generalized, low-level anxiety that what they felt to be a local, neighborhood-based, face-to-face sociability was evaporating and that this was problematic for ethical conduct (see Meeker 1994). As a 28–year-old member from Istanbul put it, recalling his early introduction to the *cemaat*,

My friend used to invite me to the mosque; it was through him that I got to know [the *cemaat*]. He was my childhood friend; he's two years older than me. So we were neighborhood friends, you know. I'm now 28, so this was about 18 years ago, and in Istanbul, you know, childhood and neighborhoods were different then. Neighborhood friendships [*mahalle arkadaşlığı*] were closer, warmer [*canlı*, lit. "lively"], not like now. These days, neighborhood friendships have declined. Why? Television, computers; kids now are shut up in their houses. But 15, 20 years ago, neighborhood friends would play ball, would play together. And there weren't many cars . . . There were more traditional types of games. So in those days, the old kinds of friendship, neighborhood friendships were more widespread, unlike today. Now this has practically disappeared. So it was one of these friends who first invited me to a *sohbet*, and we used to go to the Sunday afternoon [*ikindi*] hadith *sohbets*.

In such recountings of their introduction to the order, networks of face-to-face interaction were often the mechanism through which the speaker hears about and was encouraged to go listen to Esad hoja. The key dimension here was trust; given that one knew one's friend and trusted him, one would be likely to take his suggestion favorably.

Such ambivalences about the fracturing of neighborhood ties in general, and about the expansion of the role of mass broadcast media in one's life and alongside the absence of Esad hoja, echo longstanding, classic discourses of disappearing authentic community in the face of industrialization and migration. More recently, the well-known scholar Şerif Mardin inadvertently caused something of a storm of discussion on television talk shows and in newspaper columns when he referred to "neighborhood pressure" (*mahalle baskısı*) in influencing what many people in Turkey do and do not do. Mardin was criticized by both conservative Muslims, who thought he was suggesting that there is something illegitimate about what they take to be community norms and informal mechanisms of enforcement (which they claim all societies have), and by archsecular Kemalists, who see in discussions of the operating of such information mechanisms, and especially at the level of the neighborhood, reminders that their country is not yet modern (e.g., still a grouping of "communities" rather than a "society").[35]

STRUCTURAL TRANSFORMATION OF
A DISCIPLINARY PRACTICE

In his book *The Public and Its Problems*, originally published in 1927, John Dewey writes,

> Consideration of [the] condition of the generation of democratic communities and an articulate democratic public carries us beyond the question of intellectual method into that of practical procedure. But the two questions are not disconnected. The problem of securing diffused and seminal intelligence can be solved only in the degree in which local communal life becomes a reality. Signs and symbols, language, are the means of communication by which a fraternally shared experience is ushered in and sustained. But the wingèd [*sic*] words of conversation in immediate intercourse have a vital import lacking in the fixed and frozen words of written speech. Systematic and continuous inquiry into all the conditions which affect association and their dissemination in print is a precondition of the creation of a true public. (1984a, 371)

Dewey's point is less epistemological than pragmatic: in the constitution of a "public" it makes a qualitative difference if people come together in debate and conversation. For a particular kind of political culture Dewey calls liberal and democratic, people aiming to form a community need to be forming their tastes, habits, and dispositions through face-to-face contact with one another. While Dewey's romance of the small town is well known and problematic, we can detach his situating of authentic community in the town from his more general point that a public is not merely a space in which a preexisting community deliberates on information; it is a performative space in which a particular kind of community emerges in the first place. As such, the kinds of conversations people have among themselves are linked to the logistics and infrastructure of mediation, as certain ("vital") habits of feeling come to be formed and reinforced in public life.

This is a useful way of thinking about the changes in Islamic traditions that have occurred with the institutionalization of mass-broadcast media and, to a certain extent, literacy (Eickelman 1992). Islamic scholarly traditions, in fact, have had quite a bit to say about the epistemological and ethical dimensions of writing texts, interpreting them, and putting them to specific purposes, such as making a juridical claim (Messick 1993; Graham 1987). Habermas's treatment of the notions of the public and publicity was famously ambivalent on the issue of the kind of "social integration" necessary for a public sphere to properly function: "[Habermas's formulation] was a model resting on a distinctive dialectic between inwardness and publicness, which subverts and sometimes suppresses some fundamental characteristics of more ancient and often more complex trajectories of construction of public argument" (Salvatore 2007, 48).

As Hadot and MacIntyre have argued regarding philosophy, discourses may be part of broader programs, "practices of spiritual exercises," and not ends in themselves. Hence, such discourse is profoundly marked by the conditions in which it is produced and for which it is meant to be employed. Thus, in approaching "practices of spiritual exercise" as central to Islam, we may document concretely what is at stake in the issues attending mass broadcast media in a Muslim community.[36] Especially when central exercises work through language as discursive practice, the mass broadcast of language puts a great deal at stake. We thus can come to appreciate what is at stake in the secularization of a religious disciplinary practice in Turkey.[37] This is an example of what happens when Islamic traditions articulate with liberal politics and capitalist consumerism, showing that there is a multiplicity of reasons—including religious ones—why various groups come to see themselves as and participate in the public.[38] This renders plural and heterogeneous the temporality of this public (Connolly 2005), which is a source of anxiety for statist, archsecular people in Turkey and elsewhere.[39]

With *sohbet* being broadcast on radio, it is transformed from a multileveled, ambiguous discipline into information; the context, reception, and function of the discourse are altered (compare Benjamin 1968; Eickelman 1992). The specifically "Sufi" quality of the discourse as disciplinary practice is being transformed into generalized Islamic *content*. (Most listening to the order's radio station are probably unaware it has any relationship to a Sufi order and take it simply as a station sympathetic to Islamic traditions and sensibilities). In a sense, such transformations are not necessarily a departure from longstanding Sufi traditions, whereby Sufis' outward activities have long been oriented toward calling non-Muslims to Islam per se (rather than to Sufism specifically) and Muslims in general to greater piety and discipline in their practice. We might recall that Sufis have historically played a very major role in the expansion of the Muslim community on its frontiers (Hodgson 1974).

The processes described here are much more pervasive and important for an understanding of the nature and status of religious traditions of discourse and practice in politically and economically liberalizing environments. The public sphere does not merely include them; they are transformed, placed in different contexts, and put to different purposes. *Sohbet* on the radio sounds like simply a lesson or informational talk, which a listener changing the dials may stumble upon. The hearer, who likely has no idea that the lesson was originally an instance of disciplinary *sohbet*, may listen to the discussion, weigh its merits according to criteria of reason that may have nothing specifically Islamic about them, and may either find them "interesting" or change the channel. *Sohbet* is newly recontextualized side by side next to heterogeneous genres. Moreover, personal choice becomes foregrounded in this situation, and the shared background of Islamic norms (or "authority," to use Arendt's [1968] term) described previously can no longer be taken for granted.

Central to theoretical discussions about the nature of political modernity is the ability of participants to communicate their views to each other and to those in positions of legitimated power. As such, an important amount of work on modern political culture has been concerned with the history of communication technologies—initially printing, but more recently radio, television, and the Internet (Warner 2002). Habermas's famous formulation of the emergence of modern democratic political culture saw it as intimately bound up with the coalescence of a sphere of reasoned public debate among an increasingly economically and politically powerful bourgeois class who began to express their views on matters of public policy in writing, mostly in circulated journals, and without recourse to (especially religious) authority (Habermas 1989; Kant 2007). Thus, important aspects of the logic and form of political modernity are to be sought in the structural transformations wrought by new forms of mediation, as in the new kinds of relationships that were established between people that were in tension with older ones.[40] One of the more obvious examples of the new tensions thus created is the effect appeals to reason bracketing claims to authority based on status had on the social and political status of certain classes and groups, most notably those who came to be seen as religious specialists.[41] It turns out that how religious traditions of discourse and practice are transformed by new kind of mediation is central to debates about the nature of the public sphere in Muslim environments. It is to such debates, and the discourses and practices associated with them, we turn in the next chapter.

CHAPTER 6

LIBERAL ISLAMIC RELIGIOSITY

IN FEBRUARY 2001, ESAD HOJA WAS TRAVELING outside of Sydney, Australia, when he was killed, along with his son-in-law, in a car accident. Esad hoja's body was brought to Turkey for burial, and some controversy erupted when the then-coalition Democrat Left Party-Nationalist Action Party-Motherland Party cabinet approved plans to have Coşan buried in the cemetery attached to the Süleimaniye mosque where sheikh Mehmet Kotku and previous sheikhs in this Gümüşhanevi branch of the Naqshbandi order lay buried (and where we previously saw members of the order tending the graves and tidying up the cemetery). The decision was vetoed by then-President Sezer on the grounds that the constitution does not allow special privileges to some (Süleimaniye no longer being an active cemetery accepting burials), and Coşan was then buried in Eyüp, a center of pilgrimage and piety just beyond the historical walls of the city.[1] Funeral prayers were conducted at the Fatih mosque, led by a former imam of the Iskender Pasha mosque, Mikdat Kutu, who also announced during his homily that leadership of the community had passed to Esad hoja's son, Nureddin Coşan. Nureddin's ability to continue the life of the order in a traditional structure was somewhat unclear, and I have been told by former members that both the number of the order's adherents and the order's future were uncertain.

Why would its future be uncertain? It might have been otherwise, but I think two things were paramount in bringing about this situation. First was the relative inexperience of Nureddin and his training in non-Islamic disciplines (he obtained a MBA in the United States) and hence his relative lack of authority on Islamic topics. Shortly after Esad hoja's death in February 2001, one of his former students, who was known to have been close to him, expressed some doubts that the sheikh had left written instructions on who was authorized to succeed him (*icazet*) (Oğhan 2001). Commentators close to the community also pointed to the voluntary nature of Sufi orders; in the event that someone is brought to lead it who does not satisfy the base or core of the group, it is very likely that people will start distancing themselves from it, and it will, in time, shrink into insignificance. Speaking of Nureddin's assumption of the community's leadership, one commentator said (invoking a topic that, as we saw in earlier chapters, has been controversial among Sufis for over a century), "History has shown that as a result of 'cradle sheikhs' or 'cradle ulema'—that is appointing people not according to qualities like how deserving they are or according to their competence and authority but rather merely because they are someone's son or grandson—that so many *medreses* and Sufi lodges broke up and disappeared."[2] Nureddin was not a well-known figure in the community, though he had been prominent in the management of businesses for Server Holding—the umbrella group for the community's schools, media, travel agency, health care, and construction companies—and arguably had been trained more for business management than for leadership of the Sufi *cemaat* in the role of sheikh. It is an interesting indicator of the outlook of Nureddin's father that the sheikh should have directed his son toward training in business management rather than Islamic disciplines.

The second factor is the changed context in Turkey, in which it is arguably less important for a "parallel sphere of religiosity" to exist outside of and alongside official, state-sponsored religious institutions (often seen in the past by religious conservatives as excessively guided by principles of secular nationalism), as devout people increasingly participate in society, economy, and politics. Two attendant processes exist here. First is the liberalization of Muslim conceptions and practices of politics, whereby conservative Muslims attenuate their demand for normative hegemony (i.e., openly or subtly insisting that everyone ought to share their norms and live accordingly) and subsume adherence to such norms to the sphere of personal choice; the discourse and style of the Adalet ve Kalkınma Party (AKP) is illustrative of this (examined shortly), as are developments we will examine among scholars of Islam and in broader Islamic discourse and practice in the country.[3] At the same time, the public in Turkey is becoming more heterogeneous and plural relative to what it has been during the course of the republic, with groups that had been relatively marginal vis-à-vis official secular nationalism openly participating in the economy, in popular culture, and in politics (e.g., constituencies formed around gender issues or ethnic-minority identities). The question then arises whether there is necessarily "a single, authoritative basis of public reason and/or public ethics that governs all reasonable citizens regardless of 'personal' or 'private' faith" (Connolly 1999, 11). Debates surrounding this issue cleave along certain tendencies in political thought.

Since the 1990s in Turkey, the increasing prestige of the public-private distinction central to liberal political culture has been reorganizing preexisting conceptions and institutionalizations of these spheres, leading to a redistribution of attention and authorities regarding sentiments and conduct. Some hitherto private issues are increasingly considered public (e.g., domestic violence), while some previously public (national) ones are increasingly considered a matter of private preference or choice (e.g., religion). As we have seen, the common shorthand for the changes taking place in Turkey since the early 1980s, and more intensively since the late 1990s, is liberalization, a restructuring of politics, economy, and social life around the basic concepts of liberalism: freedom and equality of individuals, strong citizenship and civil rights, strong property regimes, transparency of the state, and so on. All of this is in line with European Union (EU) entry protocols, which the AKP had been pursuing energetically in its first five years in power. In this context, Turkey has seen an easing of regulations regarding the establishment of interest groups, associations, and to a certain extent foundations. While many observant Muslims in the country (including this Naqshbandi community) have formed such associations and foundations, some of the most important foundations are arguably research foundations. These have a significant impact on Islamic discourse and practice in the country.

This chapter, looking specifically at examples of Islam as a religion on the liberal model, examines several aspects of the changing place of religion in the transformation of politics and society in Turkey as centered on something called private belief and personal choice. As we have seen, this process in Turkey is both largely complete and quite unusual in the Muslim world, and it is a process that had its roots in calculation and reasoning by late Ottoman Islamic scholars and statesmen in a context of responsibility of rule. I argue that it is now being completed by a new cadre of Muslim citizen-politicians who consider themselves to be pursuing good governance by arguing for the institutionalization of liberal political culture, though they rarely use the terms "liberal" or "liberalism." They are reasoning for these moves both on the grounds of liberal culture (invoking concepts like the rights of citizens) and in terms of internal debates among Muslims on good governance and the history of institutional change, leading them to situate and contextualize these changes to suggest that they are in continuity with Turkey's "own history," which I have sketched out in earlier chapters. How do Muslims like those we have been discussing experience these changes?

LIBERAL MUSLIMS: THE AKP

The elections of November 2002 gave the AKP an overwhelming majority in the assembly and enabled it to form the first single-party government in 15 years.[4] With respect to foundations and the incorporation of civil groups as associations, the AKP favors liberalizing regulation, which is conveniently in line with the views of its moderately conservative supporters and with EU entry protocols. This and similar convergences between EU liberalization and the discourse of the moderate religious right (as it is known in Turkey) make the Kemalist establishment—not to mention the military—nervous.[5] It has led to the ironic situation in which a majority of observant Muslims in Turkey have been pro-EU entry (at least until roughly 2006), while the military and Kemalist establishment sought a slower reform.

AKP discourse and legislation tends to be centered on personal freedoms, civil rights, and in principle, a strengthening of civil protections through which, for example, one may sue on grounds of discrimination. Crucially, religion is also approached in AKP discourse in the liberal terms of freedom of choice and conscience. Their party program, announced at an inaugural press conference in August 2001, later the same year Esad hoja died, lays out this liberal conception of politics and religion. The atmosphere of the party's inauguration ceremony was extremely festive, with Erdoğan an extremely popular figure (though not without his enemies, of course). The inauguration opened with atmospheric music penned by the Greek-born musician Vangelis, certainly a sign that the party was stepping out of the usual lines for Turkish political parties regarding nationalism. Knowing that one of the biggest challenges for the party was going to be its relations with the Kemalist establishment, Erdoğan quickly proceeded to lay out the ethos of the new party regarding its stance toward those who hold different views from its own by citing the apocryphal line ascribed to Voltaire (though he presented it as Voltaire's own): "I do not agree with your views, however I will give my own life defending your right to freely express them," a dramatic appeal to Enlightenment liberal sensibilities of the sort that not even left-of-center parties have made in the past.[6] The quote turned the game of the Kemalist, statist establishment on its head: would they be willing to say the same thing regarding views with which they disagree? Moreover, the effect was to show the AKP—"observant Muslims"—engaging in a more sophisticated way with "Western" Enlightenment thought than has hitherto been done in analogous situations by other parties, an interesting move for a party the Kemalist establishment was adamant at dismissing as the same old Islamism the country had seen before. This was in striking contrast to Refah-Fazilet discourse; many of the country's liberals were impressed. It was also at the party's inaugural press conference that Erdoğan declared the party to be for Turkey's EU membership, in contrast to the Refah-Fazilet position, which had been to strengthen Turkey's ties with the Muslim world and merely to pursue good relations with the EU but at arms length.

The party platform presentation continued: "AKP discourse is a plain, consistent, up-to-date, and realistic one that takes both the social values which inform our cultural convictions [*bağlarımız*, lit. "ties"] and universal values as givens" (Aksoy 2001). The notion of universal values is familiar to students of Turkish history and politics, for it was in the name of this notion that Atatürk undertook many of the reforms of the early republic, such as changing to the Gregorian calendar, using "Western" numerals, and even initiating sartorial reforms. In this context, however, the referents are primarily democracy, human rights, freedom, and so on—in other words, beliefs, practices, and institutions that may have originated in the West but that have now been taken up, internalized, and are valued as universal by most of the world. Again, the appeal here is subtle but important, as it contrasts with some Refah-Fazilet discourse that was to the effect that these "universal values" are not really Turkish and can and should be disposed of in favor of authentically Turkish ones.

"The AKP sees fundamental rights and freedoms in the broadest possible limits as fundamental; it seeks the foundation of social liberation [*özgürleşme*] in individual freedoms [*özgürlükler*]. It aims to be realistic regarding fundamental rights and freedoms" (Aksoy 2001). Individual freedom and rights are the obvious cornerstone of liberalism, an indication that it will pursue a politics that takes such freedoms as its basis. Such an orientation continued a line popularized by Özal and the Motherland Party (Anavatan Partisi, or ANAP) in the 1980s and 1990s, which was significant because it meant that the AKP was aligning itself with political liberalism, echoing an ethos that had been heard in the country before—one, moreover, that was not marginal in Turkey and that had propelled parties to electoral victories before. However emphasizing the individual and his freedoms (including prominently freedom from excesses on the part of the state) can provoke a significant amount of anxiety among those who see it as the first step in the country's disintegration through regional separatism, ethnic separatism, or both. In my view, the careful qualifying phrase that they wanted to be pragmatic about this, that is, not too dogmatic or idealistic "libertarians," meant that they were realistic about the pace at which an individual freedoms based constitutional regime and political culture can be established.

"[The AK Party] accepts freedom of religion and conscience [*vicdan*], thought, expression and initiative as indispensable principles. It sees the phenomenon of religion not as something that divides society, but something that unites it" (Aksoy 2001). We have here the common liberal conception of religion, which associates it most prominently with conscience, but also thought and expression, mixed with a vague (for some, problematic and dangerous) allusion to majoritarian "community values." Some may see in the reference to religion playing a role in social unity an invocation of the kind of Durkheimian functional role of religion in social solidarity that was seen earlier in the writings of late Ottoman figures like Ziya Gökalp. On the other hand, Erdoğan's phrasing plays well to those trying to offset Kemalist anxieties that being "more religiously observant" is an attempt to be divisive and create discord in society. (Kemalist denunciations of the head scarf often take this form.) In other words, Erdoğan may be read as suggesting, "Yes, with democratization we will see that some individual citizens may be more religiously observant than some are used to seeing; this does not, however, mean that our country is any less secular, nor is the country heading toward disintegration." An attempt to address fears of disintegration while emphasizing "freedoms" can be read in statements like the following: "The AKP's conception of law consists of the supremacy of the law, which is the shared guarantee of being able to live together, as well as of the independence of the judiciary . . . The AKP sees democracy as a style [*tarz*] of politics, a kind of administration [*yönetim*] and supervision [*denetim*]. It seeks the formation of a democratic Constitution based on social agreement [*mutabakat*] . . . The AKP is in favor of a 'small but strong' model of the state. It is an advocate of strengthening local administration" (Aksoy 2001).

Rule of law, in Turkey as elsewhere, is considered to be the main guarantee of everything from equal treatment to the supremacy of elected government (over, for instance, shadowy nonelected forces who take it upon themselves to intervene in society and politics, usually in the name of the security of the state). Advocating both the rule of law and a law that is transparent and democratic, in other words, is, among other things, in Turkey code for an end to the disproportionate influence of small but well-placed groups in the military and security services, judiciary, academia, the criminal world, and the press. These groups came to work together (quite effectively, but at high costs to the country in terms of human rights abuses and corruption) in the context of the Kurdish insurgency in the country's southeast and have on several occasions lashed out when they felt reforms got too close to their ability to maintain a degree of influence over institutions and political developments. It is also worth noting that democracy was described as not only a form of administration but also a style; it involves certain attitudes and a kind of ethos. The implications here are important, for while all parties in Turkey profess their support for democracy, democracy is more than an institutional arrangement; it involves not only certain kinds of dispositions and attitudes, most basically a sensitivity toward the common person's needs and desires, but also a certain style of argumentation and disagreement.

The AKP also strongly supported secularism, though in terms that did not please militant Kemalists: "Secularism is what guarantees democracy. The AKP sees secularism as the state's neutrality regarding any religious belief. Secularism is a formulation that puts limits not on the individual, but rather on the state. Moreover, the AKP sees secularism as the fundamental principle of social reconciliation [*barış*]" (Aksoy 2001). In other words, it is not individuals who are or are not "secular" but rather states. This conceptualization of secularism has been repeatedly criticized by the Republican Peoples' Party [Cumhuriyet Halk Partisis, or CHP], who insist on a certain kind of secular subject, and anyone not pursuing the reproduction of this kind of subject is seen as contributing to projects of religious fundamentalism.

On the question of economy, the AKP unsurprisingly laid out liberal lines clearly informed by biopolitical governmentality, which sees the development of the capacities of the population through indirect managing of its welfare as a major aim of government:[7] "The AKP takes people [*insan*], which are both the source and goal of economic development, as its foundation, and it is in favor of a market economy. It aims to balance the risks and the benefits of globalization. It sees the economic role of the state as a regulatory and supervising one" (Aksoy 2001). It then came out in favor of privatization in both the health care and education fields, common neoliberal techniques anathema to the more statist traditions of parties like the CHP. In privatizing wide swaths of what was hitherto under the state's purview, its aim was the usual "freeing up" of personal, private initiative.

Alongside the common idealism of such party introductions, there is much here that is new. It is important to point out the emphasis made in AKP discourse on people with significant differences living together, beyond the usual "we seek to be everyone's party." This came up in a discussion of "social values and traditions": "Our key principles are respect for social values and traditions; love for national [*ulusal*] culture; accepting differences within society as a richness; pluralism; development of social welfare; and that youth and women should be active in social life" (Aksoy 2001). Most people in Turkey would find it difficult to oppose the ideas in this platform, though it is obvious that some of these ideas potentially conflict with others (e.g., what if "social traditions" do not encourage women or youth to be "active in social life"?). Indeed, the most common criticism in the wake of the party inauguration was not with its ideas but rather whether Erdoğan and the party leadership had "changed" from their earlier Islamist positions and identities.

One way to interpret this platform is in a performative sense: in the very act of advocating these positions, the AKP shows that it is possible for people whose Muslims credentials are solid in the eyes of the population to do so. The confidence with which this vision of the political is put forth is thus a very important part of the particular political culture being formulated. There is no defensiveness or apologetic tone; on the contrary, this program was presented as having an inevitability, as if those who espouse it are "on the right side of history." This means that "modern Muslims" are not necessarily the only ones on that side, but they are not necessarily, merely by virtue of being Muslims, on the "wrong" side either.

AKP discourse both explicitly lays out principles in which pluralism is a norm and contributes to an attempt to institutionalize this pluralism. There are debates regarding how consistent the AKP has been during its tenure in power in attempting to adhere to the principles laid out in this program. Many feel that they are not truly committed to the defense of the rights of nonreligious people who claim to suffer discrimination because of an insufficient religiosity. The difficulty in measuring this is compounded by the fact that with a change of party administrations in Turkey, the country always sees a massive removal of higher-level bureaucrats from their positions and their replacement by people from the new party. This always trickles down to lower-level positions, where firing is rare, but some considered "undesirable" by the new administration are made to feel uncomfortable.

BECOMING A MUSLIM

In 2006, as I ate lunch with colleagues in the cafeteria of the most prominent and prestigious (foundation-based) center for Islamic studies in Istanbul, the İslam Araştırmaları Merkezi [İSAM], we were joined by one of the center's founders, an Islamic scholar and former imam, former President of Religious Affairs (Diyanet İşleri Başkanı) for over ten years, and at the time, a Member of Parliament (national assembly) in the AK Party governing the country. Once introductions were finished, he let me ask him a few questions as we ate our lunches. My questions centered on debates about the EU within the AKP and among its cadres. "For the most part," he said, "there really aren't any debates anymore. Maybe ten, fifteen years ago there were [i.e., before the AKP was even founded], but not any longer. Whether we should try to enter the EU is just not debated anymore. In fact, as a matter of national policy, it's gone past the point of no return. Whatever party comes to power, whatever they might say during the campaigns, once they are briefed and really think it over, will realize that there can be no turning back on the EU [entry process]." I then asked him how his party colleagues felt about that.

He replied, "Among many of my colleagues there is a certain *keyifsizlik*, a feeling of being out of sorts and demoralized. *Başkalarca terbiye ediliyoruz* [we're being disciplined by and according to the standards of others]." The thrust of this last sentence is, in my paraphrase and not his, "It's like we couldn't get ourselves together on our own as a country and had to have others come in and put us into order." He went on to illustrate what he meant by relating several connected stories, a particular method of moral edification as we saw in earlier chapters. First, he once received a phone call to participate in a political party youth event—"somehow they managed to get my cell phone number"—and agreed, despite his immensely hectic schedule, to go. Showing up at the time they told him, he found the facility still being set up. The organizers apologized, saying that they told everyone to come at that time expecting that the invitees would be late. Second, decades ago he was in Baghdad, and learned that a famous *alim* (Islamic scholar) he had heard of was giving a course. Knowing Arabic fluently, he went to listen to his lessons. Class time came and went, but the scholar never showed up. Everyone waited around, and eventually someone went off to inquire and was told, "Come tomorrow." The students came the next day and waited. A day and several hours late, the scholar came to his class. Third, several of his older friends had studied at Istanbul University when there were still professors from Germany around who had fled the Nazi regime, and these academics had played important roles in the reorganization of the university. His friends told him how impressed they had been that their professor not only was never late to class (not to mention never missed class) but also came early, waited by the door with the students for the previous class to end, and then would go in a couple of minutes before the hour, prepare himself, and start right on time. "Now," former chief imam of Turkey and President of Religious Affairs Tayyar Altıkulaç asked all of us at the table, "which one of these three behaviors is becoming of a Muslim?"

I want to draw out here the nature of the sentiment being expressed. Altıkulaç is someone who has spent his adult life serving the religious needs of Muslims in Turkey and attempting to assist them in living in continuity with Islamic traditions; it cannot be said that he would endorse a general "Westernization" of the country, especially if this would mean a decline in the importance of Islam in people's lives. Yet clearly the timeliness Altıkulaç referred to in his anecdotes is essentially the temporal sensibility of the market and bureaucracy, the prominence of which is central to political modernity. There is thus a recognition that Islamic ways of life are now necessarily interwoven with forms of life that come from geographies to the West. In addition, according to Muslims' own standards, they may need "disciplining" from the West to live up to their own Islamic norms. Altıkulaç thus set the AKP's EU reforms in the context of broader twentieth-century reformism in Islam. I think it is important not to underestimate the historical significance of this evaluation on the part of many observant Muslims in Turkey, including many in and harboring sympathy toward the AKP. The question for many observant Muslims sympathetic to the AKP is whether they would have been as effective in combating torture, in expanding civil rights, in rendering the state more responsible to the citizens, and so on without the EU process. They think the answer is no, and so it means that they are taking

on others' discipline, leading at times to a heightened reflexivity like the one
Tayyar Altıkulaç displayed.

FROM RELIGION TO DISCURSIVE TRADITION
AND BACK TO RELIGION

It is widely known that many AKP cadres are personally close to many of
the country's leading Islamic scholars and Muslim intellectuals, embodied
in people like Tayyar Altıkulaç (though their intellectual supporters also
include a wide range of numerous liberals of various stripes). Within these
Muslim scholarly circles, profound reevaluation has been taking place, and
new schools of thought have appeared regarding the historiography of the
late Ottoman Empire and transition to the republic, such that there has been
a general change in attitude toward the republic on the part of a very large
number of these intellectuals and academics. It is definitely not, however, the
case that Muslim intellectuals in Turkey simply took up the official statist historiography. In fact, in past decades, Islamist and Kemalist historiographies
mirrored each other nicely. For many years in Islamist writings, the Ottoman Empire was authentic, Islamic, and so on, while everything republican is
Western, inauthentic, alienation, and the like; for Kemalists everything Ottoman was Islamic, backward, despotic, and so on and everything republican
represents salvation, Enlightenment, and authenticity. In more secular, liberal
circles, such official historiography is rapidly being put aside; it is important
to note that a similar process is happening among the country's Islamist historians and scholars (Silverstein 2005).

Regarding 1923, in place of the old rhetoric of revolution, the emphasis
is on continuities before and after 1923. While it is hard to say that many
of these Islamist scholars are overly enthusiastic about all of the reforms that
were carried out, it is however increasingly the case that they have a realistic assessment of why they were carried out, that is, they were aware of
the concrete circumstances the country was in during the late empire, second constitutional era, and transition to republic. This involves a review of
the imperatives and the exacting and demanding situations (*zaruret*) those
attempting to live as Muslims were acting in.[8]

This general reevaluation is matched by a heightened concern with historical methods, with archival research and memoirs, and with a heightened
critical stance regarding now-widespread notions like nationalism. These
new approaches in what we could call Islamist historiography do not have
merely academic importance. There is considerable "cross-fertilization"
between several institutions involved in the production and dissemination of
Islamic discourse and scholarship, such as private, foundation-based research
centers (where seminars and symposia are often organized) and university

theological faculties. One of the researchers at İSAM also told me that one of his colleagues who had retired from his official position at a university was at the time of our conversation an advisor to the chairman of YÖK, the High Council for Education (Yüksek Öğretim Kurulu), which plays a role in setting education policy in Turkey. These new academic approaches come to inform attitudes toward the late empire and the republic that are more subtle in their understanding of the events surrounding the establishment of the republic from the remains of the empire. Moreover, many of those involved in such seminars write columns as *araştırmacı-yazar* (researcher-writers) in Islamically oriented periodicals, where they translate for broad audiences their ongoing work, often with primary sources like unpublished memoirs from the period, passed down through families.

This reevaluation of the history of the late empire and transition to the republic has had an influence on—as it is also partially a product of—the way in which many contemporary scholars of Islam conceive of their work. In talking of the role of independent Islamic research foundations in Turkey, one observant Muslim scholar, working full time at the largest and most prestigious in the capital, set the mode of research his institution engages in against the background of transformations in institutions of scholarship and learning in the late empire and republican transition, specifically Islamic scholarship. It is worth quoting him at length:

At the core [*temel*] of [this foundation] lies the following issue: Islam and modernity; what is the situation of Muslims vis-à-vis modernity? What are the essential challenges modernity poses? In the face of these challenges, what form should Muslims put themselves into? There are many scholarly questions like this that the center has been working on. What are the opportunities modernity puts forth, what are the difficulties? In the face of these, how can we prepare and equip ourselves? How can we better make use of these experiences and improve ourselves? These issues sit before us as scholarly [*ilmî*] problems . . . How have Islamic knowledges [*İslami ilimler*] been affected by modernity? What are the issues modern understandings of knowledge create for the teaching and acquisition of Islamic knowledge?

Note here that the relation between Islam and modernity for this scholar of Islam is not merely one of tension or alterity. It is a matter of working on oneself and improving oneself through an engagement with the challenges and opportunities of modernity. One form this engagement with modernity takes, according to him, is in reworking how Muslims relate to Islamic knowledge. Here my interlocutor introduces a discussion of Islamic knowledge and scholarship in relation to modern conceptions of knowledge and scholarship.

Each, he goes on to say, has developed ways of moving forward and ways of going about its work: "There are specific methods [*yöntem*] of research and scholarship that modern science has put forth, and these methods have been integrated into *ilahiyat* [theology] education [in Turkey], into the way religious disciplines [*dinî ilimler*] have been taught. So a new kind of *ilahiyat* subject, researcher, or expert emerged. What is this? Not even thinking of it as good or bad, but how should one conceptualize [*kavramak*] this transformation? How can it be taken forward?" In a frank assessment, this scholar states that modern conceptions of research and scholarship have now been integrated into the way Muslim scholars approach their own scholarly traditions. Moreover, these modern approaches are now part of the mechanism through which Muslims teach Islamic knowledge to themselves and one another. Two issues arise here for my interlocutor, and I think we would do well to note the directions in which he heads, for they are very indicative of many Turkish Islamic scholars' positions: First, given this situation, how ought we theorize the status of the subjects, as Muslims, who emerge. Second, how, historically, did Turkish Muslims come to this point? In other words, he asks, beside a hasty judgment that the situation is "bad" or "good," what is the historical status of our ontology as Muslims in Turkey today?

Here, in a fashion I came to see as typical for Turkish Muslim scholars, he turns to a concrete discussion of the history of institutions and how they changed in the late Ottoman Empire, and then, crucially, how and why they continued to change into the republic. In discussing institutions, the concern (recalling how he arrived at this discussion) is with the present, with the ground from which Muslims in contemporary Turkey relate to Islamic traditions. But the discussion of institutional transformation displays a very sophisticated, up-to-date knowledge of recent approaches in the historiography of the late empire and transition to the republic:

> At the same time, there are problems that a kind of dual education system produces . . . On the one hand, from the nineteenth century onward, the Ottomans maintained a *medrese*-based conception of education, while on the other hand, they had modern school-based [*mektep*-based] education systems [*rüştiye, idaiye, mülkiye, harbiye,* etc.] and the people who were trained in them. Then you have the establishment of the modern university, the *darulfünun,* and theology faculties [*ilahiyat*] were established within that. So the question arises: how can we run an *ilahiyat* education based on modern pedagogical knowledge? This was a question the Ottomans were dealing with, and it continued into the republic.

The first way to think about the relationship between Islam and modernity, he suggests, is in terms of a duality, that is, Islamic and Western institutions—and by extension, subjects—side by side. Yet he heads in a different direction, suggesting that we must think concretely about what it would have meant to *live* that duality. This is a point noted by many of the Islamic scholars I encountered in Turkey, reflecting a sober, realistic assessment of what it must have been like to actually live, as an Ottoman Muslim, inside of the difficulties of that era. This is an example of the effects of recent approaches to the historiography of the late empire and republican transition as an increasing amount of work is done with sources from that period, such as unpublished memoirs and debates in journals.[9]

My interlocutor thus situates his own institution in the history of institutional reform and the structural transformation of spheres of knowledge from the Ottoman Empire into the republic. Again, the ground he speaks from is marked by an attempt to more realistically and adequately conceptualize the problems earlier generations were facing. In other words, he points to a genealogical concern: what is the status of our present? In what sense are our institutions, our subjectivities "Islamic"? There are no institutions in Turkey with the name "*medrese*"; does this mean there are no traditional institutions of Islamic learning in the country? Finally, what is the status of Muslim subjectivity in Turkey given these genealogies? Here the discussion includes the example of Egypt and the parallel situation in that country:

> So this dual system led to the formation of two kinds of selves [*insan*], and it only came to an end with the *tevhid-i tedrisat* [unification of education] law in 1923. The same things had been experienced in Egypt. On the one hand, you have al-Azhar [the centuries-old, important center of Islamic learning], and those who go through a traditional education based on the local conditions in Egypt, while on the other are the schools Mehmed Ali Pasha established, akin to the *tıbbiye* [medical college], *harbiye* [military academy], and so on [established in Istanbul] based on a modern pedagogy, or "*alamani*" as they say, a so-called secular education. This created serious tensions in Egyptian society; you know the serious critiques made by Taha Hussain. This created serious problems in our societies.

This discussion of the concrete problems the Ottomans had been dealing with in the tensions created by having two separate educational systems by the late nineteenth century takes an interesting turn. Two kinds of institutions were forming two kinds of subjects who systematically generated different kinds of normative judgments regarding what is even a problem, let alone what the solutions should be. My interlocutor sets this as the background against which one should understand the reform of institutions in the new republic:

194   ISLAM AND MODERNITY IN TURKEY

[You had] two different, in fact separate, worldviews, ways of thinking and ways of forming judgments [*muhakeme biçimleri*]. So when a fundamentally crucial issue for the country emerged, someone from Azhar comes to a completely different conclusion and judgment, by making use of different priorities, from someone from Cairo University, who reaches totally different conclusions. Now, it is practically impossible to bring such people together, not to mention coming up with a concrete course of action or expecting them to collaborate. In this regard, Atatürk occupies an interesting place. His initiatives, the unification of education—sure, we can criticize them, but I personally find them very understandable. Turkey was experiencing these same difficulties at the time. While a graduate of a modern school [*mektepli*] looked on events from a certain perspective or worldview, *medrese* graduates came at them from a totally different place. So there were these totally different worlds. Now, we can discuss the coexistence of different kinds of people; that's another issue. But when it comes to matters pertaining to the fundamental direction the country will go in, it's hard to accommodate such difference; it produces very serious difficulties for a country. So, for this reason [I think] that the unification of education was very understandable. In Egypt, the "'asal va 'almaniye" system exists, and it leads to great difficulties [in that society]. But Turkey, over a long period, more or less solved that problem. It was very understandable from the point of view of creating a common [*ortak, müşterek*] culture and worldview . . . Now, the *ilahiyat* education that this perspective led to, based on modern pedagogy, took the teaching and researching of religious disciplines [*dinî ilimleri*] to a different place. In the light of modern, scientific research, how do we do religious scholarship? It's in this framework that *ilahiyat* faculties give their education [in Turkey], and that İSAM pursues its program.

The mode in which Islamic scholarship is undertaken in Turkey and the institutions in which such work has been done in the country are, this scholar suggests, to be placed against the historical background of their emergence and the concrete issues Muslims faced at the time. This leads to a heightened awareness of the historical status of both Islamic knowledge and the subjects formed in and through it, and this awareness goes a long way toward explaining why a great many of such scholars of Islamic traditions and other observant Muslims in the country do not see the form or content of the religious sphere in Turkey as illegitimate.

Here we have an illustration of how all of the work reevaluating the late empire and transition to republic is having a subtle but pervasive influence on the attitude observant Muslims have toward the legitimacy of the republic; this work reflects an important feature of the changes in many Turks' attitudes toward religion, culture, and the state. The newer generations of scholars engaged in Islamic scholarly work at the country's most prominent foundation, and increasingly those at its theology faculties, see the status of the work they are doing and the institutions in which they do it against the background of modernization and reform of institutions. It is also in such terms that broader issues regarding Islam's relationship to modernity, and the various positions, attitudes, and judgments Muslims ought to have regarding modern ways of life and modes of knowledge, are taken up. This includes discourses about Turkey's EU bid. For instance, an emphasis on the compatibility of Islamic identity with secular tolerance in the statements of AKP cadres is an important part of the legitimation of EU entry. The AKP cadres are aware of this work (again, they have close contacts with many of the scholars doing it), and many of them situate their own political identities against the its backdrop. They do not consider themselves to be making concessions regarding their Muslim identity as they reform governance in line with EU protocols; rather they see it as positively incumbent upon them, as Muslims, to competently govern and institutionalize liberal political culture in line with the reasoned changes made by earlier generations.

ISLAMIC PUBLIC OR COUNTERPUBLIC?

We saw in previous chapters that the normative principles on which civil social and political institutions were based in the new republic were initially articulated on grounds internal to Islamic reason as they engaged with universalist discourses of "civilization." While recent scholarship on the relationship between Islamic traditions and liberal political culture has focused either on Muslims in "illiberal" states (e.g., Egypt, Iran) or on Muslims as minorities in liberal democracies, in the case of Turkey we need to theorize the situation differently. The experience of responsibility of rule over large populations of non-Muslims, as well as the impact on worldviews and daily comportment of intensive interaction between Muslims and non-Muslims were both important aspects of the context in the Ottoman Empire in which the transformations described in Chapters 1 and 2 came about. In Turkey's case, these establish a particular genealogy of the institutionalization of political liberalism and Muslims' relationship to it.

I use the term "public" in the sense of a variety of civil, social institutions, and I think it is useful to retain the classic sense of civil society that writers like Hegel and Marx used in referring to it, that is, as bourgeois society (*bürgerliche Gesellschaft*). Hegel's famous formulation of civil society, which he puts forth in the section "Ethical Life" of his *Philosophy of Right*, distinguishes it from both the family and the state (1991). In discussing transformations of the public sphere in Turkey, we also might do well to begin by recalling Kant's contribution to theorizing the public in his classic essay "What Is Enlightenment?" For Kant, "Enlightenment is man's release from his self-incurred

tutelage" (Kant 2007, 29), that is, it is having the "maturity" to not depend
on others' thinking when one can exercise reason for oneself. Kant notes that
it may happen that an isolated individual reasoning alone ("by their own
exercise of mind") may have the courage to begin reasoning and eventually
release himself: "However, that the public should enlighten itself is more possible"; all that is needed, Kant argues, is freedom (2007, 30). The real agent of
Enlightenment in Kant's essay, then, is the public, conceived in a very specific
sense: "By public use of one's reason I understand the use one makes of it as
a scholar before the reading public" (2007, 31). The details need not detain
us here, but Kant makes a distinction between private and public uses of reason. His private-public distinction can seem counterintuitive for present-day
English speakers, for a small group of people talking among themselves in a
town square, for instance, would be for Kant an instance of the private use of
reason, as would a pastor giving a sermon (i.e., doing his "duty," as Kant saw
it). While in various places in this essay Kant refers to examples of "external
direction" such as books, physicians, and pastors or clerics, he returns repeatedly to religious figures to such an extent that the place and limits of religion
are at the heart of his discussion of Enlightenment.

Political modernity—that is, rule through the modern institutions of the
state, bureaucracy, and capitalist enterprise—is usually conceived as structured around a bourgeois public, constituted by autonomous individuals exercising secular reason to deliberate on matters of common concern,
known as "policy." The ensemble of participants is considered civil society,
and in most countries in the world, this is a small minority of the population.
In republican Turkey, it has been nationalist elites who have seen themselves
as constituting the public, in this sense, and ruling in the name and for the
welfare of the population as a nation, whom they have tried to carefully bring
"into" civil society. The structural tensions and problems here are legion,
most obviously the fact that Kemalist cadres, distinctly unlike civil society's
ideal, were speaking from positions of prominence *within* the state apparatus
rather than as individual citizens with private interests.[10] In any event, there is
reason to believe that this period, at least as it has been lived over the course of
the republic, is coming to an end, not simply because of democratic electoral
politics ("the masses" making their voice heard, so to speak), or because of a
radical abandonment of the norms of political modernity, but rather because
of two connected processes. One is the undeniably extensive degree of penetration and internalization of those norms by the population (visible in the
fact that the idiom of citizenship and civil rights is increasingly employed to
press claims by groups and individuals who feel they have been wronged),
while the second is the nature of objects considered to be of political concern
and that their distribution in the field of power is changing.

Muslim ethical culture is just one of many formations (religious, class, or gender based, etc.) that has intersected with this modern civil society in the Muslim world and has tried to legitimate itself in terms of both its internal (e.g., religious) traditions and the ongoing elaboration of that civil political culture. One of the ways in which this situation has been theorized is in terms of an Islamic counterpublic. In a widely discussed article, Michael Warner has taken up an earlier discussion by Nancy Fraser of counterpublics and attempted to give the concept a more rigorous meaning: "A counterpublic maintains at some level, conscious or not, an awareness of its subordinate status. The cultural horizon against which it marks itself off is not just a general or wider public, but a dominant one. And the conflict extends not just to ideas or policy questions, but to the speech genres and modes of address that constitute the public and to the hierarchy among media. The discourse that constitutes it is not merely a different or alternative idiom, but one that in other contexts would be regarded with hostility or with a sense of indecorousness" (Warner 2002, 86). I do not think that the changes described in this book amount to the formation of a counterpublic in this sense because most observant Muslims in Turkey have taken sides in favor of the liberalization of political discourse and practice and see it as the process that allows good governance to unfold. This form of politics is relatively prestigious in Turkey, if still not entirely hegemonic vis-à-vis statist nationalism. If such observant, liberal Muslims are "counter" to anything, it is the statist, Kemalist establishment, which tends to be opposed to, or at least often cynical toward, liberalization (and often defines it immediately as neoliberalization, on the one hand, and code for the obliteration of the state through ethnic separatism invoking "cultural difference," on the other).

Largely because of the genealogy outlined in the first part of this book, then, observant Muslims do not see the major fissures regarding Turkish political culture as cleaving between authentic Islamic religiosity and liberalization. The restructuring of politics around a liberal, civil public is, in short, not something to which the vast majority of observant Muslims in Turkey seek an "alternative" or "counter" formation. The structural transformations in Turkey's society, politics, and economy are not primarily experienced by them as a conspiracy of outsiders; as we saw previously, they have ways of making sense of these changes as incremental and thus reasonable.

RELIGION, THE POLITICAL, AND SOVEREIGNTY IN TURKEY

At a conference recently, a Turkish social-scientist colleague expressed her exasperation that, in her opinion, practically the only topics one may do research on in Turkey (because these are the only topics the funding agencies support) are religion and women. I understand the frustration. It is true that for at least a century people referring to themselves as "modern" have largely done so by contrasting themselves with peoples who had a very different (prominent, public) place for religion in their lives and who were thought to treat women in particularly repugnant ways. These two issues came to be the index of modernity according to which so many non-Western societies were found "lacking." Similarly, the fact that such issues are hotly debated in Turkey stands in the eyes of some as a symbol of the debatable status of Turkey's modernity, itself also a source of exasperation. I do not, however, think it is a coherent claim that were it not for the research agendas of powerful (Western) funding agencies, religion (or women) would simply not be much of an issue in Turkey.

Why the prominence of the discussion of religion, and what does religion have to do with the political in Turkey? In December 1922 and January 1923, Ismet Pasha, a former Ottoman army officer and commander of nationalist forces fighting the invading Greek army in western Anatolia, was the lead negotiator for the new Ankara administration at the peace conference in Lausanne, Switzerland. Invitations to attend the conference had been extended by the Allies victorious in World War I to both the sultan's government in Istanbul and the Grand National Assembly, convening in Ankara. The invitation to the sultan's government enraged the nationalist leaders and hastened the Ankara assembly's moves to abolish the sultanate (discussed in Chapter 1). The conference was ostensibly called to revise and update the Treaty of Sèvres, which had brought World War I to a close but which was a dead letter since Turkish nationalist forces had regrouped, routed the Greeks, and stood ready to menace British, French, and Italian forces occupying parts of Anatolia. The Allies—namely Britain, France, Italy, and the Kingdom of Croats, Slovenes, and Serbs—having won World War I, considered themselves the victors at the conference; the Turkish nationalist forces led by Mustafa Kemal Pasha (i.e., not those around the sultan), having defended the homeland and not having surrendered, also saw themselves as victors.

For the Turkish delegation, the most important thing to be accomplished at the conference was to establish the sovereignty of a new country called the Republic of Turkey and the legitimacy of the Grand National Assembly in Ankara. By far the greatest difficulty in the negotiations concerned what would become of the infamous capitulations, or the economic, political, and juridical concessions given to foreign companies and citizens in Ottoman territories. The Ottoman authorities had declared the capitulations void in 1914, but the Allied powers now wanted to negotiate this, since they felt that the capitulations had been ratified in treaties between themselves and the Ottoman state and could not be abrogated by one party alone. All parties agreed that the capitulations as they had previously existed were now inappropriate. However, the Allies argued that many of their citizens had invested a great deal of money, had lived with their families in the country for decades, and had very much at stake in the country because they understood that they were making these investments under certain conditions. These conditions included a parallel legal system, in which consular courts handled cases involving foreign subjects, even if one of the parties involved was an Ottoman subject. The Allies now wanted to establish some other arrangement whereby their subjects would not be tried in Turkish courts by Turkish judges. The Turkish delegation flatly refused any arrangement other than a single judicial system of courts, one in which all citizens, Turkish or otherwise, would be treated equally. Ismet Pasha argued during the negotiations, "The administration of justice is one of the essential attributes of sovereignty, and therefore any interference in the exercise of that power, in the application of the law or in the organization of the courts, and any restrictions on the appointment of judges are infringements of sovereignty to which no independent state could agree . . . As Turkey forms an independent nation and state, she cannot be expected to accept in any shape or form proposals which are unjust and constitute an outrage on her sovereignty" (*Lausanne* 1923, 489, 492). The Allied delegations expressed their faith that the Turkish courts would soon "fulfill modern requirements" (482), but "changes so sweeping as those now taking place in Turkey in regard to the régime of foreigners cannot be brought into force by a mere stroke of the pen. Transitory measures are indispensable . . . We therefore suggest and demand a transitory period of this kind" (483). The Allied side began to apply extreme pressure to the Turkish delegation (which was much less experienced in diplomacy) to accept some transitional arrangement whereby foreign citizens would not be under Turkish jurisdiction.[11]

Ismet Pasha's reply was multilayered and stated at the outset that the genealogy of the capitulations must be taken into account, which led to the Turkish delegation submitting into the record an interpretation of the historical overview of the capitulations. Its key points were that the arrangements later called capitulations were granted by the sultan personally because of his power, generosity, and a sense that it would benefit his realm. Moreover, law in the empire at that time was "personal" rather than territorial, Ismet argued. The sultan gave these privileges, and he could have, in principle, retracted them. He certainly never would have given them if he thought those benefiting from them would try to use them against him or his subjects. As an example of the gap between personal and territorial law that the Turkish delegation emphasized, in another context, Lord Curzon, the chief negotiator for the British Empire (as it is officially known in the documents), at one point brought up the holy relics that the retreating Turkish authorities had removed from the Hijjaz (Western Arabia, including Mecca and Medina), asking that they be returned (Curzon and the British were keen to prop up a monarchy in the region, and all the historical trappings would have been helpful in this effort). Ismet responded that he had no competence in religious affairs and was therefore unable to negotiate the matter, but that in any event the holy relics were the personal property of the caliph and he could therefore do with them what he wished.

Most importantly, Ismet also protested that no such parallel legal regime for foreigners was being demanded of Bulgaria or Greece, two countries recently independent of the Ottoman Empire (i.e., whose legal system was the Ottoman one until recently).[12] Eventually Curzon tried a new approach: "The Turkish Civil Code may not deal with religious affairs, but it differs from that of the neighboring states in one fundamental respect, viz., that it is the product of theological jurists and is based in the last resort on Moslem religious law" (496). The ultimate reasoning, then, was that claims on limiting the sovereignty of the Turkish state were justified by the allegedly religious character of the law in Turkey; it would be illegitimate to subject non-Muslims to shari'a-based law.

Ismet's reply to Curzon argued that there were no grounds for anxiety, in general, and, specifically, that "the Turkish Civil Code, from whatever sources it may be derived, had no religious or theocratic character; that there was no appreciable difference between it and the codes of foreign countries as regards the fundamental principles and the rules of law enshrined in it; and that, as no state has a Civil Code altogether identical with that of another country, one could not in any way detract from the value of the Turkish code by pointing out certain differences between it and other codes" (489). In other words, as none of the laws in Turkey are derived from the shari'a, there is no reason why they cannot apply equally to all, citizen and foreigner, Muslim and non-Muslim alike, whereby the sovereignty of the Turkish state would not be affronted. The mere fact that the legal system is different from neighboring countries cannot constitute sufficient cause for exception from the courts' jurisdiction, for practically all countries' legal systems are different from one another. Curzon then tried to change the subject to the irregularities of the Turkish judicial system in practice. But the point to be emphasized here is that the sovereignty of the Turkish state was established—at its inception in the recognition coming from the negotiations at Lausanne—on the grounds of the secularism of its legal system. The sovereignty of Turkey and its courts, specifically the refusal to permit the functioning of parallel legal institutions in the country, was premised on the supposedly nonreligious nature of the law. The issue of religion, it turns out, is at the very heart of the question Turkey's sovereignty at its inception.

The relegation of religion to a private sphere in contrast with a public sphere of reasoned deliberation is usually central to predominant narratives of the emergence of political modernity and glossed as secularism. As we have seen, this was not experienced in late Ottoman and early republican Turkey as a philosophical problem but rather as a very practical one. The concern was that if the republic retains a portion of the legal system based on shari'a law, it will constantly be open to attacks on its sovereignty as non-Muslims claim exceptional status and exemption from its jurisdiction. This was a common occurrence in the later empire, and the new authorities were very keen to prevent this from happening again. The sovereignty of the state, expressing the will of the nation, should extend to all subjects inhabiting a certain territory equally and should not be interrupted. One immediately recognizes this as the ground of nationalism. What I want to draw attention to here, however, is how compelling this argument had become among Turkish-speaking Muslims in the remaining Ottoman territory that would eventually become the Republic of Turkey. The argument closely parallels arguments one year later regarding the abolition of the caliphate, which we examined in Chapter 1. Hence we can appreciate the scale on which anxieties about religion and politics have often been played out in Turkey.

CIVIL ISLAMIC RELIGIOSITY? VAKIF AND CEMAAT

We have seen that in the context of post–1925 Turkey, Sufi orders per se cannot exist, as they are illegal. Yet many, like the branch of the Naqshbandi order examined here, have continued to exist during the course of the republic. But in the case of this particular order, this may be changing. One of the major changes has to do with the changing role of foundations (*vakıf*) in social, economic, and religious life in Turkey.

Alongside a "*vakıf*-ication" of the Sufi orders in Turkey, whereby their most significant institutional form is the foundation, some commentators (and even practitioners) believe that one also ought to speak of a "*cemaat*-ification" of the orders, in the sense that the dynamics of their social life correspond to those informally characteristic of *cemaat*s in general. This relates to one aspect of Sufism in Turkey that may be specific to the Turkish context, namely, that the proscription of the orders—and their status and social standing on the eve of that proscription—has impacted organizational dimensions in subtle as well as more obvious ways. In particular, the notion of stages and ranks (*makam, derece*) along the path to spiritual maturity, common in many Sufi traditions, certainly appears to continue to operate, but it is much less a topic of discussion and daily concern than it was likely to have been in the past. Another way to put this is to say that the orders in Turkey have moved in the direction of "association" and somewhat away from "organization" on the continuum outlined by Michael Gilsenan (1973). It is difficult for them to show outward signs of organizational function and status in the prohibitive environment that is contemporary Turkey.

During my time with the Gümüşhanevi branch of the Naqshbandi order, I observed a number of developments that underscored the importance of foundations (*vakıf*) and communities (*cemaat*) for contemporary Sufi life in Turkey. One that was particularly striking concerned this branch's response to the crisis in Kosovo that involved upheaval and tragedy for fellow Muslims not far from Turkey. The response provided a palpable demonstration of Sufi life directly through the foundation informally associated with this Sufi order. In June 1999, comings and goings at the office of the foundation (located in the old *külliye* [school and kitchen] facilities facing the mosque where *sohbet*s were held) came to increasingly involve people with dossiers and forms and a distinctly urgent tone to their affairs. Dreadful events had been unfolding in Kosovo for months, but now a slaughter by Serb security forces and irregulars was well under way. In Istanbul, almost everyone who is not a migrant from Anatolia knows someone who has relatives from the Balkans (where the narrative of migration to Turkey is inevitably one of escaping from persecution). People in Istanbul were painfully aware of the news coming from the Balkans.[13]

The foundation's dealings with government bureaus, especially the Directorate of Foundations, were again uneasy after a period of eased tensions under the Refah-True Path coalition, and would continue to be until 1997. But what was now going on at the foundation office was a response to the tragedy unfolding a few hundred miles away in Kosovo, about which we had come to hear more and more direct and indirect reference in Friday sermons. Donations—mainly of tents, clothes, blankets, boots, and bottled water—and logistical arrangements were being coordinated through foundations across the country. These donations were organized into convoys with the Turkish Red Crescent Society that had permission from Bulgarian authorities to transport the shipments through. Because these were Red Crescent convoys to be received by Red Crescent and Red Cross officials upon arrival, there was no question of anything other than humanitarian aid being sent through these channels.[14]

During this time, one would encounter a few Kosovar refugees at the foundation office, and some of them spoke Turkish. The eyes of these young men bore the distinct, unmistakable look of gratitude for every moment of being alive. These men were quiet, polite, and entirely overwhelmed by uncertainty, having placed themselves utterly in the hands of people whom they desperately wanted to trust. Their presence at the foundation office is significant, as is the fact that it was the foundation that coordinated the collection and transport of donations. The significance of an activity "as Sufism" does not derive from the topics of conversation or the specific actions performed but rather from their link to broader traditions of Islamic discursive practice. In this case, the Kosovar visitors who the foundation assisted were not Naqsh-bandis, but the response of those in the foundation, taking Muslims from danger and caring for their welfare, is seen as action that one should take as a Muslim.

The Turkish government's Directorate of Foundations had issued directives banning private initiative in organizing transport to Kosovo. A number of reasons were given, foremost among them that by coordinating the efforts, the Red Crescent would know what had already been collected and what was still needed. Periodic announcements were made to this effect in the media. There was, however, speculation about other reasons as to why the Red Crescent wanted to monopolize the transport and logistics of this aid. Those at our local foundation office grumbled that this was typical behavior—that the state and Red Crescent wanted to keep people who "think differently" as distant from the process as possible while taking credit for the effort. As for the state itself, and others less sympathetic to perceived Islamist initiatives, the main explanation was that lack of coordination and standardized procedure signifies incompetence on the part of governmental authorities anywhere and tends to lead to inefficiency and ineffectiveness. In such a grave crisis as was then at hand, they claimed, it would be an outrageous scandal to allow such incompetence.

Another concern I heard voiced by politicians was that without centralized coordination, it would be difficult to know who was doing what. They claimed that this would lead not only to the problem of some needs being oversupplied and others unmet but also to diplomatic problems with countries receiving the aid, those through which the aid would transit, or both. Sometimes the initiatives of private individuals are taken to have official Turkish government approval, while reports go out in international media to the effect that "the Turks" are supporting this or that controversial group, a scenario that seems to have played out in the early days of the deteriorating situation in Kosovo.

That the government was ready so quickly with this response also points to the central function of foundation institutions in Turkey as a form of incorporation. Particularly among groups such as a Sufi order, which cannot exist legally as such, incorporation as a foundation enables them to have some institutional form of existence in Turkish society. Government policy toward foundations is therefore extremely important in terms of the tone of civil associational life in Turkey, as it was in Ottoman days.[15]

The chairman of the foundation informally affiliated with the branch of the order studied here graduated from university in 1993 with a degree in administration, making him barely 30 years of age in 1999 when the Kosovo developments I describe unfolded. Speaking of Sufism in Turkey, the young director said to me, "You know, most of Sufi life [*tasavvuf hayatı*] in Turkey these days is foundation [*vakıf*] activities. But most of the foundations get politicized, break up, and disappear, as I'm sure you've noticed." He was referring to the precarious nature of functioning as a foundation, that is, as a body recognized by the government, especially for religious activists. This foundation, he observed, is trying to "not be political," but rather to carry out "*hizmet*" (service to the community). Some commentators have described this as emblematic of a "*vakıf*-ication" of the Sufi orders in Turkey.[16]

While the regulations regarding what one can do with a foundation have been loosened, and as we saw, foundations can now be the institutional core of initiatives such as schools, universities, media groups, and so on, several people I talked with said that the regulations regarding the initial setup of a foundation had, in fact, become more strict, requiring a very large sum of money to be put down as the foundation's base. Thus, more than foundations, the main mode of sociality of Sufis in Turkey is as a community, a *cemaat*. No formal, public functions take place in Turkey as Sufi events, since these are, by definition, illegal. Nonetheless, Sufis come together, lessons are taught, ethical disciplines are inculcated, and even larger events are held. What matters is the status of the event. Here, a judicious equivocation is the norm. For example, a public lecture or symposium on a particular Sufi luminary may be organized, with many of the organizers belonging to a particular Sufi order. The aim of the conference is for those attending to broaden their appreciation and knowledge of the figure and his contribution to Islamic traditions. But is this a "Sufi" event?

FOUNDATIONS AND ISLAMIC SCHOLARLY CULTURE

Another important development in the production and circulation of Islamic discourse in a modernist, liberal mode in Turkey is the proliferation of research centers based financially and administratively on foundations. The impact of these on the style and quality of Islamic research in Turkey should not be underestimated. While there have been *ilahiyat* faculties at several universities for many decades (Marmara, Ankara, and Erzurum being the oldest) and new ones continued to open over the years as new universities were established, the independent research institutes seem to be playing an increasingly important role in setting the tone and agenda for research on topics relating to religion. Their approach to research and publication, and their stance toward and analysis of developments and scholarship outside of Turkey, put them in some contrast with university departments that are oriented toward similar topics in religious studies, history, social sciences, and so on. First is their structure. The establishment of such centers was enabled by changes in the laws in the 1980s and 1990s regarding foundations and their permitted activities. Previously, all educational activities were solely the purview of the Ministry of Education, and only state institutions could carry them out. Most people affiliated with research centers situate their establishment against the background of the political and economic liberalization that began in the 1980s and usually see their activities as constituting civil society initiatives. As a researcher at one of the prominent *vakıf*-based Islamic research centers told me,

> With expanding liberties in society, you see people forming more and more groups, and these groups need to manage their finances and raise funds. One tool for doing this is establishing a foundation. So there are two things here: (1) expansion of freedoms for civil society, integration into the EU, and the reformation of the legal system [and of the] political system—these expanded the domain of activity for civil groups; and (2) liberalization of the markets and privatization of the industrial institutions that used to belong to the state. All this led to an expansion of civil society. Before the 1980s, you didn't need *vakıf*s. What are you going to do with a *vakıf*? You don't have freedoms to be able to do something with it. After Özal's liberalization toward the end of the 1980s, civil society's domain of activities expanded. But before then, even if you [had] a *vakıf*, you couldn't do anything with it, you [couldn't] open a TV station, or a university, and so on. What you could do with it was very limited. After 1980, why might you need a *vakıf*? Say you want to open a university. Freedoms expanded [to allow you to open one], so now you need *vakıf*s. So just as Koç, Sabancı, and Bedrettin Dalan set up *vakıf*s and opened universities, the same goes for the more religious parts of society.[17] They can publish magazines, [set up] TV [stations], [set up a] university, schools, high schools, elementary schools, and so on. You also couldn't set up a research center [before]. So this is a structural change in politics and in the law [in Turkey]. And here we see globalization, integration with the EU, [and] the coming to power of liberal politicians.

This is an account of the formation of the sphere in which research foundations have been established, including Islamic research foundations, given by a scholar who would probably be described as an Islamist by most university academics. This scholar is a specialist on *hadith* and the category of the "human" in classical Islamic scholarship; he is fluent in Arabic and English alongside his native Turkish. Islamic research centers, such as the one where this scholar works, have been playing an important role in the production of

Islamic scholarship in the country in recent years, out of proportion to their number and size. While it is difficult to measure and quantify this role, we do have several indicators of their influence.

Let us take arguably the most influential, most important, best equipped, and most prestigious of such centers, İSAM, on Istanbul's Asian side, where we spoke with Tayyar Altıkulaç and another researcher earlier in this chapter. Established on paper in 1988, the center was originally founded with the aim of producing a Turkish-language encyclopedia of Islam, in some 30 volumes, roughly on the model of the Leiden-based one, with sometimes several months passing between the appearance of new volumes. Most people in Turkey pursuing advanced training in Islamic studies have a pronounced Muslim identity themselves, and the founders of İSAM as well as the scholars they gathered were no exception. While there is no formal rule per se, it is the case that those who become full-time scholars also share this identity. As scholars and materials were gathered to produce the entries, several things started to happen. One was that it became clear that the physical space for the project would have to be greatly expanded, and a purpose-built complex of buildings was constructed. Another was that a team was put together to constitute the core of the scholarly committee for the encyclopedia, who wrote and also farmed out entries to relevant scholars. In all, some three thousand scholars have been drawn on to produce the entries, three hundred of whom are outside of Turkey. The founders also began to rethink what could be done with such a team of researchers and with the library that was quickly growing. As one of the researchers told me, "This place [İSAM] is basically a by-product of the encyclopedia project."

The fact that the impetus for the formation of the center was the production of an extremely high-quality encyclopedia to world academic standards turned out to be very important for İSAM's scholarly culture. That this was the fundamental "agenda," as it were, meant that prominent, accomplished, as well as especially promising younger specialists from several fields (e.g., tefsir, fiqh, kelam, hadith, Sufism, sociology of Islam and religion, and various periods and geographies of history) were gathered, and that while research projects would eventually also be run on certain topics, all scholarly work would be done in relation to the encyclopedia's understanding of research and criteria of quality. The publishing schedule that entry writers had to work with also seems to have had a certain influence on institutional culture, as concrete productivity at a certain world-class standard and volume was monitored and expected. The fact that its basis was the encyclopedia's production also in a sense insulates İSAM from excessively swaying with the winds of politics or intellectual fashions, though naturally research agendas necessarily reflect both to a certain extent, as elsewhere.

All of these make İSAM quite different from a university faculty—for instance, a faculty of theology. Another difference is in the training of the researchers. Roughly half of İSAM's full-time researchers received their advanced degrees from universities abroad, mostly in Western Europe or North America.[18] However, the center maintains close relationships with researchers, faculty, and graduate students at a great many of the country's universities. One of the main draws for students and researchers from other institutions is the library, which has an excellent collection of books, periodicals, and Ottoman archival materials. The book collection is especially eclectic, with not only strengths in Islamic disciplines and Ottoman and Turkish history, naturally, but also a very large and continually growing collection of books in social sciences and humanities on topics like critical theory, historiography, and research methods. Graduate students, university faculty, and established, serious researchers are invited to become members of and use the library collections in house. As of the time of this writing, there are some six thousand members, about half of whom are or were students at Marmara University, located nearby and employing a large and prestigious faculty of theology.

The library collections and the files compiled for the purpose of producing encyclopedia entries are a resource that the center invites graduate students and academics to draw upon, either in person or through correspondence. İSAM has a program through which master's and doctoral students anywhere can request a file on a given topic, and its contents will be scanned and sent by email as an attachment at no cost to the applicant. While they do not keep statistics on such requests or their fulfillment, the director of the Documentation Department that handles both the files and requests tells me that they fulfill more than five hundred such requests per year.

Some measure of the communication between İSAM and theology faculties at the country's universities is in response to the foundation's call for dissertations to be submitted for possible publication in an İSAM monograph series. By far the greatest number of submissions was from Marmara University, just down the street from İSAM, with 29 submissions. Submissions from Ankara University's theology department followed, with eight; there were six submissions from the theology department at Atatürk University in Erzurum. These three are the oldest and largest theology faculties in the country, so it comes as little surprise that they should have submitted the most theses to İSAM. But it is also significant that there were submissions from some seven other theology faculties at as many universities; clearly, word is out and there is communication among the faculties and between them and İSAM.[19]

While it is difficult to quantify the influence İSAM and other research centers are having on Islamic scholarly culture, and even Islamic discourse more broadly, in Turkey, it is certain that such influence is disproportionately large. Their prestige; the crossover of personnel with other outlets such as newspapers; as well as the institutional give and take with university theology, history, and social science departments: all are mechanisms through which these research centers are having an impact. While it would be an exaggeration to ascribe the new approaches to late Ottoman and early republican history discussed previously solely to such foundation-based centers, I think the centers are an important part of the matrix in which such developments are taking place in Turkey.

It should now be clear why many observant, conservative Muslims have aligned themselves with EU-oriented liberalization in Turkey. Where one might have expected such Muslims' identity to predispose them to resist such Western hegemony, we see that one would have to ask, "In favor of what?" Their own history? The move to liberalize Turkish society, economy, and politics is seen by most observant Muslims in Turkey, if not entirely in continuity with their own history and Muslim identity, not as a break with them either. Among other things, this means that it will not be especially useful to conceptualize Islamic traditions as standing in a counterpublic or alternative relationship to liberalism.

A major phenomenon I have tried to examine in this chapter is the liberalization of Muslim conceptions and practices of politics, whereby conservative Muslims attenuate their demand for normative hegemony (i.e., openly or subtly insisting that everyone ought to share their norms and live accordingly). We saw this in the case of the radio station manager conceptualizing the station's work in terms of Erdoğan's regret that he had not put himself in a position to appreciate different points of view, and in the AKP's conception of itself and its formulation of politics. In this chapter, I have examined some of the implications of liberalization for the substance of politics and religion and how observant Muslims like the Naqshbandi Sufis we have been discussing experience these changes. The restructuring of politics, religion, economy, and social life around freedom and equality of individuals, strong citizenship and civil rights, strong property regimes, transparency of the state, and so on is taking place in the context of Turkey's accession negotiations with the EU. I conclude this study with thoughts on how the preceding pages might contribute to how we conceptualize the relationship between Turkey and Europe as well as Islam and the so-called West.

EPILOGUE

Citizens inhabit the domain of theory, populations the domain of policy.
—Partha Chatterjee, *The Politics of the Governed*

WILLIAM CONNOLLY, PARAPHRASING GILLES DELEUZE, HAS SUGGESTED that what is difficult about political pluralism is that it is inevitably a cultural pluralism because of the fact that significant differences are not merely differences of opinion on an agreed topic but rather radical differences in culturally and affectively coded visceral reactions and priorities in light of which issues coalesce or pass unnoticed in the first place (2006). The lives of observant Muslims attempting to live in continuity with Islamic traditions and cultivating ethical projects through consciously defining the parameters for normative judgment in terms of authoritative accounts of practice from the past are one of many modalities of everyday life in Turkey. In this book, we have employed the concept of tradition as a framework for defining an ethical stance and looked at continuities and ruptures in Islamic traditions from the late empire to republic, paying particular attention to Islamic traditions' relationships to modernity. Against this background, I argued that a productive way to conceptualize Islamic traditions and Muslim lives in Turkey is to see them as overlapping both of what Chakrabarty has called the analytical mode of the abstract universal and the hermeneutic mode of specificity and particularity (2000). This is the case, I argued, because of the Ottoman genealogy of modernity in Turkey; the absence of a colonial regime and continuities from the empire to the republic; the relative success of modernization welfare programs in Turkey during the twentieth century; and the resultant widespread legitimacy in the country of social-scientific conceptions of self and society. All of this is built into what it means to live in continuity with Islamic traditions in Turkey today. I have emphasized that there are then two important points to consider: First, Islam has been transformed into a religion on the liberal model in Turkey, that is, as a phenomenon having primarily to do with personal choice and private belief. This is a process that unfolded over a couple of centuries of Ottoman and republican reform, and the major moves were argued on grounds internal to Islamic reasoning (e.g., the abolition of the caliphate). Second, the vast majority of observant, "conservative" Muslims in Turkey—as described by themselves and others—do not see or experience this arrangement (Islam as a "religion") as illegitimate. Address-ing these issues required attention to the relationship between contempo-rary Islamic practice in Turkey, the legacies of institutional change in the late Ottoman Empire and early republic, and more recent transformations at the juncture of culture, power, and the economy. In this epilogue I want to conclude with thoughts on how these issues render plural the temporalities of the public in Turkey, a multiplicity that sits in an uneasy relationship to established political projects in the country.

TRANSFORMING THE POLITICAL: THE TERMS OF POLITICS

I have largely followed Talal Asad and others in seeing secularism as primarily a matter of how to define religion (1993). In earlier chapters we examined how prestigious formulations of what religion is and what it is not influenced the ways in which Islam came to be differentiated, organized, and institu-tionalized as a religion. The institutionalization of a distinction between the public and the private spheres is central to the functioning of liberal political culture, as is the centering of religion on something called personal (private) belief (Asad 2003; Casanova 1994). It is then the very transformation of Islam into a religion on the liberal model that is in question and at stake in many parts of the world, including Turkey, and has been for the last century or so. This transformation is not a forgone conclusion and, in fact, merits our attention as an object of inquiry—something I have attempted to do in this book—for this way of distributing things and assigning spheres is not natural or universal; rather, specific historical processes produce this arrange-ment. This transformation is, however, essentially a fait accompli in Turkey. It results superficially from the republican reforms but more substantially from centuries of Ottoman institutional reform and incremental shifts in the authority and prestige of Islamic regimes of knowledge and power vis-à-vis other regimes. Thus, as we saw in the preceding pages, the transformation of Islam along liberal lines is neither universal or natural, and any Muslim society that is structured this way is not necessarily dealing with postcolonial legacies or with some degree of alienation from Islamic traditions. I have argued that while it is useful to historicize the category of religion and set it aside for a moment in favor of the analytical purchase of other concepts—in particular the category of tradition—we need to return to examining Islam as a religion because it has been deliberately made into one in Turkey as a result of processes set in motion by reasoning on grounds internal to Islamic tradi-tions. I have outlined these processes in this book in order to suggest how we might conceptualize why there is extremely little disagreement among the Turkish public about the notion that religion should be a matter of personal choice any more than there is in many other current European Union (EU) countries.

One implication of this book is that the pluralization of Turkish society will involve the incorporation into the public, in the technical sense, of citizens whose "embodied intelligence," to use Dewey's phrase, is formed through articulation with Islamic traditions (1984a, 366). The formation and strengthening of a private-interest, civil rights–based public in Turkey is neither inevitable nor a foregone conclusion, nor are there no dangers associated with it. It was, however, probably only a matter of time before a country with Turkey's history that sought to simultaneously (1) consider itself—and convince its own people that it is in fact—a democracy and (2) pursue integration into the EU would come to the kind of situation Turkey is in now.

It is difficult to overstate the reversals that have taken place in Turkey in recent years. For practically the entirety of the history of the republic, Kemalists have had a virtual monopoly on a modern, progressive identity. Indeed, it can be argued that in the context of the 1930s, this is not an incoherent way to describe Kemalism, and the extent to which this modality of governance was prestigious and supported by the population ought not be underestimated. By the twenty-first century, however, the situation was different. Many in Turkey came to see the Adalet ve Kalkınma Party (AKP) as more democratic, transparent, and committed to citizenship and civil rights central to the liberal political culture required by the EU than the establishment parties like the Cumhuriyet Halk Partisi, Republican People's Party (CHP), who had come to appear in the eyes of much of the population to stand for nationalism and even ethnic chauvinism, statism at the expense of civil rights, and military intervention in politics—increasingly seen as a reactionary position.[1] Many Kemalist types reacted to this situation with rage, despair, and a virtual explosion of conspiracy theories, for their conception of themselves as the force in Turkey for progressive modernism has been very dear to them (Özyürek 2006).[2] We thus now have a situation where a higher number of erstwhile secularist, Westernizing Kemalists are anti-EU and even anti-West (whatever that would mean for a secular nationalist) than are more religiously oriented supporters of the AKP, who more often support the country's integration into the EU. This means that the CHP, which has prided itself on its vanguard, modernizing, politically progressive credentials, is not the sole representative of political modernity in Turkey. The fact that the AKP comes out of Turkey's Islamist movement (while diverging in important respects from it) means that there is much yet to be understood about the relationship between Islam and political modernity in the country and, more broadly, in the world. A shorthand calculus of pro-Western secularists and anti-Western

Islamists never described the cultural politics of Turkey very well, as I have tried to show, but such a framework is even more useless and incoherent than ever.

Alongside the emergence of a sphere of sociality not directly dominated by the state, arguably central to recent changes in Turkey are changes in the relationship between civil society and what we may call, following Partha Chatterjee (2004), political society. Chatterjee formulated the concept of political society out of a frustration that classic Western political theory was insufficiently attentive to the historical and cultural norms inhabiting its terminologies and the attendant weakness of the analyses done with them in non-Western contexts. In such political theory, "politics" consists of some variation of self-interested, profit-maximizing individuals forming groups, debating among themselves according to norms of secular reason, with some transmitting their will to the state by ascending to power through elections. As Chatterjee points out, this (essentially civil bourgeois) experience of the political corresponds to the actual lived experience of a relatively small minority of the world's population; Chatterjee's estimate is less than one fourth of humanity (2004, 3).

Political society, however, refers to people as individualized and politicized by having been the target of the regimes of governmental knowledge and power (Foucault 2003b), but who do not participate as full members of civil society. This situation is illustrated in Turkey by the famous (though also possibly apocryphal) headline allegedly published by *Cumhuriyet* newspaper (the mouthpiece of the CHP) in the 1930s during a particularly hot summer: "The people [*halk*] race to the sea, citizens [*vatandaş*] can't go to the beach," pointing to the contrast between the "people" (in the sense of "masses") and the "citizens," which while supposedly nonexistent in populist-nationalist discourse, has been very real in practice in the country.[3] Political society on Chatterjee's account is not merely premodern in a temporal sense; it is, rather, a product of modern governmentality, in which people are targets of state welfare and development programs but do not or cannot live fully according to the regimes of property and law, nor do they fully exercise the rights and prerogatives of citizenship. An important part of their existence is thus in a kind of legal limbo, or quasi-legality (e.g., the case of squatters is the most obvious in many areas of Turkey, especially the peripheries of cities; consider the land they occupy, the utilities they divert without paying, etc., until their status is "normalized," often on the eve of elections).[4]

Chatterjee developed the notion of political society to describe such populations, paying particular attention to the fact that they do not fully enjoy the rights of citizenship but are very intimately related to political processes; one might say that they are the "object" rather than the "subject" of politics. Democratic political culture generally sees the inclusion of such populations (e.g., their acquiring a "voice") as a goal. The difficulty, however, tends to be that they often do not "behave" politically according to norms of secular, calculating individualism, and so they are often, in practice, made to wait until they are told the right conditions exist (e.g., either the people themselves have changed in some regard or certain "dangers" no longer exist) for them to participate in citizenship, much as colonial powers used to do to those subjugated in the colonies. This is obviously an uncomfortable position in which to be for a state claiming to be democratic. The implicit (implicit because it is a fairly offensive way of talking about one's countrymen) debate, then, is about whether the population is "mature" enough to be citizens. Are they autonomous enough in their exercise of secular reason? Do they, for instance, bracket religion as being a matter of personal belief or choice and not to be forced onto others? The AKP played a strong hand *against* this attitude when they repeatedly stated that they "believed" in the people more than the other parties did and located their political legitimacy in the actual consent of the governed, claiming to be more progressive than other parties.

We see here the illiberal moments in the engineering of liberal political culture, based as it is supposed to be on the consent of the governed, and this is certainly not something specific to Turkey. Even such classic liberal political theorists as John Locke held that a politics of consent based on the natural freedom and equality of all can only be sustained by virtues such as self-denial, civility, truthfulness, justice, and courage, and that these in turn can only be acquired through a moral education that takes place in "private," in the family (Locke 1996). In other words, it is only through the careful, repetitive inculcation of certain virtuous dispositions, without worrying about the consent of those (children) in whom such dispositions are being cultivated, that liberal political culture can function. So, while the attitudes and dispositions characteristic of liberalism are neither more nor less natural than any other particular cultural system, it is a coherent system that creates the kinds of subjects it needs in order to function. The questions of the commensurability of liberalism with other assemblages of knowledge and power I would argue then becomes "What is the history through which such an assemblage has come to exist in a given environment?" What were the incremental shifts in practice and discourse, and most importantly, what were the rationales and styles of reasoning through which politics becomes liberalized in a given environment?

Regarding the idea and practice of elite-directed modernization and its inherent contradictions, Keyder writes,

> Modernization-from-above came to mean modernization of the solitary nation but not of its individual members, who were expected to continue living in their *gemeinschaftlich* universe newly constructed under state

auspices. This project did not permit the individuation of the component parts of the national unity. There thus emerged a widening gap between the declared intent of Westernization and the actual practice of limited modernization. This is why, in cases of elite-directed transformation in which nationalism is the ideological environment of modernization, it is the state elites who have to be defeated in order for modernization-from-above to be transcended by a full project of modernity. (1997, 46)

One may ask if this is indeed being attempted in Turkey, and who is—and who is not—doing or advocating it. It is against this background that commentators like Tanıl Bora (2006) have begun to use terms like "conservative Turkish republicanism" to describe the state discourse and practice, as well as that of the statist political parties. Oddly, as I mentioned previously, these parties tend to think of themselves as progressive and modernist, which Keyder refers to as the widening gap between what such parties say they stand for regarding modernization and the structural position they actually occupy. On this point, the Achilles' heel for "modernizers" in the Turkish case is democracy: Kemalists have a necessarily strained relationship to democracy because it is something both utterly critical to legitimacy in the "Western" contexts they tend to admire, but it is also something that in Turkey does not seem to return them many votes. It is on this point that AKP discourse has been oriented toward transforming segments of "political society" that have existed on the margins of Turkey's politics and public culture into civil society.

LIBERALISM, NEO AND OTHERWISE

Turkey is one of many countries where, as Chatterjee puts it, "in the course of the twentieth century, ideas of participatory citizenship that were so much a part of the Enlightenment notion of politics have fast retreated before the triumphant advance of governmental technologies that have promised to deliver more well-being to more people at less cost" (2004, 34). The enumeration and classification of population groups for purposes of welfare administration have taken the form in Turkey of a government of the social, the social being figured—in strongly emotional terms—as the nation. For most of the history of the republic, a heavy developmentalist-statist conception of state-society relations has been predominant. There was not much of a bourgeoisie left in the republic formed in 1923 after the collapse of the empire, as many had been ethnic or religious minorities and were now gone. The state took a very prominent role in the economy and even in the institutionalization of social life (people's houses [halk evleri], teachers' houses [öğretmen evleri], etc.), so that there also was not much of a civil society to speak of in the classic sense. The state sectors of the economy were large and were managed by technocrats with considerable expertise for the welfare of the nation without, however, much interest in feedback from the nation (who was presumably not well-enough informed to even know what it needed). The economic and political crisis of the 1970s, the coup of 1980, and the rapid economic and political liberalization of the 1980s and 1990s now appear, in retrospect, to have been part of a broader realigning of the relations between capital and governance along neoliberal lines.

Thus Turkey's history since 1980 is, in a sense, one local chapter in a global history of neoliberalism (Harvey 2005; Foucault 2008). Forms of neoliberalism have been described as characterized by a concern with

> the extent to which competitive, optimizing market relations and behaviour can serve as a principle not only for limiting governmental intervention, but also rationalizing government itself. [They seek] a principle for rationalizing government by reference to an idea of the market. Where [neoliberalisms] differ from earlier forms of liberalism is that they do not regard the market as an existing quasi-natural reality situated in a kind of economic nature reserve space marked off, secured and supervised by the State. Rather, the market exists, and can only exist, under certain political, legal and institutional conditions that must be *actively constructed* by government. (Burchell 1996, 23; emphasis added)

Liberalization, that is, the process of actively constructing a liberal regime for molding conduct largely through "choice," is thus by its very nature a neoliberal process. As we have seen, the AKP stands at the intersection ideologically and historically of several important transformations that have taken place in Turkey in recent decades. Economic liberalization in line with neoliberal, International Monetary Fund–directed structural adjustment programs is a well-known aspect of this period. Political liberalization—literally the increasing conceptualization, definition, and differentiation of the political along lines laid out in liberal theory—is another feature worth discussing, especially for what it implies regarding the religious sphere. The liberalization of the economy is without a doubt the mechanism through which global capitalism penetrates ever deeper into Turkish society (Harvey 2005).

The topic of (neo)liberalism in Turkey is a large one that deserves much more extensive treatment than we can give it here, but at the same time we grant what has just been said regarding (neo)liberalism in Turkey—that Turkey is increasingly integrated into global capitalism and income disparities are growing alarmingly—let us also recall that torture at the hands of the security services appears to be declining sharply, and average citizens are suing state officials for corruption and abuse of power; it has been in the name of freedom and equality (the basic principles of liberalism) that things like civil rights, transparency of the state, and protections against torture have been defended in Turkey. I think we do no one any favors by overlooking or minimizing the violence and trauma the "pre-neoliberal," nationalist order through the 1980s amounted to. Liberalization, to say the least, does not involve "less power" saturating the landscape; it is rather a different arrangement of power, and in this book I have tried to clarify what recent changes in such an arrangement implies, prevents, and enables in religious life in Turkey.

To be sure, cynicism about recent reforms is widespread, and those who are cynical about recent reforms include those who tend to identify themselves with the Left and the military.[5] The frustrating thing for many in Turkey who see themselves as Leftists may not be merely that the Left is in disarray but that one sees increasingly sophisticated self-critique coming from liberals of various (including religious) stripes, who are currently exploring the implications of the suggestion that "the art of better government [might be] the art of governing less, and that in this sense liberalism forms an autocritique of governmental reason: a governmentality which develops and corrects itself through its own critique" (Gordon in Donzelot and Gordon 2008, 57).

TURKEY AND EUROPE

The theme of rapid and profound change in Turkey is now at least a hundred years old, as is the practice of foreigners commenting on it.[6] In 1924, John Dewey was invited to Turkey to consult on education reform, a field in which he was highly accomplished, and in early 1925, he published an essay titled—note the contemporary echoes—"The Problem of Turkey."[7] The ambiguity of the title—Turkey's problems? The problem that Turkey poses?—is also perennial. To Dewey's credit, the essay addresses both of these issues with a subtlety and insight that is remarkable for someone with his presumably limited amount of experience with and knowledge about the country. After noting an almost palpable sense of uncertainty in the country, and a fairly intense suspicion toward foreigners (quite understandable, Dewey notes, once one recalls what foreigners did in the country during the Ottoman collapse), he goes on to praise "the president of the new republic" (he wrote before the law on names that saw Mustafa Kemal become "Atatürk") for his "warning against entertaining illusions" (1984b, 191). Dewey appears to have been present at several of Mustafa Kemal's speeches and notes illustrations of these warnings, such as abandoning all ambitions that interfered with the main goal of securing the unity and independence of Turkey (e.g. recovering lost territory). Dewey also noted that Kemal emphasized in his speeches that while foreigners carried some blame for what befell Turkey in its recent past, this was much less than is the blame borne by Turkey's own rulers. Difficult as the struggle against invaders was, the real difficult work was only now beginning, "the economic and social battle which must be won if Turkey was to become an integral part of the civilized world" (1984b, 191). Dewey's article is remarkably devoid of the condescension familiar to readers of foreign commentaries on Ottoman and Turkish reform movements and makes reference (as Turks did) merely to civilization, rather than, say, the "West," thus setting out from the position that this is the direction Turkey has chosen for itself. While it will be a big job, he clearly conveys his impression that they are up to it. However, he notes presciently, the attitude on the part of those in the "West" is also part of the equation:

> The military prowess of Turkey has made it possible for her to protect her independence in the final crisis . . . The handicap imposed upon [the Turks] by the old régime is enormous. It is double: part of it is real in the heritage of ignorance and lack of economic ability; part of it consists in the reputation which Turkey acquired and which, by foreign ignorance and by the design of interested foreign powers, leads other nations to deny to present-day Turkey a genuine change of spirit and aim. If refusal to admit the reality of the change persists the refusal may do much to prevent Turkey from receiving the assistance it needs to make the change effective and permanent. In that case the belief of liberal Turks that the most powerful enemies of the modernization of Turkey have been the professedly modern and democratic states of Europe, will receive another confirmation. (Dewey 1984b, 193)

It is striking that Dewey noted in 1925 a point that is very important regarding Turkey's relationship with Europe, namely, that there is a performative dimension to commentaries regarding the degree to which Turkey has or has not "sufficiently" reformed itself to be counted as a modern, European country. This is because—regardless of the referential truth-value of such a claim and whether it is true independent of its saying—such commentaries can cause such exasperation among Turks that they may begin to think that reform is pointless and will cease to pursue such reform, thereby ensuring that the country does not "become" European. Turkish reform movements do not and have not taken place in a vacuum. Domestic and international discussion and debate about the reforms have, in turn, an impact on these very reforms and apparently always have.

In the last few years, it has become clear that the stakes involved in Turkey's accession into the EU are extremely high, involving searching questioning of the very nature of both Turkey and Europe. The question of Turkey in the EU is really the question of the EU itself, that is, "What is Europe?" The matter of Turkey's accession has led to such voluminous, intense debate because Europe is forced to define itself. Will Turkey enter the EU? There are several questions built into this one question: Will Turkey be the kind of country that EU member states tend to be internally? The answer to this question is almost definitely yes. But the more important question has to do with the current EU's ability or will to accept Turkey. That Turkey's accession would lead to intense debates had been expected. Several things, however, were less expected. One was the degree to which some older EU members would experience something of an identity crisis as debate over Turkey's admission unfolded. Another was the extent to which perceptions in Turkey about the standards to which the country would be held—compared to candidates like Bulgaria or Romania—would contribute to Turkish public opinion turning against the EU project amid a dramatic upsurge in nationalism in the country. There may be reasons why Turkey does not belong in the EU in 2010, but I have tried to show why civilization, culture, and history are not among those reasons. There are two main reasons why these are not valid: (1) Turkey's history is part of the history of that thing called Europe, as much as many other EU members; and (2) Europe was never created on the basis of geography; it is a political project, aimed at forming a political community of people who share juridical norms and political culture. Turkey *is* European in both of these senses.

While many self-styled "Europeans" and "Islamists" posit a radical otherness between Islam and Europe, many in Turkey think that what is at stake in Turkey's EU bid is nothing less than the Enlightenment project, which invoked the possibility of shared juridical norms across differences of religion and the humanism of which has been the basis for several centuries of Europeans' sense of legitimacy. To claim that Turkey is outside of Europe because of its Muslim identity is to declare that religious difference is an insurmountable obstacle to political community, recalling the centuries of—now conveniently forgotten—debates about Jews in Europe and their alleged inability to be assimilated and problems of allegiance (e.g., to "society" or to their own community, etc.). In other words, many in Turkey consider that, regardless of whether adherents are aware of it, such claims of civilizational difference qua religious difference signal an abandonment of the Enlightenment project.

LIBERAL ISLAMIC RELIGIOSITY IN TURKEY

In Turkey there is a great variety of understandings of the practical implications of the meanings of secularism. When conscious efforts are made to transform the nature and substance of politics on the liberal model, what happens to Islamic disciplines? This study of transformations in Sufi practice and discourse in Turkey and their articulation with discourses, practices, and institutions of political modernity illustrates how characteristically modern social forms and techniques are now among the conditions of possibility for a great many movements that aim to extend Islamic traditions of practice and piety. There was nothing inevitable about these transformations; they are the result of conscious decisions taken in order to change society and politics in Turkey—"reflexive modernization," as it were. But it is important to appreciate that the large majority of observant Muslims in Turkey who support these transformations[8] arguably do so because, in the technical sense, political liberalization—the structuration of politics around the institutions, practices, and discourses of liberalism, that is, the natural freedom and equality of all—and economic liberalization—the "freeing up" of entrepreneurial potential through an arrangement of the legal and institutional apparatus to be conducive to competition and enterprise—(Foucault 2008) have temporally coincided. Thus, as was the case in former socialist Europe, political and economic liberalization present themselves in recent years as being two aspects of the same phenomenon. The restructuring of the economy came first (e.g., strengthening the regime of private property and establishing an environment friendly to capital), getting under way after 1981; serious political liberalization (e.g., the strengthening of civil rights, the ability of citizens to demand redress for abuses at the hands of the state, rendering the functioning of state institutions more transparent, etc.) has come more recently. While the most concrete and dramatic liberal reforms (including those regarding civil rights and minority issues) have found only lukewarm support from the left-of-center parties like the CHP (though small, far left parties have generally supported them), it is this AKP administration that has carried such reforms through.[9]

As a window on the relationship between Islam and political modernity, the issue of Sufism and the political in Turkey is arguably less a matter of the influence of the orders on party politics and more one of the relationship between ethical solidarity of the type cultivated by Sufi orders and the place of moral discourse in the liberal political culture increasingly prestigious in the country. Social and political criticism in an Islamic idiom is conducted more openly and at a more sophisticated level in Turkey today than at arguably any time previously in the history of the republic. But the rise of "Islamic" publishing, television, and radio, for instance, should not be mistaken for a generalized expansion of an unchanging tradition. Rather, as Islamic traditions flourish in Turkey, they are also transformed and articulate with modern forms of civil and political culture. These transformations of an Islamic tradition of discursive practice can be taken as an instance of the privatization of Islam in Turkey into a religion on the liberal model, centered on personal choice. However, because of the genealogy established in Part 1 of this book, this should not be taken as an abandonment of Islamic traditions.[10] Islam's transformation into a religion on the liberal model in Turkey is both largely complete and quite unusual in the Muslim world and has implications for how one conceptualizes Islamic traditions in relation to Europe and the so-called West, as well as the relationship between religion and social-scientific and political cultures associated with such concepts as citizenship, human rights, popular sovereignty, and social justice. The temporal heterogeneity of discourses and practices, and of the subjects formed in and through them, in Turkey suggests the kinds of forms pluralism has come to take in Turkey as well as in Europe. In these pages we have seen how one might arrive at such a plural public from grounds internal to Islamic traditions, among other paths.

NOTES

INTRODUCTION

1. Spoken Turkish has, compared to spoken Arabic, more vowels and fewer consonants, so that when the language was written with the Arabic script, as many as four Turkish vowel sounds were represented by a single letter (the latter-day o, u, ö, and ü all represented by the Arabic *waw*); meanwhile, spoken Turkish pronounced as many as four of the letters of the Arabic alphabet (all distinct in spoken Arabic) identically. The umlauts on some Turkish vowels are a feature familiar to German.

2. Turkey was not the first Muslim community to take up the Latin script; Albanian, Bosnian, and Caucasian and Central Asian languages like Azeri, Turkmen, Uzbek, and Kazakh were all already being written in the Latin script before 1928.

3. See, for example, Tapper (1991), Mardin (1989), White (2002), Yavuz (2003), Çınar (2005), and Tuğal (2009).

4. See Findley (1980; 1989).

5. Müge Göçek recalls that writing on the continuities from the Ottoman to the republican period has been risky for academics during most of the history of the republic, and the few works that did this mostly did so implicitly (personal communication). The seminal work of Şerif Mardin is extremely important in this regard. See the preface to the reissue of his *The Genesis of Young Ottoman Thought* (2000). The edited volume by Bozdoğan and Kasaba (1997) is one of the few works structured around a desire to place contemporary Turkey in the context of late Ottoman developments.

6. See Bowen (1993). The line of enquiry here is akin to the mode of critical history Nikolas Rose lays out, taking his inspiration from Foucault: Critical history investigates "the conditions under which that which we take for truth has been established. Critical history disturbs and fragments, it reveals the fragility of that which seems solid, the contingency of that which seemed necessary . . . It enables us to think against the present, in the sense of exploring its horizons and its conditions of possibility" (1998, 41).

7. The work of Marx and Weber has obviously been most influential on this point. In anthropology, for work inspired by the former, see, for example, Wolf (1982); influential analyses situating more recent transformations within the context of capitalism include Harvey (1989) and Jameson (1991). Weber's legacy has been more suffused throughout several bodies of literature in the social sciences; several prominent students of Ottoman and Turkish society have been influenced by Weber, including Findley (1980, 1989) and Mardin (1969).

8. In this connection, Weber (2004) discussed what he called "disenchantment." This did not mean for him that moderns had better knowledge (through science) of their own environments than "primitives" did; indeed, Weber muses that such primitives probably had much better knowledge of their own surroundings than moderns. (How many of us actually know the details of nuclear fission, or how an automobile works?) Rather, for Weber, disenchantment is the attitude that if one wanted to, one could easily find out

such things, by reading the rights books, asking the right expert, or eventually doing the right experiment. It is this attitude that Weber sees as characteristic of a modern outlook.

9. A useful overview of modernity is given in Connolly (1989).

10. See Mitchell (2000) and Abu-Lughod (1989).

11. The same argument can be made for institutionally recognizable anthropological narratives.

12. See the excellent essay on late Ottoman and republican Muslims' conceptions and experiences of history and temporality by İsmail Kara, "Tarih ve hurafe" in İ. Kara (2003).

13. Works I have found particularly useful include Abou-El-Haj (2005), Murphey (1999), Zürcher (2004), Keyder (1987), Kasaba (1988), Goffman (2002), and Aksan (2007).

14. It is at this point that the contrasts between the present study and Tuğal's recent one on Islamism become clear. Tuğal acknowledges that "there are certainly traditions of liberal and modernist religion in the Muslim world . . . [but]," he argues, "it is not continuity with these traditions that has empowered moderate Islam in countries such as Turkey. It is rather the mobilization of broad sectors under the banner of radicalizing Islam, the subsequent defeat of radicalism, and the radicals' strategic (yet internalized) change of track after the defeat" (2009, 3). I agree that we ought not interpret recent transformations in Turkey as steps toward the ultimate liberalization of Islam in general. However, I emphasize the resources for thinking and living that Muslims in Turkey find in Islamic traditions as they have been lived since the late Ottoman Empire. The compellingness of the value of an attempt on the part of observant Muslims in Turkey to be at home in a strongly centralized, authoritarian, modernizing state and then in democratic political culture, and the sincerity of these attempts, cannot be understood purely on ground external to Islamic traditions and subjectivities (e.g., as "strategic" if "internalized"). I do not deny a role for the "defeat" of "radical Islamism" in the vibrancy of moderate Islam, its leaders, and its followers in Turkey; however, I argue that without the lived continuity in Islamic religiosities and the grounds internal to traditions of Islamic reasoning and living extant in Turkey, this moderate Islam would not have been so popular and widely perceived as legitimate. Only careful attention to Islamic traditions of discourse and practice positions one to appreciate this. The chapters that follow are an extended argument in this direction.

15. This point needs to be qualified by acknowledging that Europe is itself in important respects postcolonial. Timothy Mitchell has recently recalled that the conditions of possibility for the emergence of modern forms are found in colonialism and the access to resources and new experiences it entailed (2000, xvi). World-systems theorists have made similar points; see Abu-Lughod (1989).

16. The state of the art in Turkish historiography has converged on this point and has come to emphasize the continuities from particularly the second constitutional period starting in 1908 into the early republic; see Zürcher (2004). This perspective has been elided meticulously by the vast majority of works on Islamist historiography in Turkey, according to which much of Republican history is indeed a story of alienation (Silverstein 2005). See the revisionist work by İ. Kara (2001). Michael Meeker's (2002) magisterial work on the eastern Black Sea region also emphasizes continuities from the empire to republic, though it is not centrally concerned with Islam but rather the intersection of kinship, political authority, and state institutions.

17. One may note, for instance, that while Kant's classic essay "What is Enlightenment?" initially decries settling for the answers others come up with rather than thinking for oneself in general, he ends up focusing repeatedly on religion as his main example of this (Kant 2007).

18. Iconic of this line of thought is Bernard Lewis's (2002) bestselling book *What Went Wrong?*

19. Thus many who pride themselves on their secularist religious relativism (i.e., that they see nothing wrong with Islam per se) nonetheless claim that what is problematic is that Islam somehow inhibits secularism. In other words, part of the "problem" with Muslims is not so much that their religion is Islam but that they are unacceptably (excessively) religious.

20. Talal Asad has made this point in several works; see Asad (1993; 2003). See also Smith (1991), an early forerunner of much of the recent work historicizing the category of religion.

21. See Asad (2003), Casanova (1994), Benhabib (2002), and Habermas (1989).

22. See also Silverstein (2003).

23. This is a conclusion arrived at—often to their own surprise—by a growing number among the newer generation of Islamist historians in Turkey. See the introduction to and seminal collection of primary sources in İ. Kara (1997).

24. Asad, "The Limits of Religious Criticism in the Middle East" in Asad (1993, 200–236); Mahmood (2005); Hirschkind (2006).

25. This does not detract from the importance and insights of recent work like Charles Hirschkind, Asad, and Saba Mahmood who diagnose a "counter" quality to Islamic traditions vis-à-vis the political norms of the nation-state, but it does suggest caution lest we too hastily generalize their insights to other geographies and histories from the ones they study.

26. See Chakrabarty (2000) on epistemological issues attending historical and cultural difference.

27. See the important collection of essays on Islam in Turkey in Tapper (1991).

28. For a discussion of plural temporalities and liberalism see Connolly (2005, 54–67).

29. On statist, secularist "Republicans" (Kemalists) and their nostalgia in Turkey, see Özyürek (2006).

30. The work of İsmail Kara has been especially influential and subtle.

31. The thrust of the collection was the large degree to which much that goes under the sign of "timeless tradition" is actually of fairly recent vintage or is a recent application and use of older materials. This is especially easy to show in the case of various nationalisms and their constructions of tradition, history, and culture. Turkey is no exception.

32. See also Messick (1993) on the functioning of Islamic discursive traditions.

33. It appears that while Foucault was greatly inspired in his later work on ancient Greece and techniques of the self by the work of his colleague Pierre Hadot, Hadot has some misgivings about the readings Foucault did of both Hadot's work and that of the Stoics (though Hadot is overall generally approving of Foucault's work with classical materials, see Hadot 1995). We are not concerned with the details of Foucault's take on the Stoics here, but merely his general appreciation of ethics as norm-governed work on oneself.

34. See also the argument in Bowen (1993).

35. Sheikh Baha ad-Din "Naqshband" died in 1389. However, as Algar (1990, 3) notes, "In the view of its practitioners, *tasawwuf* [Sufism] is coeval with Islam itself, in reality if not in name, for its essential doctrines and practices are derived from the twin sources of all that is Islamic—God's Book and the *Sunna* of His Messenger. It is, therefore, only approximately correct to regard a legitimate order as originating at a given point in history under the auspices of its eponym."

36. Sufis acknowledge the "schools" of techniques to be several, reflected in the various emphases of the many different Sufi orders with different legitimate lineages. Analogies abound, likening the different orders, for instance, to the many spokes of a wheel all uniting at a single hub, the many paths to the one true God. The various orders tend to be respectful toward one another, and it has been common for practitioners to be affiliated with more than one order at a time (though this appears to be less common today). The extent to which heterodox practices or beliefs—which have garnered much attention in

the West—have been prevalent among Sufis over the centuries is a point of some dispute among scholars.

37. On Sufism in the Ottoman Empire and legacies in the republic, see the essays in Lifchez (1992). The term "mysticism" as a translation for *tasawwuf*, while a useful shorthand, is technically problematic, as there is no theological "mystery" in Islam analogous to that in Christianity. The etymology of the term "Sufi" is obscure but probably related to the Arabic term "*suf*," or wool, a reference to the simple, rough-hewn cloth early Sufis were often seen to wear as a sign of their humility before God and rejection of worldly prestige. Useful overviews of Sufism are given in Knysh (2000), Schimmel (1975), and Trimingham (1998). *Ulema* are often portrayed as being relatively hostile toward Sufism.

38. See Gilsenan's (1973) study of a Sufi order in Cairo for an account of religiosity and sociality in a context in which Sufis were stigmatized but not proscribed; see also Ewing (1997) on the identification of Sufis in Pakistan with the nonmodern.

39. On the relationship between Turkey's Islamist movement and party politics since the 1970s, see Çakır (1990). See also Kafadar's (1992) discussion of the recent resurgence of interest in and practice of Sufism in Turkey.

40. See Chakrabarty (2000) on the heterogeneity of contemporary temporalities around the world.

41. While Leftist activists were rounded up, often tortured, imprisoned, and even murdered, many right-wing activists ended up being taken quietly into the services of the state security agencies as quasi-legal agents, saboteurs, provocateurs, and even assassins working against labor movements and those critical of capitalism and the North Atlantic Treaty Organization; starting in the late 1980s they were used against Kurdish activists. By the early 1990s, many commentators in Turkey lamented the "criminality of the state," which was exacerbated by the growing Kurdish separatist insurgency. One of the means the security services used to put down the insurgency was the employment of former right-wing activists and thugs—many convicted criminals and murderers—to use organized crime rings to fund and arm the state's fight and its support for (mostly Kurdish) irregulars assisting it. I was in Turkey when such direct links between the state and organized crime came to light in the mainstream press in the early 2000s. Former state officials replied that they would be willing to discuss the issue but only if the Turkish public really wanted to know what was done to defend the state against separatist terrorism and save the country. Most journalists lost their enthusiasm for the topic, and the issue was quietly dropped.

42. While 98 percent of the population of Turkey identifies itself as "Muslim," the term "Muslim businessmen" refers to observant Muslims for whom their Muslim identity is prominent. See Keyder (2004).

43. Conspiracy theories abound among secular-minded Turks as to how this capital got into the hands of these pious Muslims. Turkish branch offices of Arab (mainly Saudi, Kuwaiti, and Libyan) finance houses offering "profit without interest" became a part of the financial landscape in the mid-1980s and seem to have indeed been a significant source of capital. But most of the economic power of the Muslim bourgeoisie derives from trade, manufacturing, and state patronage (especially under Özal) of such sectors as construction and infrastructure. Speculation about the finances of various Islamist groups never abates in Turkey and is often the first comment a secular-minded Turk will make about them. See Tuğal 2009.

44. See Özyürek (2006) for a subtle and thoughtful ethnography of these Kemalists. Many of these "conservative Turkish republicans," as Tanıl Bora (2006) terms them, have gone so far as to embrace antidemocratic, authoritarian ideas, considering them a means to "save the country" from the uncertainties associated with democratic pluralization.

45. On the denial of coevalness in the anthropological construction of its objects, see Fabian (1983).

46. So, again, foreign researchers like myself are thus either being duped and taking seriously as a "local phenomenon" what has been a U.S.-hatched plot—or at the very least a U.S.-initiated process—all along, or we are ourselves part of the plot, playing our part in legitimizing Islamist movements. The aim of these plots tends to be portrayed as "weakening" Turkey in order to divide it up into pieces. For that matter, the "plot" is also taken to include such phenomena as human and civil rights. The so-called National Left sees the rise in discourses of multiculturalism; women's equality; and ethnic, religious, and gender minorities as all part of the nefarious plot against Turkey. The topic of political liberalization as conspiracy is a large one that is beginning to be addressed by Turkish researchers. See Bora (2006).

47. While not concerned with this particular order, studies of Turkish Sufi women do exist. See Raudvere (2003).

48. See Nietzsche (1998) and Foucault (2003c) on genealogy as a mode of enquiry.

CHAPTER 1

1. A recent survey found that 98.4 percent of people in Turkey respond to the question "Are you connected to a religion?" (*bir dine bağlı mısınız?*) with "Yes, I am a Muslim" (Çarkoğlu and Toprak 2006, 38). The survey was based on interviews with 1,846 people over age 18 in 23 different administrative regions (*il*) between March and May 2006.

2. The perspective developed here contrasts in important respects with the common historiography of Ottoman reform. Berkes (1998) and Lewis (1968), while meticulously documenting these reforms and reformers, insert it all into a teleology moving toward the allegedly inevitable and logical emergence of a secular nation-state. More recent work has shown that this was patently not the intent of Ottoman reformers until the final years of the empire when nationalism was rampant.

3. On the formalization of calculation and norms in what Weber called characteristically modern social forms, see the chapters titled "Bureaucracy" and "The Meaning of Discipline" in Weber (1978); see also Foucault (2003e) on the relationship between modalities of power and the subjects formed in and through them.

4. See the important work by Abu-Manneh (1994), which situates the Ottoman Tanzimat reforms within Islamic reasoning and rationales. Abu-Manneh argues that the Naqshbandi order was influential in the nineteenth-century Ottoman Tanzimat reform movement, as the personal tutors of the reformist Sultan Abdülmecid were Naqshbandis, indeed of the very suborder under discussion here. There is, in other words, arguably a long history of reasoning for modernization and reform on the part of Sufis in the Ottoman context, as in other parts of the Muslim world. See also Zarcone (1993).

5. On internal Ottoman debates about reform see Lewis (1993), Findley (1980), and Aksan (2007).

6. Much of the work of Şerif Mardin has been devoted, albeit for several decades implicitly, to the same points. See the recent collection of his essays (Mardin 2006).

7. Mustafa Kemal (d. 1938) was leader of the nationalist forces establishing the republic in 1923 out of the ruins of the Ottoman Empire. He became the country's first president.

8. See Meeker (2002).

9. One might be tempted to see the zeal of Müteferrika's "reformist spirit" as a direct result of his being a convert; however, while not minimizing the importance of his background (e.g., his upbringing in Hungarian Protestant circles, his apparent knowledge—in

addition to Ottoman Turkish—of French, Italian, German, Hungarian, and Latin, etc.), it is also the case that a very large portion of the empire's ruling class were similarly converts from the Balkans.

10. Kut gives the date as mid-February 1732 and notes that the tract was printed in 500 copies (1996, 51). On Müteferrika's printing activities, see the catalog of the exhibit *Yazmadan basmaya: Müteferrika, mühendishane, üsküdar.*

11. On reform under Selim III, see Shaw (1971).

12. See Foucault (1979); on the career of these techniques in Ottoman Egypt, see Mitchell (1991).

13. In emphasizing this point, the aim is not to celebrate prestige deriving from successful resistance or to argue for the local origin of these modern forms in the Ottoman context. Rather, as will become evident shortly, the move is in the opposite direction; upon their emergence in northwest Europe, these specifically modern forms and practices were received as foreign and often hostile by the populations (urban working classes, peasantries, rebellious peripheries, etc.) who would be subject to them.

14. For an analytic of modern social forms and practices, see Weber (1978). On the role of the emergence of the human sciences in the minute application and effectiveness of these modern modes of power and in close proximity to practitioners of *raison d'état*, see Foucault (1979).

15. On the Tanzimat and Ottoman reform, see Findley (1980).

16. The text of the Gülhane edict is given in English in Mustafa Reşid Paşa (2006).

17. The Turkish text read, "The objects of our favors are without exception the people of Islam and the other peoples [*millets*] among the subjects of our imperial sultanate," while in the French version the Ottomans distributed at the time, Muslims were not specifically mentioned (Zürcher 2004, 341).

18. These delegations were interested in visiting precisely those military schools, hospitals, and factories Foucault (1979) has described.

19. Cited in Lewis (1968, 82).

20. See Todorova (1997) for a discussion of the issue of the reification of a region into the Balkans and its representations in the West and in the region itself.

21. It will be recalled in this connection that Mustafa Kemal attended the military high school in Manastır (Bitola) in (now former Yugoslav) Macedonia, along with such figures as Ali Fethi Okyar and Kâzım Özalp, who later played prominent roles in the republic. See Mango (1999), and on continuities in personnel from the Ottoman military to the republic, see Zürcher (1984).

22. Karpat estimates that between 40 and 50 percent of the population of today's Turkey is of Balkan, Caucasian, or Crimean ancestry. If one considers that intermarriage of the immigrants with local Kurds was less common, one is left with a very high percentage of Turks of non-Kurdish origin having ancestry in these regions. It should be obvious that the point here is not to determine origins but rather to estimate what impact the experiences of these populations during the collapse of the empire, loss of territory, and migration might have had on discourse and practice in the early republic (Karpat 2000, xvi).

23. Zürcher (2004) also provides a useful brief discussion of what is known, what is not known, and what is probable regarding the fate of Ottoman Armenians in 1915. Nationalism is, of course, the main factor, including the experiences of the preceding years of nationalist rebellions in the Balkans.

24. See Butler (1997) for a discussion of these modes of subjection.

25. For example, administrative techniques and strategies of military formation had been incorporated from the Persians and Byzantines by the expanding Muslim polity as it came into contact with them; the profound Muslim engagement with Aristotelian traditions of philosophy is likewise well known.

26. The term "Islamist" in Turkish (*İslâmcı*) appears to date to 1913, when it was first used by Ziya Gökalp. The term is generally used to refer to, on the one hand, Muslim thinkers and writers who do not have a clerical education in a *medrese*, and on the other, to attempts to politicize Islam in a very precise, technical sense. The term "Islamist" in the context of its emergence refers to those who are working—on grounds that have already largely separated out the spheres of the religious and the political—to make Islam part of the political solutions to society's most pressing problems. See the introductory essay in İ. Kara (1997, vol. 1) and İ. Kara (2001).

27. See, most prominently, Lewis (1968) and Berkes (1998).

28. In arguing for, documenting, and disseminating this view among—and indeed in training a new generation of—historians and scholars, the work of İsmail Kara has been seminal. See, for example, İ. Kara (2005b, İ. Kara (1997, vol. 1), and İ. Kara (2001).

29. The Committee of Union and Progress is an extremely important feature of Ottoman history during its final decades. See Zürcher 2004. This organization built on earlier Young Ottoman circles. See Mardin (2000).

30. See, for example, Kara's long introduction to his anthology of Islamist writings in İ. Kara (1997, vol. 1).

31. It should not be forgotten that the term "intellectual" was relatively new in Western Europe, gaining popularity in France in the last years of the nineteenth century, and specifically referring to those literati who came to the public defense of Alfred Dreyfus.

32. On Kara and his work, see Silverstein (2005).

33. For the ulema-CUP alliance and ulema opposition, I draw on İ. Kara (2005b).

34. For Hanafis (which was the predominant *madhab* in the empire) something that is *wajib* is a duty, though not as obligatory as something that is *fard*. Thus the text could be translated as "all efforts to prevent this outcome are incumbent upon Muslims as a duty."

35. Şura is mentioned twice in the Quran as worthy of praise: in 42:38 and in 3:159.

36. On early generations of Ottoman reformers see the classic study by Mardin (2000).

37. Ottoman text transcribed in Yazır (1997); English translation in İ. Kara (2005b, 186).

38. An interesting overview of Egyptian attitudes toward the republican reforms is given in Hattemer (1999).

39. In the later empire, the office of the Şeyhülislam (known as the Meşihat) had three main duties: giving learned opinion on matters of Islam, directing the system of *medrese* schools and mosques, and managing the Sufi lodges. By the end of World War I, the Meşihat was doing the sultan's bidding (himself bowing to pressure from the victorious Allies) in issuing fatwas denouncing the nationalists fighting to eject Allied armies from Anatolia. In response to this, in 1920 in Ankara, a Ministry of the Shari'a and Pious Foundations was established. In March 1924, the law on the unification of education ("*tevhid-i tedrisat*") was passed, bringing all educational institutions under the auspices of the ministry of education. Also in March 1924, the Ministry of the Shari'a and Pious Foundations was changed into the Presidency of Religion. It duties were now limited to the administration of mosques and their personnel (imams and muezzins), and fatwa issuance, which was gradually translated into "informing citizens on religious matters." This remains the sphere of activity for the Presidency for Religious Affairs.

40. See the information in the next chapter on Sheikh Safvet efendi.

41. As far as I can ascertain, this text has not appeared in English anywhere before.
42. Relatively little is known and has been written about Seyyid Bey. See, however, the master's thesis by Erdem (1993), Yalçın (1936), and Guida (2008).
43. Later in his discussion, Seyyid Bey states that there are differences among the four Sunni *madhab*s regarding the requisite qualities for a legitimate caliph. The main difference is that while Shafi'is, Malikis, and Hanbalis require that a caliph be at the level of *mujtahid* (one authorized to interpret sources through *ijtihad*) in his knowledge of Islam, Hanefis are somewhat more flexible, Seyyid Bey says, in that they only require that he be an *alim* (scholar; 1997).
44. Qur'an sura *al-Shura* 42:38. See the photo in İ. Kara (1998, 45).

CHAPTER 2

1. A phrase I heard on numerous occasions. On early laments among Sufis of the degenerated condition of Sufism as internal critiques see the interesting article by M. Kara (1991).
2. Members tended to think of the United States as a religiously conservative, or at least observant, place, with the state minimally interfering in one's practice of one's religion.
3. On Sufism in neighboring Syria in recent years see Pinto (2004).
4. On the social, political, economic, and architectural aspects of the *tekke* and *zaviye* in the later empire, see the essays in Lifchez (1992).
5. In 1882 and 1890, there were 260 and 305 *tekke*s respectively in Istanbul, of which 52 and 65 were Naqshbandi (Karpat 2001, 107). Kreiser estimates that between 60 and 85 percent of these were continuously occupied (1992, 49).
6. In tandem with these transformations, in the mid-nineteenth century, the nature of taxation in the empire also changed from being assessed to neighborhoods and communities (with the distribution usually calculated by neighborhood imams) to being due from individuals through a process administered by the newly established *muhtar*s. See Behar (2003, 79–80).
7. The rise of the Naqshbandis to preeminence is related to several phenomena, including the proscription of the Bektashi order in 1826, whereupon Bektashi property was given over to the Naqshbandis, as well as the success of a Naqshbandi sheikh, Mevlana Khalid, in placing his disciples and deputies in positions of influence.
8. A great deal of work has been done on the history, ideas and practices of the Naqshbandiyya. See, in particular, Algar (1976; 1990); the essays in Gaborieau, Popovic, and Zacone (1990); Hourani (1981); Abu-Manneh (1982); LeGall (2005); and Knysh (2000, 218–34). On Naqshbandis in republican Turkey, see also Mardin (1991).
9. On this lodge and the Fatma Sultan mosque to which it was attached, as well as some of the social activities of attendees and affiliates, see Eyice (1987).
10. In April 1828, Sultan Mauhmud II had the leading Khalidi Naqshband sheikhs of the Ottoman capital rounded up, taken by rowboat to the suburb of Kartal, and from there, sent into exile in Sivas (Gündüz 1984, 151).
11. It is some index of the spirit of the times, so difficult to even conjure up today, that Mehmet Ali Aynî dedicated his 1923 volume *Why I Love the Great Sheikh* (Ibn Arabî) to "Gazi Mustafa Kemal Pasha." Aynî was a Naqshbandi.
12. See the texts of such debates from this period in İ. Kara (1997, vol. 2). On debates about schools in this period, see Fortna (2002).
13. On these new schools, their role in reform programs and relation to alternative regimes of knowledge (especially Islamic ones), and their relative prestige, see Fortna (2002).
14. On Ottoman *medrese* programs, organization, and reforms, see Atay (1983).

15. Although suppression of the Bektashis was quite severe, with many Babas executed and exiled and *tekkes* confiscated and given over to Naqshbandis, the real targets in 1826 were the Janissaries. By the 1850s, Bektashis were again associating and holding their ceremonies in a public secret fashion; by 1870, books of Bektashi poetry and doctrine were being published. However, the Bektashis never regained their licit status, and their *tekkes* were never officially allowed to reopen (Birge 1994, 74–86).

16. İ. Kara cites a decree from 1793 that represents, in a sense, a precursor to the 1812 decree (2003, 326–27). However, this did not concern the orders' finances and was mainly concerned with maintaining standards of knowledge and ethical conduct among sheikhs.

17. There were exceptions to this general rule, as in cases where a sheikh's appointment to a certain lodge would entail his simultaneously being a preacher (*va'iz*) in a related mosque. In such cases, the appointment was approved by the ulema. See Kafadar (1989, 139–40).

18. Başbakanlık Arşivi, Cevdet Evkaf, No. 11874, cited in Gündüz (1984, 193–94). See also M. Kara (2002, 30).

19. See Barnes (1986, 92–101; 1992, 42).

20. See the classic study by F. de Jong (1978).

21. For a more detailed account of these specifically modern forms and the attendant subjects formed in and through them see, Foucault (1979).

22. See Gündüz (1984, 205) and M. Kara (1980, 301–18). The original *nizamnâme* (charter) dating from the founding of the assembly has not been found. See also the discussion of the Meclis in Zarcone (1993, 139–43).

23. For the text of the 1917 reorganization (*Meclis-i meşayih nizamnamesi*) published in *Takvim-i vekayı*, see M. Kara (1980, 389–93).

24. İlmiye Salnamesi, 1334/1915–1916, 596.

25. In rural areas, Councils of Sheikhs (*encümen-i meşayih*) were established to carry out this function, composed of the region's mufti (who chaired it) and two sheikhs (Aydın 1998, 98); see also M. Kara (2001, 15).

26. From the 1840s onward, the role of the imam in neighborhood social life was structurally transformed with the creation of the administration position of the *muhtar* to attend to matters of neighborhood-level security and representation to and communication with wider authorities and administrative bodies. These duties had hitherto been performed by local imams (Behar 2003, 78–83).

27. Cited in Aydın (1998).

28. Ibid., 99.

29. See, for example, Lewis (1968, 409).

30. See İ. Kara (2001, 66–81) and Tunaya (1962, 94–96).

31. İ. Kara (2001, 71). Interestingly, Gümüshanevi wrote that he was Naqshbandi by *tarikat*, Shadhili (another Sufi order) by disposition (Gündüz 1984), while İsmail Hakki İzmirli is known to have been in possession of an *icazetname* (certificate) from the Shadhili order (M. Kara 1985, 991). These facts are certainly due to the standing of this particular *tarikat*, widespread in North Africa but almost entirely without adherents in Anatolia and the Balkans, during the later part of the reign of Abdülhamid and his cultivation of it, most likely as part of his efforts to strengthen ties to the Arab provinces.

32. For general accounts of the relations between the orders and Abdülhamid, see Zarcone (1993) and Deringil (1998).

33. Lewis describes the Naqshbandis as characterized by "aggressive fanaticism" (1968, 406).

34. An account of life in Esad efendi's Naqshbandi *tekke* in Istanbul during two weeks in the months before the proscription of the orders and closing of their lodges in 1925 is given by the Danish esotericist Carl Vett in his *Dervish Diary* (1953).

35. *Tasavvuf* 8 (1911), 3.

36. See Brummett (2000). An account of the trials and tribulations of newspaper publishing in the later empire, and an especially lively account of the proliferation of papers in the wake of 1908, is found in Tokgöz (1993).
37. A very brief overview of the journals and their publishers is given in Kreiser (1985).
38. See Mitchell (1991, 128–60) and Foucault (2003g, 377–91).
39. See Tanpınar (2001, 249–52) and Türköne (1991, 43–45).
40. See Findley (1982) for a treatment of the emergence of a notion of ideology as emblematic of the new form of politics. For a discussion of the new field of *siyaset* in the Arab provinces see Mitchell (1991, 100–104).
41. *Tasavvuf* 1 (1911), 5–7.
42. The inclusion of the term "*ittihadiye*" is no doubt an indication of support for the new atmosphere brought by the Committee of Union and Progress. Zarcone suggests two possible reasons for the failure of the United Sufis Association, namely, its relatively severe attacks on the practice of *evladiyet* and its lack of a powerful patron (particularly among the ulema; 1993, 149).
43. Cited in M. Kara (1980, 284).
44. Ibid.
45. Ibid., 285.
46. There was considerable controversy surrounding the failure of the United Sufis Association and the founding of the Sufis Association, with bitterness expressed in the pages of the journal *Muhibban*, close to the figures central in organizing the United Sufis Association. See the discussion in Zarcone (1993, 144–54).
47. A fascinating and controversial individual, Musa Kâzım efendi was a member of the CUP, a Naqshbandi, and in all probability a Mason, in addition to being sheikh ul-Islam four times between 1910 and 1917. He was a very articulate and sophisticated intellectual and author of numerous books and treatises on Islam and the problems of the modern world. See İ. Kara's introductory remarks and the texts by him in İ. Kara (1997, vol. 1).
48. See also Ülker and Bahadır (2003).
49. İsmail Hakkı would go on to play a prominent role in the reorganization and reform of the education system in the early republic. See the discussion in Jäschke (1972) and the entry on him in Ülken (1979, 275–78). A selection of his writings is in İ. Kara (1997, vol. 2).
50. *Tasavvuf* 8 (1911), 3. Several Naqshbandi communities in contemporary Turkey continue the organization of seminars and symposia at which the results of scholarly research on Islamic topics are presented.
51. Ibid.
52. Aynî is another fascinating scholar and bureaucrat of the late Ottoman environment who was active well into the republican period. Born near Monastır (Bitola) in former Yugoslav Macedonia, he went to the *rüşdiye* school in Sana'a, Yemen, when his father was transferred there, then finished in the Gülhane Askeriye and Mülkiye schools in the capital. He then taught in schools in Edirne, Aleppo, and Diyarbakır, among other places, and went into the Ottoman administration, working in posts including Kosova, Kastamonu, Taiz (Yemen), Basra, Lathakiyye, and Albania. He then worked in several capacities in the new republican administration. See the texts by Aynî in İ. Kara (1997, vol. 2) and Kara's comments on him.
53. Cited in M. Kara (1985, 986).
54. Ibid.
55. On debates about Sufis and their autocritiques, see İ. Kara (2005a) and M. Kara (1991).
56. Cited in M. Kara (1985, 985).
57. See the chapter titled "Bureaucracy" in Weber (1978).

58. For the texts of the surveys and responses, see Albayrak (1996).

59. This cooperation between the nationalist forces and the Sufi orders is generally interpreted as being based on the fact that Turkish nationalism was relatively new to the majority of Turkish-speaking Muslims in Anatolia, especially among the illiterate masses, and that there could consequently be difficulties in mobilizing the population in its name. Portraying the struggle with the invading powers as a jihad, however, in the name of expelling infidel invaders, was more compelling, as was the authority of Sufi sheikhs. In other words, there is little evidence that the nationalists had much personal admiration for the Sufi orders but rather tended to use them instrumentally, much as Sultan Abdülhamid had done in the closing decades of the empire. See Zürcher (1984; 2004), M. Kara (1980), and İ. Kara (2001).

60. On debates about the status of the orders and of Islamic institutions and personnel associated with them, during what ended up being the closing years of the empire through the war of independence and into the republic, see Jäschke (1972) and İ. Kara (1997, vol. 2).

61. For a transcript of the deliberations in the Grand National Assembly, see İ. Kara (2008, 279–89).

62. For the text of law 677, see M. Kara (2002, 151). For the debates on the orders' proscription see M. Kara (2002, 144–161) and M. Kara (1980, 328–33).

63. First- and secondhand, publicly and privately expressed accounts of sheikhs' reactions to the closure of the *tekke*s are given in İ. Kara (2008, 239–63).

64. Cited in M. Kara (2001, 16).

65. See, for example, the memoirs of Mehmet Şemseddin efendi in M. Kara (2001), and see the comments by Abdülaziz efendi in İ. Kara (1991, 20).

66. I heard this expression several times, leading me to suspect that it is something of a formula used among Sufis to express how, contrary to what many may think, the formal closing of the lodges was not in fact that much of a shock to Sufis themselves. It is also the case, however, that among Naqshbandis, the relative lack of importance of specialized lodges to their practices has been documented for centuries. See Le Gall (2005).

67. The recent work of Mustafa Kara and his students has been important in this regard, as has the work of İsmail Kara.

68. For a summary of these views and source materials, see M. Kara (2002).

69. Cited in M. Kara (2001, 16).

70. An interesting account of this period and how it was experienced by sympathizers of the orders is given in Zarcone (1993).

71. See the extremely important collection of writings by prominent Islamist intellectuals from this period in the two volumes of İ. Kara (1997).

72. Cited in M. Kara (2001, 16–17).

73. See Weber's (1978) discussion of rationalization in the bureaucratization of administration, very useful in interpreting Ottoman reform, including that of the Sufi orders.

CHAPTER 3

1. See later in this chapter on these Sufis' work in the Süleymaniye garden.

2. *Keramet* are to be rigorously distinguished from *mücize*; while these latter are solely acts of a prophet, *keramet* pertain to acts of "friends of God" or *veli*s, such as Sufi sheikhs.

3. I did not pursue systematic research on the topic, but it seems that their discouragement on this issue may be a residue of the processes discussed in the previous chapter, whereby Sufis in the closing decades of the Ottoman Empire were the object of scathing and widely accepted denunciations for their obscurantism and hocus-pocus charlatanism.

4. For a discussion of the *Futuhat*, including *karamat* and habits, see Chittick (1989). See also Uludağ's entry on *keramet*, where he writes, "The greatest charismatic gift [*keramet*] is getting someone to abandon bad dispositions, and embrace good ones" (1995, 307).

5. On Bediüzzaman Said Nursi and the Nurcus, see Mardin (1989), Yavuz (2005), and Yavuz and Esposito (2003).

6. Hadot uses "spiritual exercises" to translate the Greek "ascesis," exercises in the art of living. Hadot suggests that Ignatius of Loyola in fact made the same translation in the sixteenth century, putting the term to Christian purposes.

7. On this topic see Charles Taylor's (2002) *Varieties of Religion Today*, in which he revisits James' classic *Varieties of Religious Experience*, noting that one of the reasons it is still so remarkably readable today over one hundred years after its publication is that James was expressing a modern, secular, and somewhat romantic sensibility (one that sees the authentic essence of "religion" in a personal relationship to the transcendent, by-passing authority) that became predominant among most English-speaking academics in the twentieth century.

8. See, for example, the series of booklets *Tasavvufî Ahlâk* by Mehmed Zahid Kotku.

9. Several fine histories of the Khalidi suborder are available; see especially the essays in Gaborieau, Popovic, and Zarcone (1990); Algar (1990); and Hourani (1981).

10. Zeyrek was also the site of the first Naqshbandi center in the Ottoman capital, when 'Abd Allah Ilahi of Simav established one there in the fifteenth century.

11. Accounts of republican era *sohbet*s prior to those of Mehmed Zahid Kotku are few. In addition to the references cited here see Gürdoğan (1996, 34–36) and M. Kara (2002, 262).

12. Coşan was born in 1938 in Çanakkale and raised in Istanbul in an observant family of Naqshbandis. He graduated from the faculty of Arabic and Persian literature at Istanbul University, moving to Ankara University's faculty of theology in 1960, where he completed his doctorate in 1965, became docent in 1973, professor in 1982, and retired in 1987. He married Kotku's daughter and succeeded him upon his passing in 1980. Coşan's two daughters studied in Turkey, while his son studied business in the United States. See Çakır (1990) and Yavuz (1999).

13. Mention of Özal here is a reference to his university training as an engineer. While some in Turkey are convinced that Özal was a Sufi initiate, I never heard this from anyone in this order, and I know of no evidence that he was. He is, however, generally considered by many in this order to have had a certain sympathy for Sufism, reflected in the fact that he arranged for his mother to be buried in the Süleymaniye cemetery where Mehmed Zahid Kotku and several earlier sheikhs of the order are buried.

14. Interestingly, Schimmel (1975, 366) writes of a Naqshbandi-affiliated journal called *Sohbet Dergisi*, published in Istanbul in 1952 and 1953.

15. See the discussion of neoliberal reform in later chapters, as well as Foucault (2008) on neoliberalism and enterprise as an ethos.

16. See the discussions among secular Turks during this period in Navaro-Yashin (2002).

17. In January 2001, retired general and former secretary of the Joint Chiefs of Staff, Erol Özkasnak, referred to February 28 as a "postmodern coup" (2001). See also the useful discussion of the period in Raudvere (2003).

18. It is difficult to overstate how much the overriding concern of these Sufis is to align with the sunna of the Prophet Muhammad, that is, orthodoxy. Those I worked with would find the "rejection of the Sunni pattern" Trix documented (1993, 105) among the Bektashis she worked with to be a grave straying from the fold of Islam and error. While I do not wish to cast suspicion or doubt upon Bektashi devotions, my work with Naqshbandis is, in part, attempting to effect a minor corrective to Western emphases on

heterodoxy among Sufis, while the evidence regarding how widespread such heterodoxy has been among those considering themselves to be Sufis is unclear.

19. Translation from the Turkish by Hamid Algar, cited in Algar (1976).

20. For the *silsile* (initiatic chain of descent) of this order's sheikhs see appendix B to Özal (1999).

21. See the discussion in Chapter 4.

22. Followers of the teachings of Said Nursi (1876–1960), a revivalist and modernizer of Islamic traditions (Mardin 1989).

23. See Schimmel (1975) for a discussion of *nefs* (*nafs*).

24. Arabic calligraphy of this phrase can be seen inlaid in wooden wall hangings in rooms and offices of the order, and it was put on lapel pins, posters, and brochures. An example appears on the cover to this book.

25. "That's what we've heard" has the effect here of negating any pretense to authoritative knowledge on the speaker's part. In other words, while he is giving an account of the teachings of the order, he is not intending to put himself in the place of someone at a high station, let alone a sheikh. This was commonly the stance from which disciples would speak of the ethical programs of the order.

26. The Quran frequently uses the term *zikr* to refer to revelation, as a "reminder" of God, and the prophetic function has often been commented as one of reminding, to which the appropriate human response is to remember and take heed (Izutsu 2002). The *zikr* was commonly one hundred "Estaghfur al-Azim," one hundred Kelime-i Tawhid, one hundred Lafza-i Jelal ("Allah"), one hundred Salavat-i Sherife, followed by one hundred times Sura al-Ikhlas, and sometimes one hundred Sura al-Inshira. See Algar's (1976) discussion of Naqshbandi *zikr* and its relative "sobriety" in comparison with its function in other orders (e.g., its role their inducement of certain types of "ecstatic" states).

27. These techniques are all the same for women and men. As those I worked with and interviewed were all men, for smoothness of exposition I hereafter use the masculine pronoun.

28. The term used here is *tutucu*, which is generally translated as "conservative." While this sense of the term is meant here as well, the verb *tutmak* (from which *tutucu* is derived) also refers—in addition to "holding" something—to being a partisan of something, someone, or a group, such as a sports team. Thus the term here combines the meanings of conservative and zealot.

29. The literature on the initiatory process in Sufism is enormous; a useful overview is provided in Schimmel (1975).

30. A mufti is a scholar who has the authority to give his opinion (*fetva*) on matters brought to him. In the Ottoman Empire, alongside their religious functions, muftis had many administrative duties. In Turkey they are the representatives of the Presidency for Religious Affairs, presiding over the imams in a given county of the country. This is, in other words, a very high-level official for someone in Ahmet's situation to present himself to.

31. (9:5); emphasis added.

32. For an exhaustive treatment of *fitne*, see the discussion in Pandolfo (1997).

33. Sohbet at İskender Pasha mosque, June 13, 1999.

34. For a generally sympathetic account, see Yavuz and Esposito (2003).

35. When I met her, she wore a monochrome overcoat over her clothes and covered her hair with a colorful silk scarf.

CHAPTER 4

1. It appears that the *sohbet*s began to be held on Sunday during Kotku's tenure as sheikh, instead of Friday like they had under the previous sheikh Abdülaziz Bekine.

2. The Iskender Pasha mosque is a relatively small but historic stone structure constructed in 1506. Its role in the devotional, social, and even political life of Turkey since the late 1960s is out of all proportion to its modest physical stature, however.

3. For a study of women's experience of Sufism in Turkey, see Raudvere (2003).

4. On reading hadith as a devotional practice among Naqsbandis, see Algar (1990, 33). Until very recently, the hadiths were read from Ahmed Ziyaüddin Gümüşhanevi's concordance, *Ramuz el-Ehadith*, compiled from the six authoritative collections and originally published in 1858 with many Latin-script transliterated versions published since the 1970s. The *Ramuz* became a kind of handbook for the Gümüşhanevi branches of the Naqshbandi order in Anatolia and the Balkans and is known to have been the basis of *sohbet* lessons in the main Gümüşhanevi Naqshbandi lodge in Istanbul up until the closure of the lodges in 1925. However, as of summer 2006 and reportedly at the suggestion of Coşan's son Nureddin (discussed in Chapter 6), some of the *cemaat* has taken the significant step of abandoning *Ramuz* in favor of the six "*sahih*" collections that "all Muslims agree upon" (as I was told by a senior member), who admitted that a very few of the hadith in the *Ramuz* were disputed as "weak."

5. The precise formulation varies depending on those present and the leader of the *zikr* but was commonly the same as that noted in the previous chapter.

6. The sense of *terbiye* as synonymous with (and a translation of) the French and English "education" was an innovation of the nineteenth century (Mitchell 1991, 87–89). In the later decades of the nineteenth century, Redhouse (1996) recorded several senses of the word in the Turkish-speaking parts of the empire; these are in order: rearing, nursing, training or educating, culture, good manners, good breeding; a correction, chastising, admonition; regulating or improving by the use of chemical or other agents, including seasoning for food; bringing up or training; and correcting or punishing. Sufis use *terbiye* in the older sense of "breeding" and "cultivating" through correction (as in tying a growing plant to influence its formation). The term is now synonymous with education and training in the Arab world, but in Turkey it is falling out of use with regard to education and tends to be associated with parents' upbringing of children.

7. Among Naqshbandis specifically, the practice of *sohbet* has been emphasized since at least the time of 'Ubaidullah Ahrar (d. 1490) and Ahmad Sirhindi (d. 1625) and was also by the major sheikh in the chain of initiation of the order I studied, Mevlana Khalid ("al-Baghdadî" d. 1827; Abu-Manneh 1990).

8. In Trix's (1993) study of the performative aspects of attunement between Baba and devotee, there is no evidence of the Baba guiding her toward the restructuring of her desires, hopes, fears, and sentiments generally along the lines of the exemplary traditions of Prophet Muhammad.

9. This was the only discussion (and implicit at that) of Salafi tendencies I heard during my fieldwork.

10. A. Ziyauddin Gümüşhanevi (d. 1893) is a luminary in the *cemaat*'s *silsile* and a major Islamic scholarly personality of the Ottoman nineteenth century. See Algar (1990).

11. Shi'a Muslims consider that it was, in fact, Ali who was favored by the prophet, and that the first three caliphs before him, including Abu Bakr, were usurpers. A chain of initiation passing through Abu Bakr rather than 'Ali thus represents a heightened Sunni identity.

12. This was more often the case in Urfa, possibly due to the relatively greater familiarity of the city's population with Arabic.

13. Some exceptions to this are documented. Algar (1971) relates that, as of the early 1970s, Naqshbandis in Bosnia were often combining silent and voiced formulations of *zikr*.
14. On the content and modality characteristic of contemporary debates among some prominent scholars of Islam in Turkey, see Silverstein (2005).
15. Aristotle's term was hexis. Habitus was a term Mauss (1979) used.
16. Hirschkind (2001) and Asad (1993) also note that not treating habitus as part of a conscious attempt to form certain kinds of selves dissolves its quality as a resource for the ongoing elaboration of tradition and, possibly, for resisting Western hegemony. This latter point is not one I echo in this chapter, for reasons that will be made clear in the conclusion.
17. Irvine (1989, 255).
18. For a critical account of logocentrism in Western thought see Derrida (1976, chaps. 1 and 2). See also the discussion in Messick (1993). Meeker argues that "for much of the provincial population [in Turkey], official nationalism stood to Islamic social culture as 'printed' to 'oral'" (1994, 33). On written texts as particular kinds of cultural technologies see Basso (1989).
19. The notion of presence that subtends Sufi practice here contrasts with that which Derrida (1973) has identified as characteristic of Western metaphysics, whereby meaning and knowledge have been idealized as the presence of a pure origin to an identical meaning. It is rather a metaphysic of "influence" that is at work here, and to the extent that there is a theory of knowledge operative, it is one that assumes the pragmatics of context as central to the formation of dispositions to perception. It is less a question of signification (which nonetheless is a field in play here, recalling that these *sohbet*s are structured around the lecture of hadith) than of ethical practice.
20. All quotations are from Plato (1995).
21. Among the more important studies on this issue see Eickelman (1978), Graham (1987), and Messick (1993), as well as the "Quranic Dialogics" in Fischer and Abedi (1990).
22. A similar point, though not in reference to Islam, is made by Basso (1989).
23. Logocentrism has been identified and critiqued by Jacques Derrida as that metaphysic that assigns "the origin of truth in general to the logos: the history of truth, of the truth of truth, has always been . . . the debasement of writing, and its repression outside 'full' speech" (1973, 3).
24. Sirhindi wrote in his *Maktubat*, "Saya-i Rahbar bih ast az dhikr-i Haqq" (The Shadow of the Guide is Better than the *zikr* of God), referring to the importance of being in the presence of a sheikh. On the influence of Sirhindi on Naqshbandis in the Ottoman world, see Algar (1976, 143).
25. Based on his fieldwork in the Black Sea region in 1970, Meeker draws a contrast between what he defines as a local, oral culture of "intimacy, loyalty, interpersonal transparency and affection" on the one hand and secular nationalism on the other (1994, 37–38).
26. The nature and role of love in Islam is an exceedingly large topic. For a useful treatment on love in Sufism, see Schimmel (1975).
27. *Sohbet* at İskender Pasha mosque, June 13, 1999.
28. A similar point was made by Abu-Lughod (1999, 236–38). See also Scott (1991).
29. See Scott (1991) and Rosaldo (1982).
30. Arendt (1968) analyzed this particular modality of power as part of a diagnosis of its decline among "moderns."
31. This is in marked contrast to the conception of the citizen in the deliberative public sphere and its constitution around rational, critical argument in which the status of participants is not supposed to matter. See Habermas (1989).
32. See Keane (1997) on recontextualization in religious language.

33. There is a current in recent liberal political theory that seeks to affirm, recover, and revive work within the liberal tradition on virtue and the cultivation of specific qualities of character considered to subtend a politics of natural freedom and equality. See Berkowitz (1999).

34. Meeker's work on face-to-face Islamic sociality contrasted with official nationalism documents interesting tensions, as he argues that establishment Republican People's Party functionaries upheld secular norms in public while maintaining an Islamic based ethic of sociality in informal situations, a bifurcation of public versus private he argues had nonetheless already been eroded by the early 1970s, leading by the 1990s to "the representation of local and oral Muslims in a new Islamist media culture" (1994, 38). Some of the structural tensions inherent in this move are discussed in the next chapter.

35. Incorporation as a foundation (*vakıf*) is one of the most important (indeed, one of the only) forms of civil association in Turkey. Government policy toward foundations, therefore, is extremely important to the tone of civil associational life in the country. There being of course no Sufi orders per se in Turkey, to the extent that a group of people wishes to congregate at a locale with an official status and permission to do so, they will do this as an association (*dernek*) or a foundation.

36. For historical perspective on these changes in prestige, see Chapters 1 and 2.

37. See the essays in Calhoun (1992) for an overview of the nature of the public sphere as a feature of a specific political culture.

CHAPTER 5

1. The name reflects the common practice of station names ending in "ra," short for "radio." In this case, the station would be known as "ak radio," or "white/pure radio." The station has existed since before the AK Party, and many saw significance in the fact that the party's acronym was the same as the radio station's name.

2. While it cannot be taken to directly measure the number who object to radio on such grounds, or even who reject it, a recent survey found that 9.7 percent of people in Turkey think that radio is harmful to religion and morals (*din ve ahlak*; 7.8 percent of women interviewed and 11.7 percent of men). Similarly, 7.8 percent of people interviewed agreed with the statement "Radio degrades our culture and traditions" ("*kültür, örf ve âdetlerimiz*"; 5.9 percent of women; 9.7 percent of men; (RTÜK 2007, 125–29).

3. At the time of my fieldwork, I was told that roughly half of the employees and volunteers at the station were directly involved with the Sufi order; most of the rest had a general but pronounced Muslim orientation and identity.

4. *Hizmet* can be more meritorious of God's reward (*sevab*, from the Arabic *thawab*) than *nafilah* prayers, the voluntary one, two, or four *rak'ats* performed before and after canonical worship (Bukhari 1971, 140–41).

5. This team was headed by Esad hoja (himself a professor retired from the Ankara theology faculty) and included teachers and academicians. One of the station managers said to me, "If we have any hesitations [on a matter of policy], we ask them, 'We have such and such a situation, what are the standards on this? What are the criteria? Is something *haram* [forbidden]? If so, due to what?' We get the criteria from them, and act accordingly. So we can't just do things according to our own knowledge."

6. I was repeatedly told that several of these sympathizers establishing receivers had been women. At the time of my research, the Islamist-leaning media company Channel 7 had rented one video feed and around five audio feeds on a satellite, using the video and one audio and subleasing the other audio channels, one of which this station rented.

7. That women constituted the primary audience during the daytime is also suggested by the homemaking nature of several of the programs during these hours. In addition, on several occasions I saw the mail as it was being sorted after arriving at the studios, and many of the envelopes were written in a hand typically associated with adolescent girls, often with flowers and similar designs drawn on them. Several men I interviewed in Anatolian cities told me that their local repeater, allowing AKRA to be received in their area, had been set up through the initiative of women. I was unable to follow up on either the role of women in establishing local receivers or on their listening habits and the influence this had on their practices. This is an important topic and merits systematic work.

8. While rating statistics for radio stations have been kept regularly in recent years, I have been unable to find statistics from the relevant earlier years that would corroborate this claim.

9. What the survey means by "religious programming" is not stated in the survey itself. This study, carried out by the research department of the Turkish Supreme Council for Radio and Television (RTÜK) between January and February 2007, includes interviews from all seven of Turkey's major regions; however, the regions appear to be disproportionately represented. For instance, the Marmara region represents 40 percent of interviews; the Aegean (which includes Izmir), 11.4 percent; and Central Anatolia (including Ankara), 20 percent. Also 85.5 percent of respondents live in cities, and 53.5 percent were men (RTÜK 2007, 29–30). Twenty-five percent of all respondents said they listen to "religious programs," 11 percent listen "sometimes," while 64 percent never listen to them; 24.5 percent said they listen to "religious music," 10.5 percent listen sometimes, while 65 percent "never" listen to religious music. For both religious programming and religious music, the most widely reported station was TRT, the national Turkish Radio and Television—an odd choice, since there is practically no programming on TRT radio's three channels with religious content, nor is there much musical content that would be associated with Sufism, which is the music most commonly referred to as "Islamic" in the country (RTÜK 2007, 137–41) It is quite possible that in years before the Adalet ve Kalkınma Party (AKP) came to power, most of those listening to such religious programming would have listened to private channels instead of TRT, which is a state channel; with the AKP in power (and thus exerting influence over TRT) perhaps some of these listeners switched to TRT. It is still puzzling that most respondents cited TRT as the station they listened to for religious content, given that there is little over an hour a week of either "religion and morals" or "Sufi music" programming on its four channels.

10. In fact, during the course of my fieldwork, the group's television channel failed and closed, followed by the newspaper, a severe blow to the morale of the group.

11. Interestingly, "Sağduyu" has recently appeared as the name of a political party in Turkey. One of the founding members is Nureddin Coşan. An announcement on their website before the 2007 elections stated that while the party had supported the AKP, they would not be doing so this time, due to what they saw as the AKP's failure to live up to its promises regarding "liberties."

12. Most respondents to an AKRA online survey said they listen in the evenings between 6:30 and midnight (51 percent), while 33 percent listen between 10:00 a.m. and 6:30 p.m. AKRA website accessed November 2007.

13. This appears to have been especially the case after the radio station's website was established and started to archive *sohbets* for access anytime; 49 percent of 5,966 online respondents said they listen to AKRA at home, 18 percent in the car, 27 percent at work, and 5 percent elsewhere (AKRA FM website, accessed November 2007).

14. *Sohbet* broadcasts appear to continue to be important to listeners of the station; 38 percent of respondents to the online survey said they mostly listened to *sohbets*, which would

make them the most-listened-to programs. This was followed by music (35 percent) and then news (11 percent; AKRA website).

15. It appears that at the time of this writing, the number of people who regularly tune into AKRA on the radio is relatively small, even among the 25 percent of radio listeners who is listening to religious programs and religious music. Again, it is possible that there has been a shift on the part of such listeners from private stations such as AKRA to TRT under the current government, but there seems to be little basis for this as there is practically no religious programming on TRT at all, and there is very little "religious" music (TRT broadcast schedule on http://www.trt.gov.tr accessed 11/07).

16. I note in passing that this discussion of technology echoes in some respects Heidegger's discussion in his classic essay "The Question Concerning Technology," where he emphasizes that "the essence of technology is by no means anything technological" (1977, 4), thereby displacing the discussion to issues of historical and social forms associated with various relationships to techne, or "craft." In our discussion that follows, parallels can be drawn between his focus and mine on the relationship between particular forms and ways of life and kinds of technologies of mediation; I do not, however, wish to take a stand regarding what Heidegger puts as the "liberating" or "dangerous" aspects of techne as bringing forth versus techne as placing before.

17. Ibn Sina (d. 1037) was a polymath from Khorasan in Central Asia especially known for his contributions to medical knowledge; he is known as Avicenna in the West.

18. It appears that despite the general prohibition, some ten works in Arabic (including a book of Psalms of David) were printed in Aleppo, that is, in Ottoman lands, in the first decade of the eighteenth century. Erginbaş (2005, 15).

19. For a translation of the text of the decree see Atiyeh (1995, 283). A transliteration of the original into Latin script, as well as select pages of the printed originals, can be found in *Yazmadan basmaya: Müteferrika, mühendishane, üsküdar* (34–35).

20. The first printed work in Arabic appears to have been produced in Rome in 1514, a book of hours for Melkite Christians; four years later, in 1518 a section of the Quran was printed. The first work printed in Turkish was the bilingual text of capitulations ceded to France by the Ottoman Empire, printed in Paris in 1615 (Kuneralp 1992, 2).

21. For an English translation of the petition, see the Appendix to Atiyeh (1995, 286–92). For a Latin script transcription of this petition and the sultan's *firman*, see *Yazmadan basmaya* (30–33).

22. Interestingly, and entirely in character for the empire at that time, Ibrahim had been born into a Hungarian-speaking Christian family in present-day Romania and entered Ottoman lands during Magyar prince Tököly's rebellion against the Habsburgs (incited by Ottoman forces retreating from Vienna), as the Austrians regained control of the Kolozsvár region.

23. There is some doubt about Müteferrika's authorship of the Risale (Erginbaş 2005). The Risale is usually described as an apology for his newly embraced faith; however, its content is mainly a polemic against papism and the trinity, which has led Berkes to conclude that he had, in all probability, previously been a Unitarian and thus subject to considerable persecution at the hands of the Catholic Austrians. The sheikh of the Sufi order discussed here, Esad Coşan, wrote a short book on the Risale, in which he is aware of the critiques Berkes has brought to bear on the reading of the Risale as Islamic apologetics, but nonetheless sees in the work a sincere account of Müteferrika's rationale for embracing Islam, namely that Christians and Jews had been careless with the dogmas (*akide*) revealed to them and had, over time, falsified their scriptures (Coşan 1993, 37–38; Berkes 1998, 36–50).

24. Firman of Ahmet III, 1139 AH/1727 CE, in Atiyeh (1995, 285).

25. The proofreaders named in the *firman* are the *kadıs* (judges) of Istanbul, Selanik, and Galata, along with the sheikh of the Kasımpaşa Mevlevihane (Mevlevi dervish lodge; Atiyeh 1995, 285).

26. On the supervisory role of the ulema in early Muslim printing, see Mahdi (1995).

27. Anderson only alludes to this in passing, when he mentions that "before the age of print, Rome easily won every war against heresy in Western Europe *because it always had better lines of communication than its challengers.*" Lines of communication imply important infrastructure and not just literacy (1991, 39; emphasis added).

28. The very different impact of print in places like the Philippines and Yemen are two cases that have been especially well documented; see Rafael (1993) and Messick (1993).

29. In 1974, Keith Basso wrote an essay, "The Ethnography of Writing," in which he suggests that we need to be attentive to "what kinds of information are considered appropriate for transmission through written channels, and how, if at all . . . this information differ[s] from that which is passed through alternative channels such as speech" (1989, 431). See also Derrida (1976).

30. In this context, Basso's (1989) point about writing being merely one mode, or "channel" of communication, among others is well put.

31. See the discussion in previous chapters.

32. For an analogous argument see Woolard and Schieffelin's (1994) critique of speech-act theory's claims to universal validity, specifically regarding the centrality of intention.

33. Cited in Woolard and Schieffelin (1994, 57).

34. A precedent to these relatively recent changes in communication technologies in relation to Islamic discourse and practice is the emergence of printing among Muslims in the central Ottoman lands in the early eighteenth century and then the proliferation of journals and newspapers—including publications by Sufis, such as *Tasavvuf, Ceride-i Sûfiye*, and *Muhibban*—in the 1910s.

35. Professor Mardin expressed to me his surprise that his comments—made in passing during an otherwise not particularly sophisticated interview with a mass-circulation daily—became so debated and created so much anger in some circles (personal communication, November 2007).

36. See the discussion of these different epistemes in Messick (1993) and Mitchell (1991, 128–60). Thus the various manuals of everyday ethics, compiling teachings of scholars from the early centuries of Islam, and even those summarizing the teachings of Sufi sheikhs from over the centuries are to be analyzed in the contexts in which they were meant to be *used*, not merely in terms of content.

37. See the important collection of essays on Islam in Turkey in Tapper (1991).

38. For a discussion of plural temporalities and liberalism, see Connolly (2005, 54–67).

39. Debates in France surrounding the Swiss Muslim scholar Tariq Ramadan similarly involved archsecularist denunciations of his "religious" reasons for strongly embracing democracy, multiculturalism, tolerance, and an ethic of citizenship among Muslims in Europe. According to their norms (and those of many nonreligious people in the so-called West), one is apparently supposed to both act according to liberal private-public norms *and* have nonreligious reasons for doing so. On statist, secularist "republicans" (Kemalists) and their nostalgia for the days of their clear hegemony in Turkey, see Özyürek (2006).

40. Recent work has shown the centrality of specific technologies to the emergence of a particular kind of exercise of reason and power and their link to the fact that criteria for participation were thoroughly gendered and class based (propertied men being the players initially). See Ryan (1992) and Eley (1992); see also Mazzarella's (2004) discussion of media and mediation.

41. See Arendt's chapter titled "What is Authority?" in Arendt (1968).

Chapter 6

1. Esad hoja was accompanied to his grave by some ten thousand mourners. Among the politicians attending the funeral were Recep Tayyip Erdoğan and Abdullah Gül, at the time of writing Adalet ve Kalkınma Party (AKP) chairman and prime minister, and president of the republic, respectively. "Sevgi Seli," *Yeni Şafak,* February 10, 2001; "Yerini Oğluna Bıraktı," *Radikal,* February 10, 2001. Erdoğan also published a condolence message in the *Yeni Şafak* newspaper.

2. A "politician known to be close to Sufi circles," quoted in Oğhan 2001. See our discussion of the problem of cradle sheikhs in Chapter 2.

3. In September of 2002, the Sağduyu (Commonsense) Party was formed with the prominent participation of Nureddin Coşan (recall that the newspaper affiliated with the order had also been called *Sağduyu*). The public profile of this party was very low in Turkey, with few even knowing of its existence. They apparently supported the AKP in the November 2002 elections ; however, Nureddin made a public statement (placed on the Sağduyu Party website, http://www.sagduyu.org/) that in the July 2007 elections, they would not be supporting the AKP, due to what they saw as the AKP's failure to address issues of freedom and rights (most probably the head scarf issue).

4. On the AK P era in Turkish politics, see Yavuz (2006), Keyder (2004; 2006), and Tuğal (2007).

5. Beginning in 2008, the country was shaken by a deepening investigation into a shadowy group allegedly known as Erkenekon, apparently formed by hard-line Kemalists among active-duty and retired military personnel and people close to them in academia, the media, "civil society" associations, and business circles. They are accused of plotting one or more coups and of using the media and academia to turn public opinion against the AKP and to orchestrate street protests against the AKP administration. Particularly shocking to some is that it is special counterterrorism police units that are leading the investigation, marking the most prominent group calling itself "patriots" as terrorism suspects, as Leftist and Kurdish groups have been.

6. This and following quotes from Erdoğan's speech at the inauguration are taken from Aksoy 2001.

7. See the discussion in Foucault (2008).

8. To give an example, most such scholars would agree with other, not particularly "religious" people in the country that the reason why Istanbul still carries that name and not Constantinople, while the main language spoken in the city now is not Bulgarian or Greek, is the military.

9. We have seen examples of this kind of work in earlier chapters, such as the fact that the vast majority of the *ulema* and Sufi sheikhs in the major Ottoman cities enthusiastically supported the Committee of Union and Progress (CUP) coup against Abdülhamid and are on record saying and writing so; or that when the Sufi orders were abolished in 1925, many sheikhs wrote their memoirs, and a great many expressed sympathy with the decision on grounds either that Sufism's degeneration was extensive or that it was a luxury that Muslims could not afford given their general educational, infrastructural, economic, and military situation.

10. See Keyder (1987; 1997) on the significance of the relative absence of a bourgeoisie in the formative decades of republican Turkey.

11. Interestingly, among the delegates pressing Turkey for such a concession was the Japanese Baron Hayashi, who outlined the recent history of his country whereby such a transition regime had been established "with success" (Lausanne Conference 1923, 492–93).

12. An independent Greece had existed since 1831, but the northern part of the eventual Greek country only became independent of the empire after the Balkan Wars of 1912 and 1913.

13. Again, we recall that Karpat (2000, xvi) estimates that between 40 and 50 per cent of the population of today's Turkey is of Balkan, Caucasian, or Crimean ancestry.

14. Arms and financing for Kosovar Albanians were certainly being organized quietly by the Albanian diaspora around the world, including in Istanbul (where I met an Albanian American allegedly doing just that). But the Turkish authorities had committed themselves to coordinating their responses through the North Atlantic Treaty Organization, and such material support was done discretely in Turkey. Emotional ties to Kosovo and the rest of the Balkans run high in Turkey, however, and the Turkish authorities flew in several thousand Kosovar Albanian families to temporarily shelter them in camps set up by the military near Kırklareli, in Thrace.

15. It is also through foundations that religious minorities such as Armenian and Greek Christians and Jews are to provide for the administration of their communities' facilities, such as houses of worship, schools, lands, and archives. Again, the importance of regulations on foundations can hardly be overstated, and indeed the liberalization of such regulations is a part of the reforms being undertaken by authorities in line with European Union–accession protocols.

16. On foundations and associations in the corporate life of Naqshbandis in Turkey, see Yavuz (2003, 133–50); on observant, non-Sufi communities in Turkey, see White (2002, 178–211).

17. These are prominent industrialists and businessmen in Turkey, who established Koç, Sabancı, and Yeditepe Universities, respectively.

18. Many of the center's researchers have also spent time abroad in language courses in the Arab world, or English-speaking world, or both, and as visiting fellows in centers in North America, Western Europe, or Malaysia.

19. These universities, all of which had between one and five submissions, were the following: Dokuz Eylül (Izmir), Erciyes (Kayseri), Selçuk (Konya), Süleyman Demirel (Isparta), Cumhuriyet (Sivas), Harran (Urfa), and Uludağ (Bursa).

EPILOGUE

1. Some of these circles went so far as to openly support a coup, such as the former head of the Kadıköy branch of the Atatürkçü Düşünce Derneği (Kemalist Thought Association), Birol Başaran, who said in speaking to a so-called seminar on law and politics in February of 2008, "I think days are coming when the law's boundaries will be stepped out of [hukuk dışına çıkılacağı]. In certain situations the law can be suspended. [Some are saying] 'Let's call in the army, they should do a coup, and so on.' [It is said that] now is not the time. Why isn't it the time? After watching for five years the AKP's treason [vatan hainliği] and their betrayal [lit. "selling"] of the country, if we take the country into our own hands at this moment we'll also get a grip on the crisis. This is the problem. The Turkish military should be on stand-by, they know what to do" (quoted in "Kim kimdir?" Radikal, July 2, 2008). Başaran is also a member of the CHP and sought to lead the party, though he received only a handful of votes in the party's 2001 delegation. As this book went to press, there were signs of significant changes within the CHP, involving among other things its distancing itself from views expressed here by Başaran.

2. The (then) chief of the general staff, General Yaşar Büyükanıt, said in a speech, "There is a topic about which no one should have any doubts—and we in the military are

emphasizing this once again—and that is that there are things that we support and that we cannot abandon. These are the Republic of Turkey's unitary state structure, its nation-state structure, its secular state structure, and that the established organization of the armed forces not be damaged through political, emotional or prejudiced attitudes. However, we are seeing that now just such an atmosphere is emerging as well as tendencies to prune away the state while exalting the individual. Now, of course the individual is important. But how democratic and reasonable is it to erode the state while promoting the individual?" ("Yaşar Büyükanıt: Konuşmak için taslağı bekliyoruz." *Radikal,* October 2, 2007).

3. Many people in Turkey have heard this anecdote, and I found several vague references to it having been either a headline in *Cumhuriyet* in 1933 or a radio announcement at around the same time. However, I have been unable to verify either of these.

4. The Turkish state, like most others, has been very reluctant to simply massively incorporate such people into active citizenship, for example, by legalizing the status of squatters, for fear of destabilizing the whole property regime; at the same time, the state must display a degree of responsiveness to the needs of its titular citizens, for to do otherwise risks political instability. Their situation usually becomes a issue in party politics, as parties try to curry favor with such populations by promising to issue titles and deeds to the properties they inhabit, to extend municipal services like utilities and transportation to their hitherto marginal neighborhoods, and so on.

5. An interesting discussion of cynicism as a modality of the political in Turkey is in Navaro-Yashin (2002). Most prominent among the cynics are many supporters of the CHP, who see liberalism as merely a mechanism for the penetration of capitalism and the dismantling of the Turkish state through treachery and collaboration on the part of lackeys within Turkey. I must set aside discussion of the so-called National Left phenomenon in Turkey, which, on these topics, is often indistinguishable from the Right.

6. Indeed, this may be part of the reason why anthropologists have given scant attention to the country; with so much reform and modernization, Turkey had simply ceased to be exotic enough. (It is also true that for many decades, access of foreigners to conduct research in rural areas and "villages"—the locus of anthropological objects par excellence for decades—was restricted by the state.)

7. First published in *The New Republic* 41 (January 7, 1925): 162–63, reprinted in Dewey (1984b: 189–93).

8. See Çarkoğlu and Toprak (2006).

9. What has become of the political Left in Turkey since the 1990s is itself a large, important topic deserving of attention. For our purposes, it will suffice to say that many political commentators in Turkey note that after 2002, they saw very little difference between the discourses of the self-proclaimed Left (like the CHP) and the nationalists (MHP) and declared that for all intents and purposes the Left has ceased to exist. The nationalist hysteria and conspiracy theories coming from the so-called Left in Turkey (especially those structured around the notion of the "National left" [*ulusal sol*]) can appear utterly foreign and bizarre to those more familiar with Leftist politics in Western Europe.

10. I reiterate here that I am not arguing that every instance of articulation of Islamic and liberal norms and practices around the world is such an internal unfolding of Islamic traditions. That this is the case in Turkey is because of the status of political modernity in the country (see earlier chapters of this book). Nor am I suggesting that processes in Turkey could or should be "models" for other Muslim societies (a suggestion the current government in Turkey also politely refuses, incidentally), since the grounds from which reasoning is undertaken, as well as the historicity of regimes of knowledge and power intersecting at such grounds, will differ.

REFERENCES

Abdo, Geneive. 2000. *No god but God: Egypt and the triumph of Islam.* New York: Oxford University Press.

Abou-El-Haj, Rifa'at Ali. 2005. *Formation of the modern state: The Ottoman Empire, sixteenth to eighteenth centuries.* 2nd ed. Syracuse, NY: Syracuse University Press.

Abu-Lughod, Janet L. 1989. *Before European hegemony: The world system A.D. 1250–1350.* New York: Oxford University Press.

Abu-Lughod, Lila. 1999. *Veiled sentiments: Honor and poetry in a Bedouin society.* Updated ed. Berkeley: University of California Press.

Abu-Manneh, Butrus. 1982. The Naqshbandiyya-Mujaddidiyya in the Ottoman lands in the early 19th century. *Die Welt des Islams* 22: 1/41–36.

———. 1990. Khalwa and Rabita in the Khalidi suborder. In *Naqshbandis: Cheminements et situation actuelle d'un ordre mystique musulman,* ed. Marc Gaborieau, Alexandre Popovic, and Thierry Zarcone, 289–302. Istanbul: Isis.

———. 1994. The Islamic roots of the Gülhane rescript. *Die Welt des Islams* 34 (2): 173–203.

Adanır, Fikret, and Suraiya Faroqhi. 2002. *The Ottomans and the Balkans: A discussion of historiography.* Leiden: Brill.

Ágoston, Gábor. 2005. *Guns for the sultan: Military power and the weapons industry in the Ottoman Empire.* Cambridge: Cambridge University Press.

AKRA FM radio. Website http://www.akradyo.net/.

Aksan, Virginia. 2007. *Ottoman wars 1700–1870: An empire besieged.* Harlow, England: Longman/Pearson.

Aksoy, Ergun. 2001. Ve bir ampul yandı, *Radikal.* August 15.

Albayrak, Sadık. 1996. *Son devir osmanlı uleması.* Istanbul: Büyük Şehir Belediyesi Kültür İşleri Daire Başkanlığı.

Algar, Hamid. 1971. Some notes on the Naqshbandi Tarikat in Bosnia. *Die Welt des Islams,* 13 (3–4): 168–203.

———. 1976. The Naqshbandi order: A preliminary survey of its history and significance. *Studia Islamica* 44: 123–52.

———. 1990. A brief history of the Naqshbandi order. In *Naqshbandis: Cheminements et situation actuelle d'un ordre mystique musulman,* ed. Marc Gaborieau, Alexandre Popovic, and Thierry Zarcone, 3–44. Istanbul: Isis.

———. 1992. Devotional practices of the Khalidi Naqshbandis of Ottoman Turkey. In *The dervish lodge: Architecture, art, and Sufism in Ottoman Turkey,* ed. Ramond Lifchez, 209–27. Berkeley: University of California Press.

Anderson, Benedict R. 1991. *Imagined communities: Reflections on the origin and spread of nationalism.* Rev. and extended ed. London: Verso.

Arendt, Hannah. 1968. *Between past and future: Eight exercises in political thought.* Enlarged ed. New York: Viking Press.

Armbrust, Walter, ed. 2000. *Mass mediations: New approaches to popular culture in the Middle East and beyond.* Berkeley: University of California Press.

Asad, Talal. 1986. *The idea of an anthropology of Islam.* Washington, DC: Center for Contemporary Arab Studies, Georgetown University.

——. 1993. *Genealogies of religion: Discipline and reasons of power in Christianity and Islam.* Baltimore: Johns Hopkins University Press.

——. 2003. *Formations of the secular: Christianity, Islam, modernity.* Stanford, CA: Stanford University Press.

Atay, Hüseyin. 1983. *Osmanlılarda yüksek din eğitimi: Medrese programları, ıcazetnâmeler, islahat hareketleri.* İstanbul: Dergâh.

Atiyeh, George N. 1995. *The book in the Islamic world: The written word and communication in the Middle East.* Albany: State University of New York Press.

Austin, J. L. 1975. *How to do things with words.* 2nd ed. Oxford: Clarendon Press.

Aydın, Bilgin. 1998. Osmanlı devlet'inde tekkeler reformu ve meclis-i meşayih'ın şeyhülislâmlık'a bağlı olarak kuruluşu, faaliyetleri ve arşivi. İstanbul Araştırmaları 7: 93–109.

Barnes, John. 1992. The dervish orders in the Ottoman Empire. In *The dervish lodge*, ed. Ramond Lifchez, 33–48.

——. 1986. *An introduction to religious foundations in the Ottoman Empire.* Leiden: Brill.

Basso, Keith. 1989. The ethnography of Writing. In *Explorations in the ethnography of speaking*, ed. Richard Bauman and Joel Sherzer. Cambridge: Cambridge University Press.

Behar, Cem. 2003. *A neighborhood in Ottoman Istanbul: Fruit vendors and civil servants in the kasap ilyas mahalle.* Albany: State University of New York Press.

Benhabib, Seyla. 2002. *The claims of culture: Equality and diversity in the global era.* Princeton, NJ: Princeton University Press.

Benjamin, Walter. 1968. *Illuminations.* New York: Schocken Books.

Berkes, Niyazi. 1998. *The development of secularism in Turkey.* New York: Routledge.

Berkowitz, Peter. 1999. *Virtue and the making of modern liberalism.* Princeton, NJ: Princeton University Press.

Birge, John Kingsley. 1994. *The Bektashi order of dervishes.* London: Luzac Oriental.

Blumenberg, Hans. 1983. *The legitimacy of the modern age.* Cambridge, MA: MIT Press.

Bora, Tanıl. 2006. *Medeniyet kaybi: Milliyetçilik ve faşizm üzerine yazılar.* Istanbul: İletişim.

Bourdieu, Pierre. 1977. *Outline of a theory of practice.* Cambridge: Cambridge University Press.

——. 1990. *The logic of practice.* Stanford, CA: Stanford University Press.

Bowen, John. 1993. *Muslims through discourse: Religion and ritual in Gayo society.* Princeton, NJ: Princeton University Press.

Bozdoğan, Sibel, and Reşat Kasaba, ed. 1997. *Rethinking modernity and national identity in Turkey.* Seattle: University of Washington Press.

Brummett, Palmira Johnson. 2000. *Image and imperialism in the Ottoman revolutionary press, 1908–1911.* Albany: State University of New York Press.

Bukhari, Muhammad ibn Ismail al-. 1971. *Sahih Al-Bukhari: The translation of the meanings of Sahih Al-Bukhari.* Trans. Muhammad Muhsin Khan. Medina: Islamic University.

Burchell, Graham. 1996. Liberal government and techniques of the self. In *Foucault and political reason*, ed. Andrew Barry, Thomas Osborne, and Nikolas Rose, 19–36. Chicago: University of Chicago Press.

Burnyeat, M. F. 1980. Aristotle on learning to be good. In *Essays on Aristotle's "Ethics,"* ed. Amélie O. Rorty, 69–92. Berkeley: University of California Press.

Butler, Judith. 1997. *The psychic life of power: Theories in subjection.* Stanford, CA: Stanford University Press.

Çakır, Ruşen. 1990. *Ayet ve slogan: Türkiye'de İslami oluşumlar.* Istanbul: Metis Yayınları.

Calhoun, Craig J., ed. 1992. *Habermas and the public sphere.* Cambridge, MA: MIT Press.

Carey, James. 1992. *Communication as culture: Essays on media and society.* New York: Routledge.

Çarkoğlu, Ali, and Binnaz Toprak. 2006. *Değişen Türkiye'de din, toplum ve siyaset*. Istanbul: Türkiye Ekonomik ve Sosyal Etüdler Vakfi.

Casanova, José. 1994. *Public religions in the modern world*. Chicago: University of Chicago Press.

Cemiyet-i Sûfiye. 1911 [14 April 1327 Rumî]. *Tasavvuf* 6: 7–8.

Cemiyet-i Sûfiye. 1911 [28 April 1327 Rumî]. *Tasavvuf* 8: 3–4.

Chakrabarty, Dipesh. 2000. *Provincializing Europe: Postcolonial thought and historical difference*. Princeton, NJ: Princeton University Press.

Chang, Ruth, ed. 1997. *Incommensurability, incomparability and practical reason*. Cambridge: Harvard University Press.

Chatterjee, Partha. 2004. *The politics of the governed: Reflections on popular politics in most of the world*. New York: Columbia University Press.

Chittick, William C. 1989. *The Sufi path of knowledge: Ibn Al-'Arabi's metaphysics of imagination*. Albany: State University of New York Press.

Çınar, Alev. 2005. *Modernity, Islam, and secularism in Turkey: Bodies, places, and time*. Minneapolis: University of Minnesota Press.

Comaroff, John L., and Jean Comaroff. 1992. *Ethnography and the historical imagination*. Boulder, CO: Westview Press.

Connolly, William E. 1989. *Political theory and modernity*. Malden, MA: Blackwell.

———. 1999. *Why I am not a secularist*. Minneapolis: University of Minnesota Press.

———. 2005. *Pluralism*. Durham, NC: Duke University Press.

———. 2006. Europe: A minor tradition. In *Powers of the secular modern*, ed. David Scott and Charles Hirschkind, 75–92. Stanford, CA: Stanford University Press.

Coşan, Esad. 1993. *Matbaacı İbrahim-i Müteferrika risale-i İslamiye*: Tenkidli metin. Istanbul: Seha.

Davidson, Donald. 2001. *Inquiries into truth and interpretation*. Oxford: Oxford University Press.

Deringil, Selim. 1998. *The well-protected domains: Ideology and the legitimation of power in the Ottoman Empire, 1876–1909*. London: I. B. Tauris.

Derrida, Jacques. 1973. *Speech and phenomena, and other essays on Husserl's theory of signs*. Evanston, IL: Northwestern University Press.

———. 1976. *Of grammatology*. Baltimore: Johns Hopkins University Press.

Dewey, John. 1984a. The public and its problems. In *The later works, 1925–1953*, Volume Two, 1925–1927, ed. Jo Ann Boydston, 235–372. Carbondale: Southern Illinois University Press.

———. 1984b. The problem of Turkey. In *The later works, 1925–1953*, Volume Two, 1925–1927, ed. Jo Ann Boydston, 189–93. Carbondale: Southern Illinois University Press.

Donzelot, Jacques, and Colin Gordon. 2008. Governing liberal societies: The Foucault effect in the English-speaking world. *Foucault Studies* 5: 48–62.

Eickelman, Dale F. 1978. The art of memory: Islamic education and its social reproduction. *Comparative Studies in Society and History* 20 (4): 485–516.

———. 1992. Mass higher education and the religious imagination in contemporary Arab societies. *American Ethnologist* 19 (4): 643–55.

Eickelman, Dale F., and Jon W. Anderson. 1999. *New media in the Muslim world: The emerging public sphere*. Bloomington: Indiana University Press.

Eley, Geoff. 1992. Nations, publics and political cultures: Placing Habermas in the nineteenth century. In *Habermas and the public sphere*, ed. Craig J. Calhoun, 289–339. Cambridge, MA: MIT Press.

Erdem, Sami. 1993. Seyyid bey: Hayatı ve eserleri. PhD diss., Marmara University.

Erginbaş, Vefa. 2005. *Forerunner of the Ottoman enlightenment: Ibrahim Muteferrika and his intellectual landscape*. Master's thesis, Sabancı University.

Ersöz, Ahmed. 1992. *Abdülaziz bekkine hazretleri*. Izmir: Nil Yayınları.

Ewing, Katherine Pratt. 1997. *Arguing sainthood: Modernity, psychoanalysis, and Islam*. Durham, NC: Duke University Press.

Eyice, Semavi. 1987. İstanbul'un kaybolan eski eserlerinden: Fatma sultan camii ve gümüşhaneli dergâhi. In *Prof. Dr. Sabri Ülgener'e armağan*. Istanbul: Üniversitesi İktisat Mecmuasi.

Fabian, Johannes. 2002. *Time and the other: How anthropology makes its object*. New York: Columbia University Press.

Faroqhi, Suraiya, and Fikret Adanır. 2002. Introduction. In *The Ottomans and the Balkans: A discussion of historiography*, ed. Fikret Adanır and Suraiya Faroqhi, 1–56. Leiden: Brill.

Faubion, James D. 2001. Toward an anthropology of ethics: Foucault and the pedagogies of autopoiesis. *Representations* 74 (Spring): 83–104.

Findley, Carter V. 1980. *Bureaucratic reform in the Ottoman Empire: The sublime porte, 1789–1922*. Princeton, NJ: Princeton University Press.

———. 1982. The advent of ideology in the Islamic Middle East. Parts 1 and 2. *Studia Islamica* 55–56: 143–69; 147–80.

———. 1989. *Ottoman civil officialdom: A social history*. Princeton, NJ: Princeton University Press.

Fischer, Michael M. J., and Mehdi Abedi. 1990. *Debating Muslims: Cultural dialogues in postmodernity and tradition*. Madison: University of Wisconsin Press.

Fortna, Benjamin C. 2002. *Imperial classroom: Islam, the state, and education in the late Ottoman Empire*. Oxford: Oxford University Press.

Foucault, Michel. 1978. *The history of sexuality*. Trans. Robert Hurley. New York: Vintage.

———. 1979. *Discipline and punish: The birth of the prison*. New York: Vintage Books.

———. 1980. Two lectures. In *Power/knowledge: Selected interviews and other writings, 1972–1977*, ed. Colin Gordon, 78–108. New York: Pantheon.

———. 2003a. The ethics of the concern for self as a practice of freedom. In *The essential Foucault*, ed. Paul Rabinow and Nikolas Rose, 25–42. New York: The New Press.

———. 2003b. Governmentality. In *The essential Foucault*, ed. Paul Rabinow and Nikolas Rose, 229–45. New York: The New Press.

———. 2003c. Nietzsche, genealogy, history. In *The essential Foucault*, ed. Paul Rabinow and Nikolas Rose, 351–69. New York: The New Press.

———. 2003d. Questions of method. In *The essential Foucault*, ed. Paul Rabinow and Nikolas Rose, 246–58. New York: The New Press.

———. 2003e. The subject and power. In *The essential Foucault*, ed. Paul Rabinow and Nikolas Rose, 126–44. New York: The New Press.

———. 2003f. Truth and power. In *The essential Foucault*, ed. Paul Rabinow and Nikolas Rose, 300–18. New York: The New Press.

———. 2003g. What is an author? In *The essential Foucault*, ed. Paul Rabinow and Nikolas Rose, 377–91. New York: The New Press.

———. 2007. *The politics of truth*. Ed. Sylvère Lotringer. Los Angeles: Semiotext(e).

———. 2008. *The birth of biopolitics: Lectures at the Collège De France, 1978–79*. Trans. Graham Burchell. New York: Palgrave Macmillan.

Friedmann, Yohanan. 2000. *Shaykh Ahmad Sirhindi: An outline of his thought and a study of his image in the eyes of posterity*. New Delhi: Oxford University Press.

Gaborieau, Marc, Alexandre Popoviç, and Thierry Zarcone. 1990. *Naqshbandis: Cheminements et situation actuelle d'un ordre mystique musulman*. Istanbul: Editions Isis.

Gay, Peter. 1973. *The Enlightenment: An interpretation*. New York: Vintage.

Gilsenan, Michael. 1973. *Saint and Sufi in modern Egypt: An essay in the sociology of religion*. Oxford: Clarendon Press.

Goffman, Daniel. 2002. *The Ottoman Empire and early modern Europe*. Cambridge: Cambridge University Press.

Goffman, Erving. 1981. *Forms of talk*. Philadelphia: University of Pennsylvania Press.

Graham, William. 1987. *Beyond the written word: Oral aspects of scripture in the history of religion*. Cambridge: Cambridge University Press.

Guida, Michelangelo. 2008. Seyyid Bey and the abolition of the caliphate. *Middle Eastern Studies* 44 (2): 275–89.

Gümüşhanevi, Ahmed Ziaüddin. n.d. *Veliler ve tarikatlarda usul* [Turkish translation of *Jami' al-Usul*]. Istanbul: Pamuk Yayınları.

Gündüz, İrfan. 1984. *Osmanlılarda devlet-tekke münasebetleri*. Istanbul: Seha.

———. 1995. Mehmed zahid kotku'nun tarikat ve İrşad anlayışı. In *Mehmed zahid kotku ve tasavvuf*. Edited by Hüseyin Erkaya, 85–94. Istanbul: Seha.

Gürdoğan, Ersin. 1996. *Görünmeyen üniversite*. Istanbul: İz.

Habermas, Jürgen. 1989. *The structural transformation of the public sphere: An inquiry into a category of bourgeois society*. Cambridge, MA: MIT Press.

Hadot, Pierre. 1995. *Philosophy as a way of life: Spiritual exercises from Socrates to Foucault*. Malden, MA: Blackwell.

Hanioğlu, M. Şükrü. 2008. *A brief history of the late Ottoman Empire*. Princeton, NJ: Princeton University Press.

Harvey, David. 1989. *The condition of postmodernity: An enquiry into the origins of cultural change*. Malden, MA: Blackwell.

———. 2005. *A brief history of neoliberalism*. Oxford: Oxford University Press.

Hattemer, Richard. 1999. Atatürk and the reforms in Turkey as reflected in the Egyptian press. *Journal of Islamic Studies* 11 (1): 21–42.

Hegel, G. W. F. 1991. *Elements of the philosophy of right*. Trans. H. B. Nisbet. Cambridge: Cambridge University Press.

Heidegger, Martin. 1977. *The question concerning technology, and other essays*. New York: Harper & Row.

Hirschkind, Charles. 2001. Civic virtue and religious reason: An Islamic counterpublic. *Cultural Anthropology* 16 (1): 3–34.

———. 2006. *The ethical soundscape: Cassette sermons and Islamic counterpublics*. New York: Columbia University Press.

Hobsbawm, Eric J., and Terence O. Ranger. 1983. *The invention of tradition*. Cambridge: Cambridge University Press.

Hodgson, Marshall G. S. 1974. *The venture of Islam: The expansion of Islam in the middle periods*. Chicago: University of Chicago Press.

Hourani, Albert. 1981. Sufism and modern Islam: Mawlana Khalid and the Naqshbandi order. In *The emergence of the modern Middle East*, ed. Albert Hourani, 75–89. Berkeley: University of California Press.

İlmiye Sâlnâmesi, 1334/1915–1916. Matbaa-i Amire: Istanbul.

Irvine, Judith. 1989. When talk isn't cheap: Language and political economy. *American Ethnologist* 16 (2): 248–67.

Izutsu, Toshihiko. 2002. *Ethico-religious concepts in the Qur'an*. Montreal: McGill-Queen's University Press.

Jameson, Frederic. 1991. *Postmodernism, or, the cultural logic of late capitalism*. Durham, NC: Duke University Press.

Jäschke, Gotthard. 1972. *Yeni Türkiye'de İslâmlık*. Trans. Hayrullah Örs. Ankara: Bilgi Yayınevi.

Jong, F. de. 1978. *Turuq and Turuq-linked institutions in nineteenth century Egypt: A historical study in organizational dimensions of Islamic mysticism*. Leiden: Brill.

Kafadar, Cemal. 1989. Self and others: The diary of a dervish in seventeenth century Istanbul and first-person narratives in Ottoman literature. *Studia Islamica* 69: 121–50.

————. 1992. The new visibility of Sufism in Turkish studies and cultural life. In *The dervish lodge*, ed. Ramond Lifchez, 307–22. Berkeley: University of California Press.

Kant, Immanuel. 1991. *Political writings*. Cambridge: Cambridge University Press.

————. 2007. What is enlightenment? In *The politics of truth*, ed. Michel Foucault, 29–38. Los Angeles: Semiotext(e).

Kara, İsmail. 1991. Sonuç yerine: Tekkeler kapandı mı? *Dergâh* 16: 14–15; 20.

————. 1998. Ulema-siyaset ilişkilerine dair önemli bir metin: Muhalefet yapmak/muhalefete katılmak. *Divan* 1: 1–25.

————. 2001. İslâmcıların siyasi görüşleri. 2nd ed. Istanbul: Dergâh.

————. 2003. *Din ile modernleşme arasında: Çağdaş Türk düşüncesinin meseleleri.* Istanbul: Dergâh Yayınları.

————. 2004. Bir kâseden bin neşve peyda. *Dergâh* 173 (15).

————. 2005a. Çağdaş Türk düşüncesinde bir tenkit/tasfiye alanı olarak tasavvuf ve tarikatlar. In *Osmanlı toplumunda tasavvuf ve sufiler*, ed. Ahmet Yaşar Ocak, 561–86. Ankara: Türk Tarih Kurumu.

————. 2005b. Turban and fez: Ulema as opposition. In *Late Ottoman society: The intellectual legacy*, ed. Elizabeth Özdalga. London, 162–200: Routledge.

————. 2008. *Cumhuriyet Türkiyesi'nde bir mesele olarak din*. Istanbul: Dergâh Yayınları.

Kara, İsmail, ed. 1997. *Türkiye'de İslâmcılık düşüncesi*. Vols. 1–3. Istanbul: Kitabevi.

Kara, Mustafa. 1980. *Din, hayat, sanat açısından tekkeler ve zaviyeler.* 2nd ed. Istanbul: Dergâh Yayınları.

————. 1985. Tanzimat'ta cumhuriyet'e tasavvuf ve tarikatlar. In *Tanzimat'tan cumhuriyet'e Türkiye ansiklopedisi,* 978–94. Istanbul: İletişim.

————. 1991. Sûfilerin tenkidleri ve tasavvufu ihya faaliyetleri. In *Tanımı, kaynakları ve tesirleriyle tasavvuf,* ed. Coşkun Yılmaz, 67–90. Istanbul: Seha.

————. 2001. Bir şeyh efendi'nin meşrutiyet ve cumhuriyet'e bakışı. *Dergâh* 134: 14–18.

————. 2002. *Metinlerle günümüz tasavvuf hareketleri, 1839–2000.* Istanbul: Dergâh Yayınları.

————. 2005. İkinci meşrutiyet devrinde dervişlerin sosyal ve kültürel etkinlikleri. In *Osmanlı toplumunda tasavvuf ve sufiler*, ed. Ahmet Yaşar Ocak, 533–44. Ankara: Türk Tarih Kurumu.

Karpat, Kemal. 2000. *Ottoman past and today's Turkey*. Leiden: Brill.

————. 2001. *The politicization of Islam: Reconstructing identity, state, faith, and community in the late Ottoman state*. New York: Oxford University Press.

Kasaba, Reşat. 1988. *The Ottoman Empire and the world-economy: The nineteenth century.* Albany: State University of New York Press.

Keane, Webb. 1997. Religious language. *Annual Review of Anthropology* 26: 47–71.

Keyder, Çağlar. 1987. *State and class in Turkey: A study in capitalist development*. London: Verso.

————. 1993. The dilemma of cultural identity on the margin of Europe. *Review* 16 (1) 19–33.

————. 1997. Whither the project of modernity? Turkey in the 1990s. In *Rethinking modernity and national identity in Turkey*, ed. Sibel Bozdoğan and Reşat Kasaba, 37–51. Seattle: University of Washington Press.

————. 2004. The Turkish bell jar. *New Left Review* 28: 65–84.

————. 2006. Moving in from the margins? Turkey in Europe. *Diogenes* 53 (2): 72–81.

Kim kimdir? İşadamı, gazeteci, profesör, emekli komutan. 2008. *Radikal*, July 2.

Knysh, Alexander D. 2000. *Islamic mysticism: A short history*. Leiden: Brill.

Koselleck, Reinhart. 2004. *Futures past: On the semantics of historical time*. New York: Columbia University Press.

Kosman, L. A. 1980. Being properly affected: Virtues and feelings in Aristotle's "*Ethics.*" In *Essays on Aristotle's "Ethics,*" ed. Amélie O. Rorty, 103–16. Berkeley: University of California Press.

Kotku, Mehmed Zahid. n.d. *Tasavvufî ahlâk* [Sufi ethics]. Istanbul: Seha.

Kreiser, Klaus. 1985. Derwischscheiche als publizisten: Ein Blick in die Türkische religiöse Presse zwischen 1908 und 1925. *Zeitschrift der Deutschen Morgenländischen Gesellschaft* 6 (supplement): 333–41.

———. 1992. The dervish living. In *The dervish lodge*, ed. Ramond Lifchez, 49–56. Berkeley: University of California Press.

Kuneralp, Sinan. 1992. Les débuts de l'imprimerie à Istanbul au XVIIIe siècle. In *Turquie: Livres d'hier, livres d'aujourd'hui*, ed. Paul Dumont, 1–4. Istanbul: Isis.

Kut, Turgut. 1996. Türk matbaacılığı. In *Yazmadan basmaya: Müteferrika, mühendishane, üsküdar*. Istanbul: Yapı Kredi Yayınları.

Lausanne Conference on Near Eastern Affairs 1922–1923: Records of Proceedings and Draft Terms of Peace. 1923. London: H.M. Stationery office.

Le Gall, Dina. 2005. *A culture of Sufism: Naqshbandis in the Ottoman world, 1450–1700*. Albany: State University of New York Press.

Lewis, Bernard. 1968. *The emergence of modern Turkey*. 2nd ed. New York: Oxford University Press.

———. 1993. Ottoman observers of Ottoman decline. In *Islam in history*, ed. Bernard Lewis, 209–22. Peru, IL: Open Court.

———. 2002. *What went wrong? Western impact and Middle Eastern response*. New York: Oxford University Press.

Lifchez, Raymond. 1992. *The dervish lodge: Architecture, art, and Sufism in Ottoman Turkey*. Berkeley: University of California Press.

Locke, John. 1996. Some thoughts concerning education. In *Some thoughts concerning education and of the conduct of the understanding*, ed. Ruth Grant and Nathan Tarcov. Indianapolis: Hackett.

MacIntyre, Alasdair C. 1984. *After virtue: A study in moral theory*. 2nd ed. Notre Dame, IN: University of Notre Dame Press.

———. 1989. *Whose justice? Which rationality?* Notre Dame, IN: University of Notre Dame Press.

Mahdi, Muhsin. 1995. From the manuscript age to the age of printed books. In *The book in the Islamic world: The written word and communication in the Middle East*, ed. George Atiyeh, 1–16. Albany: SUNY Press.

Mahmood, Saba. 2005. *Politics of piety: The Islamic revival and the feminist subject*. Princeton, NJ: Princeton University Press.

Mango, Andrew. 1999. *Atatürk: The biography of the founder of modern Turkey*. New York: Overlook Press.

Mardin, Şerif. 1969. Power, civil society and culture in the Ottoman Empire. *Comparative Studies in Society and History* 11 (3): 258–81.

———. 1989. *Religion and social change in modern Turkey: The case of Bediüzzaman Said Nursi*. Albany: State University of New York Press.

———. 1991. The Naqshbandi order in Turkish history. In *Religion in modern Turkey: Religion, politics and literature in a secular state*, ed. Richard Tapper 121–42. London: I. B. Tauris.

———. 2000. *The genesis of young Ottoman thought: A study in the modernization of Turkish political ideas*. Syracuse, NY: Syracuse University Press.

———. 2004. Religion and secularism in Turkey. In *The modern Middle East*, ed. Albert Hourani, 347–74. London: I. B. Tauris.

———. 2006. *Religion, society, and modernity in Turkey*. Syracuse, NY: Syracuse University Press.

Marx, Karl. 1990. *Capital*. Trans. Ben Fowkes. New York: Penguin.

Mauss, Marcel. 1979. *Sociology and psychology: Essays*. London: Routledge.

Mazzarella, William. 2004. Culture, globalization, mediation. *Annual Review of Anthropology* 33: 345–67.

Meeker, Michael. 1994. Oral culture, media culture, and the Islamic resurgence in Turkey. In *Exploring the written: Anthropology and the multiplicity of writing*. ed. Eduardo Archetti, 31–64. Oslo: Scandinavian University Press.

———. 2002. *A nation of empire: The Ottoman legacy of Turkish modernity*. Berkeley: University of California Press.

Messick, Brinkley. 1993. *The calligraphic state: Textual domination and history in a Muslim society*. Berkeley: University of California Press.

Meyer, Birgit, and Annelies Moors. 2006. *Religion, media, and the public sphere*. Bloomington: Indiana University Press.

Miller, Flagg. 2007. *The moral resonance of Arab media: Audiocassette poetry and culture in Yemen*. Cambridge, MA: Center for Middle Eastern Studies, Harvard University Press.

Mitchell, Timothy. 1991. *Colonising Egypt*. Berkeley: University of California Press.

———. 2002. *Rule of Experts: Egypt, techno-politics, modernity*. Berkeley: University of California Press.

Mitchell, Timothy, ed. 2000. *Questions of modernity*. Minneapolis: University of Minnesota Press.

Morson, Gary. 1981. *The Boundaries of genre: Dostoevsky's "Diary of a Writer" and the traditions of literary utopia*. Austin: University of Texas Press.

Murphey, Rhoads. 1999. *Ottoman warfare, 1500–1700*. New Brunswick, NJ: Rutgers University Press.

Mustafa Reşid Paşa. 2006. The Gülhane Edict. In *Discourses of collective identity in Central and Southeast Europe (1770–1945): texts and commentaries*, Volume 1. Balázs Trencsényi and Michal Kopecek, eds, 332–39. Budapest: Central European University Press.

Navaro-Yashin, Yael. 2002. *Faces of the state: Secularism and public life in Turkey*. Princeton, NJ: Princeton University Press.

Necatioğlu, Halil. 1990. İslam alimlerinin tartışılmaz değeri ve üstünlüğü. İslam (January).

Nietzsche, Friedrich Wilhelm. 1998. *On the genealogy of morality: A polemic*. Trans. Maudemarie Clark and Alan J. Swensen. Indianapolis, IN: Hackett.

Oğhan, Şehriban. 2001. İcazet tartışması, *Hürriyet*, 11 February.

Öncü, Ayşe. 1995. Packaging Islam: Cultural politics on the landscape of Turkish commercial television. *Public Culture* 8 (1): 51–71.

Ong, Aihwa. 1995. State versus Islam: Malay families, women's bodies, and the body politic in Malaysia. In *Bewitching women, pious men: Gender and body politics in Southeast Asia*, ed. Aihwa Ong and Michael Peletz, 159–94. Berkeley: University of California Press.

Outram, Dorinda. 2005. *The Enlightenment*. 2nd ed. Cambridge: Cambridge University Press.

Özal, Korkut. 1999. Twenty years with Mehmed Zahid Kotku: A personal story. In *Naqshbandis in western and central Asia*, ed. Elizabeth Özdalga, 159–85. Istanbul: Swedish Research Institute.

Özkasnak: 28 Şubat postmodern darbeydi. 2001. *Radikal*, January 15.

Özyürek, Esra. 2006. *Nostalgia for the modern: State secularism and everyday politics in Turkey*. Durham, NC: Duke University Press.

Pandolfo, Stefania. 1997. *Impasse of the angels: Scenes from a Moroccan space of memory*. Chicago: University of Chicago Press.

———. 2000. The thin line of modernity: Some Moroccan debates on subjectivity. In *Questions of modernity, ed. Timothy* Mitchell, 115–47. Minneapolis: University of Minnesota Press.

Pinto, Paulo. 2004. The limits of the public: Sufism and the religious debate in Syria. In *Public Islam and the common good*, ed. Armando Salvatore and Dale Eickelman, 181–204. Leiden: Brill.

Plato. 1973. *Phaedrus and letters VII and VIII*. Trans. Walter Hamilton. New York: Penguin.

Polanyi, Karl. 2001. *The great transformation: The political and economic origins of our time*. 2nd ed. Boston, MA: Beacon Press.

Rafael, Vicente L. 1993. *Contracting colonialism: Translation and Christian conversion in Tagalog society under early Spanish rule*. Durham, NC: Duke University Press.

Raudvere, Catharina. 2003. *The book and the roses: Sufi women, visibility, and zikir in contemporary Istanbul*. Istanbul: Swedish Research Institute in Istanbul.

Redhouse, James. 1996 [1890]. *A Turkish and English lexicon*. Beirut: Librairie du Liban.

Robbins, Joel. 2004. *Becoming sinners: Christianity and moral torment in a Papua New Guinea society*. Berkeley: University of California Press.

Rosaldo, Michelle. 1982. The things we do with words: Ilongot speech acts and speech act theory in philosophy. *Language in Society* 11 (2): 203–37.

Rose, Nikolas S. 1998. *Inventing our selves: Psychology, power, and personhood*. Cambridge: Cambridge University Press.

Radyo ve Televizyon Üst Kurulu [RTÜK]. 2007. *Radyo dinleme eğilimleri araştırması*. Ankara: Kamuoyu Yayın Araştırmaları ve Ölçme Dairesi Başkanlığı.

Ryan, Mary. 1992. Gender and public access: Women's politics in nineteenth century America. In *Habermas and the Public Sphere*, ed. Craig Calhoun, 259–88. Cambridge, MA: MIT Press.

Said Halim Paşa. 1997. İslâm'da siyasî teşkilat. In *Türkiye'de İslamcılık düşüncesi*, ed. İsmail Kara, 160–93. Istanbul: Kitabevi.

Salvatore, Armando. 2007. The exit from a Westphalian framing of political space and the emergence of a transnational Islamic public. Theory, Culture & Society 24 (4): 45-52.

Salvatore, Armando, and Dale F. Eickelman. 2004. *Public Islam and the common good*. Leiden: Brill.

Salvatore, Armando, and Mark LeVine. 2005. *Religion, social practice, and contested hegemonies: Reconstructing the public sphere in Muslim majority societies*. New York: Palgrave Macmillan.

Schimmel, Annemarie. 1975. *Mystical dimensions of Islam*. Chapel Hill: University of North Carolina Press.

Scott, Joan. 1991. The Evidence of Experience. *Critical Inquiry* 17 (4): 773–97.

Sevgi Seli, in *Yeni Şafak*, 10 February, 2001.

Seyyid Bey. 1997. Hilafetin şer'i mahiyeti. In *Türkiye'de İslamcılık düşüncesi*, ed. İsmail Kara. Istanbul: Kitabevi, 259–300.

Shaw, Stanford J. 1971. *Between old and new: The Ottoman Empire under Sultan Selim III, 1789–1807*. Cambridge, MA: Harvard University Press.

Silverstein, Brian. 2003. Islam and modernity in Turkey: Power, tradition and historicity in the European provinces of the Muslim world. *Anthropological Quarterly* 76 (3): 497–517.

———. 2005. Islamist critique in modern Turkey: Hermeneutics, tradition, genealogy. *Comparative Studies in Society and History* 47 (1): 134–60.

Smith, Wilfred Cantwell. 1957. *Islam in modern history*. Princeton, NJ: Princeton University Press.

———. 1991. *The meaning and end of religion*. Minneapolis, MN: Fortress Press.

Somers, Margaret R. 1995. What's political or cultural about political culture and the public sphere? Toward an historical sociology of concept formation. *Sociological Theory* 13 (2): 113–44.

Stokes, Martin. 1992. *The arabesk debate: Music and musicians in modern Turkey*. Oxford: Clarendon Press.

Tanpınar, Ahmet Hamdi. 2001. *19 uncu asır Türk edebiyatı tarihi*. Istanbul: Çağlayan Kitabevi.

Tapper, Richard. 1991. *Islam in modern Turkey: Religion, politics, and literature in a secular state*. London: I. B. Tauris.

Tasavvuf ve Meşrutiyet. 1911 [10 March 1327 Rumî]. *Tasavvuf* 1: 5–7.

Taylor, Charles. 1989. *Sources of the self: The making of the modern identity.* Cambridge, MA: Harvard University Press.

———. 2002. *Varieties of religion today: William James revisited.* Cambridge, MA: Harvard University Press.

Tedlock, Dennis. 1983. *The spoken word and the work of interpretation.* Philadelphia: University of Pennsylvania Press.

Tilly, Charles. 1985. War making and state making as organized crime. In *Bringing the state back in,* ed. Peter Evans, Dietrich Rueschemeyer, and Theda Skocpol, 169–91. Cambridge: Cambridge University Press.

Todorova, Maria. 1997. *Imagining the Balkans.* New York: Oxford University Press.

Tokgöz, Ahmed İhsan. 1993. *Matbuat hatıralarım.* Istanbul: İletişim.

Trimingham, J. Spencer. 1998. *The Sufi orders in Islam.* New York: Oxford University Press.

Trix, Frances. 1993. *Spiritual discourse: Learning with an Islamic master.* Philadelphia: University of Pennsylvania Press.

TRT [Türk Radyo ve Televizyon]. 2007. *Radio broadcast schedule.* http://www.trt.gov.tr (accessed November 7).

Tuğal, Cihan. 2007. NATO's Islamists. *New Left Review* 44 (March–April): 5–34.

———. 2009. *Passive revolution: Absorbing the Islamic challenge to capitalism.* Stanford, CA: Stanford University Press.

Tunaya, Tarık Zafer. 1962. *İslâmcılık cereyanı.* Istanbul: Baha Matbaası.

———. 1998. *Türkiye'de siyasal partiler.* Vol. 1. Istanbul: İletişim.

Türköne, Mümtaz'er. 1991. *Siyasi ideoloji olarak İslâmcılığın doğuşu.* Istanbul: İletişim.

28 Şubat postmodern darbeydi. 2001. *Radikal,* 15 January.

Ülken, Hilmi Ziya. 1979. *Türkiye'de çağdaş düşünce tarihi.* Istanbul: Ülken Yayınları.

Ülker, Mustafa, and Faruk Bahadır. 2003. Şeyh mustafa safvet (yetkin) ve tasavvuf dergisi. *Müteferrika* 24 (Winter): 145–57.

Uludağ, Süleyman. 1995. *Tasavvuf terimleri sözlüğü.* 2nd ed. Istanbul: Marifet Yayınları.

Vett, Carl. 1953. *Dervish diary.* Trans. Elbridge Hathaway. Los Angeles: K. K. Mogensen.

Vološinov, V. N. 1986. *Marxism and the philosophy of language.* Cambridge, MA: Harvard University Press.

Warner, Michael. 1992. The mass public and the mass subject. In *Habermas and the public sphere,* ed. Craig Calhoun, 377–401. Cambridge, MA: MIT Press.

———. 2002. Publics and counterpublics. *Public Culture* 14 (1): 49–90.

Weber, Max. 1978. *Economy and society: An outline of interpretive sociology.* Ed. Guenther Roth and Claus Wittich. Berkeley: University of California Press.

———. 2004. Science as a vocation. In *The vocation lectures,* ed. David Owen and Tracy Strong, trans. Rodney Livingstone, 1–31. Indianapolis: Hackett.

White, Jenny B. 1999. Amplifying trust: Community and communication in Turkey. In *New media in the Muslim world,* ed. Dale F. Eickelman and Jon Anderson, 162–79. Bloomington: Indiana University Press.

———. 2002. *Islamist mobilization in Turkey: A study in vernacular politics.* Seattle: University of Washington Press.

———. 2005. The end of Islamism? Turkey's Muslimhood model. In *Remaking Muslim politics: Pluralization, contestation, democratization,* ed. Robert Hefner, 87–111. Princeton, NJ: Princeton University Press.

Williams, Raymond. 1992. *Television: Technology and cultural form.* Hanover, NH: Wesleyan University Press.

Wittgenstein, Ludwig. 2003. *Philosophical investigations: The German text, with a revised English translation by G. E. M. Anscombe.* 3rd ed. Malden, MA: Blackwell.

Wolf, Eric. 1982. *Europe and the people without history.* Berkeley: University of California Press.

Woolard, Kathryn, and Bambi Schieffelin. 1994. Language ideology. *Annual Review of Anthropology* 23: 55–82.

Yalçın, H. C. 1936. Tanıdıklarım: Seyyid Bey. *Yedigün* 183.

Yaşar Büyükanıt: Konuşmak için taslağı bekliyoruz. 2007. *Radikal*, October 2.

Yavuz, M. Hakan. 1999. The matrix of modern Turkish Islamic movements: The Naqshbandi Sufi order. In *Naqshbandis in western and central Asia*, ed. Elizabeth Özdalga, 125–42. Istanbul: Swedish Research Institute in Istanbul.

———. 2003. *Islamic political identity in Turkey.* Oxford: Oxford University Press.

———. 2006. *The emergence of a new Turkey: Democracy and the AK Parti.* Salt Lake City: University of Utah Press.

Yavuz, M. Hakan, and John L. Esposito. 2003. *Turkish Islam and the secular state: The Gülen movement.* Syracuse, NY: Syracuse University Press.

Yazır, Elmalılı Muhammed Hamdi. 1997. İslâmiyet ve Hilafet ve Meşihat-ı İslâmiye. In İ. Kara. 1997. Vol. 1, 521–25. Istanbul: Kitabevi.

Yazmadan basmaya: Müteferrika, mühendishane, üsküdar. 1996. Istanbul: Yapı Kredi Yayınları.

Yerini Oğluna Bıraktı, *Radikal*, February 10, 2001.

Yılmaz, Murat, ed. 2005. *Liberalizm.* Istanbul: İletişim.

Yusuf Ali, Abdullah. 1992. *The meaning of the holy Qur'an.* New rev. ed. Brentwood, MD: Amana Corp.

Zarcone, Thierry. 1993. *Mystiques, philosophes et francs-maçons en Islam.* Paris: Maisonneuve.

Zürcher, Erik. 1984. *The unionist factor: The role of the Committee of Union and Progress in the Turkish national movement, 1905–1926.* Leiden: Brill.

———. 2000. Young Turks, Ottoman Muslims and Turkish nationalists: Identity politics 1908–1938. In *Ottoman past and today's Turkey*, ed. Kemal H. Karpat, 150–79. Leiden: Brill.

———. 2004. *Turkey: A modern history.* 3rd ed. London: I. B. Tauris.

INDEX

Italicized page numbers refer to a figure on that page.